UNDERSTANDING EVANGELICAL MEDIA

The Changing Face of Christian Communication

Edited by Quentin J. Schultze
and Robert H. Woods Jr.

Foreword by Clifford G. Christians

An imprint of InterVarsity Press
Downers Grove, Illinois

InterVarsity Press
P.O. Box 1400, Downers Grove, IL 60515-1426
World Wide Web: www.ivpress.com
E-mail: email@ivpress.com

InterVarsity Press® is the book-publishing division of InterVarsity Christian Fellowship/USA®, a student movement active on campus at hundreds of universities, colleges and schools of nursing in the United States of America, and a member movement of the International Fellowship of Evangelical Students. For information about local and regional activities, write Public Relations Dept., InterVarsity Christian Fellowship/USA, 6400 Schroeder Rd., P.O. Box 7895, Madison, WI 53707-7895, or visit the IVCF website at <www.intervarsity.org>.

Design: Cindy Kiple
Images: Kiyoshi Takahase Segundo/iStockphoto

ISBN 978-0-8308-2882-1

Printed in the United States of America ∞

InterVarsity Press is committed to protecting the environment and to the responsible use of natural resources. As a member of Green Press Initiative we use recycled paper whenever possible. To learn more about the Green Press Initiative, visit http://www.greenpressinitiative.org

Library of Congress Cataloging-in-Publication Data

Understanding evangelical media: the changing face of Christian communication / edited by Quentin J. Schultze and Robert H. Woods, Jr.
p. cm.
Includes bibliographical references.
ISBN 978-0-8308-2882-1 (pbk.: alk. paper)
1. Communication—Religious aspects—Christianity. 2. Mass media—Religious aspects—Christianity. 3. Evangelicalism. I. Schultze, Quentin J. (Quentin James), 1952- II. Woods, Robert, 1970-
BV4319.U53 2008
261.5'2—dc22

2008008912

P 21 20 19 18 17 16 15 14 13 12 11 10 9 8 7 6 5 4 3 2 1
Y 25 24 23 22 21 20 19 18 17 16 15 14 13 12 11 10 09 08

Contents

Foreword

I read this book and hear the New York Philharmonic. The aesthetic harmony of a symphony orchestra sounds from its pages. Each chapter features a maestro at work, with the editors the legendary Leonard Bernstein. The biblical worldview when taken seriously makes our thinking distinctive, and this is dramatic evidence of it.

As an educator in communications research, I celebrate. While my heart sings, my mind is on fire. In this book I find meticulous research wall to wall, throughout every chapter and across the book; data and analysis an integrated whole; the overall purpose crystal clear—evangelical media in the context of the digital revolution; and here in sparkling prose a comprehensive, encyclopedic work on tribal popular culture, heretofore unequalled and henceforth the research standard. This is living proof that academics of faith working in concert create surplus value for the common good.

But this is a signature book in a deeper sense. Yes, the aesthetic magnificence of the Himalayas, but more profoundly an icon of daring epistemology. Tribal media systems as defined in chapter one are grounded in belief, not empirical neutrality. Rather than escape into subjectivist dualism, *Understanding Evangelical Media* is a treasure of presuppositional epistemology. It is rooted in core commitments instead of noncontingent rationality. This audacious book is "in our face" without apology—overarching beliefs about the world are the very condition through which cognition is possible. Critical analysis is not an examination of external events, but the creative power that gives an inside perspective on reality. Popular culture, that value-saturated domain, is simultaneously our human home and the arena of divine providence.

Through the editors' ingenuity and the authors' gifts, this book operates on another order of magnitude. Its contributors recognize that to think deeply does not in itself dispose us to value beliefs as indispensable. The media issues presented are rooted in convictions about the nature of human beings and the meaning of life. The discussions of media technologies—radio, film, books, internet, gaming and the rest—are a venue for the permanent questions about our place in the universe. They rightly see the Herculean obstacle as not the ignorance of fact but the illusion of knowledge. The meaning and purpose of human existence become the context within which analytic skills are honed and specific issues resolved. The twenty-one chapters are first of all an intellectual enterprise, not for exposing the deficiencies in others but for struggling with the rationale of human existence. The subject matter is not explained epistemologically, but in terms of the ultimate questions about which ideas are true and whether they warrant commitment.

Parsimony is important in every chapter, as it has been since William of Ockham, but only in its arising from an animated worldview. Know the tribal media historically and sociologically, we are told. But discerning readers will recognize that to the authors throughout, the foundations of knowledge are of incalculable importance. The perspective on mediation represented here is not content with superficial claims regarding socially produced selves or lingual assertions about symbolic constructions. The book's thick reading is not merely an analytic strategy but a public philosophy.

In the mystery of human intelligence, presuppositional knowledge releases us from epistemology and focuses relentlessly on the nature of the human. In this way, *Understanding Evangelical Media* commands an inescapable presence in communications research. No theorizing is more vital for the field at present. While our research has specialized in the nature of knowledge, the constitution of the human is the pathway of the future. And in concentrating here on the communicating human, the spiritual dimension becomes inescapable. The philosophical anthropology of Professors Schultze and Woods and their cohorts works deeply and persistently out of spirituality as intrinsic and inescapable. Humans are not simply biological or psychological entities, but spiritual beings seeking expression in culture. In enhancing rather than suppressing the spiritual, a normative strategy is made transparent for acting virtuously in the twenty-first century's mediated world. A spacious framework is unveiled by including spirituality within philosophical anthropology rather than adhering to the conceptual boundaries of epistemology. The book has thematic integrity—from presuppositions to humans to spirituality and then to holism.

Spirituality refers to those sacred times and spaces so engrained in human community that history becomes an empty shell if viewed without it. Spirituality rejects the naiveté that the religious realm can be isolated and established independently. It presumes that all explicit operations of the mind presuppose an inexplicit worldview. One of the human species' most intriguing problems is why something exists and not nothing, why we find ourselves living on a tiny particle of the vast universe in a minute fragment of time. Our intrinsic spirituality is the arena for answering that, though our yoke is not easy or our burden light in doing so.

The spiritual domain is a polyphonic world that prevents both sterility and cacophony. It finds the nonempirical not only meaningful but necessary. Spirituality is the human response to unconstrained reality and the ultimate sphere, or in Rudolf Otto's terms "the numinous."[1] In so arguing, spirituality fundamentally reorients philosophical anthropology. It insists on the need for a transcendent center to prevent arbitrariness in human relations. In these terms, our important threat is not physical survival but the uncanny. The ultimate menace occurs when lingual systems start disintegrating. By contrast, human beings are elevated to their highest and noblest by nurturing the supersensible. We are connected to the history of the human race, and set alongside the digital, through the realization that ritual and symbolism are not extraneous but intrinsic to humankind as a species.

Insisting on spirituality enables this book to define communicating beings holistically. The human species is understood to be an indivisible, organic unity with multisided spiritual, mental and physical capacities. Contrary to the rational being of Greece and the Enlightenment's Descartes, the body, mind and soul are developed in concert. In these terms, an ideal popular culture awakens the unity of our whole being. Ultimately we are exposed to the largest possible vision of what it means to be a human being inhabiting the cosmos. Therefore, the analyses in this book do not center too narrowly on intellectual development or behavior control that ignores human growth in holistic terms. This book advocates our pursuit of a spiritual life amid the dominant voices touting efficiency, production and management. It turns people's eyes to the unitary picture of beings in congruence—from oneness with the eternal to solidarity with others created in God's image.

Holistic humans as the golden subtext throughout gives this volume phosphorescence. It sets the standard for authentic disclosure in tribal media programming. Moreover, it exposes the truncated individual self of the mainstream media. Instead of *secular* or *non-Christian* media, this book correctly chooses *mainstream* as the descriptor. Rather than condemnation and belligerence toward mediated communications as a whole, the authors are charitable in spirit and busy themselves with the prospects for the tribal media in a digital age. Their unrelenting commitment to holistic humanity, however, amounts to a fundamental critique of the emaciated human in nontribal systems.

In the mainstream media, a person's moral and political obligations are dependent on a contract or agreement among society's members. Contractual models have come to inform a vast variety of interactions in contemporary Western society, and discourse about popular culture generally assumes them. And what kind of person is this precisely? Typically we call it the liberal self—individualism in which independence and self-reliance are supreme. Rights are nonnegotiable with fierce opposition to external control. The self draws together all other dimensions of life, and only through an aggregate of personal preferences does commonness exist. The well-being of individuals ultimately justifies society and government. Community describes a possible aim of individuated selves but is not a constituent of human identity. People are distinct from their ends, so the domain of the good is extrinsic. The autonomous self floats independently of the historical and moral orders, and freedom is defined as liberty from external and arbitrary restraints.

The liberal individual is purported to be universal—raceless, classless and gender neutral—and is taken to represent a generalized model of humanity above cultural differences. Many political thinkers have argued that when we investigate carefully the characteristics of the liberal self, we find not a universal human being, but a historically located, specific type of individual—actually a bourgeois man that characterized early modern Europe. He is radically solitary, not owing any of his qualities or even his very existence to anyone else. Such liberal individuals enter into the social contract as a means by which to maximize their own interests individually considered.

Thus the dramatic appeal of *Understanding Evangelical Media.* Its holistic human being challenges the one-sided, historically contingent person assumed in the mainstream media. While it does not do so self-consciously, it calls liberal selves to be exorcized and replaced by holistic beings instead. It insists on an empathic rather than contractual approach to community life. In so doing it centers on tribal media, as communication research comes to grips with the necessary and sufficient conditions of being human.

However, this book's holistic ontology has an impact on the field in even more far-reaching terms. Regarding the new media technologies, a fundamental debate is still unresolved. The issue is whether communication is most productively oriented (1) to the epistemology of virtual reality (What does it mean that our relationships are disembodied?), (2) to the nature of the human (What is authentic humanness in virtual space?), or (3) to social structures (Are political and social formations offline and online fundamentally different?).

Understanding Evangelical Media makes the case for the second alternative, with such luminosity, in fact, that other alternatives seem indefensible. The issues are complicated and the details serpentine. But this is a testament to philosophical anthropology as the appropriate framework, rather than epistemology or social constructionism. In working out the human/digital interface, this book properly emphasizes communal stewardship. Its theorizing is not driven by technology per se, but by "tribal communities of discourse" making "shared sense of the media landscape" and the tribe's roles in it.

Philosophical anthropology is relentless in refusing secondary questions. In totalizing our concentration on humanness, it disposes us within this intellectual space toward the religious dimension. And spirituality in turn effectively leads to a richer definition of the human as holistic beings. Through presuppositional knowledge, this book's contributors think and act beneath mediated structures and thus lay the groundwork for revolutionizing them.

Clifford G. Christians

Acknowledgments

Collaborative works of this magnitude require many hands and voices working in concert. Our debts are considerable.

With the generous support of the DeKruyter Chair in Faith and Communication and especially the Gainey Institute for Faith and Communication at Calvin College, we were able to conduct important research for the book early on in the process, provide valuable professional and academic experiences for students, and host a book-related conference at Calvin College that helped authors clarify and unify their contributions to the project.

Calvin College's Prince Conference Center staff provided first-class service during the book-related conference in July 2007.

Kim Chimienti and Ruth Remtema skillfully coordinated the summer workshop and provided top-flight administrative support at all stages of the project. Rachel Van Klompenberg and Scott Tanis ably assisted them and us at the conference.

The many chapter and sidebar-essay authors contributed immeasurably to the overall quality of the book. They charitably commented on each other's work and tirelessly revised their own contributions. We are very grateful.

Prior to the July 2007 workshop, reference librarians Stephanie Davis (Spring Arbor University—SAU) and Francene Lewis (Calvin College) organized an intensive training session for the student researchers who collected thousands of resources that were eventually compiled and distributed to chapter authors. They also provided ongoing advice to the researchers and editors. Researchers included Kelly Cleaver, Sarah Shirlen, Jennifer Timm, Megan Wilhelm and Rachel Van Klompenberg. The financial aid office at SAU provided accounting support.

Several colleagues, students and friends reviewed various chapters to help make them more readable and compelling: Mark Fackler, Samuel Ebersole, Brian Walrath, Scott Johnson, Le-Toya Averhart, Connie Britner, Rachel Decker, Julie Devine, Kyle Ferguson, Tiffany French, Jeff and Suzanna McGraw, Jillian Moller, Amy Palmer, Sarah Shirlen, John and Lissa Strodtbeck, Scott Tanis, Jennifer Timm, Stella Tippin, and Rebekah Woods. Spring Arbor University librarian Dave Burns provided much needed research support.

Marsha Daigle-Williamson quickly and expertly copyedited the draft of the large manuscript with its nearly one thousand endnote citations. Art Bamford checked and rechecked the many notes and tracked down numerous hard-to-find sources.

Our spouses (Barbara and Rebekah) demonstrated patience as we exchanged thousands of emails and phone calls over a two-year period. They even let us bring our work along on a vacation or two.

Dave Zimmerman of InterVarsity Press championed this project from the beginning, providing wise feedback and marshalling the publisher's resources on our behalf.

To one and all, far beyond this short list—many thanks. Especially to the triune One in whom and through whom the concert of grace abounds.

Introduction

Each book has its own life. This one was born in conversations I had with co-editor Robert Woods. He encouraged me to put together an updated version of a volume of essays I had edited in the late 1980s. That book, *American Evangelicals and the Mass Media,* broke some new ground by assessing some of the scope of evangelical media efforts primarily in North America. Until then, nearly all the books on the topic had looked at particular historical periods or specific media and media forms, such as televangelism and Christian book or tract publishing.

I was uncertain about being able to cover in one book the range of developments in evangelical media in the nearly twenty years since *American Evangelicals* appeared. A lot has changed since 1990. The idea of mass media has been replaced by networked media. Narrowcasting has replaced broadcasting. Media power has become democratized; low-cost digital production lets younger evangelicals tell stories in multiple venues. And this only begins to scratch the surface.

Besides, how could we find authors to address everything from high-tech evangelical theme parks to worship media, and from graphic comic books to YouTube and blogs? Moreover, I thought that any new book on the topic of evangelical media needed to do what nearly all previous books had ignored, namely, provide historical perspective back to the early church and even ancient Hebrew culture. I imagined an outlandishly big project that connected the psalms to contemporary worship music and email to the New Testament epistles. Impossible, I thought to myself. This project would require an encyclopedia, not a mere book.

Then there was the issue of working with a lot of different authors since so few scholars could write expertly about the entire gamut of evangelical media entrepreneurship. I had been involved previously in a number of these kinds of multiauthor projects with mixed success. The editorial work is like directing a symphony. You need a score, or a script, and you have to have a gifted conductor. Finally, the whole enterprise requires a wide range of talented musicians—in this case, writers.

But Robert talked me into it. Or I talked him into it. Or we both talked each other into it. I would not have done it alone. Nor could I have done it without Robert. I needed someone like him, a gifted conductor, to develop the script, especially the theme, and to help keep the musicians playing together. Besides, Robert is also an attorney. This project was going to be a contractual concert. Somehow the two of us would have to manage all the paperwork with a couple dozen or more authors on the one side and a publisher on the other.

After various discussions in person over many cups of coffee, we had hammered out the details. We determined media and topics to cover and authors (musicians) to invite to the concert. As explained in chapter one, we identified two overarching frameworks to direct authors' efforts and make the chapters hang together. First, we told authors to identify fans, critics and critical friends of their respective media. Then we asked them to reflect on Cicero's three basic purposes for public communication[1]—*instructing*, *delighting* and *persuading*—and determine how evangelicals' media use fit these functions. Along the way, we asked authors to make connections to ancient communication roots and to consider the ways evangelicals copy or mimic mainstream media endeavors.

Thanks to support from the Gainey Institute for Faith and Communication at Calvin College, we could pay authors to write their chapters and sidebar essays. More than that, we could try to bring them all together to assess one another's ideas. So in the summer of 2007 about forty of us met at Calvin College to begin the manuscript-driven conversations that led to this book. We all began to see our strengths and weaknesses in the challenging task of interpreting the evangelical media landscape. We listened and learned from one another.

Then we all redrafted our chapters based on the collective wisdom of the group, not just our own, personal penchants. We also began soliciting, reviewing and redrafting sidebar essays to increase the number of voices, the range of perspectives and the sorts of practical illustrations that would give the historical perspective additional contemporary relevance.

In the end, however, Robert and I had to make the difficult decisions about wording and sometimes tone within the various chapters and sidebar essays. So if any of the work in this volume disappoints or even offends readers, we two are responsible. Our goal has been to ensure that the level and style of the writing were somewhat consistent throughout the book, with a bit greater latitude in the sidebar essays. We were very pleased with the work of all of the authors, but we also had to make some tough editorial decisions. Most scholars like to write more than they should! We had to edit down material, by 50 percent in a few cases. Otherwise this book would have gotten so long that only scholars would read it. We hope that the resulting brevity will serve a wide range of readers, including pastors, students, teachers, communications professionals and journalists.

I suppose that the goal of every author is to write something that serves readers for a long time. As editors, too, Robert and I hope that this volume will teach, delight and persuade readers for years to come. As we state in chapter one, we seek to encourage informed conversations about evangelicals and the media. We hope—and pray—that the resulting conversations will continue long after the death of this book. Where there is faith, life continues.

Quentin J. Schultze
Calvin College, 2008

1

Getting the Conversation Going About Media and Culture

QUENTIN J. SCHULTZE AND
ROBERT H. WOODS JR.

When reports surface that a secular music group is made up of Christians, many evangelical fans head for the Internet to read the latest news. Soon cyberspace crackles with comments about faith and music.

In the case of U2's Bono, discussions never stopped. Email connected fans around the world. Websites linked to unfolding U2 news and interviews. Blogs examined the band's latest efforts and discussed the meaning of Christian music.

After Bono used the f-word during an internationally televised award ceremony, fans responded online. Was the language appropriate for TV? Did Bono step over the line? Should he apologize? Was he *really* a Christian?

As time went on, however, Bono expressed his faith even more openly during public speeches about world debt, famine and HIV/AIDS epidemics. Many secular (or mainstream) media did not know how to respond. If Bono was a Christian, they wondered, why was he so concerned about social justice? Aren't Christians right-wing, preachy, self-righteous moralists? Many Christians and non-Christians alike were puzzled. Unable to chat with Bono personally, all they could do was track the latest news reports and converse among themselves.

"Mediating" Views of Reality

The case of U2 shows how communication "mediates" our views of reality. We all learn to interpret reality—e.g., the reality of the f-word on TV—by communicating with others. For instance, we talk with friends, relatives, teachers, pastors and acquaintances. We surf the Web, play recorded music, read books, watch TV and view films—all the while forming views of people and places that we don't know firsthand. In the process of communicating interpersonally and via mass media, we form views of reality: Bono *is* an evangelical—depending on how we define the word.[1] *The Simpsons is* antifamily. Christian theme parks *are* Disney wannabes. Praise and worship music *is* better than traditional hymns for meaningful worship. Really? Who says so?

Why do we form views of reality without firsthand experience? Partly because we get lazy—it is easy to be opinionated and hard work to become informed. Partly because we want friends to like us, so we just agree with them instead of challenging their views. And partly because we all think that the world revolves around our own opinions and feelings.

In other words, we are inclined to use communication, including media, to support our existing views of reality. We pick and choose media according to what *we* want, what *we* enjoy, what *we* like to discuss with others. For instance, Christian contemporary-music fans download more of it than do the music's detractors. We use media to mediate *our* experience of reality in tune with our interests and desires, even our religious beliefs. If we don't like U2 or Amy Grant, we spend time with friends who share our criticisms. We like to know that we have got it right, even self-righteously so!

Human communication, then, is not primarily a sure-fire way of influencing others. We humans don't just hypodermically inject messages into passive receivers who react the way we want them to react every time. Instead, we use verbal and nonverbal communication to form communities that define reality for us and for others who are like us. We use peer groups, for instance, to share what we like and to enjoy it with others. We select a church to attend based on what we like in music and worship style, and presumably what our friends like too. Then those shared definitions of reality function like shared maps that help us navigate life by making judgments about faith and culture, including popular culture.[2]

FORMING TRIBAL COMMUNITIES OF DISCOURSE

Our self-selective mediation of reality is both good and bad. On the good side, it equips us to form communities that share particular values and beliefs. We don't have to interpret and evaluate culture by ourselves, without the wisdom and experience of others. God created us as social rather than instinct-driven creatures. We are free to affiliate with others in *tribes*—unique, reality-defining groups within larger societies and communities.[3]

One type of mediating tribe is *evangelicals, who believe in Jesus Christ for personal salvation, view the Bible as the Word of God and seek to share their faith with others. Christians* is a term that we can use to talk about everyone who follows Jesus Christ; Christians are Christ-followers—even though some groups within that broader category tend to use the word *Christian* to refer only to those who believe exactly what they believe. (For instance, some evangelicals use the phrase "Christian media" to refer only to evangelical media, not to Roman Catholic media.) Evangelicals are a subgroup of Christians, and they reside within many denominations: there are evangelical Roman Catholics, Presbyterians, Methodists and others. Some entire denominations define themselves as evangelical (the thirteen hundred associated congregations in the Evangelical Free Church of America, for example). Many independent Protestant congregations without denominational ties consider themselves evangelical; the phrase "Bible Church" nearly guarantees it.

Because evangelicals emphasize *evangelization* (converting unbelievers to faith

WHO OR WHAT IS AN EVANGELICAL CHRISTIAN?

Thus saith *The Associated Press Stylebook and Briefing on Media Law,* the journalist's bible:

> Historically, evangelical was used as an adjective describing dedication to conveying the message of Christ. Today, it is also used as a noun, referring to a category of doctrinally conservative Christians. They emphasize the need for a definite, adult commitment or conversion to faith in Christ. . . . Evangelicals stress both doctrinal absolutes and vigorous efforts to win others to belief.[a]

The problem is agreeing on the evangelical "absolutes." When *Time* listed "The 25 Most Influential Evangelicals in America," the editors even included two Roman Catholics—an activist priest and a U.S. senator.[b]

Evangelical has become so vague that the world's most famous evangelical cannot define the term. In 1987, I asked the Reverend Billy Graham for a definition and he bounced the question back at me. "Actually, that's a question I'd like to ask somebody, too," he said. The term has "become blurred. . . . You go all the way from the extreme fundamentalists to the extreme liberals, and, somewhere in between, there are the evangelicals."

We do know that many journalists are convinced *evangelical* is a political word. Thus, journalists struggle to interpret exit polls where many voters call themselves evangelicals. Thus, evangelical voters reelected an evangelical president to pursue an evangelical agenda—whatever that means.

Graham stressed doctrine. He finally defined an evangelical as someone who believes the doctrines in the ancient Nicene Creed. Graham stressed the centrality of the resurrection and belief that salvation is through Jesus, alone. "I think there are evangelicals in the Roman Catholic Church and the Eastern Orthodox churches," he said. Thus saith Saint Graham—if evangelicals believe in sainthood.

TERRY MATTINGLY, WASHINGTON JOURNALISM CENTER

[a]Norm Goldstein, ed., *Associated Press Stylebook and Briefing on Media Law,* 39th ed. (New York: Basic Books, 2004), p. 213.

[b]*Time,* February 7, 2005 <www.time.com/time/covers/1101050207/photoessay/22.html>.

in Jesus Christ), they have been among the world's most innovative users of media. They also tend to be some of the harshest critics of secular media. The idea that particular media are Christian and others are merely secular, however, does not work very well for understanding the real world. It simplistically suggests that Christian media are entirely godly while secular media are entirely godless.

The trinitarian God—three persons in one God!—created humankind with the ability to form tribelike religious communities that differentiate themselves from other religious and nonreligious communities. For example, we form churches and denominations, differentiating Lutherans from Baptists, and one congregation of American Baptists from another congregation of independent or Southern Baptists. Often believers in Christ use the word *holy* (meaning "set apart") to refer to tribes that seem to be godlier, or at least more like they themselves!

Each tribal community—whether an avid group of *Star Trek* fans or a denomination—equips members to *share* and *evaluate* reality. Tribes give us a place to stand, beliefs to affirm, values to hold, friends for fellowship. They help us to interpret and judge the world around us. In short, tribes provide us with *communities of discourse* so we can decipher, discuss and debate reality with others. A self-defined Christian tribe, for instance, has its own theological and biblical language for conversing about popular culture. It might use phrases like "crossover music," "redemptive themes" and "family values."

On the negative side, tribal communities of discourse can limit how members perceive reality, and can even confirm members' simplistic or false conclusions. Each tribe has preexisting assumptions that limit the questions it asks and even the media it uses. How can a tribe understand print media—such as comic books—without reading them personally? How can it evaluate Super Bowl commercials without viewing and discussing them?

RELATING CHRIST TO CULTURE

The relationship between Christian tribes and the broader society is often called the Christ-and-culture paradox.[4] How should followers of Jesus Christ relate to the world around them, even to their own churches and local communities? In short, how should Christians live *in* the world without being fully *of* the world? Should they dwell in isolated, rural tribes, like some Anabaptists? Should they restrict which media they consume or produce? Should they go to work in Hollywood or mainstream book publishing—or stay within "safer" tribal communities, producing and consuming only tribal media?

These are critically important questions for all Christians who seek to discern with others what it means to live faithfully. For instance, Christians' conversations about U2's beliefs, music and social activism raise questions about the relationship between faith and culture (or ways of life). How should Christians consume, produce and evaluate various forms of media? Are there distinctly tribal—even evangelical—ways of defining *Christian* media? How can evangelicals engage media artists such as U2?

As influential shapers of culture and faith, the mass media take center stage in this book. All the chapter authors invite you to ask important questions about the media without assuming simplistic, one-approach-fits-all answers. Our goal is not to tell readers what to think about the media but to encourage conversations about living faithfully in the age of iPods, YouTube, on-demand publishing and social-networking websites.

We aim in the rest of this chapter to get the conversation going by offering language to use in discussions about evangelicals and media. We hope that readers will talk about how Christian and mainstream media mediate their views of reality for good and for bad, and how evangelicals can form communities of discourse to equip them to understand, examine and even produce media faithfully.

To get the conversation going, we show that contemporary Christ-and-culture questions about new media have ancient roots. First, current debates about the latest media elicit age-old questions about how to define Christian, or even evangelical, media. Second, opposing views of the media today often hinge on various long-standing assumptions about the proper role of both tribal and main-

GUESS WHO'S COMING TO DINNER—A WARRING EVANGELICAL!

John Bunyan. Charles Colson. The apostle Paul. Bill O'Reilly. Strange bedfellows. Yet each one uses war as a metaphor to describe public conflicts between faith and culture.

Wars are bloody and violent. They produce innocent victims. Are evangelicals warlike? Yes, according to the culture-wars rhetoric. Mainstream media repeatedly depict evangelicals as frightening people with scary agendas. Evangelicals respond by playing the part: the tribe assumes an us-versus-them mentality.

What would happen if evangelicals invited others to dinner rather than challenged them to war?

Pope John Paul II said that Christians should not *impose* their morality on others but *propose* a more excellent way. Martin Luther King Jr. said we must love people if we want them to change.

Jesus used peaceful metaphors. He spoke of God as a farmer scattering the seed and as a loving father searching for a lost son. He invited himself to dinner at sinners' homes. At the dinner table, each member gets to speak, be heard, and be considered family.

Suppose evangelicals approached those they disagreed with as their neighbors and friends, sharing the common goal for a better community and society. Jesus said that his followers will be known by the way that they love others. Bury the hatchet and come to the table.

ELIZABETH W. McLAUGHLIN,
BETHEL COLLEGE, INDIANA

stream media. Third, ongoing disagreements about the media point once again to the need for collective wisdom and discernment, not just for personal likes and dislikes.

OLD QUESTIONS IN NEW MEDIA SKINS

Most media-related questions go all the way back to the early church. The main issue back then was how to relate Jesus' teachings to mainstream Roman and tribal Jewish culture. Early Christians discussed whether they should go to Roman games, sports events and theater. They wondered if they should read the pagan philosophy of Aristotle or the mythic tales of the *Iliad* and *Odyssey*. Or dance at non-Christian festivals.

The apostle Paul soon joined the ongoing discussions among Jesus-followers. He wrote letters to churches, endorsing Christian freedom against excessive Jewish legalism. He also cautioned Christians against becoming too conformed to the ways of the world. Believers "have the right to do anything," he said, "but not everything is beneficial" (1 Cor 10:18-23). Paul stimulated local churches to think about how to relate Christ to their own cultures, such as whether to go to particular theatrical productions or to read pagan philosophy.

Today the dilemmas include not just how to engage mainstream theater and books but also how to approach new media, such as social-networking websites, audio and video podcasting, blogging, and high-tech worship. Christians face a bewildering array of media, from high-tech Bible theme parks to fantasy computer games, online banner advertising, and intense public relations campaigns for political candidates and megachurch celebrities.

As Paul suggested, the place to begin the Christ-and-culture discourse is not with legalistic prohibitions against culture but instead with a healthy, positive view of the opportunities for relating Christ to culture. Human communication—in all forms and media—is an enabling gift from God. In fact, God is a multimedia communicator, employing everything from sunsets to burning bushes and majestic mountains in order to demonstrate glory, power and love.

Of course, humans misuse God's gift of communication. Pride, ego, selfishness and other enduring human problems affect people's media production and consumption. Human beings mediate reality self-interestedly, half-heartedly, sloppily. Christians, too, living in imperfect communities of biblical discourse, create celebrity idols, misinterpret Scripture, confuse faith with politics and produce bland media content.

Ancient biblical wisdom is this: everything that Christians do with media is part of their witness to the world. Christians' involvement in tribal and mainstream media speaks to *what* and *who* they believe. This is partly why non-Christians' opinions of the church and even of Jesus Christ are mediated by their views of

USES OF PHILIPPIANS 4:8-10

Evangelicals frequently quote Philippians 4:8 in support of their decision to avoid objectionable media content: "whatever is true, whatever is noble, whatever is right, whatever is pure, whatever is lovely, whatever is admirable—if anything is excellent or praiseworthy—think about such things."

But if we use this verse strictly as a media filter, even portions of Scripture such as Judges 19 and 20 seem unacceptable! Perhaps the apostle Paul's advice is not a legalistic filter as much as a perspective for gaining insight into culture. Paul urges us to think about truth, beauty and morality, and to put them into practice, letting them shape our attitudes and action. In other words, these things are meant to serve as guides for Christian discernment, not prohibitions against particular content.

Seen in this light, the oft-quoted Philippians passage opens up culture to Christian engagement, which does not necessarily result in uncritical acceptance. We still are responsible for protecting the weak because some cultural products might lead them astray (Rom 14). There are movies, for example, that are too mature in theme and graphic in treatment for the intellectual and emotional capabilities of children. Nevertheless, contemplating truth will require us to confront cultural expressions of the harsh realities of our fallenness—the waste and ugliness of war, injustice and racism, the depths of human despair, the chaos and confusion of life—all the while seeing these as distortions of the way things are supposed to be in God's good world.

We also have to explore the beauty, grace, mercy, forgiveness, order and certainty that reveal the original goodness of created life and testify to God working through his people to bring about cultural renewal as well as biblical salvation. Philippians 4:8 presents us not with otherworldly ideals but with norms to be lived out in the here and now. Christian interpretations of cultural products then are going to be variously influenced by myriad factors, including theological and ideological beliefs, ethnicity, gender and many more. Increased awareness of the complexity of communication combined with a measure of openness can lead to genuine cultural engagement with Christian media criticism embracing the tension between conviction and humility.

WILLIAM D. ROMANOWSKI, CALVIN COLLEGE

publicly available tribal media. Non-Christians form their views of Christians partly by scanning religious TV and radio and by surfing religious websites.

WHAT MAKES MEDIA CHRISTIAN?

Christian tribes like to insert the adjective *Christian* in front of nouns—as we just did in this sentence! One of the authors of this chapter conversed with a woman who worked at a "Christian wallpaper" company. She was convinced that by printing Bible verses on wallpaper she was creating Christian wallpaper. What does the adjective *Christian* mean when it describes media or the arts? Is there really such a thing as a Christian *medium* (singular) or Christian *media* (plural)?

Tribes often disagree about the meaning of the word *Christian* as applied to culture. For instance, one tribe might assume that U2 is secular. Another one believes that U2 is a prophetic witness to God's truth. One Christian tribe might say that believers should attend only Christian theme parks, whereas another one finds it completely acceptable to visit secular ones. Some say the news is liberal, whereas others say it is primarily entertainment or business. One set of tribes holds that Christian news is news about Christians, whereas others contend that it is news reported from a Christian perspective.

KEY DEFINITIONS

Christian media: all media claimed by one or another Christian tribe, whether evangelical, mainline Protestant or Roman Catholic.

Evangelical media: media that evangelicals produce and consume, often called Christian media by evangelicals themselves.

Mainstream media: media that none of the Christian tribes would call Christian in their everyday use of the term and that evangelicals typically call secular.

Broadly speaking, evangelical tribes tend to use the adjective *Christian* to refer to media that are produced and consumed primarily by evangelicals. To them, *Christian* and *evangelical* are nearly synonymous adjectives. This language can offend other Christian groups. But North American evangelicals are able to get away with this usage largely because they are the most public creators and consumers of distinctly tribal media. It is not easy to come up with nonevangelical examples of religious radio, for instance.[5]

In this book, we use the phrase *Christian media* to refer to the larger grouping of all media claimed to be Christian by one or another Christian tribe—including Roman Catholic and mainline Protestant media (mainline Protestants being those who would not describe themselves as evangelicals). We use the phrase *evangelical media* to refer to media that evangelicals consider their own. We call non-Christian media *mainstream* rather than *secular* to avoid making superficial tribal judgments about media that do not seem to be very religious, at least on the surface. Using the term *mainstream* opens up rather than closes off a discussion about Christian media. The word *secular* carries negative connotations, as if there is nothing of value in such media.

Of course human beings communicate one on one for many practical purposes all day long—on the job, at home, during shopping trips and over coffee. But when it comes to our public communication, the ancient Roman orator Cicero's three categories—teaching, delighting and moving—are helpful.

For instance, media do try to delight audiences, sometimes just by entertaining them. Watching TV shows and movies, and reading novels, can be lots of fun. So can writing a blog or designing a website. We enjoy a good story, funny lines, a beautiful picture, a happy ending and joyous worship.

Admittedly, what delights one person or group might not delight others. Not everyone laughs at a preacher's joke or a blogger's sarcasm. We all grow up in particular cultures marked by things like ethnicity, social class and race. We communicate through gender, personality and personal experiences. We implicitly learn to think of our own tribe as superior to other cultures, making us more or less elitist about things like musical, dramatic and literary taste.

HOW PEOPLE USE PUBLIC COMMUNICATION

Before the birth of Christ, the great Roman orator Cicero (106–43 B.C.) identified three basic purposes for public communication: *teaching, delighting* and *moving* (or persuading) audiences.[a] Augustine of Hippo (A.D. 354–430), one of the most accomplished public communicators in the history of the church, agreed.[b]

[a]Cicero *The Orations of Marcus Tullius Cicero* 4.11[1].

[b]Augustine *De doctrina christiana* (Christian Instruction) 4.27[74].

Teaching and persuading are easier to grasp. For instance, Christians have always loved to instruct people in the faith and to evangelize nonbelievers. Evangelicals occasionally emphasize persuasion as *the* purpose for Christian media; they fall into the trap of thinking that if a message is not meant to convert people to Christ, implicitly or explicitly, it is not Christian communication. Or they assume that a public message has to teach audiences about Jesus or promote Christian values. The idea of just delighting audiences makes them uncomfortable.

Evangelicals' bias toward persuasive communication might result partly from their emphasis on Jesus' Great Commission: "Therefore go and make disciples of all nations, baptizing them in the name of the Father and of the Son and of the Holy Spirit" (Mt 28:19-20). They make personal religious conversion the beginning and end of media activity, equating Christian media with missionary media. Sometimes they justify popular art only as evangelism; they worry that enjoying a musical recording or drama in worship might be sinful. They convince themselves that as long as the message is biblically true, the production is good—no matter how bored the congregants might be!

The instructional-persuasive emphasis in evangelical media also demonstrates fear of emotions, especially sensual emotions. Evangelicals rightly teach, learn and worry about sin. In tune with Scripture, they admit that human beings can go astray in their feelings, not just their minds. Even lusting after someone is like committing physical adultery. For many evangelicals, delight is sometimes too sensual, possibly even carnal. According to an old joke, unholy music leads to dancing, which is a vertical expression of a horizontal desire.

Shying away from delight, evangelicals have tended to support media that preach and teach audiences. Their church libraries are loaded with instructional recordings by pastors and other religious experts. Evangelicals even justify watching delightful stories like the VeggieTales series based on what the recordings teach, not the fact that they entertain as well as instruct. The same instructional-persuasive bias is true for other media products produced by evangelicals—from novels to theme parks and blogs.

Isolating or elevating one of the three major purposes for public communication—teaching, delighting and persuading—underestimates the complexity of human communication. Blogging for one audience might be more instructional than blogging for another audience—especially if one audience wants to be taught and the other one is surfing the Web for fun. Writing a video script to persuade audiences to live faithfully will differ from one that is intended to teach or primarily to entertain. In essence, we have to determine the actual ways that messages work in peoples' lives—not the ways we *think* they will function among mere outsiders to the Christian or mainstream tribes. This applies both to producing and to consuming media.

FAITHFUL MEDIA STEWARDSHIP

The ultimate test of Christians' use of media is applied faithfulness. Do particular tribal media messages represent the faithful efforts of grateful people seeking to love God and neighbor as themselves? Moreover, we can discern such faithfulness in media makers' God-honoring motives, biblical discernment and honed skill.

Market size is not an adequate standard for faithful use of media. A film might become a box-office smash. A novel could be a bestseller. A blog could be top-listed on Google. So what? Spiritually speaking, market success is not necessarily a sign of faithfulness. Neither are examples of unpopular media, of course.

Critical acclaim is insufficient, too. Who says that reviewers are necessarily faithful critics? Are they boosting their own careers? Trying to make friends with media artists? Telling tribal audiences that they want to hear? Floundering about from review to review? Pleasing donors or advertisers?

Audience impact is similarly inadequate. How do we measure media effects?

Which effects are good? What about mixed effects? Some TV preachers undoubtedly bless some viewers, but many of them offend viewers, too. Anecdotal evidence suggests that the more popular TV preachers seem to confirm non-Christians' stereotypes about evangelicals being political operatives, if not self-righteous, lower-class religious hucksters.

Rather than focusing too narrowly on market size, critical acclaim or audience impact, Christians are called to faithful media stewardship. Stewards are caretakers of something owned by someone else. Christian stewards take care of media as God's gifts. They see every medium as another opportunity to praise God by using it to love their neighbors as themselves.

ARE EVANGELICALS' BLOGS A WASTE OF TIME?

Like stadium litter after a game, blogs clutter cyberspace—more than one hundred million of them.[a] A blog (Web log) is a chronological posting of personal thoughts and links to other websites that interest the author. At their best, blogs allow citizen-journalists to break news stories and highlight sources ignored by mainstream media. At their worst, blogs are personal rants without original research or deep analysis.

Evangelical blogs—and there are thousands of them, including networks devoted specifically to faith-based issues—can help writers and readers (1) grow in their faith and (2) find conversational partners who share similar thoughts and struggles. However, tribal bloggers are not the only ones addressing faith. Mainstream counterparts also use strong opinions, humor and personal anecdotes to discuss faith and culture. Often it's not clear to the reader whether a blogger is an evangelical or even religious.

Blogging can help evangelicals strengthen critical-thinking skills while articulating what they believe. Some of the best blogs are online versions of "iron sharpen[ing] iron" (Prov 27:17). They demonstrate a blogger's courage of convictions. Tribal blogs can also help readers learn to discern the wheat from the chaff, worthwhile from worthless content.

It's easy to surf from one blog to another before discovering that it's late at night and the adventure has largely been a waste of time—or that one or two great blogs merit further exploration another day. Personal online time is always a stewardship issue since there are plenty of other things to do!

What if you were responsible to someone for every minute you spent writing and reading blogs—for "every empty word" (Mt 12:36) spoken—or blogged? Would your blogging habits change? What if that person were God? How would it change your blogging habits?

PHYLLIS ALSDURF, BETHEL UNIVERSITY

---

[a]"About Us," Technorati <http://www.technorati.com/about/>.

This *faithful media stewardship* involves at least five actions.

1. Using our time wisely. We all have limited time, so we make media choices implicitly as well as explicitly. Is tonight a good time for consuming a movie, browsing the Internet or conversing with friends? For writing a blog or producing a video for YouTube? We cannot make such decisions wisely unless we understand the opportunities and pitfalls for media in our personal, family, church and community lives.

2. Using our money wisely. Money, like time, is a valuable, God-given resource. It is easy in relatively affluent, materialistic cultures and tribes to squander financial resources on the latest, most impressive and most popular media products. We like demonstrating to others that we have state-of-the-art technologies, even while much of the world does not even have telephone service. We spend a

IS IT TIME TO STOP PLAYING AND START VOLUNTEERING?

Christian critiques of media often focus on bad content: Any offensive language? Violence? Nudity? Innuendo? Disrespectful portrayals of parents, churches, teachers? But some researchers are focusing instead on the media *form*—the ways a medium affects individuals and society regardless of content. For instance, how does playing video games affect children's mental abilities regardless of the specific game they play? Social relationships? School performance? Does cybersurfing promote or inhibit real community?

In *Bowling Alone,*[a] Robert D. Putman labeled TV a chief culprit in the decline of volunteerism because it led people to stay at home. He also speculated that cyberspace might even worsen this problem.

Think about video gaming. In college, men play such games (and watch sports) significantly more than women; they volunteer less than women, too.[b] Is there a connection?

Around the world, there are increased reports of people, especially young males, isolating themselves from society and even their families. (In Japan, they are called *hikikomori.*) Digital technologies such as the Internet and video games seem to be connected to this behavior. At colleges, for instance, some men lock themselves away in their rooms after dinner, playing online network games all night long, and then sleep half of the following day. Unlike bookworms, they don't even go to the library or a café to read and thereby chance upon meeting a friend.

Time is a zero-sum reality. We have only so much of it to use. Yet we need entertainment. What form should our lives take, especially as we seek to love others as ourselves?

MICHAEL JINDRA, SPRING ARBOR UNIVERSITY

[a]Robert D. Putnam, *Bowling Alone: The Collapse and Revival of American Community* (New York: Simon & Schuster, 2000).

[b]Robin Wilson, "The New Gender Divide," *Chronicle of Higher Education* 53, no. 21 (2007): A36.

tremendous amount on entertainment without thinking about the consequences for ourselves, others and God's physical creation.

3. Being discerning critics. Evangelical and mainstream media tend to view audiences as mere consumers. They see us as relatively passive message receivers rather than active audiences who think critically with others about media forms and content. By contrast, as discerning critics we realize that God created us to engage culture, to ponder and evaluate the kinds of lives we are living and the messages we mediate. We refuse to allow ourselves to become mindless, heartless consumers. We care about what we do *with* media, and what the media are doing *to* us. We are vigilant and skeptical about tribal as well as mainstream media.

4. Being purposeful producers. Every human being produces communication and culture. Today many more people produce their own public messages via new technologies. Individuals can publish their own books on paper as well as online, promote personal videos, launch their own Web columns and file their own blog-based news reports about local events. Producing media content is becoming almost as common as interpersonal conversation. Faithfulness requires us to be rightly purposeful, not purposeless producers. We need to ask ourselves repeatedly, What's the point?

5. Participating in Christian communities of discourse. We cannot live faithfully on our own. We cannot become lone media stewards. We all know that we need God's help. We forget, or deny, that we need to communicate with other faithful people about how to communicate faithfully. We need to be reading, writing, producing, listening, viewing and performing with others who seek to love God and their neighbors as themselves.

Conclusion

More and more evangelicals are media makers. Omnipresent computers—cell phones, personal digital assistants, still and moving-image cameras, and word processors, for instance—offer more possibilities for making messages. Websites, blogs, YouTube and other cyber-media outlets provide means for individuals, churches and parachurch groups to circumvent traditional media gatekeepers. It is not so easy to be narrowly tribal anymore, as if we can stick our heads in the sand and ignore mainstream media.

At the same time, we need tribal communities of discourse to make shared sense of the media landscape and our roles in it. Our high-tech media environment, in particular, is heating up with increasingly instantaneous communication among and within tribes. We are all making speedy, often erroneous judgments about others' motives and actions, creating growing conflicts among and within religious faiths.

In order to become better-informed, wiser and more skilled media stewards, we need to discourse with the fans and critics of mainstream as well as tribal media. Otherwise we will tend to assume that God's mixed-up world merely matches our mediated views of it, however right or wrong. We need both interpersonal and mass media to help us together make sense of the world we inhabit. By first listening and conversing—and only then making humble judgments—we can gain a better sense of the real value of new media in church and society. Then we are much better able to use our God-given abilities to make a difference. If we cut off the conversations too quickly, we end up making hasty judgments, poor decisions and fewer audience-serving messages.

U2 is but one example of a group of media makers who, however imperfectly, have evaluated culture through various communicative forms, from musical and video recordings to concerts and websites. The group has instructed, delighted and persuaded tribal and mainstream audiences. It has sought to be faithful to its vision of what it means to be media stewards. By listening to them and others, engaging in ongoing conversations, we too might become wiser media makers. So let the conversations begin!

2

Looking Beyond Radio for Listeners

PAUL A. CREASMAN

A few years ago I began my first radio production class as a new professor at an evangelical university. I asked the students how they used radio. After a long silence, I rephrased the question. What were some of their favorite things about listening to radio? Again, no response. Eventually, one student spoke up, "We don't listen to the radio much."

The students' apathy toward broadcast radio is common. Armed with MP3 players and laptops, young media consumers are turning to personal audio players rather than broadcast radio for music, comedy and other material. The same is true for many evangelicals. Evangelical radio stations and networks are slowly adopting technologies such as satellite radio, webstreaming and podcasting, yet they are scantly attracting younger audiences. The reason? Evangelical radio's programming choices appeal mostly to an aging (and aged) demographic tribe—particularly those fifty-five and older.[1]

Preaching to the Senior—and Conservative—Choir

Radio technology and content diversified significantly in the early years of the new millennium. Traditional or *terrestrial* radio—using the electromagnetic spectrum to broadcast signals from earth-based antennas to homes and autos—increasingly competed with newer technologies like webstreaming, satellite radio and personal digital music players. These new media gave listeners more selection and the freedom to start making their own radio-like programming choices.

Rather than slowly die, terrestrial radio stations created unique content for these new media, like podcasts featuring their most popular DJs or live, commercial-free streaming on the Internet. In some cases, broadcast radio networks provided programs to satellite radio channels. By adapting to new technologies, broadcast radio began tapping into a newer generation of listeners to ensure its survival.

Evangelical broadcast radio semi-adapts. Evangelical stations and networks have adapted somewhat by streaming their broadcast signals online, but without the creativity necessary to attract younger audiences. Evangelical radio—including terrestrial radio, satellite radio, webstreaming and podcasting—still emphasizes only two types of content (or formats): (1) contemporary Christian music (CCM) and (2) preaching/teaching programs.

Instead of creating unique content for new technologies, tribal stations use podcasts, webstreams and satellite radio channels typically to retransmit programming they are already broadcasting over local airwaves. Why? Partly because of evangelical stations' stable ownership. Whereas mainstream radio networks and stations regularly change hands, evangelical ones are sometimes family businesses or parachurch ministries with very loyal, older owners and boards of directors. Thus, tribal radio is driven by conventional ways of doing things—practices meant to appease audiences and owners who have grown up listening to the programming and venerating older on-air celebrities. The result is small, older audiences that prefer conservative programs.

Tiny audiences. Terrestrial tribal radio has long captured only 1.5 percent of all radio listeners.[2] While stations playing contemporary music have slowly but steadily gained listeners, those emphasizing preaching/teaching programs have steadily lost listeners.[3] The exact number of tribal stations in the United States is hard to determine, although estimates suggest that over two thousand stations broadcast at least twenty hours of religious programming weekly.[4] Religious fare can include anything from Southern and traditional gospel to a handful of Arabic and Hindi programs.

Gray-haired listeners. Nearly 60 percent of the tribal audience for preaching/teaching programs are fifty or older—almost 90 percent are older than thirty-five. Surprisingly, the audience for CCM radio is only moderately younger—almost 70 percent are thirty-five and older with an average age of forty.[5] One study observed that "religious young people seem to be underserved" by evangelical radio.[6]

Evangelical radio serves the tribe. The leading national radio network aimed primarily at evangelicals is Salem, ranked seventh largest among all radio companies with ninety-seven owned-and-operated stations—a majority of them in the twenty-five largest U.S. markets.[7] Salem produces everything from preaching and teaching programs to contemporary music and a few politically oriented talk shows, some hosted by non-Christians. The for-profit Salem competes with both conservative mainstream talk radio and other nonprofit evangelical stations, mixing faith and right-wing politics. The management sees its growing group of stations as a platform for political influence as well as evangelization. Salem's owners note, "We seek to be a positive influence on our culture. As Christians, we have an obligation to be involved and politics is part of that involvement."[8]

Apart from Salem's talk format, contemporary music dominates tribal radio. Contemporary Christian music is the seventh most programmed radio format in the United States with nearly 700 full-time stations.[9] Salem started the FISH format, featuring an upbeat but predictable mix of current and older Christian music, from Jars of Clay to Mercy Me and Amy Grant. The K-Love radio network focuses exclusively on playing CCM on over 250 U.S. broadcast stations and translators (largely rural radio transmitters that merely retransmit programming from another frequency in a different city or even state). CCM channels are available on the major satellite radio and cable TV systems. CCM gained popularity in the early 1990s, replacing some of the preaching/teaching formats that had long been the staple of tribal radio.

The typical preaching/teaching radio format is a continuous flow of sermons and lessons in half-hour segments that mimic shortened church services: announcements, a song, a sermon and sometimes an "opportunity" for an offering. Nonpreaching programs, like James Dobson's popular *Focus on the Family,* often address current social issues with a guest or mimic the call-in style of mainstream talk radio. Popular personality-oriented programs have included the following:

Focus on the Family with Dr. James Dobson
Insight for Living with Chuck Swindoll
In Touch with Charles Stanley

WHAT IS EVANGELICAL RADIO?

Professional mainstream radio research organizations do not define *evangelical* as a distinct radio format. Instead they use the generic term *religious* along with a few subcategories. Why? Partly because evangelical-oriented programming can take a myriad of forms and cross various subcategories, such as contemporary Christian, contemporary inspirational, gospel, and Southern gospel. Perhaps it is also a result of mainstream organizations failing to understand evangelicalism's tribalism.[a] The phrase *evangelical radio* as used in this chapter is defined by the most popular religious format, namely, contemporary Christian, along with a secondary religious format which focuses on biblical preaching and teaching.

[a]See *Broadcasting and Cable Yearbook 2006* (New Providence, N.J.: R. R. Bowker, 2005), p. D-682, and Karen M. Hawkins, ed., *Directory of Religious Media* (Manassas, Va.: National Religious Broadcasters, 1996), pp. 199-206. The mainstream *Yearbook* defines the religious format as Christian, the gospel format as evangelical music and leaves the Christian format undefined. The evangelical-oriented *Directory* identifies nineteen distinct radio formats used by religious and evangelical broadcasters, including adult contemporary, inspirational, sacred, praise and worship, teaching/preaching, Southern gospel, and urban contemporary, among others. While later editions of the *Directory* combine or eliminate some categories, this is perhaps indicative that evangelicals view their broadcast efforts to be quite diverse and sophisticated, in contrast to nontribal groups, who lump evangelical broadcasting into just a few broad categories (or spread it around among those categories).

Grace to You with John MacArthur
Hour of Decision with Billy Graham
Thru the Bible with J. Vernon McGee
Bible Answer Man with Hank Hanegraaff
Love Worth Finding with Adrian Rogers

These shows require a likable, high-profile personality who can engage older listeners. Thus, many programs feature a grandfatherly host. Such recognizable, friendly personalities create strong listener loyalty. Some producers continue distributing sermons even after the preacher passes away—as in the cases of McGee and Rogers.[10]

Shedding the choir robes. A small cadre of evangelicals uses webstreaming and podcasting exclusively to distribute creative, unique content to younger audiences not served by typical tribal broadcasts.[11] CMRadio.net streams various genres of Christian music, from heavy-metal to Celtic and punk, through its website and via iTunes. Tastyfresh.com, dedicated to Christian club and dance music, uses the Web to discuss and distribute programs that otherwise would not be broadcast on conventional stations.[12] Young pastors such as Rob Bell of Mars Hill Bible Church in Michigan post downloadable sermons online, extending their teaching beyond the local congregation without the expense of purchasing airtime.

CONVERTING AND EDIFYING AUDIENCES

Many evangelical leaders, station and network officials, and program personalities believe that radio powerfully communicates the gospel. In fact, evangelicals have held this faith in the power of the medium ever since the first regularly scheduled radio broadcast in 1921—which originated from a church. Radio broadcasting was the miracle that supposedly would transform the world, reaching every corner of the globe for the sake of the gospel. Modern evangelical radio fans still see broadcasting (and now by extension, satellite radio, webstreaming and podcasting) as an electronic means of converting the unsaved and teaching the faithful.

Teaching. While evangelical radio expends considerable effort to convert unbelievers, it spends more time teaching the tribe. Broadcasts often are edited directly from Sunday sermons; programs such as *Insight for Living* and *Back to the Bible* focus on scriptural instruction and practical Christian living. Often, broadcasts will direct listeners to the ministry's companion website, where one can download program outlines, sermon notes and other learning resources.

Some Christian musicians whose songs are played on radio believe that they are essentially teachers who nurture believers with "songs of exhortation" to "keep the Christian on the narrow path."[13] Evangelical radio's supporters recognize that music can be instrumental in the "growth" and "nourishment" of believers.[14]

Delighting. Early evangelical radio broadcasters worried about radio's "potential for entertainment" and "prideful display that elevated the self."[15] As they got more involved in the medium, however, tribal leaders wrestled with how to discern appropriate uses of broadcast entertainment.[16] By and large, broadcast entertainment is no longer an issue since most evangelicals readily accept Christian music as "sanctified entertainment."[17]

One study reveals that some members of the tribe enjoy Christian music radio more when it mimics the reverence of the church service.[18] Comedy interviews or discussions of secular issues detract from the worshiplike setting that the genre affords them. Not everyone agrees, however, that Christian music radio or evangelical radio as a whole should maintain this churchlike attitude.

Persuading. Evangelism is at the heart of tribal radio, whose history is filled with stories of broadcasters concerned "fervently about the need of every person to find eternal salvation in Jesus Christ."[19] Early radio evangelists such as Paul Rader, Walter Maier and Charles Fuller were passionately drawn to radio to "reach people with the gospel of Christ."[20] Even after the rise of TV in the 1950s, these early broadcasters "never wavered in their commitment to a single overriding goal: the conversion of the unsaved American public."[21]

While mainstream broadcasters view radio as entertainment, tribal stations view it primarily as "ministry."[22] As the title of a leading evangelical media magazine said: "CCM and Teaching and Talk Programmers Agree! Stay on Mission with the Great Commission."[23] Generally speaking, evangelicals believe converting souls to Jesus Christ is the most important, God-honoring, effective purpose for using radio.

Tribal radio's supporters also hope that it can shape culture. Programs such as *Focus on the Family* seek to persuade evangelical audiences to social action, particularly on political and moral issues. They urge listeners to get involved in the political process to influence legislators on issues such as abortion and gay rights. The American Family Radio (AFR) network maintains an extensive website of news about social issues, potential product boycotts and daily issue-oriented podcasts—all of which correspond with AFR's own radio broadcasts.

Mired in Tradition . . . and Mediocrity

While older tribal audiences seem content with evangelical radio's offerings, many younger evangelicals and mainstream critics are not so pleased. They charge tribal radio with boring, predictable mediocrity aimed at the "gospel ghetto."[24]

Tribal radio is still based largely on program styles that go back at least to the

IT'S ALL JUST TRIBAL PROPAGANDA . . .

Propaganda is a slippery word for a slippery concept. If I don't like someone, his efforts to change minds are propaganda. If I agree with him, he is practicing the "art of persuasion, beautiful and just."

The word has religious origins. In 1622, Pope Gregory XV founded the Sacred Congregation of Propaganda, which was to spread Catholicism in the New World and combat Protestantism in Europe. In the twentieth century, the word *propaganda* has been applied primarily to persuasive efforts by governments and political parties. However, a Google search finds nearly 50,000 pages with the phrase "Christian propaganda." Most are unflattering.

To be useful, the propaganda can't simply be a synonym for persuasion. Jacques Ellul, a leading Christian social theorist, describes it as "techniques of psychological influence combined with techniques of organization and the envelopment of people with the intention of sparking action."[a] In other words, modern propaganda is a large-scale persuasive effort using multiple media, often conducted by people more interested in success than truth.

It's also *not* helpful to refer to the persuasive efforts of a single person, a small group or the average church as propaganda. Few Christian groups in North America have the resources to compete with governments, major political parties or huge corporations. And that's good, since Christians are guided not by propaganda's goal of success through any means but by faithfully presenting the gospel. When evangelicals depart from such faithful communication, they provide traction for the idea that "it's all just Christian propaganda."

RANDALL L. BYTWERK, CALVIN COLLEGE

[a]Jacques Ellul, *Propaganda: The Formation of Men's Attitudes* (New York: Knopf, 1968), p. xiii.

1930s and 1940s, when phenomenally popular radio preacher Charles E. Fuller hosted his national *Old Fashioned Revival Hour.*[25] His religious variety show offered a little singing and chit-chat, notably with Fuller's wife, Grace, who would read a few short listener letters each week. Toward the end of the program, Fuller offered a sermon in his down-home, folksy style. Many radio preachers mimicked this approach through the years. Some added controversial elements such as miraculous healings and aggressive fund raising. One critic argues that such programs rarely make "severe intellectual demands on either pastor or flock."[26]

As one tribal critic said regarding evangelical TV, teaching/preaching programs demonstrate that evangelical broadcasters "drift along on imaginary clouds," fooling themselves that their shows actually engage mainstream audiences.[27] Tribal radio might have drifted along even more than TV since there have historically been so many more radio stations than TV stations. In any case, it is hard to imagine a non-Christian listening seriously to these programs; instead, he or she might find them more entertaining or silly than instructional.

Evangelical radio got itself into this tribal ghetto partly because of its narrowly conceived ministry rationale, which suggests that as long as believers produce programs with the right motive—i.e., "for the Lord"—quality is not especially important. According to a Christian music industry insider, this rationale is merely an "excuse for mediocrity."[28] An opponent of tribal radio says that a "driver who listened to Christian radio on the road was in danger of falling asleep at the wheel."[29]

Amazingly, the tribal music radio industry recently criticized itself for not being adequately ministry-oriented. Trying to shed perceptions of its bland backwardness, some evangelical broadcasters decided to operate more like for-profit stations with higher production values and more professional-sounding program hosts. One national study urged the industry to shed its preachy tendencies and go "mainstream."[30] Yet when stations try to compete directly with mainstream radio they often end up losing their distinctive, tribal ethos and audience. One Christian music artist laments, "Now, when you scan the dial, you can't find the Christian radio station. Not a lot of the big songs are identifiably Christian."[31]

Efforts to update evangelical radio for younger audiences do not sit well with its loyal but aging listeners. A single change to the broadcast day—moving program times, for example—can elicit hundreds of complaints from listeners, including donors to nonprofit stations. In particular, modernizing music on Christian music stations sets off audience alarms: "It sounds like secular music!" After a few vehemently negative listener calls about heavy rock or hip-hop music, for instance, most station managers will reconsider, if not change, their airplay policies. An early tribal rock radio DJ recalled that some evangelicals who heard his show "started making so much of a hassle [about the music] that stations began to back off, because they were afraid of offending the constituency."[32]

Opponents also complain about evangelical radio's tendency to push old-fashioned moral, political and cultural agendas. According to such critics, evangelical broadcasters tend to put down those that do not believe the same things they do. Self-righteous program hosts engage in militaristic us-versus-them (usually conservatives versus liberals or Christians versus unbelievers) rhetoric because it plays well with their donors and advertisers. Such rhetoric often alienates the very non-Christians that the stations are supposedly evangelizing.

Some evangelical and mainstream broadcasters have criticized a few evangelicals' bullying tactics to gain new radio stations in markets. The AFR network acquired more stations by assuming the translator frequencies of some National Public Radio (NPR) stations. Apparently such tactics "riled NPR listeners" and irked "rival Christian broadcasters."[33] In some cities, there is no longer an NPR station. Even more irritating for evangelicals, however, is the way that some for-profit

CHRISTIAN RADIO'S IDENTITY CRISIS

Encouraging. Positive. Safe for the whole family. Listen to any evangelical radio station and you're bound to hear one of these identifiers in the station's taglines.

I've worked for years in evangelical radio and seen many stations do a lot of good for a lot of people. Most parents understandably don't want their little children to be exposed to the crude humor of shock jocks or to lyrics that promote loose living. But the squeaky-clean lingo often signifies merely what a station stands *against,* not what it stands *for.* Is the only goal of Christian culture to be safe and sanitized?

What do most evangelicals really want from the radio? Authenticity. They want to hear about real life, real struggles, real people who share the same kinds of messy experiences and tough choices that they do. After all, the church is a hospital for sinners, not a museum for saints.

Evangelicals are tired of robo-Christianity, political agendas, fake-sounding DJs and laundry lists of alleged sins—like voting for a Democrat or attending a liberal church. They want programming that helps their communities flourish here on earth—not incessant infomercials for eternal life after death. That's why a lot of young people are tuning out radio and listening to podcasts and recorded music instead. They're crying out for authentic programming that is relevant to *everyone,* Christian or not.

SCOTT TANIS, INSIDER CRITIC OF CHRISTIAN RADIO

tribal companies have bought stations in markets with existing nonprofit tribal stations, thereby reducing the nonprofits' listenership, donations and revenue. Often the result is a splitting of the already small tribal audience of older listeners, not the cultivation of a significantly younger audience on the newer station.

Broadcasting Extends the Ancient Church

When radio broadcasting emerged in the 1920s, it captured the human imagination with the grand promise of communicating across geographic space with the speed of electricity. Media theorist Marshall McLuhan noted that all media extend some aspect of the human—physical or psychological—in spatial and temporal dimensions.[34] Radio expands humans' ability to speak and listen beyond their local communities. Audio recording devices, from records to iPods, also enable people to communicate through time by preserving modern voices for future generations.

The Hebrew and Christian faiths already believed in cross-spatial communication. Worship and prayer always involved cross-spatial, cross-temporal communion with God. Moreover, ancient worship included elements of praise, prayer and instruction.[35] Most contemporary evangelical radio extends these ancient worship practices across space.[36] Much of the early public rhetoric about wireless technology used biblical imagery and claimed that the world would become one large, unified family of believers.[37]

Competing with Shock Jocks While Pleasing the Tribe

Evangelical music stations imitate mainstream radio. Salem's contemporary music format includes hip DJs, long music blocks, catchy jingles, boisterous morning cohosts, local promotional events with said cohosts or other station personalities, call-ins, shout-outs, countdown shows, request lines, etc. The imitative list goes on and on.

These stations avoid musical and DJ references to sex and drugs. Sometimes they mention prayer requests and remind listeners their programming is "safe for the whole family"—likely a reference to mainstream radio's sometimes sordid nature. In addition, commercials tout Christian everything: chiropractors, mortgage lenders, real estate agents, high schools and colleges, car salespersons, and lawyers. The adjective *Christian* becomes a marketing device and a badge of tribal loyalty.

Furthermore, stations playing contemporary Christian music enjoy a special synergy with the evangelical product marketplace—becoming a gateway for evangelical popular culture. Christian music and book-publishing companies value CCM radio because it often provides ample exposure for their products. Evangelical product companies sometimes pay less in advertising costs because evangelical radio stations are willing to feature the latest Christian book, Christian film or Christian concert as part of their programming. One observer noted that CCM's growth as a genre has been due at least in part to the number of radio stations playing the music that drives listeners to local evangelistic bookstores.[38]

Moreover, such stations tend to be dedicated to Christian music megastars, recognizable to mainstream audiences, much to the promotional detriment of newer musicians and performers. Tribal stations play a fair share of recognizable hits from Christian music's past. As with preaching programs, the CCM radio industry tends to recycle its most popular songs and artists. But even these selections are limited to overtly Christian lyrics or inspirational praise tunes, such as Amy Grant's "Thy Word" and Michael W. Smith's "Friends," which are played over and over again. Listeners seem to delight in the predictable, safe, praise-oriented music, rather than more secular genres as jazz, hip-hop and, oddly enough, classical music. In the process, these stations seem to end up "rocking the flock" rather than reaching the lost.

Tuning in Creative Stations and Listeners

Broadcast radio has survived challenges from new technologies such as television, satellites and iPods by creating innovative content adapted to new cultural, social and economic realities. In the 1950s, radio adapted to television by creating new music programs and emphasizing the local DJ. In the 1990s, it adapted to the Internet by forging online stations featuring music not heard elsewhere. In the twenty-first century, satellite radio has established itself as a haven for broadcasters—like Howard Stern—who dislike terrestrial radio's governmental restrictions on content. With every new technological innovation, radio has found new, often more intriguing means of competing.

This is vital in today's fragmented media landscape. Radio has to compete with media such as TV, the Internet, video games and comic books for the attention of audiences moving from the home, to the car, to work and back again. Frequently, radio takes a secondary role in the lives of listeners, who may be driving, doing homework or cooking dinner as they listen. In order to maintain audiences, radio stations have to create ever-more-compelling programs. Evangelical radio fails to do so.

Radio's strengths. Radio effectively generates community based on a "sense of camaraderie and mutuality."[39] Radio brings people together to share experiences. It can bring joy, like being among the first to hear a new song with other listeners. In times of trouble, such as after Hurricane Katrina, radio can offer mutual comfort.[40] Such moments bond audience members together. The best radio allows individuals to contribute to that community, such as through a talk show or call-ins.

Radio also excels at stimulating the imagination, often called "the theater of the mind." In the absence of visual cues, listeners are left to picture what they are hearing, such as the DJ at the microphone. NPR excels at this technique, using natural sounds to heighten otherwise typical news stories.

Evangelical radio's weaknesses. Tribal radio, by comparison, lacks imagination. Both CCM and preaching formats are filled with direct, overt and often simple expressions of the Christian faith. Such lackluster programming hardly builds community among those outside the faith and possibly taxes the patience of those within. Even tribal listeners can tire of being preached at constantly.[41] New audio technologies do not automatically alleviate this problem. Making programs available online or via download might demonstrate evangelicals' technical competence, but it does not mean that the tribe understands how to use radio to connect well with others.

Much tribal radio seems like a college lecture class without PowerPoint. Surely there are artful, innovative ways to tap into the sense of community and imagination afforded by radio without resorting to moralistic bullying and dogmatic preachiness and without sacrificing the core tenets of the tribal faith.

Previous attempts to reinvent Christian radio have not fared well. Several radio stations in the 1990s toyed with a hybrid format—mixing wholesome mainstream songs with contemporary Christian ones. The highest-profile attempt lasted only

AN INTERNET ALTERNATIVE TO REGULAR RADIO

Like many nonreligious tribes, evangelicals love to circumvent mainstream media with their own means of reaching the public. One alternative model to regular broadcast-radio distribution of programs is the Public Radio Exchange (PRX, found at <www.prx.org>).

Like YouTube, but with higher-quality fare, PRX enables anyone to pay a small annual fee to post audio files online for others to hear and review, and even for radio stations to license and broadcast. The site's Vox Pop gives listeners a way to comment on programs, even by posting their own video responses. PRX is a "bottomless grab bag full of radio pieces," said one newspaper writer.[a]

"In some ways, PRX is an example of radio done Internet style, where the content is bottom up," explained Steve Schultze, Calvin College graduate and PRX project director from 2003, when it began, until he left in 2006.[b] He said PRX's supporters hope to reinvigorate mass media and encourage program contributions from all kinds of people.

Although explicitly religious content is sparse on the site, programming is remarkably diverse: *Anatomy of a Wrongful Conviction,* a thirty-minute documentary about the causes and impact of wrongful convictions, and "The Pol Walk," a four-minute documentary about a Montana politician going door to door to meet voters.[c]

Headquartered in Boston, PRX is funded by grants as well as by fees from the radio stations that license content. Maybe evangelicals should consider such an open policy, allowing all comers to slip their perspectives under the door to be heard and examined.

MICHAEL RAY SMITH, CAMPBELL UNIVERSITY

[a]Alex van Oss, "New Exchange Aims a Kick at Public Radio," *The Washington Post,* July 6, 2004.

[b]Personal communication, Aug. 27, 2007.

[c]"MacArthur Foundation provides $350,000 for public radio exchange; online service to link producers, public radio stations, listeners throughout the country." AScribe Newswire, January 27, 2004.

six months before listener outrage and a lack of advertising doomed the station.[42]

The balance point. Evangelical radio is divided by age. Broadcast programming is governed by older station owners who play staid, preachy shows that appeal to their loyal, older listeners. Nonbroadcast audio programming, especially Internet streaming and audio downloading, is used primarily by younger evangelicals. In the end, the most innovative content gets marginalized to the edges of the evangelical radio industry or pushed underground.

All radio formats must determine how to rebuild their audience when listeners go elsewhere. Evangelical radio is at this critical juncture. Today's Christian music audiences are only slightly younger than preaching/teaching audiences, which are dying off. Evangelical stations, by continually playing to older audiences, are alienating the next generation of listeners—those with the most potential skill and drive to use modern technologies effectively and to engage mainstream culture more openly. If evangelical radio does not determine how to attract a new, younger audience, the format risks disappearing.

Case in point: between 1999 and 2006, the radio audience for adult standards

A CHRISTIAN, AN ATHEIST AND A RABBI WALK INTO A BAR . . .

At first, it seems like a regular radio talk show. Instead it's North America's first competition talk show. It's *The Hub.*[a] Each week, panelists discuss politics, religion, philosophy, regional and national news, and popular culture. Panelists might be Christians, atheists, even the average man on the street or "pledges."

Here's the twist: pledges face off on particular issues, after which listeners call in and vote off a pledge—à la *Survivor.* Only pledges who outwit and outlast the others get to return for the next program.

The wild show, broadcast on a mainstream news/talk radio station and streamed live on the Web, originates from a bar. Get this: the program's host and co-creator are both Christian college graduates. Is this any way to run a radio program? You bet. It might just be what dull tribal radio needs.

Evangelical radio is full of worship, preaching and teaching. It doesn't provide forums for believers to interact with people of other faiths. It doesn't really entertain. It doesn't attract many people from outside the tribe—not even most people from inside the tribe!

The Hub reveals new possibilities for evangelical radio. It creatively engages panelists and listeners with faith-based dialogue that appeals to those outside the tribe. It doesn't rely on the right-wing spin and rants common in existing Christian talk radio. In fact, the big-name tribal radio hosts would probably get booted off *The Hub* faster than listeners could recite the Lord's Prayer.

The Hub is a fresh approach to talk radio created by Christians. It is drawing listeners, ratings and advertisers by appealing to a wide audience, not just Christians.

PAUL A. CREASMAN, AZUSA PACIFIC UNIVERSITY

[a]www.thehubradioshow.com.

(easy listening, nostalgia) shrank from 3.8 percent to 0.9 percent.[43] Adult standards programming shares one important characteristic with evangelical radio—older listeners.[44] As the adult standards audience ages and dies, the format's presence on the radio dial diminishes accordingly. Evangelical radio faces the same fate. In fact, it has already begun. Since 1998, the preaching/teaching format has lost half its audience.[45]

Contemporary tribal radio does serve an important role by teaching and edifying primarily older, eager Christians. At the same time, allowing evangelical radio broadcasting to slowly die is not good stewardship. Faithful media stewardship means conversing with others in the faith about how to communicate wisely and well. Intergenerational conversations about the future of evangelical radio are sorely needed. Evangelical media owners, businesspersons and church leaders must relinquish some control over their for-profit and nonprofit industries if they expect tribal radio to innovate and increase listenership.

One possibility is to reinvent evangelical radio from the outside in, rather than inside out. Working from outside the established tribal radio industry may awaken others to the possibilities of faith-based radio. This has its own potential pitfalls, such as evangelical entrepreneurs creating programs without adequate biblical and theological wisdom. Such attempts might create unnecessary waves of conflict, schism and controversy. On the positive side, it might prompt a spiritual and artistic renaissance—perhaps even a redefinition of evangelical radio.

Conclusion

The first week of my college teaching career, I asked my radio production class, "How could you NOT listen to radio?" I stood in amazement as they explained that they preferred their mix tapes to radio broadcasts.

I hope that younger evangelicals will rediscover the joy of radio even as it assimilates itself into new technologies. I learned from my students that the lines between broadcast radio and personal audio might be a thing of the past. I also learned they can be passionate, creative producers. They and others like them are the future of evangelical radio.

3

Thinking Outside the Tribal TV Box

KATHY BRUNER

Tim Scott and Will Decker, twentysomethings passionate about evangelism, launched a worldwide missionary journey. With a mini-DV camera, the two captured their adventures in *Travel the Road (TTR),* their own entertaining cross between *Survivor* and a missions documentary. They pitched their production to TV networks, but only the Trinity Broadcasting Network (TBN) risked launching the series that followed Scott and Decker through twenty-five countries.

MTV later expressed interest in picking up the program because of its engaging plot, although the network's producers wanted to downplay the gospel and spice up the stories. MTV suggested either adding sexy female companions or adding a Buddhist monk, a Muslim imam and a Jewish rabbi who could compete for converts. Scott and Decker understandably turned MTV down in order to keep the gospel in the picture.[1] Episodes continued on TBN for additional seasons, with past seasons available for purchase online.

Travel the Road represented a new approach to Christian video and TV at the beginning of the twenty-first century. The show was higher quality and more creative than most previous evangelical fare, emphasizing stories about real lives shaped by the gospel, healings and miracles. The style appealed to younger viewers, encouraging them to share their faith. But because many episodes were overtly evangelistic, some viewers were undoubtedly turned off.

For years, evangelical critics have blasted Christian TV for preaching to the choir. Now, because of audience fragmentation and a proliferation of channels, some tribal TV is actually thriving *because* it reaches a particular market segment. Evangelicals are being forced to compete for both mainstream and tribal audiences in a media environment with digital formats, more channels, widescreen home entertainment systems, handheld shooting and playback devices, and consumers-turned-producers of their own YouTube productions.

THE RANGE OF CHRISTIAN TV

About 45 percent of all American adults watch some type of Christian TV monthly, about the same percentage of the population that attends church services.[2] That figure includes Roman Catholic, mainline Protestant and evangelical programs via broadcast, cable and satellite. It also includes those who tune in only briefly because they happen to be tuning across the channels. When all Christian media—radio, television, Web and publications—are included, the figure rises to 67 percent, suggesting that more people tune in, however briefly, to some form of Christian media than actually attend church monthly.

Catholics and mainline Protestants have long been producing TV programming. Notable past shows included the Lutherans' long-running drama *This Is the Life* and Catholic Bishop Fulton Sheen's prime-time talking-head teaching show, *Life Is Worth Living,* which landed him on the cover of *Time* magazine in 1952.[3] Pope Paul VI once said that "the Church would feel guilty before the Lord if she did not use these powerful means that human skill is daily rendering more perfect,"[4] and true to that mission, the Catholic Eternal Word Television Network (EWTN), begun by Mother Angelica, distributes conservative Catholic programs from a TV studio/monastery in Alabama.

Nevertheless, evangelicals dominate the religious TV landscape. Thanks to broadcast, cable, satellite and Internet programming, most Americans have access to evangelical TV. Programs include news and talk shows, magazine shows, sitcoms, reality TV, and cartoons.

Evangelicals educate through devotional programs, Bible studies such as Kay Arthur's *Precepts for Life,* prophecy shows, and seminars on faith and family issues such as the Family Enrichment series on FamilyNet. Many Bible certificate programs, training workshops and degree programs advertise during broadcasts and often feature ministry leaders as teachers.

Evangelism is the goal of most revival and crusade broadcasts and televised preachers, whereas political persuasion dominates tribal public affairs programming. Jay Sekulow's weekly program defends a conservative understanding of constitutional law and religious freedom, encouraging viewers to make their opinions known to local and national leaders.

Evangelical entertainment includes sitcoms and comedies like *Pastor Greg* on Cornerstone TeleVision and *Bananas,* a stand-up comedy show. Other entertaining genres include Bible game shows, music video programs and late-night variety shows. Talent contests (e.g., the Inspiration Network's *Christian Artist Talent Search*), modeled after *American Idol,* seek out new talent for Christian recording labels.

MAINSTREAM IMITATION WORKS

Evangelicals have always imitated mainstream TV. But so has mainstream television! TV producers tend to copy other successful programming rather than risking innovative shows. For evangelicals, copycat programming might give viewers the sense that they can be "in the world" without being "of the world" (Jn 17:13-16).[5]

For instance, evangelical TV news such as the news segment on *The 700 Club* is conservatively slanted. Evangelicals produce imitation magazine/lifestyle shows including *Living the Life* and *Life Today.* Some female-oriented tribal talk shows resemble the popular mainstream morning show called *The View.* They feature attractive hosts chatting about health, family, fashion and household tips. While teaching and delighting daytime audiences, they sometimes encourage women to embrace traditional female roles.[6]

Tribal children's programming includes preschool learning programs with animation, puppets, songs and lessons that resemble *Playhouse Disney.* Evangelical cartoons feature characters overcoming physical and moral danger. Adventure programming is similar to that seen on *Discovery Children.* Children's shows combine entertainment with spiritual instruction.

Programming for teenagers includes mainstream-styled music, celebrities, comedy and extreme sports. *Steelroots* mirrors an MTV music show. *InTune with Tara* is a celebrity feature and talk show on iLifetv. Music programs mirror all pop culture genres, including Christian hip-hop, hardcore rock and punk. Extreme sports programs can feature young Christians combining their love of surfboarding or skateboarding with a service-oriented ministry trip. Teens who enjoy *Late Night with Conan O'Brien* can watch imitation fare like *The Logan Show,* hosted by a former Nickelodeon personality.[7]

SUPPORTERS OF THE SMALL SCREEN

Evangelicals are perhaps the most enthusiastic Christian fans of television. They cite the medium's capacity to accomplish several goals.

Fulfill the Great Commission. Evangelicals have often seen TV as a means to "go into all the world and preach the gospel" (Mk 16:15; Mt 28:19-20) or to do what one scholar has called "missionary television."[8] The programming can reach people who do not attend church and who might not otherwise hear the gospel. Given that "slightly more than one-fourth of the unchurched—about 20 million adults—tune in these shows monthly,"[9] their claims about audience reach reflect North American optimism about the power of media to influence people.[10] One Christian television executive says the media have developed "beyond people's wildest dreams, and the best is probably yet to come."[11] Another says his network's transition to high definition television (HDTV) "will help us fulfill our mission better."[12] Fans of evangelistic TV often point to the apostle Paul's assertion that he became all things to all people so that he might "by all possible means" save some (1 Cor 9:22).[13]

The Great Commission relates to evangelical end-times prophecy, since only those who are saved will be carried up to heaven when Christ returns. "We may not have much time left," says the founder of a Christian television network.[14] Many evangelicals believe that Jewish control over Israel will culminate in Christ's return, so securing Israel's future is paramount.[15] Many Christian TV programs point prophetically to the formation of the nation of Israel as the beginning of the end times in Scripture, although it is hard to determine if such programming

DOES TRIBAL TV EVANGELIZE?

"Right now . . . bow your head and pray with me. . . . Turn your life over to Jesus Christ!"

Can a TV message like that elicit real repentance and salvation? Or are TV evangelists kidding themselves or puffing up donors?

Evangelist Billy Graham set an all-time attendance record at a crusade in New York City in 1957, but soon after he began focusing instead on TV evangelism. "TV is the only way to reach the non-churched," he said, and through the years, a higher proportion of his TV viewers reportedly made decisions for Christ than those at his live crusades.[a]

Some TV evangelists claim they average ten thousand salvation decisions for every evangelistic appeal on TV. But do these decisions really mean much? Do they stick?

Many evangelicals imagine that if Jesus were alive today, he would use modern media to draw people to him. It's a great image. But the Holy Spirit is the prime mover until Jesus returns. We can't see the Spirit on TV. Or can we?

Evangelicals are split on the issue of TV evangelism. Some are understandably wary of superficial televangelist messages. Others believe that it would be a sin not to use the tools God has given believers to communicate truth. One evangelical writes, "To not use TV as a medium for the gospel . . . is to make a conscious choice to be half-hearted in our attempt to fulfill the Great Commission."[b] But being committed to using a medium is not the same as using it well, in tune with the greatest Creator of all.

KATHLEEN SINDORF, CORNERSTONE UNIVERSITY

[a]Verified by Melany Ethridge, a spokesperson for the Billy Graham Evangelistic Association, in a phone interview on August 8, 2007.

[b]Jason Dulle, Letters, ninetyandnine.com, February 10, 2003 <www.ninetyandnine.com/Archives/20030210/letters.htm>.

significantly shapes evangelicals' understanding of biblical prophecy—or if tribal TV merely reaffirms what evangelicals are taught by pastors and through other media such as books and radio.

Teach and disciple. Proponents of evangelical TV value the medium's apparent teaching and discipleship potential. The increased use of DVDs in churches has made more believers accustomed to media teaching. Fans also point to audio and video podcasting for mobile discipleship, recognizing that believers will increasingly be able to download the latest episode of a favorite preacher or teacher and then exercise, drive or ride the commuter train while listening or viewing.[16]

Calm believers in turbulent times. Terrorist attacks on the World Trade Centers in New York City in 2001 immediately increased public interest in spirituality, and tribal broadcasters began providing more faith-related news.[17] In 2005, evangelical networks established a news cooperative as a means of pooling footage and improving global coverage. "We don't just tell them what the news is," explains one leader. "We tell them what it means. And that's appealing to people, especially in moments of cultural instability."[18] The coverage avoids lurid topics and affirms a world in which evangelical faith is a normal, essential part of life.

Provide wholesome, family-friendly fare. Fans of tribal TV say the programming is morally safe and offers a "Christ-centered alternative to standard television fare."[19] They stress that evangelical programming provides audience-desired spiritual themes and clean plot lines often unavailable on mainstream programs. Moreover, as consolidating mainstream media organizations continue to be on "the cutting edge of degradation," evangelical leaders believe they have "a vested interest in promoting clean programming."[20]

WHY THE CRITICS CRINGE

British writer and TV personality Malcolm Muggeridge once wrote an essay, titled "The Fourth Temptation," in which Christ resists the devil's offer to star on prime-time TV.[21] Over the top? No doubt. But Muggeridge nevertheless argued persuasively that a camera always lies because it cannot capture everything—only what is shot. Christians need to be careful about how they use the medium.

Cheap grace. Detractors still claim that evangelical TV tends to turn the gospel into entertainment. Viewers learn cheap grace rather than self-sacrifice; they wrongly believe that faith is a ticket to earthly health and wealth rather than a call to deny oneself and carry Jesus' cross.[22] Other critics say TV gives a lopsided view of Christianity because the medium has a bias toward charismatic, overly emotional formulations of the faith rather than more thoughtful, liturgical traditions.[23]

Politicization. Opponents also worry that TV ministries promote right-wing political agendas on hot-button issues such as abortion, the environment, health care and gay rights while ignoring important topics such as racism and poverty.

(AIR)TIME IS MONEY

Need more cash? Physical healing? A way out of debt? Just send money to a TV evangelist who promises you victory over poverty, sickness and joblessness. What's the catch?

Sow a "seed offering" by sending a donation to their TV ministry. Credit cards accepted. Just call this toll-free number!

Sadly, many donors remain sick and in debt, while the televangelist lives in lavish luxury. These hawkers offer prayer cloths, anointing oil and other gimmicky trinkets, and every direct mail letter seems very personal: "Dear Partner: I pray for you regularly." Really?

Without telethons and viewer donations, most TV ministries couldn't buy airtime, upgrade their equipment or pay employees. One evangelical TV executive says that if his network just wanted to make money, it would sell advertisements instead of asking for viewers' contributions. But with advertisers comes control. His network strictly limits programs to two minutes of fund raising per half-hour program—much less time than the major networks allot for commercials!

Thankfully, there are TV evangelists who are genuine and major ministries that thrive *without* begging for money or selling ads. But they are usually supported by a large church or denomination. Still, what kind of image of Christianity do non-Christians get from the TV evangelists who are constantly soliciting money and promising God's blessings in return? Maybe it's time for a new paradigm for supporting evangelical media. Perhaps younger evangelicals, who are turned off by most tribal TV, will discover a better way.

KATHLEEN SINDORF, CORNERSTONE UNIVERSITY

Popular tribal personalities promote conservative politics and urge viewers to take right-wing political action.[24] The late TV preacher Jerry Falwell said that "there's no need for the church of Jesus Christ to be wasting its time gullibly falling for all of this global warming hocus-pocus." Instead, he urged keeping focus on "reaching this world with the Gospel of Jesus Christ."[25] Not surprisingly, self-described conservatives are twice as likely as self-described liberals to watch Christian TV.[26]

Servants turned into celebrities. Perhaps evangelicals have always been susceptible to "a cult of personality" that is "magnified by television."[27] The TV screen favors close-up shots and confers celebrity status on those who take the national stage.[28] Of the "50 Most Influential Christians in America," nearly half are on TV.[29] Outside the tribe, however, evangelical media celebrities are largely unknown.[30]

Questionable fund raising. Critics also say that hawking products on TV and exaggerating a media ministry's impact are evidence of viewer manipulation and putting riches before God.[31] Households that make less than the national income average are the heaviest users of Christian media, fueling the critics' accusations of manipulation of lower-income viewers.[32] And when ministry leaders lead lavish lives, it makes their extensive on-air fundraising more suspect.

Constraints on creativity. Related to the fund-raising problem is the critics' concern that excessive reliance on viewer contributions reduces the creativity of programming.[33] Ministries must tell already-loyal viewers what they want to hear—morally, politically and spiritually. Many of these devoted viewers will contribute only to overtly evangelistic fare, not to less evangelistic shows that ironically might appeal to a wider range of viewers. Opponents of evangelistic programs wish that tribal audiences had a broader view of the popular arts as a means for delight, not just instruction and persuasion.[34]

Preaching in the mirror. Regardless of its claims about evangelism, tribal TV attracts overwhelmingly older, already committed evangelicals, according to its detractors.[35] Viewers of religious TV are older, more likely not to have completed high school, and are Catholic or conservative Protestants.[36] Nearly half are "born again" (43 percent) or believe in a literal interpretation of the Bible (38 percent). Older, female and Southern audiences consume more Christian media, including TV.[37]

Lamenting little impact. Critics lament that tribal TV has so little positive impact on mainstream culture. Many evangelical shows are unknown to most mainstream viewers—except in the spoofs on *Saturday Night Live* and other shows. Tribal TV hosts with wacky hairdos, heavy makeup, gaudy studio sets and tacky product giveaways paint an unfavorable view of all believers, not just evangelicals. Moreover, mainstream news media often look to evangelical TV leaders as spokespersons for all of evangelicalism; they fail to report that even a highly visible personality such as M. G. "Pat" Robertson receives only a marginally favorable rating (fifty-five out of one hundred) among evangelicals.[38]

Diluting face-to-face evangelism. Finally, critics worry that TV evangelism is replacing face-to-face outreach by leading believers to fund media professionals rather than share the gospel themselves. One TV ministry boasts that it "costs just 20 cents, two dimes, to present the gospel face-to-face and help change a person's life forever! That means a gift of $40 helps present Christ to 200 people, $80 will present Christ to 400 people and your gift of $120 will present Christ to 600 people!"[39] In an era when about half of all born-again adults do not share their faith with others, religious media have become the primary means of evangelization.[40]

CENTURIES OF VISUAL STORYTELLING

Christian TV can trace its ancient roots to oral culture, for which the spoken word and in-person storytelling were the primary modes of communication. Advocates for tribal TV point to Jesus' own use of parables for evangelizing and discipling.

Frescoes on the ceilings and walls of churches during the medieval period taught illiterate believers the stories of the Bible, although disputes arose in the Byzantine churches during the mid-eighth century over the use of iconography.[41] Rank-and-file believers revered icons, while religious leaders and Emperor Leo III wanted them removed because of the Ten Commandments' prohibition of idolatry. While the controversy may seem far removed from contemporary evangelical TV, the class-based prejudice over religious imagery bears some parallels to the ways that educated Christians today bemoan some viewers' apparent veneration of tribal TV and its stars.

As the fifteenth-century Reformation brought increased literacy and access to the written Scriptures, visual media's preeminence gave way to the Enlightenment's modern, print-based aesthetic. Martin Luther said that the ears are the only organ for the Christian.[42] Visual storytelling suffered as Protestantism emphasized the preaching and reading of the Word. Not until the twentieth century would Christians attempt to reclaim visual media.

On the Shoulders of Radio and Film

Just as mainstream radio of the 1920s and 1930s birthed TV twenty years later, some early televangelists started in radio. Walter Maier, a major Lutheran radio preacher, preached the first religious TV program on Easter in 1940. Billy Graham, whose *Hour of Decision* radio ministry made him a household name, began telecasting the show in the 1950s.[43]

Christians began experimenting with TV drama when the Lutheran Church–Missouri Synod launched *This Is the Life* on nearly five hundred stations in 1952, featuring parables about contemporary believers. Although even many of the denomination's leaders did not own TVs then, the show's creator, Herman Gockel, "believed television was truly the daughter of cinema, so that the story itself should carry the audience along."[44] Today similar optimism about the power of visual media is evident in the so-called emerging church, which aims, among other things, to engage popular culture and the arts.[45]

Mainstream TV Goes Spiritual

Beyond tribal fare, however, some younger and older Christians work in mainstream media, sometimes quietly for fear of reprisal in a religiously sensitive industry. Former Disney executive Ken Wales managed to see *Christy,* the popular novel of faith, made into a TV series. David McFadzean executive-produced the highly successful sitcom *Home Improvement,* while various Christian support groups in Hollywood have added momentum to a spiritual thaw.[46] Perhaps Hollywood today is hungrier for spiritual, if not theological, dialogue since "popular entertainers aren't shying away from spiritual conversations" in an industry that has long glamorized "sex, money and power."[47]

In the early 1990s about 6 percent of shows had identifiable religious affiliations,[48] but prime-time religion was either a largely invisible institution or portrayed in denigrating ways.[49] However, positive response to the 1990s drama

TYLER PERRY'S REDEMPTIVE STORIES IN DRAG

What does well-made entertainment with faith-friendly content look like? Maybe like an angry, silver-haired black woman named Madea—the character played by entertainment entrepreneur Tyler Perry in such films as *Diary of a Mad Black Woman* and *Tyler Perry's Madea's Family Reunion.*

These two low-budget but profitable independent films opened the door for Perry's TV sitcom, *Tyler Perry's House of Payne.* With more movies on the way, Perry is a brand name for his devoted audience, which loves his unique mixture of raucous humor, family melodrama and church themes.

What's the appeal of a Perry production—whether screen, tube or stage? For starters, it serves the audience. Perry's early success came when urban audiences responded to the way his plays addressed their neighborhoods' concerns. In Perry's stories, African American communities beset by family strife, drug use and other problems find hope and healing in the context of a dynamic local church.

Moreover, Perry's plays, films and TV work earn the right to be heard. His sometimes earthy humor—best exemplified by the loud and bossy Madea, played by Perry in drag—keeps audiences laughing. Faith-based messages don't seem preachy but feel like natural expressions of authentic religious experiences. Perry's work demonstrates the necessity of both knowing and delighting your audience to gain those teachable moments—moments that remind them of the truths that protect community life and faith that fights despair.

ALEX WAINER, PALM BEACH ATLANTIC UNIVERSITY

Touched by an Angel and the public's surging interest in spirituality encouraged networks to introduce more spiritually themed programming, including *7th Heaven*, *Joan of Arcadia* and the short-lived *Three Wishes,* featuring Amy Grant. Big Idea's animated children's series VeggieTales ran on NBC in 2006, albeit with most spiritual content removed. The Turner Broadcasting System even consulted with African American ministers before the launch of Tyler Perry's 2007 TV comedy *House of Payne.*[50]

Some celebrity Christians have been outspoken about their faith, including Patricia Heaton, former star of *Everybody Loves Raymond,* and Dean Batali, producer for *That '70s Show*. Joseph "Reverend Run" Simmons, formerly of the hip-hop group Run-DMC, even launched a clean reality show—*Run's House*—on MTV. He said that "the show is like my pulpit. I want the world to get into spirituality and lead people to Christ."[51]

PROGRAM PREVIEWS

For years, critics accused tribal TV of preaching to the choir. Yet, in an era of technological democratization—that is, the erosion of mainstream network dominance, a proliferation of channels, less expensive production equipment, and personal viewing technologies such as cell phones and personal digital assistants—preaching to a niche audience has become key to almost all media success. So when an evangelical network available on two thousand U.S. cable systems targets "the millions of Americans who embrace inspirational values," it could potentially hit its mark.[52] It is now theoretically easier to serve particular markets, both Christian and mainstream.

Still, major challenges lie ahead. Ministries can reach more eyeballs if they buy time on mainstream networks, but the time is expensive and those viewers are less likely to provide financial support than are viewers of tribal networks.[53] Federal Communication Commission–imposed digital TV standards pose an ongoing financial burden to stations and networks; the cost of high definition might put some ministries out of business.[54] Further, the concept of à la carte cable programming, in which consumers get to select which specific channels they want to pay for, rather than having to buy packages of channels, could reduce ministries' reach considerably by removing religious networks from many homes.[55]

Pundits and consultants believe that the winners in the new media environment will be producers who offer viewers an "elegant, robust experience" for highly targeted advertising.[56] One mainstream network executive says broadcasters must transform their brands into destinations, serving their targeted audience "better and in more ways than anyone else."[57] Tribal TV faces the same challenges.[58]

Somehow evangelical TV producers, too, will have to practice an "open business model" for rapid decision making, innovation, participation with customers, convergence between business units and sharing of resources.[59] Yet, over 80 percent of religious broadcasters said as late as 2001 that they were not planning to change their business model or audience. Even of those who said going digital would change the economics of tribal broadcasting, 85 percent indicated they would still seek viewer contributions as their primary source of revenue.[60]

Mainstream and evangelical TV organizations will probably have to practice "radical transparency," keeping few secrets and letting the public know what they are doing, both right and wrong.[61] Such transparency is a long way from the practices of some tribal TV ministries, especially regarding fundraising practices.

Christian TV has taken small steps toward innovating. Some networks are launching programs online first, building interest, then encouraging fans to write to their cable operators requesting carriage. A few cell-phone companies have collaborated with Christian content providers to offer mobile religious content, and many television networks are offering program episodes as video on demand. Both mainstream and evangelical TV will need to respond quickly to an eroding mass-market broadcast model.

One opportunity is user-generated content, where viewers create and share programming, like the YouTube and social networking models. In fact, *Time* magazine's 2006 Person of the Year was "you," referring to the personalization of media.[62] As younger viewers turn increasingly to the Internet and mobile content,[63] broadcast ministries will have to consider such new programming and distribution strategies.[64] Says one mainstream TV executive, "The viewer

TRIBAL TV'S OWN SHOCK JOCK

Is there a place on TV for deep religious conflicts? Ask the Florida station that sold an hour of time to televangelist Bill Keller so he could broadcast the gospel nightly at 1:00 a.m.[a] Unhappy with his rhetoric, they yanked the time slot from him. Why?

Apparently Keller offended just about every other influential religious group in the area, including Muslims, Mormons, Jehovah's Witnesses and Scientologists. Keller said the station caved in to pressure from the local Islamic council, which practiced "religious terrorism" by infringing on his free-speech rights.

Maybe so. But apparently he said on the air that "Islam is a 1,400-year-old lie from the pits of hell. It's leading a billion peoples [*sic*] to hell. . . . Those who follow this false religion will die and be lost for all eternity." The "false religion of Islam is about hate, lies and death."[b]

Keller's *Live Prayer* show had its supporters. He paid the station about $400,000 annually for the time slot and claimed to have helped nearly 200,000 viewers find Christ.

Keller told reporters that "it is never my intent to offend anyone with my remarks." Yet he admitted that he stands "for the truth based on the worldview that the Bible is the infallible and inerrant word of God. And based on that, those who follow other gods are on a sure path to hell."

How can a station deal with such basic religious conflicts—other than canceling religious programs, no matter how financially beneficial they might be?

QUENTIN J. SCHULTZE, CALVIN COLLEGE

---

[a]Keller's website <www.liveprayer.com> provides his own Christian testimony.

[b]"WTOG Cancels Infomercial *Live Prayer* Amid Controversy Surrounding Show," *Tampa Bay Tribune,* August 29, 2007 <www.tbo.com/entertainment/tv/MGBISGR8X5F.html>.

is speaking and the smart broadcasters are listening."[65]

Will tribal TV harness the creativity of younger producers by drawing from church media and Christian college pools? Young producers are already creating some of the most significant evangelical programming, independent of networks and often backed by large, supportive churches or wealthy individuals.[66] New talent is evident in church podcasts, redemptive and faith-based film festivals, and the growing variety of video resources for churches.[67]

A growing number of cell-phone subscribers watch TV or video on mobile handsets.[68] But will most consumers pay extra for such services? How will it be produced and formatted for tiny screens? Will long-form television continue, or will programming be "snack sized"?[69] Will programming be delivered on-demand, streamed, downloaded or all of the above? The answers are unclear, but the challenge for evangelicals will be to innovate in prayerful, God-honoring ways regardless of how such TV-like media eventually develop.

In one form or another, TV is a fixture in American popular culture. And "despite the disdain of some intellectuals . . . [it] has become a fabricator of public meanings" as well as a symbol system through which viewers interpret their world.[70] This meaning-making function is key for Christian producers and viewers who seek ways of teaching, delighting and persuading in tune with their faith—who seek discernment, artistry and ways to offer up their talents as grateful stewards.

CONCLUSION

The young producers of *Travel the Road* began their missionary journey out of a sincere passion for the lost. Most mainstream viewers will never see the program because it is run on a religious network. If mainstream viewers do tune in, the overt proselytizing might turn them off. Yet this remarkable story of two creative storytellers points to a future that will open up more means of distributing original productions. It is not hard to imagine a group of evangelical university graduates producing a less tribal program with more mainstream appeal.

Unless evangelical TV rethinks its business model and finds ways to attract younger viewers, it could face major challenges. Youthful, innovative evangelicals like the creators of *Travel the Road,* Tim Scott and Will Decker, who create compelling stories and sell them to both Christian and mainstream networks, may create the most influential tribal fare in the future. Ultimately, the goal remains the same as ever—to develop creative, meaningful and entertaining programming that embodies the truth and beauty of the gospel.

4

Moving from Film to Digital Movies

TERRY LINDVALL AND
ANDREW QUICKE

Paul Schrader and Wes Craven were enterprising Christian college students who rebelliously headed to Hollywood to make films. Schrader's screenplays include *Taxi Driver, Hardcore* and *The Last Temptation of Christ.* Craven's creations include *Nightmare on Elm Street* and *Scream.*

Coming of age in the 1960s, they could not reconcile mainstream moviemaking with their inherited faith. And their tribes were not happy with their movies either.[1] Yet, as this chapter will show, for decades evangelicals had been making movies without leaving their tribes. In fact, they were producing them for evangelicals and sometimes even mainstream audiences.

Evangelicals have always had love-hate relationships with the movies, shunning and embracing this powerful medium. They learned early on that movies can communicate what is good, lovely and true. But they also realized that films can deceive and abuse people with false or perverse sentiment, eroticism, violence, venality, cupidity or downright meanness.[2]

Evangelicals Enter MGM's Lions' Den

In the mid 1940s three diverse filmmakers sensed a calling to produce films. James K. Friedrich, an Episcopal priest, sought to tell the stories of Jesus and Paul to a new generation of Christians. Carlos Octavia Baptista wanted to evangelize people who had never heard the gospel, making simple parable films like *The Story of the Fountain Pen,* in which a pen is redeemed for a price even as Christ paid the ultimate price for sinners. Irwin Moon inaugurated the Moody Science films, using amazing special effects such as time lapses to delight audiences and to teach about a Creator-God.

Friedrich started Cathedral Films after concluding that what people see impresses them more than what they hear. "If I can rouse in them an interest to read the Bible," he said, "then, thank God, I shall have done something worthwhile."[3] Although Baptista's films tended to be crudely illustrated sermons with tribal jargon, he hoped to translate them into other languages for worldwide distribution. The Moody Institute of Science saw its films as an effective way to penetrate mainstream institutions such as public schools and the military. From this threesome sprouted a small evangelical moviemaking industry alternately teaching and scaring church audiences.

Mark IV Pictures, birthed by two filmmakers from the original *Blob* movie, found phenomenal success with their independent scare-the-hell-out-of-them rapture film, *Thief in the Night.* Ministers and parents hoped that the fear of being "left behind" would keep their hormonal adolescents away from sin.

Gospel Films (GF)—the only studio in Michigan—emerged in the 1970s under the self-proclaimed "godfather of Christian films," Billy Zeoli. GF recruited creative mainstream film-school graduates such as Mel White (Charley Churchman series and Psalm 23 series on suffering) and John Schmidt (*SuperChristian* and *Kevin Can Wait*). Grounded in the Youth for Christ movement, White and Schmidt appealed to the growing evangelical youth market, seeking to teach morality through entertainment.

Internationally, Billy Graham's film production unit, WorldWide Pictures, invested in feature films and four-wall distribution and exhibition channels (renting mainstream theaters and selling tickets to local churches). Such films aimed at teaching people how God used Graham crusades to win people to Christ. As spiritual journey films, they inevitably led back to a preaching scene with Graham.

The blockbuster that really opened the tribal floodgates was an emotional adaptation of David Wilkerson's *The Cross and the Switchblade* (1970), starring clean-cut Pat Boone as the inner-city street evangelist. Now that it was acceptable to watch movies, evangelical churches starting buying or renting hundreds of educational films not nearly as dramatic but nearly always preachy. Among the most popular series were Francis Schaeffer's *Whatever Happened to the Human Race?* and Dr. James Dobson's *Focus on the Family.* Later, ministers like T. D. Jakes, Beth Moore and Joyce Meyer benefited from the Dobson effect, which softened churches to the idea of showing videos.

Film Fans

Christians have always made similar arguments about the value of movies for teaching and evangelizing audiences, even if the arguments are sometimes overdone. In the early 1900s a minister wrote *The Religious Possibilities of the Motion Picture,* arguing that movies could teach audiences by using effective storytelling as Jesus used parables. He suggested that the story of the good Samaritan, for instance, could be recast thematically using stories from the news of the day,

THE ART OF MOVIE MISINTERPRETATION?

The apostle Paul says that we all "see through a glass darkly." We view reality through our own, narrow lenses. Maybe this affects how we interpret films, too?

Consider two evangelical critics with wildly different interpretations of the same movie—*Harry Potter and the Order of the Phoenix.*

One is Ted Baehr, who condemns the film as an example of "witchcraft with sophomoric aphorisms."[a] The movie apparently casts a demonic worldview and suffers from immature sayings or clichés.

Meanwhile, Marc Newman, of MovieMinistry.com, praises the film for exploring "how people react to the unveiling of evil in their midst."[b] Using the writings of C. S. Lewis, Newman argues that *Phoenix* positively illustrates the importance of fighting evil and the necessity of making the right choices. He concludes that the spiritual truths "embedded in the story of the boy wizard . . . magnify its allure."[c]

How can two critics who profess the same biblical faith come up with such opposing interpretations? One possibility is that critics bring personal assumptions to their interpretations. Critics grow up in different families and churches and have varied educational backgrounds. Baehr earned a law degree. Newman has a doctoral degree in communication.

Another possibility is that critics write for different audiences. Perhaps Baehr's audience is more conservative, so he obliges with reviews in tune with such assumptions. Maybe Newman writes for an audience that is less tribal and more open-minded about the redemptive value of mainstream fare.

What else might account for such differences in interpretation? Is it possible that one critic's interpretation is better than the other's?

TOM CARMODY, VANGUARD UNIVERSITY

---

[a]Ted Baehr, "*Harry Potter and the Order of the Phoenix:* Uninspired Witchcraft with Sophomoric Aphorisms," *Movieguide* <www.movieguide.org/index.php?s=reviews&id=7499> (password required).

[b]Marc T. Newman, "C. S. Lewis, Spiritual Warfare, and *Harry Potter and the Order of the Phoenix,*" Movie Ministry: See the Truth <http://www.movieministry.com/articles.php?articles=all&article_view=102>.

[c]Ibid.

something like *Adventures of the Samaritan and the Highwaymen.*[4] In other words, movies could translate biblical stories and truths into the current vernacular, the moving picture narrative.

For at least a hundred years, then, some evangelicals have held that moving pictures could teach both by precept and by example. The famous vamp Theda Bara once boasted that she kept many young girls from sin by her films, which showed the wages of sin as death for loose-living people. The Moody Institute of Science's *Sermons from Science* even prefigured the intelligent design movement, portraying the amazing order within God's creation—from bees working together in colonies to the blood flowing through arteries.[5] Dobson's *Focus on the Family* used his counseling experience and personal anecdotes to demonstrate how parents can faithfully raise teenagers. He understood implicitly that films can provide people with "equipment for living,"[6] not just entertain them.

The national Lutheran Council distributed a film titled *Answer for Anne,* in which a young girl was assigned to write a school essay exploring whether displaced European refugees should be allowed in her town. Ken Curtis's Gateway Films provided an amazing array of historical dramas and documentaries, including films on William Carey's missions work in India *(Candle in the Dark)* and the Moravian missionaries *(First Fruits).*

The most-watched film ever produced by any company in the world has been Campus Crusade's *Jesus* film, translated into over one thousand languages and viewed by six billion people in rented metropolitan theaters and in outdoor screenings in remote villages. According to the Jesus Film Project website, "200 million people have indicated decisions to accept Christ as their personal Savior and Lord."[7] A similar venture was the Indian version of Jesus' life, *Dayasagar (Oceans of Mercy).* The producer was struck by how the Indian audience "responded to the film. They talked to each other, and talked back to the movie, throughout the showing."[8] The film itself became a worship service.

WorldWide Pictures' president explained that "the central purpose of all our films, whether dramatic or documentary, is to demonstrate that Jesus Christ, and He alone, is the answer to mankind's problems and needs; that a personal, vital relationship with Him is not only possible, but necessary, if we are to fulfill the purpose for which we are created."[9] This strategy was clear in the popular 1975 dramatic film of Corrie ten Boom's experiences in a Nazi Germany concentration camp, *The Hiding Place,* in which ten Boom appeared at the end to persuade people to seek the God who loves everyone.

In spite of the tribe's instructional and evangelistic emphases in filmmaking, evangelicals share with mainstream audiences a desire to be delighted by engaging stories, not by heavy-handed preaching. Christian inspired, written or produced films as diverse as *Holes, Facing the Giants* and *The Lion, the Witch and the Wardrobe* contributed to a revival of interest in films, providing an alternative in film viewing for evangelical families. Evangelicals still produce tribal films like *One Night with the King, The Nativity* or *Left Behind,* but they seem to be more and more open to less educational or instructional material.

In hopes of avoiding offensive mainstream movies while discovering tribe-satisfying gems, evangelicals who like movies increasingly gather online to discuss and review films, creating a more vibrant national and even international community of tribal discourse.[10] Many evangelicals write movie-related blogs, serving as nonpaid critics for friends and congregations.

TRIBAL CONCERNS

Evangelicals have always worried about where motion pictures were shown, and to whom, along with film content. They did not want their own family and congregations going to the seedy parts of town where movies were shown—although no doubt their White-Anglo-Saxon-Protestant biases were somewhat directed at urban ethnic groups, perhaps especially Irish and other Catholics. Evangelicals denounced some movies that supposedly taught boys how to become petty crooks or exploited the violent world of boxing.[11]

Charles M. Sheldon extended his popular 1896 novel, *In His Steps,* into a subsequent the essay titled "What Would Jesus Do with the Drama?"[12] In it, Jesus confronts not only the director, producer and actor for their films, but the writer, the exhibitor and the public audience. All of them, Sheldon suggests, are culpable for the low-quality and negative content of movies. With colleagues at *Christian Herald* magazine, Sheldon unsuccessfully attempted to launch a religious film production company. Some Christians were undoubtedly sneaking into movie houses, but churches were not ready to pay for and show films.

Sheldon's arguments against mainstream movies echoed the criticisms of the early church fathers against the theater. John Chrysostom (349–ca. 407) denounced those who would go to the theater and see a titillating flash of female flesh (and then, he said, take that whore home with them, in their imagination). Others believed that the stage was a school for revenge, greed and other vices, as well as lust.[13]

Tribal critics warned believers even into the mid-1900s that a real Christian would not want to be caught in a theater when Jesus returned. Ministers attacked Hollywood companies as sewage factories, spewing forth toxic evils that would contaminate any who came in contact with them.[14] They worried that religious movies turned faith into entertainment, and that motion pictures were opposed even to the idea of godliness. They claimed movies portrayed lasciviousness, generated sexual arousal, modeled criminal activity, glorified smoking and drinking, and even taught teenagers how to make out.[15] More recent evangelical critics argue that movies challenge family values and evangelical worldviews—although such tribal critics sometimes use a quasi-scientific method of movie criticism that merely counts bad words, highlights offensive images and hunts for heresies.[16]

Even though evangelicals generally attend mainstream movies, the tribe has always believed that the medium can be a significant menace to church and society.[17] Tribal critics emphasize how films promote promiscuity, mock parents and other authority figures, glorify violence, use obscene or profane language, celebrate material success, and malign religion and religious leaders.[18] By offering such criticism publicly, increasingly on the Internet through blogs and church websites, evangelical critics also create publicity for the very movies they condemn. Evangelicals are not so quick to publicly praise films that uphold what the apostle Paul calls goodness, beauty and truthfulness (Phil 4:8). One exception is *Christianity Today* and its accompanying website, which have offered more balanced film criticism since early 1956, when it first reviewed Graham films.[19]

One of the most intriguing trends is cross-promotion of mainstream movies to evangelical leaders and audiences. The leading promoter is Grace Hill Media, owned by Jonathan Bock. *Premiere* suggested Bock might be "the most powerful Christian in Hollywood, but you'd never know it."[20] Bock has publicized films like *The Lord of the Rings: The Two Towers, Signs, The Rookie* and *A Walk to Remember.* He argues that many Christian-themed movies are "horribly acted,

CHATTING WITH THE APOSTLE PAUL ABOUT MOVIES

"Only watch what Jesus would watch." "Don't view anything you don't want your children to see." Some evangelical adults use these and similar mini-sermons to instruct their children and limit their own moviegoing. Do such sayings make any biblical sense? Not if we agree that evangelicals often disagree about what Jesus would watch—let alone how to raise their children as entertainment consumers.

One balanced alternative is to look for what is apparently beneficial in movies, not just what is seemingly detrimental. Imagine a continuum between the beneficial and detrimental aspects of a movie. Most movies are somewhere in between.

- Beneficial aspects? The truthfulness of the story's message, the beauty and entertainment value derived from the film, and maybe even how a movie might impact someone's faith.
- Detrimental aspects? The usual things like excessive or unnecessary sex and violence, unwarranted obscenity and profanity, and the more complicated issue of message.

What a family decides to watch would then be a matter for conversation, discernment and informed conscience. In some cases there might not seem to be anything beneficial. Why watch it, then? The tough choices occur when good and bad are side by side, confusingly intermingled. Maybe the best choice is a food metaphor: have a healthy diet, don't eat poison, but an occasional dessert won't hurt you.

Just like our diets, many of us consume far too much unbeneficial media. The apostle Paul says, "I have the right to do anything" but adds that he "will not be mastered by anything" (1 Cor 6:12). He refuses to become a slave to things that are merely permissible and not really beneficial. He captures the middle ground between outright rejection and mindless acceptance. It would be interesting to chat with him today about what he would watch.

PETER KERR, ASBURY COLLEGE

shot on a shoe-string budget, and you always know how they're going to end. . . . When the day comes, we as religious people better be prepared to offer more than end-of-the-world Bible prophecy movies."[21]

But evangelism might still be the rationale for getting churches behind filmmaking, as witnessed in the tribe's glowing optimism about Mel Gibson's *The Passion of the Christ* in 2004. Now that movie theaters have moved to suburban malls, DVDs are so readily available, and online reviews and movie trailers are so easily accessed, evangelicals have a hard time keeping the tribe as concerned about the evils of Hollywood. Some congregations even rent mainstream films to show in their sanctuaries as a means of getting the unchurched inside their doors. And a growing number of evangelical pastors refer to popular, mainstream movies in their sermons.

MINING THE EGYPTIAN GOLD

In defending the idea that God gave the gift of persuasion to his people for God's service, Augustine (354-430) argued that because the Egyptians had not used their resources for the glory of God, they were undeserving. Israel should be able to take and transform the raw materials of Egypt to use in their holy journey.[22]

Today, many evangelicals see Hollywood films as gold in the hands of unworthy Egypt. They want to transform moviemaking into a means of glorifying God. But the road to this openness about using images to glorify God has been very rocky throughout the history of the church because of the seemingly iconic nature of movies.

The place of visual communication in the church became extremely controversial in the eighth century. Against the backdrop of the Byzantine empire, some iconoclastic church leaders not only forbade the making of religious images but destroyed statues and other art in their passion to purify the church—almost like some evangelical churches in recent years have burned members' popular record (album) collections as a protest against apostate culture.

Once again, however, some church leaders confronted this one-sided fanaticism with creative discourse about good and bad use of images, including the difference between worship and mere veneration of images (the latter being similar to the use of a photograph to remind a person of a loved one, not substituting that photo for the loved one). One of the key defenders was John of Damascus (ca. 676–ca. 770), who argued that although some pagans made images into gods, such foul use of man-made things should not prevent Christians from employing images correctly to direct believers' worship toward the one, true God.[23] Pope Gregory III and Bonaventure similarly defended the value of images on three grounds:

1. Images helped to teach the simple and the ignorant. The uneducated who were unable to read Scripture could learn about the stories of the faith through statues and paintings.
2. Images moved viewers emotionally. Because of the sluggishness of the affections, images (especially of judgment and hell) worked to arouse devotion in lazy or indifferent hearers of the Word.
3. Images enabled people to remember better. Bonaventure argued that "those things which are only heard fall into oblivion more easily than those things which are seen."[24]

This triad of visual functions served as cures for human weaknesses: for ignorance, sloth and forgetfulness.[25] Images in the churches were the *libri idiotarum* (the books of the illiterate), a truth repeatedly emphasized by Pope Gregory the Great: "We do no harm in wishing to show the invisible by means of the visible."[26]

Another protest against religious images broke out during the radical days of the fifteenth-century Reformation, when Zwingli and his disciples tried to shatter crucifixes and whitewash cathedrals. Believers later won back much of Protestantism to an appreciation of the role of images in teaching, persuading and delighting. Nineteenth-century evangelicals somewhat reclaimed pictures for personal piety and devotions, particularly in the image of Warner Sallman's 1940 popular painting of Jesus.[27] Nevertheless, the anti-image undercurrents still exist among evangelicals, as is evident in the lack of visual decoration, let alone statuary, paintings and stained glass artwork, in so many tribal church sanctuaries.

If You Can't Beat 'Em, Copy 'Em

Evangelicals' love-hate relationship with mainstream filmmaking demonstrates the tribe's amazing ability to adapt and borrow, reject and embrace Hollywood culture. Evangelicals frequently imitate mainstream movie techniques (editing, narrative, cinematography, etc.), but they also imitate content. They realize that Hollywood is Hollywood; it sets the trends, and successful filmmakers had better learn from the pros. Even an evangelical must apprentice to the great movie artists if he or she hopes to communicate clearly and creatively through the medium.

Most obvious has been evangelicals' exploitation of the Hollywood horror genre. The evangelical scare-them-into-heaven blockbuster *Thief in the Night* tinkered with the mainstream dream (or nightmare) structure to cause viewers to question what is real. Did the rapture occur? Was she left behind? Subsequent apocalyptic films such as *Left Behind* and the *Omega Code* series were big-budget films but lacked the personal stories of the earlier shock-and-schlock film. More artistically impressive are independent filmmaker Danny Carrales's end-times films that develop characters and focus on their spiritual destinies.

In the 1980s, the evangelical John Schmidt produced and directed a series of comic moral stories that blatantly, playfully parodied Hollywood styles and titles. Schmidt sought to attract movie-savvy young audiences who would not likely find the end-times films very engaging.

With the spread of DVD and other digital formats, some evangelical filmmakers load extra, educational material onto their movie disks. Some directors and screenwriters have been providing running commentaries on their films, explaining not only why they framed certain shots in a particular way but how their faith and vision intersected with the material they were shooting.

THE ANGLE ON CHRISTIAN MOVIES

What makes a great rather than a mediocre film? Box office? Possibly. A powerful story? Sure! But what makes a story work, besides the script?

Where moviemakers place the camera and how they edit the resulting images are critically important for filmic storytelling. The way the story is told visually often makes the difference to fans and critics, whether they are aware of it or not. For instance, shooting from ground level and knee level upward made members of the Nazi German Olympic team look heroically large and imposing in the film *Olympia* (1938).[a] The choices made on how to shoot the athletes said as much as who was in the frame. No one had to say "we believe the Ayran race is superior" because the pictures said it.

What happens when you put the camera above people and shoot down at them? Do they still look strong or in control? Notice how the hero of your favorite film is framed when he or she is in control as opposed to when that person is vulnerable.

If you are shooting a large group of people on the street, which persons should you capture in the center of the frame? On the margins? Frequently in movies, things and people are marginalized—often by race, ethnicity, gender, disability and religion. Does this make a difference in how a sinner or a hero should be portrayed?

Many evangelical movies fail to consider the impact of camera angles. In doing so, they may inadvertently say things they do not intend. But that is no excuse. Good films are more than just good stories on film; they are good stories, well told.

JEN LETHERER, SPRING ARBOR UNIVERSITY

[a]Leni Riefenstahl's film *Olympia* is considered by some to be Nazi propaganda, although it is not clear that she intended it to be used this way. I believe she was caught up in the ideas of the era, but her film is really more a celebration of all human forms. In fact, Jesse Owens is often viewed as the "hero" of part one.

Faith in Mainstream Moviedom

While some evangelicals continue producing films for the tribe, others seek broader venues that include nonevangelical and mainstream audiences. Producer Ralph Winter guides films such as *X-Men* and encourages tribal youth to enter the film industry.

Others on the fringe of the church, like director/actor Robert Duvall, appear on religious TV to promote evangelically themed pictures such as *The Apostle*. Other Hollywood directors like Scott Derrickson and Tom Shadyac shoot horror and comedy films, respectively, such as *The Exorcism of Emily Rose*, *Bruce Almighty* and *Evan Almighty*. While criticized by some tribe members, the two have integrated Christian themes and issues into their films.

YOUTUBE TO HOLLYWOOD?

Web surfers initially thought lonelygirl15 was an angst-ridden teenager's video blog. They later discovered that the videos' real creators were semi-professional filmmakers hoping to attract the attention of major movie studios.

Fifty years ago, the membrane between amateur and professional filmmakers seemed impermeable protection against such hoaxes. Now, cheap cameras, free software and websites like YouTube level the field, crowning almost anyone a director. So what?

Here's what: filmmaking has been legitimized, not just democratized. Anyone can enter film festivals specializing in cell-phone videos—no kidding! Digital Web-vids are eligible for Emmy Awards. Ordinary Americans question presidential candidates via YouTube on CNN. The medium—whatever forms and formats it takes—has arrived.

What about media evangelism? YouTube itself goes "into all the world." But who's evangelizing whom? Where are the Christians with captivating content? Some have decided to join evangelicals' tribal knockoffs instead, apparently to view each others' productions. Worthwhile, but hardly evangelistic.

Why not produce actual church worship videos for shut-ins? Critics worry that twentysomethings might decide they don't need corporate worship if they can praise God on their desktops. Maybe so, but that never really happened with TV and radio.

Imagine a Romanian missionary's field report video played for a North American congregation within minutes of being uploaded. Or a clever poseur with a camera in his basement impersonating a Christian, flinging heresy as far as the Internet reaches. What are Christians doing in the uncharted land between YouTube and Hollywood? What should they be doing? Let's get the conversation going. Just use your cell phone or camera and avoid the names lonelygirl and lovelyguy.

BRIAN FULLER, CALVIN COLLEGE

The tremendously unexpected success of Mel Gibson's *The Passion of the Christ* opened the floodgates of evangelically themed moviemaking in the early 2000s.[28] It stands as a watershed film not only for its explicit, controversial portrayal of the killing of Jesus Christ but also because of its phenomenal success at the box office. It sparked frantic discussions in Hollywood boardrooms about the potential market of religious viewers that the industry had neglected. *The Passion of the Christ* made so much money that no studio in Hollywood could ignore the implications that there could be a Christian crossover market to which they should cater. Fox formed a new division called Fox Faith, and other studios like Sony formed their own religious films division. Sony Columbia even bought the existing rights to the Left Behind series.

Most significant of all, a generous entrepreneurial tycoon, Philip Anschutz, bought movie theater chains and started several mainstream movie production companies, even hiring some successful Hollywood non-Christians to advance an implicitly Christian perspective via moral messages. He acknowledged, "My friends think I'm a candidate for a lobotomy, and my competitors think I'm naive or stupid or both." But he pressed on to become a major player in the early twenty-first-century movie business, bankrolling films such as *Holes, Because of Winn-Dixie,* the C. S. Lewis fantasy *Chronicles of Narnia: The Lion, the Witch and the Wardrobe*, *Ray* and many others, many of which connected with the family market. Unlike his under-funded predecessors, Anschutz sought to make uplifting and wholesome family films that could be marketed widely and promoted extensively through "grass-roots campaigns that would reach teachers, librarians, and church groups."[29]

CONCLUSION

With the advent of new technologies, the art of filmmaking has become even more democratic, since nearly anyone can make his or her own film. Mini-movies, digital video streaming, YouTube and other outlets invite small filmmakers to try out their abilities. At the same time, new film and video festivals (e.g., Damah, Heartland and the Reel Spirituality/Biola Conference) highlight redemptive films that apparently promote biblical values without being evangelistic. In fact, the films might not be made by evangelicals specifically or Christians more generally. Although most Christian colleges do not have film programs, the evangelical Council for Christian Colleges and Universities launched the Los Angeles Film Studies Center in 1991 for its more than one hundred member schools to gain internships in Hollywood.

While some tribal critics continue to harp about the contamination of evangelical communities, many younger believers are part of a grassroots, creative rebirth of media arts. A prime example has been the successful low-budget film

THE PASSION OF . . . DAVID AND BATHSHEBA?

Imagine Mel Gibson producing *The Passion of David and Bathsheba* with the same graphic detail he put into *The Passion of the Christ.* Instead of Jesus dripping sweat and groaning under the whip, King David would be perspiring and moaning as he caresses Bathsheba. Would evangelical Christians support that kind of passion? Probably not. Graphic sexuality is taboo among most American evangelicals, while British evangelicals are more troubled by graphic violence, including the hardcore brutality in Gibson's *Passion.*[a] Who's right?

Roger Ebert called *The Passion of the Christ* the most violent film he had ever seen. "If it had been anyone other than Jesus up on that cross, I have a feeling that NC-17 would have been automatic," the film critic wrote in his review.[b] Why do North Americans give a thumbs-up to violence but not sex? Perhaps evangelicals have succumbed to what Walter Wink calls the myth of redemptive violence—the belief that we can save by destroying.[c]

The Bible, in its storytelling, doesn't shy away from violence—or sex. But it always depicts them to highlight their consequences. David's lust, for example, leads to murder and eventually to the death of his beloved infant son—and to David's repentant plea in Psalm 51.

So should Christians endorse cinematic depictions of violence or sex? I say yes to both, but only when they're cast in the full context of their consequences. Otherwise, the violence or sex becomes merely entertainment.

The death of Jesus without the Sermon on the Mount. The adultery of David without Psalm 51. To be sure, both would be titillating and entertaining to watch—but also immoral in the truest sense.

KEVIN MILLER, HUNTINGTON UNIVERSITY

[a]Andrew Quicke, interview by Kevin Miller, Calvin College, July 13, 2007.

[b]Roger Ebert, review of The Passion of the Christ <http://rogerebert.suntimes.com/>. Ebert estimated that 100 of the 126 minutes of The Passion of the Christ were given to capturing the gory details of Jesus' torture and death. "We get only a few passing reference to the teachings of Jesus," which leaves the film, he noted, "superficial in terms of the surrounding message."

[c]Walter Wink, *Jesus and Nonviolence: A Third Way* (Minneapolis: Augsburg Fortress, 2003).

from Sherwood Baptist Church in Albany, Georgia, *Facing the Giants,* a film that entertained even as it evangelized. Fans of the movie organized online, blogged their thoughts, reviewed aspects of the movie and together imagined that they, too, could be moviemakers—perhaps even via their churches.

In fact, some local churches in the digital age could raise sufficient financial backing to produce a mainstream film without the cost of seemingly old-fashioned celluloid film stock, film processing, manual editing and all the rest of the time-intensive efforts of traditional Hollywood moviemaking. It just might be that creative media stewardship, combined with innovative storytelling, could usher in a renaissance of evangelical filmmaking. If so, the Wes Cravens and Paul Schraders of today might not be so quick to escape the tribe for Hollywood. Instead they might become role models for tribal youth who are more inclined to pay at the local mall to watch a Hollywood film than to see a free one in the local church basement.

5

Pursuing New Periodicals in Print and Online

KEN WATERS

Dan Malachuk had an ambitious plan. In 1975, he launched *National Courier*, an implicitly Christian national newspaper.[1] He already had succeeded with Logos Books and *Logos Journal* for charismatic evangelicals. He hired experienced mainstream journalists who were Christians and bought an old newspaper plant in New Jersey as the *Courier*'s new headquarters. Recent journalism graduates jumped at the chance to work for a cutting-edge paper that would allow them to integrate faith and work. "We wanted an intellectually honest place to be, to examine what was going on from a Christian perspective," one said at the time.[2]

Sadly, the *National Courier* lasted only two years. It failed to find an audience among evangelicals, and a lack of business know-how kept it from reaching beyond the tribe. Malachuk learned the hard way that when "religious interest publications attempt to tell the whole story, advertisers and church member subscribers apply an economic boycott."[3]

With a large potential audience, a grand vision, and a commitment to integrating faith and journalism, how could the *National Courier* fail? After all, hundreds of distinctly tribal periodicals are succeeding—in-print and online publications aimed exclusively at Christian rather than mainstream audiences. Some of these publications are more than 150 years old. The publisher of the *National Courier* later learned that the future of traditional Christian publishing is tenuous. Few young adults subscribe to Christian magazines and newspapers, preferring instead to learn and connect with others online.

The Lay of the Land

Hundreds of print-based Protestant and Catholic periodicals are regularly published. The most vibrant ones are associated with the evangelical movement in American history. The Evangelical Press Association (EPA) estimates that millions of readers consume their four hundred member publications each year. The Southern Baptist Convention (SBC) and some other denominations are not EPA members, and thus the number of evangelical readers is even higher than EPA estimates. The Associated Church Press (ACP), which represents mostly mainline Protestant publications, and the Catholic Press Association (CPA) account for hundreds more Christian periodicals. Dozens of new print and online publications begin annually.

Some Christian publications boast remarkable distributions: *Decision* is an 800,000-distribution publication of the Billy Graham Evangelistic Association; *World Vision* magazine is published by the missions agency that bears its name and is sent quarterly to just over 500,000 people; *Relevant,* an edgy, independent publication for eighteen- to thirty-four-year-olds has 80,000 print subscribers and more than 100,000 unique visitors to its website monthly.

Denominational publications include *Holiness Today,* a forty-page monthly with 60,000 subscribing members of the 2,600,000-member Church of the Nazarene; *The Banner,* the monthly publication of the Christian Reformed Church in North America, which is sent to all homes in the 290,000-member denomination; and the *Methodist Reporter,* a newspaper for hundreds of readers interested in national and local church news. Nearly half of all Christian periodicals are published by mission agencies, parachurch groups like Focus on the Family or seminaries and Christian universities.[4] Additionally, several geographic areas like Minneapolis and Southern California are served by vibrant, locally produced newspapers with abundant news and advertising from local Christian churches and businesses.

Most of the vibrant publications rely solely on circulation and advertising revenues rather than corporate or denominational subsidies. Free from bureaucratic control, these include publications that "have inherited a sense of journalistic freedom or those who have championed movements within various sections of the church."[5] They include news and information magazines such as *Christianity Today, World, Sojourners* and *Christian Century.* These publications are admired for taking risks and creatively saying things that some readers or church officials might not like but others see as a breath of fresh accountability.

In addition to national newspapers published by denominations like the Methodists, other groups—notably the Baptists—publish statewide newspapers for their members. These papers include national news supplied by news services like Religion News Service, the Evangelical News Service and the Baptist Press service. In a number of major cities, enterprising journalists have started geographically focused publications such as the Minnesota *Christian Chronicle* (for the Minneapolis/Saint Paul area), the *Christian Examiner* (of Southern California), and the Charlotte (North Carolina) *World.* These successful papers feature

IS YOUR JESUS A REPUBLICAN OR DEMOCRAT?

Not sure? Pick a Christian magazine.

If your Jesus is a Democrat, try the most influential mainline Christian magazine, *Christian Century,* published in Chicago. You'll learn that Jesus cares about social justice, that war is justifiable only in defense of one's own country or to help other nations combat hostile takeovers by belligerent autocrats, and that the far right is imposing its values on everyone else!

But if you lean to the right, try *World Magazine* out of Asheville, North Carolina. According to this *Newsweek* or *Time* knockoff, readers should elect right-leaning Republicans in order to please Jesus. Want to help the poor? Promote responsibility. Volunteer. Praise the Lord for conservative Supreme Court justices! Take back America from the liberals!

Not sure where Jesus would stand politically? Try the evangelical *Christianity Today,* launched in the 1950s with the support of Billy Graham and theologian-journalist Carl Henry as first editor. Or consider *Charisma,* which publishes some political pieces but mostly inspirational stories and self-help articles aimed especially at charismatic believers.

The circulation leader in this batch of publications is the ideologically edgy, provocative and downright feisty *World Magazine.* It entertains. It sells subscriptions if not a lot of advertising. It knows how to draft conservative readers with extensive promotion, especially old-fashioned postal mailings. And it maintains a fairly robust blog site for readers to post comments and interact with one another.

Still, no magazine has the market on Jesus' politics. Just as it should be.

MICHAEL LONGINOW, BIOLA UNIVERSITY

local church news and advertising by Christian businesses and services.

Nearly all such publications speak to a specific, narrow audience intensely interested in their content—to a tribe within the larger Christian tribe. In other words, tribal readers prefer periodicals that reinforce their existing moral, theological and cultural attitudes. Tribal audiences are also limited because potential readers cannot purchase copies in mainstream bookstores, newsstands or Wal-Mart. By and large, tribal publishers have to generate new readers through Christian bookstores, direct-mail solicitations, the magazine's website or word of mouth. This makes them "vibrant but invisible" magazines that most mainstream readers have never even heard about.[6] The same is true for online periodicals; few attract enough readers to elevate their efforts to the attention of the culture at large. While many evangelicals might want to read a national publication with a Christian worldview, the niche status of tribal publications simply mirrors the national trend—the publishing of magazines targeted toward avid readers who devour both the specialized content (be it reviews of new books or conservative political commentary) and the targeted ads for products and services of interest to the readers.[7]

RALLYING READERS

Evangelical editors say their top five editorial priorities are (1) inspiring believers; (2) persuading readers to act on behalf of a Christian social cause such as world hunger, evangelization, or the opposition to abortion, war or pornography; (3) providing news about missionary activities; (4) offering how-to advice on interpersonal relationships or church issues; and (5) helping people better understand and interact with mainstream culture.[8] Like the book-publishing world, niche publications provide targeted information for children, youth, singles, married couples, and those facing retirement or living as senior citizens. Others aim at readers interested in theology, worship, contemporary music, home schooling, parenting, gender studies or sports.

Informing readers. Tribal periodicals often stress news and information. They responded quickly, via print or especially online editions, when thirty-two students were slain at Virginia Tech University (VT) in 2007. *Christianity Today* (moderate), *World* (conservative) and *Sojourners* (progressive) editorialized as well as reported the national events surrounding the tragedy. The *Christian Chronicle,* affiliated with the Churches of Christ, described the struggles of a fledgling campus minister at VT who began his work there only weeks before the massacre.[9]

Delighting audiences. Historically speaking, American Protestants are cautious about leisure and fun, partly because of the Puritan work ethic and partly because of the moral issues they perceive in mainstream entertainment. This might be why fiction rarely appears in Christian publications.

Evangelical editors know that print and online periodicals have to compete with television, films and now visually entertaining websites like YouTube. Their periodicals must offer interesting, engaging writing and attractive graphic design with telling illustrations. For decades most Christian and especially evangelical publications fell behind mainstream design, looking outdated even if their writing was pithy and captivating. Even today the advertisements and some of the editorial content are graphically inferior to top-notch magazines, but some of today's best magazine designs can be found on the pages of tribal periodicals.

In recent years, some publications hired professional firms to improve their graphic design. Beefed-up publications include those published by World Vision, Campus Crusade for Christ *(Worldwide Challenge),* Strang Publications *(Charisma & Christian Life)* and the Salvation Army. Sometimes, evangelical publications reconsider their design when they launch online versions since some network connection speeds cannot sustain the same types of graphic-intensive elements used in print.

Persuading readers to get involved. Only about 5 percent of editors say that they publish content aimed to persuade nonbelievers.[10] Instead, tribal periodicals attempt to persuade their readers to evangelize others or to serve those in need. Others attempt to persuade readers to begin mobilization efforts of their own—like starting pro-life rallies, protesting nuclear arms or war, or manning voter registration booths.

> **WHAT WOULD MOHAMMED DRIVE?**
>
> "How do we know God is a man? How do we know she isn't?" "Jesus was a homeless bum!" These headlines are from the print and online version of the *Wittenburg Door*[11] (intentionally misspelled), a 1970s-styled humor magazine started by church youth workers and attracting a small but remarkably loyal group who love to see fun made of Christians' foibles.
>
> The editors roast TV evangelists, churches with goofy advertisements, silly merchandise like little Bible heroes and a "loser of the month." The latter has included a mainstream book publisher that censored a Christian cartoonist's book of cartoons. One of the cartoons removed from the book portrayed a sheik driving a "Ryder Moving Services" truck with an enormous bomb sticking out the back. Caption: "What Would Mohammed Drive?"
>
> But even the *Door* includes fairly serious interviews with interesting and often influential Christians, from mainstream rock stars like Bono to high-profile pastors and writers, laced with a few tongue-in-cheek comments added by editors. On some Christian college campuses it is the most stolen library periodical. What does that say about other evangelical publications stocked in their reading rooms?
>
> *KEN WATERS,* PEPPERDINE UNIVERSITY

Drawing in New Readers

As with many other evangelical media, periodicals generally lack younger audiences. Although many high school students do not read traditional periodicals and college students often are too busy to read for pleasure, new print magazines and ezines (electronic magazines) hope to captivate a new generation of readers.

A trendsetter among a new generation of evangelicals is a publication and website called *Relevant.* Cameron Strang, the son of *Charisma* publisher Stephen Strang, discovered how irrelevant Christian periodicals seemed to younger readers when he tried to find a magazine to help him answer the inevitable questions students ask, like "What is the meaning of life? What are my calling and career supposed to be? Why is there human suffering? How should I relate to popular culture?" He and his entrepreneurial parents concluded that they could not reach potential young subscribers through traditional direct mail, church solicitations or tribal bookstores. Advertising seemed to be a lost cause, too. So he and friends began a print and website design business. Then they began publishing books by edgy young authors like Chris Seay, who wrote *The Gospel According to Tony Soprano,* and David Crowder, whose books include *Everybody Wants to Go to Heaven, but Nobody Wants to Die.* They launched *Relevant* <www.relevantmagazine.com> in 2002 with most of the content, commentary and testimonies submitted by readers. Only nine months later the online community had attracted 100,000 participants.

A year later, a print edition of *Relevant* appeared, targeted to 3,500 early subscribers who paid $10 annually. The magazine was immediately profitable and soon boasted over 80,000 readers. Its success spawned *Radiant* <www.radiantmag.com> for eighteen-to-thirty-four-year-old evangelical women. Advertising revenues allowed both magazines to offer reasonable subscription rates. There

CRAFTY COLLEGIATES TURN BEACON INTO BACON

Students at one Southern Christian college anonymously published their own online paper, *The Bacon,* competing with the official, school-sponsored paper, *The Beacon.* Administrators were not happy—though a few of them privately enjoyed some of the parodies of campus sacred cows, as I discovered when visiting the campus.

One article joked about the school's decision banning wine at campus chapel services. Catholic students supposedly had a loophole: once the priest blesses the wine, it's no longer wine but the blood of Christ. So Catholics were going to have their own Communion services at the campus "Smoker Wall" (supposedly where students who smoke would gather at a "safe" distance from the more "righteous" non-smokers).

Another story reported on a near miracle related to the new campus library building. As the headline put it, "Inspired by new library, 18 communication majors learn to read." The new library-going literates were going to meet with a tutor thrice weekly in hope of reading an entire Left Behind novel in ninety days.

Bacon editors quipped, "Never before have you seen such a devotion to truth, accuracy, might and valor embodied in the written word and occasional picture. . . . If you did not hear it from us, it's probably true." The editor added, "We strive . . . to highlight those trouble areas that are worth talking about. We hope to start conversations about issues that may never have reached the surface without us. We think that the *Bacon* (or something like it) is an essential voice in the campus conversation."

Is this a compelling vision of good, faith-informed community journalism?

QUENTIN J. SCHULTZE, CALVIN COLLEGE

are not many other media for tribal book publishers and other product marketers to reach younger Christian audiences.

"We're not afraid of talking about issues head-on or taking a stand, but the issues and importance of them may be different from my parents' generation," explained Strang. *Relevant* even interviews non-Christian recording artists like Matisyahu and Ben Folds, who talk candidly about Christianity and their own spirituality. "We don't want to be finger pointing," Strang says. "But we do want to examine situations and ask, 'How could this be? Here is something challenging, and here is how we could fix it.'"[12]

Another successful online periodical is found at ChristianityToday.com, a more timely version of the monthly *Christianity Today.* The Web version includes some of the print material along with daily news and reviews of everything from books to movies and music. It breaks down news into "hot topics" and lists the week's most-read articles. Bloggers give the online magazine a bit of editorial edge. Moreover, some articles clearly are pitched at younger readers who would not likely subscribe to the print version: "The Chewing Tobacco Diet: God Used My Student's Addiction to Teach Me Something About My Own" and "What Is My Calling?"

In addition, Christianity Today.com adds links to other websites and combines content from the company's thirteen other publications, such as *Today's Christian Woman, Ignite Your Faith* (formerly *Campus Life*) and *Books & Culture. Relevant*'s founder, Strang, says that his website fulfills its mission as a user-generated source of information and encouragement for its readers.[13] The print version of *Christianity Today,* on the other hand, provides more editor-controlled, in-depth discussions of contemporary culture.

Given the growing cost of printing and mailing offline periodicals, as well as the difficulty of generating younger print subscribers, Christian publishers are now deciding whether it makes financial sense to stay in print. Focus on the Family cut back some of its publications to Web-only and eliminated others. InterVarsity stopped publishing the highly acclaimed *Student Leadership Journal* in 2005, substituting an online-only site, studentsoul.com. Denominations that subsidize their periodicals may continue to do so. Some consider the increasing difference between the dwindling income they derive from ads and subscriptions and the accelerating costs of producing and mailing the publication to be a public relations expense, money well spent on strategic communication that attempts to strengthen tribal bonds and boundaries. Others may decide that denominational funds could be better spent on other endeavors and move to Web-only communication.

The Strengths of Evangelical Publications

Christian publications have fulfilled significant roles in church and society. They will likely continue to provide the same services in online media.

Strengthening tribal identity and bonds. Religious journals can foster "communion and discernment that help the tribe to locate itself at the intersection of tribal tradition and the public interest."[14] Not only are the tribal bonds strengthened; these publications serve a prophetic role for their readers, helping them to see mainstream culture critically, through the lens of tribal faith. The fact is that without "a shared religious language and common core labels, tribal media cannot sustain significant prophetic conversation."[15] They will lose their own, special perspective on the world around them.

Reporting from a tribal worldview. Tribal news helps believers to better understand issues reported in the mainstream press and to discern how a person with a biblical worldview should analyze and understand current events and controversies in politics, economics and culture. Periodicals can "engage clergy and lay members of churches in vigorous conversations about important events, ideas and artistic expressions that are shaping culture far beyond the boundaries of the ecclesiastical channels."[16] *Christian Century* has served this function for mainline Protestants, while *Christianity Today* and its online counterpart have done so for evangelicals.[17] The latter is recognized as the primary voice of evangelicalism, a forum for opinion and discussion that has helped shape the modern-day movement and enhanced readers' understanding of key political, cultural and religious issues. Articles and editorials have addressed all the major social issues in America, from race relations to war, abortion, worldwide poverty and nuclear weapons as a result of discussions contained on the pages of these and other periodicals.

Transcending time and space. Because tribal publications typically are circulated nationally and internationally, and now worldwide online, their discussions transcend time and space. People from around the world can engage in discussions that increase faith or empower individuals to form together for common causes. The influential Sojourners movement, for instance, started in Chicago in the 1970s as a vehicle for expressing a progressive social agenda and lifestyle choices within a broadly Christian but also primarily evangelical framework. *Sojourners* magazine became a leader in challenging believers to become more active in issues of social justice, overcoming poverty and protecting the environment.[18] Moreover, in 2007 the periodical and its influential movement succeeded at organizing the first televised national American presidential primary debates specifically addressing issues of faith as they related to candidates' personal lives and their stands on major issues.[19]

Strengthening personal faith. Articles that stress personal piety can strengthen the faith and prayer life of believers during the week, when they are not at church, and provide valuable advice for how to live as a Christian in a world that often

HWJRN = WWJD?

How would Jesus run a newspaper? (HWJRN?)

Charles M. Sheldon got his chance to run a newspaper like Jesus would—or so he thought. In 1896, he published *In His Steps,* considered by some to be the best-selling novel of all time, then got a call to be guest editor of the mainstream *Topeka Daily Capital* for one week.

"What would Jesus do?" (WWJD?). That's the hymn-based question Sheldon had asked in his novel. Now he was asking it about all content that appeared in the Topeka paper.[a] The mainstream press dubbed his experiment "The Jesus Newspaper."[b]

Sheldon believed that Christian-run papers could reach people who found religion irrelevant. To do that he scoured the news pages for opportunities to insert a message of redemption and purged all display advertisements of exaggeration and misleading claims. Sheldon also boldly addressed social ills like alcoholism and championed famine relief for drought-plagued East India. Worldwide contributions for East India poured into the paper.

But when his week ended, the mainstream press—and the church—said the experiment failed. Really?

Sheldon had already convinced the newspaper industry to examine advertising claims to make sure they were truthful. He also had shown journalists that readers do respond to calls for social reform in the name of faith. Moreover, Sheldon had launched a paper that implicitly served God by loving readers as neighbors. For him, being honest, persuasive and informative were keys to good journalism.

So what would Jesus do? Would he really provoke social reform by telling well-crafted, engaging stories that make readers think and lead them to servant-action? Or would he preach sermons?

MICHAEL SMITH, CAMPBELL UNIVERSITY

[a]Michael Ray Smith, *The Jesus Newspaper, the Christian Experiment of 1900 and Its Lessons for Today* (Lanham, Md.: University Press of America, 2002). The WWJD question is from a hymn sung in England before the turn of the nineteenth century.

[b]John P. Ferré, *A Social Gospel for Millions: The Religious Bestsellers of Charles Sheldon, Charles Gordon, and Harold Bell Wright* (Bowling Green, Ohio: Bowling Green State University Popular Press, 1988).

seems hostile to tribal beliefs. For instance, short Bible studies and daily devotionals still attract hundreds of thousands if not millions of evangelical readers to publications such as *Our Daily Bread, 21st Century Christian* and *The Upper Room. Guideposts* boasts a readership of more than a million people for its "good news" stories of human faith and courage. This role of strengthening personal piety is probably more important to older readers, but the audience might grow as younger readers age.

Learning to live faithfully at work, school and play. Specialized tribal publications for professionals and students encourage believers to apply Christian beliefs at work, school and play. The titles tell the stories: *The Journal of Christian Nursing, Christian Computing, CCM, Christian Ministry, Church Secretary Today, Christian Retailing, Relationships, Infuse* and the British young lifestyle online magazine *Soteria.*

STOP THE PRESSES

For all their strengths, evangelical periodicals continue to face challenges. As mentioned earlier, one of them is unimaginative writing and design. But there are two others.[20]

Lack of editorial freedom. The idea of editorial freedom that is cherished in the mainstream press is generally absent in both print and online evangelical publications. Few tribal newsmagazines would get a scoop on a sexual scandal by a high-profile minister, parachurch leader, musician or book author; some might ignore the story even after it appears in mainstream news media. These periodicals gladly hire idealistic journalism graduates, who disappointedly discover that their bosses and editorial boards will squelch articles on controversial subjects as well as bad news, embarrassing tribal mistakes and failed evangelical initiatives.[21]

Inability to directly engage mainstream society and culture. Few evangelical publications directly impact mainstream culture. By and large, evangelical magazines and newspapers fail to reach out beyond their tribal audiences. Instead, at best they connect evangelical themes and constituencies with the larger, nonevangelical world.[22]

DECLINING INFLUENCE

Some of the most potent criticism of Christian periodicals comes from church and media historians who wish to see tribal publications assume the visibility and influence they demonstrated at other times in history. The written word has been a powerful force in the advancement of Christianity and the continual dialogue over how believers should live. The dialogue began as the first believers discussed the Gospels and the written letters of the apostles. The advent of the printing press spurred increased dialogues, eventually fueling the revolutionary thinking we know now as the Protestant Reformation.

American Christians have always been prolific publishers of magazines and newspapers. Between 1730 and 1830, for instance, 590 different Christian periodicals were published in the United States.[23] "For much of the nineteenth century, they outnumbered strictly secular magazines, newspapers and cognate periodicals."[24] The first English-language publications served some of the same purposes as today's tribal periodicals.

News and information. Christian History (1743-1745) supplied colonists with information of a religious revival known as the Great Awakening, aiming to see how far "their pious Principles and Spirit are at this Day revived, and may also guard against all Extreams [*sic*]."[25]

Education and assimilation. Ein Geistliches Magazien (A Religious Magazine), for German-speaking immigrants in the late eighteenth century, helped readers in understanding their new culture with news of the day and essays on how to nurture children with a Christian worldview.

Advocacy. The *Christian Recorder* magazine, still published by the African Methodist Episcopal Church, began in 1852 and strongly fought against slavery. Pro-slavery forces saw it as "a very dangerous document or sheet and was watched with a critical eye. It could not be circulated in the slave states."[26]

Reconciling faith and work. Christian Scholar's and Farmer's Magazine was dedicated "to promote religion, to diffuse useful knowledge, and to help farmers in their work."[27]

Cultural and gender discussions. Women were among the early publishers of missions and temperance publications, making them forerunners of later female editors of mainstream publications.[28]

Missions. Early in the 1800s, mission societies started the first truly mass media in America, led by the American Bible Society's mass printing and distribution of millions of tracts.[29]

Influencing culture. Henry Raymond founded the *New York Times* in 1851 (yes, that *New York Times*!!) on Christian principles.[30] Media historians often cite the Reverend Elijah Lovejoy, editor of Illinois's *Alton Observer*, as America's first martyr of the First Amendment. Lovejoy was killed in 1837 while protecting his printing press from a mob of pro-slavery advocates angered over his anti-slavery editorial positions.[31]

Even as such publications sometimes became nationally circulated, their audiences became more specialized and focused on individual tribal concerns. That is especially true during the first half of the twentieth century when tribes divided over how much they should accommodate to and adopt the ideals of biblical criticism, the scientific method and Darwinism. Groups committed to upholding biblical inerrancy and a focus on "the fundamentals of the faith" disappeared from engagement with mainstream culture. Magazines played an important role in keeping marginalized believers tied together to fight against their common enemies. "By 1925, Christians were often voiceless, except in publications that largely preached to the choir."[32] They even gave their journals "militant-sounding names: *The Conflict, The Crusader's Champion, Dynamite, The Defender*."[33] To varying degrees, evangelicals inherited this kind of Christ-against-culture tribalism.

After World War II, the rise of youthful evangelists, many of them affiliated with Youth for Christ, reenergized and mobilized the adherents of biblical Christianity. In 1956, Billy Graham announced the launch of *Christianity Today,* which set the tone for a new evangelical thinking that both confronted and accommodated modern culture. (The editors used the word *evangelical* to distinguish themselves from the more militant, anti-intellectual and separatist *fundamentalists.*) Using news, commentary, staff editorials, and book and music reviews, the magazine redefined evangelicalism, earning a spot as a key publication that melded together a movement and represented its thinking to mainstream culture and mainstream media.[34]

Christianity Today quickly became a journal of opinion countering the liberal

NEWS + ANYTHING = BIAS

Is a news story about a disastrous building fire liberal or conservative? How would we know? Suppose the report says that owner did not have insurance. Maybe the implication is that the owner is at fault—possibly a conservative slant based on a bias toward *personal* responsibility. Or perhaps the government is at fault for not requiring fire insurance—maybe a liberal slant based on a bias toward *public* responsibility.

Most journalism educators agree that reporters tend to be reform-minded partly because they are taught to promote the common good, not personal interests. The idea of seeking the truth for the sake of positive social change is probably journalists' primary calling. Nevertheless, some critics of mainstream journalism believe that reporters and news media should reveal their biases. What, then, should reporters disclose about themselves when covering a fire? Or school board elections? And who should decide what reporters need to report about themselves, from their religious beliefs to their political affiliations and personal income?

A few periodicals do reveal some biases. *World* magazine says it aims "to report, interpret, and illustrate the news in a timely, accurate, enjoyable, and arresting fashion from a perspective committed to the Bible as the inerrant Word of God."[a]

Should mainstream media offer similar self-disclosure? Maybe. But mainstream newsrooms are not as monolithic as most tribal media—and perhaps not as biased. Mainstream reporters who seem to be pushing their own agendas are likely to lose their jobs.

Perhaps it's time to dump simplistic categories like liberal and conservative media in favor of educating citizens how to read all news critically, with charity and suspicion. Otherwise critics might be trying to extinguish a lit match with a fire hose.

MICHAEL RAY SMITH, CAMPBELL UNIVERSITY

[a]*World Magazine* mission statement, Dec. 22, 2007, p. 2.

political and doctrinal stands of mainline Protestantism's influential *Christian Century*. The growth of Americans' disposable income, the development of desktop publishing and the spread of improved printing options fueled an explosion of evangelical magazines in the latter half of the twentieth century. Meanwhile, mainstream Protestant periodicals lost readers.

TRIBAL CONSUMERISM

Many tribal publications appear to be thinly veiled attempts to copy market-successful mainstream publications. This phenomenon is called *twigging*, or "creating a world-within-the-world which is more like the world than their parents ever envisioned inhabiting. Does adding 'in Christ' to these themes excuse the fact that their treatment of them looks just like the world's?"[35] The twiggers are found in several categories.

Women's magazines. Today's Christian Woman, *Christian Women Today*, *Just Between Us*, *SpiritLed Woman* and *Radiant* provide essays on family, relationships, homemaking and work, much like their mainstream counterparts found at supermarket checkout stands. Some venture into topics like sex that used to be taboo for Christian women but are still addressed in a tamer fashion than a reader would see in *Cosmopolitan* or even *Redbook*.

Men's magazines. New Man, founded by Promise Keepers, provides encouragement in Christian living for men. While it does not dispense advice on how to seduce a woman, like *Men's Health, Esquire* and *GQ,* it is not unusual to find cover lines like these from the May/June 2001 issue: "Porn Again," about sexual addiction in the church, followed by "A Porn King Finds God."

Sports magazines. The *Sports Illustrated* reader can read *Sports Spectrum,* which seeks to "highlight Christian athletes of all sports and levels to help motivate, encourage and inspire people in their faith through the exciting and challenging world of sports."[36] *Christian Motorsports* recently featured "outlaw bikers" and an interview with a fuel drag champion.

Children and youth magazines. These often offer advice on fashion, dating and relationships. They include *Clubhouse* (eight- to twelve-year-olds), *Brio* (teen girls) and *Breakaway* (teen boys) from Focus on the Family, and *Ignite Your Faith* from Christianity Today.

Perhaps a deeper reading of evangelical media history will show that some of this kind of specialization occurred first in tribal rather than mainstream periodicals. Maybe mainstream publications copied earlier tribal publishing.

CONCLUSION

Tribal periodicals have served individuals, families, communities and nations. But they now struggle to adapt to tribal and mainstream cultural and technological changes. For one thing, they need to become more relevant to younger believers. For another, they will have to be delivered through whatever medium is most appropriate—print or online—for given audiences and purposes. The success of newer print and online publications, like *Relevant* and *Radiant,* and the continued strength of older publications, like *Christianity Today* and *Sojourners* that have added online features, show that changes can be made successfully.

Future editors will need to do more to keep in touch with their readers and to respond to the breakneck speed in which cultural interests change, all without watering down their Christian message. Editors may need to become more involved with their readers, undertaking the sometimes costly practice of surveying readers, meeting with focus groups and talking individually with readers at public gatherings. As we are seeing with the success of *Relevant,* successful periodicals in the future will likely be more interactive, featuring a mixture of edited and reader-submitted content. That is certainly true with popular ezines and websites like The OOZE, Emergent Village and *Next-Wave.*[37]

The *National Courier* failed partly because it tried to be all things to all Christians. Its initial readership consisted of people who had subscribed to the charismatic *Logos Journal,* but they did not want to read a story about how difficult it was to deal with an unwanted pregnancy, the pros and cons of getting an abortion, or the shortcomings of evangelical leaders. Because the content of the *National Courier* did not mirror their existing tribal preferences, readers refused to renew their subscriptions.[38]

For centuries, dedicated people have attempted to use printed periodicals to change society—to combat sin, edify believers and change the course of history. Millions of their readers have benefited from those efforts, and it is likely that future Christian editors will continue to teach, delight and persuade readers.

6

Publishing Books for the Tribe and Beyond

MICHAEL A. LONGINOW

August is over. As a returning college student, you unpack the boxes in your dorm room and set up the essentials. You click through the college website for course syllabi, jot down required titles and head to the campus bookstore. But when you get to the textbook section—sticker shock! You shove the book list in your pocket and head back to your dorm to visit an old friend: Amazon.com. It is quick, prices are lower, used copies are available, and with the money saved you can buy a couple of evangelical books the campus store does not carry.

Books are one place evangelicals turn to escape into fantasy, wrestle with ideas, learn to know and serve God, or just hang onto their faith. And evangelical books are selling everywhere from Amazon to Wal-Mart—in some cases defying the traditional evangelical label. Additionally, evangelical books are showing up not just on paper but on computer screens and in earphones as we walk, run, drive, bike or fly.

Though the number of mainstream book publishers is declining, books are selling well. Mainstream companies are buying out evangelical book publishers to get a piece of the action—and the rights to electronic versions of classic books as well as upcoming titles by new Christian authors.[1] As paper and multimedia publishers know, there's money to be made in tribal books.

Books Everywhere

Except for Bible studies or faith-based teaching books, the marketing of evangelical books mimics mainstream publishing. Evangelical publishers have used a grid structure, packaging books by demographics such as age, gender, marital or, occasionally, ethnic demographics. They tackle adolescence, new marriages, singlehood, divorce, gay issues, anorexia, recovery from addiction, reentry to life after prison—and many, many more topics that represent just about everything imaginable.[2]

Some of the biggest tribal bestsellers in the early twenty-first century were written by celebrities, often known for their broadcast ministries, megachurch leadership, news or talk-show program appearances, musical recording careers, speaking gigs, or politics.[3] Book publishers call this the author's "platform" or ability to reach likely buyers via media interviews, speeches and the like. Tribal publishers increasingly prefer to come out with books by celebrity authors. Clearly evangelicals use books partly to find out what trusted tribal authorities think about an issue or what advice they offer. They want to identify with the leader and become part of the community of similarly interested readers.

Younger evangelicals, often less tribal and more engaged with mainstream culture than their parents, are adapting new reading technologies faster than the tribal publishing industry. Many enjoy Podio books "read" on a music player. Online books include newly self-published volumes and the types of Christian classics now online at the Christian Classics Ethereal Library and the Digital

DEMONS IN THE CHRISTIAN BOOKSTORE

The apocalyptic demon-hunting novel—*Left Behind, This Present Darkness* or *The Shack*—borrows the spiritual warfare imagery once typical of classic missionary biographies.

I once helped a retired missionary pilot to write his memoirs. The Christian publisher wanted more tales of spiritual conflict and weird happenings. My pilot friend wasn't happy to find that his life story needed spicing up! For him, a faithful servant's job well done consisted of safe flying, orderly cargo storage and friendly communication—nothing terribly apocalyptic about any of it.

Young evangelical writers haven't missed this trend. A college student I know is writing a novel she describes as "a thriller/romance" about a serial killer and several Christians—a blend of Stephen King and Grace Livingston Hill. Does such writing reflect Christian dissatisfaction with the mundane ordinariness of real life in our culture?

C. S. Lewis's *Screwtape Letters* helped readers see the spiritual in everyday life over sixty-five years ago. Maybe the current trend is doing something similar—a much-needed corrective to a culture that ignores or denies spirits. Where once the corners of our maps read "here be dragons—beware," they now read "here be Prozac—demons be gone." Although these aggressive, fast-paced and often entertaining accounts may help restore the dragons to the map, do they fuel unreasonable expectations about the spiritual life among young Christians?

Spiritual growth tends to be slow and measured, much like my pilot friend's careful loading of his seaplane. Do readers come to expect accelerated rates of spiritual growth, more like the growth of cancer cells than of normal cells?

LARRY M. LAKE, MESSIAH COLLEGE

2,900 AUTHORS LEFT BEHIND—SELF-PUBLISHING TO THE RESCUE?!

When I worked in book publishing, we received more than 3,000 manuscripts yearly from eager authors trying to get in print. But we published only about 100 of them, and many from authors we recruited. How many of those 2,900 disappointed authors would be tempted to self-publish today, using the new digital tools at their disposal?

The digital revolution has changed not just printing but also promotion and distribution—how people learn about books and order them. For some authors, self-publishing looks attractive. But what can a publisher do that an individual author using a digital book printer and Amazon cannot do?

First, skillful editors improve almost every manuscript—no matter what authors think. More important, the in-house screening process that decides which books to accept makes a book "legitimate" for booksellers and chain buyers. And "being legitimate" also translates into marketing. Getting the right people to display your book is nearly impossible for individual authors.

So why self-publish? Certain works have a targeted but limited audience (e.g., my book on how to help missionaries produce better videos). The digital revolution will allow your manuscript to get before the eyes of these people, and that is wonderful.

But if you think your self-published novel about the second coming of Christ is better than the Left Behind series, you may be right. Still, don't expect the buyers at Wal-Mart or Borders to think so. Hey! Your grandmother will still love you, no matter who refused to publish your book.

Would you buy someone else's self-published book? If not, why should they buy yours?

PAUL MOUW, JUDSON COLLEGE

Christian Library. The latter includes book reviews as well as computerized versions of the Bible (English only), an alphabetized listing of "Christian Works of the Ages," a listing of works by "heretics," a listing of "legends and fairy tales," along with reference works for research. In the website's store, readers can buy a 1560 Geneva Bible in CD format consisting of pages saved as digital images.[4]

Self-publishing, once known as vanity press for its appeal to ego-driven authors, has grown among evangelicals and mainstream writers. Moreover, authors, illustrators or photographers can "publish" their work on the Web. One evangelical media giant offers self-publishing with a turnaround of ninety days and marketing through 250,000 bookstores and on the Web.[5] What would a prolific early Protestant reformer like Martin Luther (1483-1546) have thought about today's innovations? As an advocate for early mass printing of Bibles and

Christian tracts (like short paperback books), he likely would have championed the new media.[6]

Persuasion sells. Evangelical books often call believers to go deeper—deeper in their faith in God, their understanding of life issues facing them and their enjoyment of reading more recent fiction. Publishers generally assume that readers want and understand the kind of tribal jargon used in sermons, retreats and other events. Readers from outside the tribe may think that evangelical books are overly preachy if not cultlike. Tribal books call readers to become a "contagious Christian," a "new kind of Christian," a spiritual Christian, a devotional Christian, a "culturally savvy" Christian in an age of "Christianity Lite," and on and on.

Yet some of the most popular tribal books also draw mainstream readers by

SHOULD CHILDREN READ THE BIBLE?

Sex. Mass murders. Magic. It's all there—in the Bible, not just on TV or at the movies.

Evangelical response? "Safe" Christian imitations for mainstream media products. Christian rap music. Christian movies. Christian romance novels. These harmless imitations supposedly protect children and teenagers by omitting foul language, sex scenes and graphic violence—the world's pollution (Jas 1:27).

But Scripture makes it difficult to define *safe* this way. The Song of Songs describes graphic, intimate, erotic sex. Biblical violence ranges from stonings to war. The apostle Paul uses the Greek word σκύβαλα, often translated "rubbish," but better rendered as "excrement," "dung" or "sh**"!

Scripture and a hot new mainstream film might *portray* the same scene, such as a couple in bed together, but the contextual *point of view* (what the whole story says about that scene) is often radically different. When King David seduces another man's wife, Scripture points to the error of his ways rather than glorifying the act. Sex between married persons (which the Bible affirms) is contextually different from sex outside of marriage.

Similarly, biblical violence does not condone all violence and certainly doesn't glorify it. Violence for a just war is not the same as gang violence or mass murder.

So Scripture frequently reports seemingly sinful occurrences without *condoning* them. The moral of the story becomes clear only when the reader understands the G- or R-rated context—so to speak. In other words, the Bible is safe for young readers only when adults help them understand it by addressing the contextual points of view, the "rest of the story."

Might this be the same issue with mainstream media? Are evangelical communities of discourse obligated to equip their youth with the critical skills necessary to interpret secular stories from a biblical point of view?

DAVID BEDSOLE, SOUTHERN WESLEYAN UNIVERSITY

minimizing the jargon. Billy Graham's 1953 bestseller *Peace with God* and his classic *How to Be Born Again* (1977) were straightforward appeals to a personal relationship with Christ. That formula still works, even with readers already in the tribe. Former journalist and now popular Christian apologist Lee Strobel was ranked in the top twenty-five of the Christian Booksellers Association list in mid-2007 for his *The Case for Easter* (his *The Case for Christ* made the top thirty). Josh McDowell's thirty-year-old book *More Than a Carpenter* hit the top fifty in 2007 for a simple but thorough defense of the deity of Christ.[7] Don Miller's *Blue Like Jazz*—the softly evangelistic story of his conversion—sold upwards of a million copies in the mid-2000s.

Bibles sell best. The Bible is the hottest-selling book in any evangelical bookstore, outstripping sales in other bookstores of popular fiction like *Harry Potter* by two-to-one or better.[8] Why? First, despite massive change in belief systems around the world, the Bible remains central to Christian as well as evangelical belief. Second, Bibles have been marketed aggressively, promoted by both evangelical publishers and tribal leaders and as part of American educational systems that make it central to their teaching.[9] Third, specialized, annotated Bibles help particular kinds of buyers apply Scripture practically to their lives. They include the *Princess Bible,* the *2:52 Boys Bible,* the *Archaeology Bible,* the *Women's Devotional Bible,* the *Adventure Bible,* the *Student Bible* and Bibles in other languages aimed at cross-cultural ministry.[10]

Even fun reading sells. Mainstream culture might view evangelicals as dour people, but tribal book publishing suggests otherwise. Evangelicals like humorous, engaging, romantic or just plain interesting fiction and nonfiction. *Boogers Are Blessings*—a hot-selling children's book in 2005—is hardly a classic, but it does delight children, parents and grandparents.[11] Author Barbara Johnson became a tribal celebrity with personal, story-filled books like *Stick a Geranium in Your Hat and Be Happy, Where Does a Mother Go to Resign?, Humor Me: I'm Your Mother,* and *Living Somewhere Between Estrogen and Death.*

When Tribal Publishing Misses the Mark

Critics sometimes see evangelical books as watered-down imitations of the real things—at best barely worth reading, at worst dangerous to intelligent people. They claim that tribal publishing is a superficial, celebrity-driven, moneymaking propaganda machine.[12] In the view of such critics, evangelical books offer simplistic half-truths about complicated issues. Supposedly tribal authors—including celebrities' ghostwriters—sell naiveté to naive readers. Evangelical publishers simply shy away from the ambiguities of life in a fallen world and from the darkest recesses of human existence. Take Mel White as one example. Now an openly gay minister in a lifelong relationship, he once ghostwrote for

AN EVANGELICAL WRITES ABOUT HER GAY SON—AND FACES PRAISE AND CRITICISM

Tribal author Barbara Johnson sold over a million copies of *Stick a Geranium in Your Hat and Be Happy.* Her book included the story of her gay son's "return to the Lord" after spending eleven years "wandering in the gay lifestyle."

According to Johnson, when she told the story publicly "every mom in the room identified with my joy, and one mother, who had wanted to die after recently learning that her son was gay, got up and shared how she now had new hope because of what had happened."[a]

Comments on Amazon by those who read the book were not so kind:

> [I]f you're looking for a role model in dealing with homosexuality in your family, do look beyond this author.
>
> This person has no business counseling parents of homosexuals, as it is clear she has no understanding of them. . . . I have news for you, Ms. Johnson. God doesn't make mistakes.
>
> As a gay Christian . . . I find Mrs. Johnson's writings decidedly disturbing and un-Christian.

But another reader wrote on Amazon, "This book is a breath of fresh air. It keeps you laughing and thinking positively in spite of whatever comes your way in life. It is a GREAT book for a no good very bad day."

A book that persuades and entertains some Christians can offend others, so evangelical publishers review submitted manuscripts partly for potentially offensive content. They are less committed than mainstream publishers to freedom of the press. Does this self-regulation reinforce negative stereotypes against the tribe, or does it enable evangelical publishers to better serve their tribal audiences?

QUENTIN J. SCHULTZE, CALVIN COLLEGE

[a]Barbara Johnson, *Stick a Geranium in Your Hat and Be Happy* (Nashville: Thomas Nelson, 2004), pp. 165-66.

bestselling authors Jerry Falwell, Billy Graham and James Dobson. Then he stunned the tribe in 1998 with the mainstream book *Stranger at the Gate: To Be Gay and Christian in America.*[13] Even though White is a minister, no evangelical publisher would have released such a book.

The critics are correct that evangelicals need to hear critical voices from outside as well as inside the tribe. Why wouldn't an evangelical publisher release a book like Anne Lamott's *Tender Mercies,* in which she uses the f-word in conjunction with her conversion, or Andrew Beaujon's *Body Piercing Saved My Life,* a critical, detailed picture of the contemporary Christian music scene?[14] Beaujon's appeal includes his deep research into the culture, money and politics of Christian rock music, even his willingness to ask the tough questions that the tribe is too embarrassed or too worried to ask. It is edgy stuff. But evangelical books do not appeal to some tribal readers because they lack such an edge. Life is more complicated than some tribal authors admit.

People of the Book

Evangelicals are known for being people of the book—the Bible. They claim to know Scripture—along with a wealth of companion literature. This is not surprising since evangelicals' patterns of teaching and learning about the Bible go back centuries. It is partly an oral tradition (drawn from preaching and teaching) but also one that puts enormous importance on reading the published word. So, from the very beginning, Christians have written about faith in Christ, not as a substitute for reading the Word but to extend biblical reading so that those who follow Jesus Christ can make biblical sense of the world in which they find themselves, and then act accordingly.

In the fourth century, early Christians Origen and Eusebius created what was then cutting-edge media content by writing about others (not just writing their own views). In effect, they blogged about other Christian and non-Christian writers, recorded their views, then gathered into libraries (perhaps the earliest databases) the best of others' writings. Their collections of written work became a foundation for Christian learning for centuries to come.[15] These early Christian leaders took seriously the apostle Peter's admonition to be ready always to give a defense *(apologia)* for the faith (1 Pet 3:15). The Italian Renaissance and later Protestant Reformation repeatedly mined these ancient libraries as part of a well-rounded, liberal arts education. To be educated was to be well read, and to be well read included a working knowledge of the Bible and other classics.

Early American Faith in Books

In the United States, books were part of a push by early American Protestants to train ministers and bring up believers in their tribes' faiths. Harvard University, for instance, the oldest institution of higher learning in the United States, was founded in 1636 by Puritans who sought "to Advance Learning and perpetuate it to Posterity, dreading to leave an illiterate Ministry to the Churches."[16] Ministers were among the best-educated members of early American society. These early schools established the best libraries on the continent, even as they eventually moved away from Christian faith as a platform for learning. The role of ministers was, and still is, to teach congregants in the faith, to instruct them into the ways of the tribe, and to interpret the surrounding world—with all its changes.[17]

Americans celebrated books beyond the Bible as means for teaching, delighting and persuading. Popular volumes like Thomas à Kempis's fifteenth-century theological devotional, *Imitation of Christ,* became popular reading that inspired and convicted readers, and gave ministers and the laity common texts to discuss. Similarly, collections of Charles Wesley's hymns stood next to the family Bible on many American nightstands—along with practical books like *Ten Nights in a Bar Room,* a temperance melodrama published in 1854 and performed for decades around the country.[18]

Since bookstores could be hundreds of miles from readers, mail-order books were common. Today many tribal and mainline buyers prefer the convenience of buying books online and having them shipped directly to their residences or offices. If they trust the author or know about the book, such inexpensive purchases seem like a no-brainer.

HOW SACRED IS YOUR E-BIBLE?

What should we do with old or unused Bibles? Trash 'em? Give 'em to Goodwill? What about unwanted or outdated versions of digital Bibles? Is it blasphemy to delete them from our hard drives and iPods?

Downloadable audio Bibles include Samuel L. Jackson declaring himself as God to Moses at the burning bush and Jim Caviezel *(Passion of the Christ)* delivering the Sermon on the Mount.[a] You can listen while driving in your car or running on the treadmill. Sound great?

Think again. What happens when your eBible is in the same iPod rotation as *The Rolling Stones*? ("I can't get no satisfaction," moans Mick Jagger. Jesus promises, "Come to me, all you who are weary and burdened" [Mt 11:28].) Does the context affect how we interpret and use Scripture?

Also, will the easy erasure of digitized Bible files lead us to devalue digital more than printed Scripture? We might feel uncomfortable trashing a paper Bible, but would we have the same misgivings about deleting memory-hogging audio or text versions on computers, PDAs, audio players and cell phones?

Even more complicated: What is sacred Scripture when high-tech printing and multimedia technologies make it easy to produce specialized versions? You don't like it when Jesus talks about judgment on sin? Just delete those nasty verses! (Why not? The Jesus Seminar did when it concocted its own cut-and-paste Gospel.)[b]

Does your e-Bible give you easier access to the God who wrote it? Or are the new technologies inviting us again to play God?

MARK E. TAYLOR, LOYOLA UNIVERSITY CHICAGO

---

[a]*The Bible Experience: The Complete Audio Bible* (Grand Rapids: Zondervan, 2007); *The Word of Promise: New Testament Audio Bible* (Nashville: Thomas Nelson, 2007).

[b]N. T. Wright assesses the Jesus Seminar at <www.ntwrightpage.com/Wright_Five_Gospels.pdf>.

Romance fiction has long been popular in North America. Nevertheless, popular, tribal fiction never took off until the 1980s, when largely sex-free romance novels began topping the Evangelical Book Publishers Association's bestseller lists.[19] Apparently evangelicals wanted safe fiction without steamy sex scenes. Once tribal publishers started releasing such books, the market boomed.

Teaching the Tribe

The instructional, even preachy, bent in evangelical publishing reflects the strong influence of preachers and teaching on the history of modern religious book publishing. The printed sermons of nineteenth- and early-twentieth-century public preachers like Dwight L. Moody (1837-1899), Charles Grandison Finney (1792-1875) and Billy Sunday (1862-1935), a former major league baseball player who used his celebrity status to attract crowds to evangelistic rallies, were hot among evangelicals. Moody, a street-smart former shoe salesman in the Civil War era, knew how fast listeners forgot what he proclaimed in the stadium-style rallies he hosted across the United States and Great Britain. So he hired covered wagons loaded with free or low-cost books to reinforce his teaching.[20] His approach to distribution somewhat resembled the way modern churches publish on the Web their ministers' sermons free for reading or download.

As they scanned the pages, readers who snapped up such preachers' books and printed sermons could hear the preachers' voices—enormously influential voices—rising from the narrative. Celebrity status, wit, humor, tie-ins to current events—all the aspects so foundational to today's evangelical book market—were part of this draw in the late nineteenth and early twentieth centuries. Today teaching/preaching celebrities include Charles Swindoll, Max Lucado and up-and-comers like Rob Bell.

Used by preachers and others hoping to influence people, Christian books in the early 1900s became instructional weapons in ideological wars. The minds of youth, especially liberally educated students, were presumably at stake. Books became one means of fighting back against liberalism as American schools pushed a near-religious devotion to "evil" materialism, empiricism and humanism.[21]

As today, tribal publishers in the early twentieth century took to the presses to fight such seemingly pagan trends. Between 1910 and 1915 bound weapons included a series of books called *The Fundamentals: A Testimony to the Truth.* Such books birthed the labels *fundamentalist* and *modernist* (called *liberal* today), groups that were splitting Protestantism into two broadly defined camps over such things as evolution and biblical inerrancy. From both camps came books that defended particular biblical interpretations and outlined "correct" views of cultural customs, such as prohibitions against tobacco, alcohol, gambling and social dancing.[22]

Although books helped the various groups form new identities within Protestantism and evangelicalism, they helped tribes form new alliances as well: Baptists aligned with Pentecostals, Methodists with Presbyterians. The result was a renewed emphasis on the unifying power among different conservative tribal groups of their shared relationship with Christ. Books helped evangelically minded Christians build new bridges even though they differed on some key doctrinal issues such as sanctification, predestination and the second coming of Jesus Christ.[23] Today the whole idea of evangelical books and authors—rather than just the Lutheran or Reformed or the you-name-it tribe—owes much to the power of book publishing to shape people's personal and group identities. Somehow evangelicals have managed to agree that there is something distinctly called a Christian book even as they debate which books merit publication.

Although overall book sales have declined in recent years, even the mainstream industry predicts a steady climb in Christian or at least spiritual fiction.

LETTERS VERSUS EMAILS—WHERE ARE THE "KEEPERS"?

Late one summer night an oncoming speeding car hit a van in which our daughter Maggie, 21, was riding. Amid twinkling cubes of shattered glass bright in the pulsing beacons of emergency vehicles, she was secured to a backboard and helicoptered to a hospital. Soon her face was swollen with stitches and bruises, puffy lips hiding broken teeth. She was to be a bridesmaid in her brother's wedding in three weeks.

Then envelopes for Maggie filled our mailbox. Most of them were traditional cards with printed greetings signed by the giver. One, though, was different. It was from a friend. Neatly handwritten, a thoughtful, compassionate letter was squeezed into three panels of a card, with no cliché like "get well soon" to be seen. Maggie still has it. That's the kind of letter we call "a keeper." What letters or cards have you received that might be keepers?

Keepers are rare in these days of emails, instant messages and text messages, when people can stay in contact more immediately than they ever could through letters. In some cases, quantity has replaced quality.

What are some occasions on which a letter to a friend or family member might be more appropriate than a quick text message? Have you thought about ways to express interest in friends' lives that are more emotionally charged than "'sup" (What's up)?

Is the slowness of snail mail perhaps part of its power and its seduction? Maybe the time taken to compose a thoughtful letter or even a note is part of the gift to its receiver. The effort won't go unnoticed. In fact, the keepers might end up in a self-created book of remembrances.

LARRY M. LAKE, MESSIAH COLLEGE

In a pattern that has been evident many times through American history, the nation's collective passion for God bubbles up into stories it tells itself—ranging from mysteries to romances.[24] Faith infects books, for good and for bad, and in one genre or the other, again and again. This is obvious today in Christian romance—even chicklit—fiction titles available at mom-and-pop tribal stores, not just the big book chains or Wal-Mart. But it is also evident in the growing number of tribal how-to, self-help and motivational titles on the shelves at places like Target, Barnes & Noble, and Borders in the sprawling suburban centers where most Americans buy their books.[25] At most of the bigger stores the religion sections include a Christianity subsection, with a further subsection for fiction.

While evangelicals try to define who they are by communicating with one another in books and other media, mainstream authors also are trying to help evangelicals and nonevangelicals understand themselves and other groups in society. Joel Kirkpatrick's *A Field Guide to Evangelicals and Their Habitat* is both informative and mildly critical as it chuckles over quasi-biblical business names like Last Days Auto Repair and describes heaven as "the ultimate gated community"—perhaps just enough truth to make most evangelicals stop and think! Another, more trenchant and empathetic look at the tribe is

SCRATCHING THE SELF-HELP BOOK ITCH

Whatever our problems, self-help books have the answer—or *many* answers. Need love? Happiness? Faithfulness? You name it. Books offer answers.

Publishers say that best-selling self-help books scratch where people itch or come from well-known presenters/speakers. Consider how one of the most successful Christian self-help authors got started. He was a psychologist who became concerned that people weren't willing to discipline their children. He wrote *Dare to Discipline,* encouraging parents to practice stronger, more biblically-oriented discipline.

While promoting his new book on radio shows, he discovered that he had an excellent ability to converse with callers. Talk-show hosts loved him. He sold more books, got on more programs.

Next came his books *What Wives Wish Their Husbands Knew About Women* and *The Strong-Willed Child.* His books were in demand everywhere, not just in tribal bookstores. This author became a bestselling author.

Several years later, the original publisher gave this psychologist/author a significant advance on royalties to start a radio program. And sell more books. James Dobson could scratch where people itched. And speak well. He had personality, even charisma. Thus was born *Focus on the Family.*

Where do you itch? What kind of self-help book would scratch your itch?

PAUL MOUW, JUDSON COLLEGE

Mark Pinsky's *A Jew Among the Evangelicals: A Guide to the Perplexed.*[26]

But who is most perplexed, evangelicals within their own tribes or outsiders trying to understand the tribal matrix? In spite of the Internet, books still seem one of the best places to figure out who evangelicals are and how they might be different theologically and culturally from other groups in society. The evangelical author of *The Christian Culture Survival Guide: The Misadventures of an Outsider on the Inside* explains confusing concepts like altar call, the Holy Spirit, accountability groups, Christian entertainment, a salvation experience and baptism—the latter in a section titled "So Why Get Dunked?"

THE NEXT CHAPTER

Does evangelical publishing have a future? The easy answer is yes—as long as any publishing has a future. Still, critics of evangelical book publishing raise important concerns. Publishers and authors have too often gone where it was easy, pandering to the tribal or mainstream marketplace in ways that have betrayed evangelicalism's intellectual and spiritual legacy. What if evangelical book publishing survived but at the expense of being evangelical?

The fact is that tribal publishers are not just money-hungry businesspersons who will sell anything to naive tribal readers. Most of them sense that they have a calling or a mission to serve God. Some of the most creative ones have figured out ways of freeing themselves from bondage to tribal moralism, preachiness and mediocrity. For instance, evangelical publishers have started special imprints—such as Baker Publishing Group's newer Brazos Press, aimed at thoughtful works by Christians who might otherwise buy the more scholarly mainstream books.

Tribal companies do publish some books that merely tell the tribe what it already knows and what it wants to hear again—the same old stuff even if in new publishing skins. But not every title is a matter of money and market. In fact, they even publish books about how to reclaim a distinctly Christian vision of evangelical communications. In 2005 Baker published a book titled *The Great Giveaway: Reclaiming the Mission of the Church from Big Business, Parachurch Organizations, Psychotherapy, Consumer Capitalism, and Other Modern Maladies.*

No one really knows what American evangelical book publishing will look like in a few decades because no one knows what America or evangelicalism will look like. But one thing is clear: technologies are changing the ways that books are written, published, distributed and read. Tribal books will not disappear, but they will look and feel and read like some type of emerging evangelical tribalism. Evangelical book publishers are largely market-oriented. In pragmatic American fashion, they will figure out what works.

Conclusion

Evangelical book publishing is beginning to draw new lifeblood from a reformation taking place, especially in evangelical circles. Tribal celebrity Rick Warren, who in the tradition of earlier American revivalists published his purpose-driven thoughts about Scripture, cites numerous causes for this apparent reformation: a push-back from nihilism of the post-1960s era, an extended response to the attacks of September 11, 2001, and the steady growth of the emerging church movement.[27]

Is he right? Maybe. The growing flock of younger, edgier evangelical authors is one sign of such vital reforming of the tribe into a new tribe. At the same time, evangelical publishing is a complicated landscape of writers, agents, publishers, publicists, editors, readers, graphic artists, celebrity endorsers and so much more. This landscape can give birth to books on just about everything imaginable—as long as the resulting books do not offend too many tribal leaders whose criticisms can cause significant bad publicity and financial problems for publishers. But even in such situations an author can always self-publish a book and sell it online through Amazon.

The Christian college bookstore mentioned in this chapter's introduction—the one carrying the high-priced textbooks but not what students really cared about—adds one more piece to this complicated landscape. The most important issue might be whether tribal publishers can think like the new kinds of readers who grew up watching LCD TVs and blogging as well as reading online. In other words, publishers will have to think like readers rather than merely like ministers or accountants.

7

Practicing Worship Media Beyond PowerPoint

BRIAN FULLER

While I was shooting a documentary in rural Ecuador, indigenous elders took me through their small village. Few could afford power to illuminate a single incandescent bulb. Most shared living space with livestock. In the community center grew a two-story cinderblock structure, exposed rebar sprouting from its flat roof like unruly cowlicks of hair. Piled in a corner of the building's dirt floor was an impressive collection of amplifiers, keyboards, electronic musical instruments and drums. Noting the film crew's astonishment, the elders explained simply, "For church." From the Andes to the Canadian north, this Circuit City approach to worship media demands discernment.

WHAT ARE WORSHIP MEDIA?

Plasma screens direct visitors to classrooms or members to potlucks. A video highlights the congregation's food distribution project. Sunday school teachers tell Old Testament stories via PowerPoint. But the target audience of these communiqués is not a throne-sitting God receiving the praise of his people. Confusing adoration of the Almighty with information and logistic support for his servants mistakes pitcher for batboy.

This measuring stick of divine audience necessarily challenges the Ciceronian model described in chapter one. Humans cannot teach God anything, but faithful people can call on God to invite them to worship. Thus, the highest remaining aim of worship is to delight God.

As used today, do *worship media*—that is, live productions, art, artifacts and other technology used to communicate with and about God during church services—usually foster authentic worship?[1] Do they equip people as a community of faith to adore their triune God? Do they lay an unblemished lamb on his altar? If worship media makers imagined their work either as an offering or as a conduit through which other congregants offered themselves, how would that affect the morality, truth and beauty of banners, PowerPoint slides and hymns?[2]

Surveying the Electronic Landscape

Unfortunately, curiosity and popular trends frequently narrow worship's potentially broad menu to a high-profile trio of digital novelties: live production, slideware and full-motion video. These are insufficient but worthy worship media.

Live production. Multitrack amplification and mixing render the performances of choirs and praise bands audible and their lyrics intelligible. Gels, gobos and directional lighting create moods and direct attention. Dimmers jockey between the darkness worshipers need to see projected media on a screen and the light they need to read Bibles in their laps.

In a particularly large church, cameras trained on the pulpit and feeding screens flanking the platform can make an infant dedication visible to the balcony's nosebleed section, or even transmit the service to nursery workers via closed circuit. Multisite churches share the same preacher, feeding the sermon live from a central sanctuary to satellite locales. Typically, each site has its own emcee, praise band and sacraments but is unified with sister churches by simulcast preaching. An event shot for JumboTron visibility is easily recorded and archived to tape or hard drive for distribution via conventional broadcast, DVD or Web.

Slideware. Despite the money sometimes spent on live production technology, projected images are used increasingly as a visible hub of the worship wheel.[3]

USING TECHNOLOGY IN WORSHIP—FOUR CHOICES

1. *Rejection*—Don't use slideware and other technologies in worship because they are bound to promote entertainment and detract from true worship.[a]

2. *Adoption*—Go ahead now with new technologies since people have already figured out how to use them well in settings outside of worship, like education and business, and presumably the technologies can be used similarly in worship.

3. *Adaptation*—Go slowly and carefully, using new technologies only when you can discern how, when, where and why to use them appropriately in worship.

4. *Creation*—Don't just mimic or adapt mainstream uses of technology, but instead invest in the persons and organizations that will invent the next generation of technologies specifically for worship, breaking ahead of mainstream society.

Which of these approaches are evangelicals most likely to take? Why?

QUENTIN J. SCHULTZE, CALVIN COLLEGE

[a]These choices are adapted from Quentin Schultze, *High-Tech Worship?* (Grand Rapids: Baker, 2004), p. 45.

PowerPoint and its kin[4] command the attention of congregants more or less constantly from before the service (with a preshow loop of announcements, prayer concerns or Scripture meditation) through the postlude (with reminders to tidy the pews or welcome visitors).

Microsoft's omnipresence ensures widespread use of PowerPoint to project worship texts. Microsoft's major limitation for worship was once the lock-step linear structure of presentations, making it difficult to skip a stanza or adapt spontaneously to Spirit-led preaching. That problem has been addressed by multiple video cards and monitors that allow operators a fluid preview of upcoming slides while a congregation sees only one image displayed on its sanctuary screen.

Films and videos. Despite its simple animation, PowerPoint cannot satisfy the hunger of congregants raised on the moving image. Thus, an expanding number of churches integrate (1) locally produced, (2) centrally produced or (3) theatrically released full-motion video into worship.

Locally produced. A service of commission starts with a choral call to worship, accompanied by edited footage of a church's supported missionaries at work. Or maybe a sermon-supporting skit (that would have been performed live a decade ago) is opened up on the big screen. The video centerpiece of an annual service of remembrance combines home movies of members who have passed away in the preceding year. All are produced at the local level, intentionally having the same limited relevance of a family album.

Centrally produced. The second type of video might be purchased from or provided by some Christian media service, shared by church networks (chiefly on websites) or provided as a denominational resource. Generically themed clips might be pregrouped by liturgical season or holiday (Christmas, Mother's Day) or by some biblical theme that is likely to recur in sermons across Christendom ("The Fruit of the Spirit" or "Marriage and the Family," for example).[5]

Theatrically released. Finally, some culture-engaging pastors employ movie clips, frequently provided to preachers with film tie-ins that support concurrent theatrical or DVD releases. Excerpts from *Rocky Balboa*, for example, were distributed to churches in "outreach boxes." Sermon ideas (a three-part series on "The Heart of a Champion") and discussion guides were made available through a website.[6]

Evangelical groups prepared magazine readers for the 2007 release of the poorly made *Evan Almighty.* Their one-page ad read, in part:

> ArkALMIGHTY is a good deeds initiative inspired by the hilarious family film *Evan Almighty.* Random Acts of Kindness shock and amaze people, and provide a window into the grace and love of God. Launch ArkALMIGHTY right in your

own church. Do Good—it's easy, it's fun, and it totally freaks people out! To receive your Ark Kit (valued at $125) for FREE, sign up.[7]

Creative Fans

Clearly a banner-bearer for digital devotees, Father Juniper Schneider recalls that projected video appealed to him both as parish priest and as principal of the church's affiliated school. "I decided on a Thursday that we needed to go in that direction. The equipment was installed that Saturday. You hang a screen in the barren box of a Protestant church, and everyone takes notice. In a Catholic church, it's just one more thing on the wall. Have you seen the Sistine Chapel . . . ? We've been doing multimedia worship for a couple thousand years."[8] Schneider sees microphone and projector as contemporary heirs to paintbrush, loom and censer—tools of art with which the church has adored her Lord for centuries.

Access. While Father Schneider's congregation may have initially plugged in to become relevant to youth, worshipers in their seventies and eighties instantly realized an unplanned benefit. When an African priest with a thick accent started projecting his homilies, "the screen made it so much easier for worshippers to understand. That plus wireless hearing aids in the pew racks. If technology can do anything to help even one person worship better, I'm all for it," declares the church liturgist.[9]

Seattle pastor Karen Ward reports that the first time she led a service with projected readings from the *Book of Common Prayer* older worshipers were initially among the most skeptical. Later, though, they said, "'I really liked it.'" Ward recounts one woman's astonished grin after the service: "'I'm older now and I don't see so well. It's easier to focus on the screen's big letters. And my hands. I didn't have to work to hold a heavy hymnal.'"[10]

Focus on worship. Music ministers frequently claim that projected lyrics aim voices up instead of into the acoustic dead end of a hymnal. Freed from the need to hunt for Bible passages or responsive readings, congregants devote themselves more fully to the uplifting service. "The screen isn't a distraction," says a recent college graduate. "The perfume of the woman next to me . . . *that's* a distraction. Cute boys are a distraction. If worship gives me something to look at, something to smell, something to do with my body, I don't have time to be distracted. I'm worshiping better."[11]

Multimedia as multigenerational. "I'll pick you up after school, and we'll work on PowerPoint at your house." So begins the collaboration between a seventy-year-old worship committee member and a sixth-grade boy. When the elder suggests green backgrounds for the week's slideware, the young computer whiz asks, "Why?" He does not know he is opening a dialogue on colors of the liturgical calendar—but the elder does. Later in the same work session, the youngster chooses photos for slides of the middle school's pool party to be shown as worshipers meander out of the sanctuary. The elder looks over his shoulder as he flips through the files on a camera's memory card. The unlikely pair talks about the modesty of swimwear and the appropriateness of wet T-shirts in church.[12] Incorporating media technology into worship can thus offer an unlikely springboard for intergenerational faith-talk.

Multimedia as fully gendered. A church commissioned me to direct the play *The Beams Are Creaking* in cooperation with a local Christian college. Pastor and elders swiftly approved funds for this innovative script about the theologian Dietrich Bonhoeffer's collaboration in a plot to assassinate Hitler.

I researched the Third Reich, designed sets and announced auditions. A surplus of women showed up, enough to cast Bonhoeffer's mother, sister and fiancée many times over. Some volunteered to provide refreshments for intermission, grow opening night roses and host a fundraising dinner.

But the play's *dramatis personae*—soldiers, government officials, seminary students—required many men. I extended tryouts, pled from the pulpit, printed a bulletin insert, eventually working my way through the entire church directory, personally telephoning every man in the church. Sadly, I was not able to press into service even elected church leaders. I cancelled the show.

Females compose 61 percent of the American churchgoing population[13] and probably most of the nation's crafts artists. Women are the banner-making, praise-dancing, potluck-planning, flower-arranging, poster-painting, choir-joining backbone of the church. Yet with male decision makers often holding the purse strings, liturgical art is frequently underfunded and underused.

Happily, electronic worship media frequently foster an unexpected gender reunion. Button-pushing, photo-taking, mouse-clicking, video-camera-wielding men are following the Pied Piper of personal computing across art's digital bridge.[14] They realize that photos can be projected backdrops for church drama, that videos can accompany offertory hymns, and that hardware and software long in the service of commerce are newly welcome in the pulpit.

Multimedia as multisensory. Many churches report the surprise of discovering that slideware and video constitute a gateway to worshipful communication through *all* the senses. "What we're finding today with these high-tech churches is they're not just high-tech. They're multisensory, taking things from throughout the history of the church and reintegrating them into worship."[15] Hang a projector in your sanctuary and you may just start a renaissance of ancient worship, complete with calligraphy, prayer labyrinths and incense.[16] "While we were occasionally open to liturgical dance or drama or multisensory elements in traditional services, you see it more often now in our digital services."[17] According to a church member in Michigan, "People get PowerPoint; all of a sudden they do the wipes and the swipes and they think that's great multimedia. It's a starting point. But involving all the senses . . . is actually going away from the screen and incorporating other things that help to make your encounter with God real."[18]

In this new form of multimedia worship, the concept of "liturgy" is not just a style of worship with responsive readings, formal sacraments like weekly communion and colorful vestments. Instead, all worship is reclaiming its liturgical status as "the work of the people" (the literal meaning of *liturgy*). All media can contribute to this "work" of worship. In fact, worship is liturgy.

Multimedia as multiethnic. A team in California gathered to plan liturgical art based on Romans 12. The chapter enumerates a variety of gifts (prophecy, service, teaching, encouragement, philanthropy and leadership) at work in a unified body of believers. Someone suggested it sounded like a Christian spice

DIRTY DANCING ON EVANGELICAL COLLEGE CAMPUSES

Dance—possibly the most feared five-letter word on many evangelical campuses. Why? Such movement can be sensual and lead to sinful behavior. Or it can resemble crude dance hall or club behavior. Some denominations consider dancing valid in specific Old Testament contexts only. The list goes on. The default response is simply "no dancing."

Even this volume—a book devoted to understanding evangelical media—offers no discussion of dance as a medium in its own right. But in recent years, tribal students have formed dance clubs under the administration's nose, while other dance groups have popped up as part of praise and worship teams. The Step Team is one dance organization. A sacred dance group calls itself Shekinah Glory. Both wisely chose to avoid the word *dance*.

In 2003, Wheaton College in Illinois lifted the ban on students dancing, although students were advised to avoid behavior "which may be immodest, sinfully erotic or harmfully violent."[a] Other tribal schools recently added dance courses,[b] although one Midwestern college had to avoid *dance* in titles, preferring ballet and jazz technique classes in the theater department. Another college indicates that the study of dance promotes "creative expression through the art of liturgical and expressive dance," an "alternative language for the worship of Jesus Christ."

Maybe this is the beginning of a new era in the role of the body in worship. Perhaps the renaissance in liturgical traditions will get more evangelicals dancing "clean" in classes if not in chapel.

SCOTT P. JOHNSON, BETHEL COLLEGE, INDIANA

[a]"Wheaton College Lifts 143-year Dance Ban," Education, CNN.com (November 14, 2003) <www.cnn.com/2003/EDUCATION/11/14/wheaton.dance.ap/index.html>.

[b]"Dance Grows as Field of Academic Study Within CCCU," Council for Christian Colleges & Universities News (December 8, 2006) <www.cccu.org/news/newsID.497,parentNav.Archives/news_past_detail.asp>.

rack. They agreed they would represent Romans 12 with digital photos of spices, complemented by a spread of spices instead of a more traditional floral arrangement at the base of the pulpit. Recipes featuring the spices would be printed on cards included in bulletins.

An East Indian woman on the team offered recipes for curry and tandoori. An Hispanic man grew, dried and photographed a brilliant rainbow of chilies. A pair of Jamaican sisters assembled jerk seasonings. No one in the group or in the congregation made a special attempt to be programmatically multicultural; multicultural inclusion was simply and naturally a consequence of collaborating to make liturgical art.

CONCERNS

Cautious—even fearful—church members wonder whether multimedia technologies (or indeed *any* change) might weaken or even supplant trusted forms of proclamation and worship. Many voice reasonable criticisms of stewardship, logistics, theology and philosophy of multimedia worship.

Architecture. Loudspeakers and lighting fixtures can clash with existing church architecture or detract from meaningful worship symbols already in place. Even crosses get covered up by screens. Without training in informed aesthetic compromise, church leaders fear that constructing new or retrofitting existing facilities may stir a hornet's nest of offended congregants.

Money. Sticker shock is at the top of a list of reasons churches give for rejecting visual media.[19] Technology purchases often beget others: (unfriendly) locks and alarms, training, professional salaries, repairs, software upgrades. Thoughtful stewards understand that multimedia worship is not a one-time expense but an ongoing line item, just like Sunday school or building maintenance.

A poor planning fit. Lectionary traditions—Catholic and Lutheran, for example, which typically follow a list of Bible readings planned a year in advance—already employ media-friendly, long-range calendars.[20] But improvisational, Spirit-led traditions may find original, high-quality multimedia difficult to achieve. Full-motion video in particular, requiring more extensive planning and collaboration than weekly music rehearsal or sermon preparation, may demand a preproduction lead time of several months.

Frustratingly, some of the church's savviest media producers are least willing to bind themselves to far-sighted production timetables. It seems the surest way to estrange an artistic teenage "computer wiz" is to ask him to join a committee. Some church members might not even want minors in a worship planning group.

Artless or other unprofessional results. Too often the responsibility for creating worship media is shouldered by aesthetically challenged technicians (who know which function keys to press), not artists (skilled in composition or audio mixing). This is a bit like expecting piano tuners to perform concerts or making quarry owners carve sculptures. Doing the best they can on short deadline with a mismatched skill set, technicians pressed into artistic service are frequently overworked and underappreciated. Their resulting product is sometimes embarrassingly amateurish: distracting PowerPoint slides cluttered by a ransom note of fonts, muddied by unmotivated screen transitions only a game show could love, and filled with pixilated background images of syrupy landscapes lifted last minute from the Internet.

Business models. A business model—keeping up with the Joneses of mainstream media—guides many churches. "If we don't have it and another church down the street does, well, people, young families will go there, won't they? I mean that seems to be the logic."[21] With success increasingly described in terms of congregational size, worshipers seldom challenge a competitive rationale of utilitarian democracy and capitalism.

> Vendors [of computers, projectors and slideware] have turned their attention . . . to the church as their number one market. It's why most of what's being written [to encourage the use of technology in churches] doesn't offer aesthetic or theological guidelines. It's all about equipment's technical specifications. All of the "how," none of the "why."[22]

Frequently accepted without examination, forces of marketing and manufacturing drive evangelicals' multimedia paradigm. The church also imports from corporate life technology's rapid rate of innovation. The corporate crowd prides itself on cutting-edge adaptation of new technologies, and some churches do the same. Because the church ultimately should value the thoughtful embrace of unchanging truths, not mere trendiness, there are bound to be missteps between the corporate and church trains moving at different speeds.

Ironically, neither churches which embrace electronic media as fashionable[23] nor those which reject it as fleeting and faddish seem to know that projected song lyrics are as contemporary as the movie palaces of the 1920s. Immigrants, fresh from Ellis Island, sought respite from New England sweatshops in twice weekly outings to motion picture shows. Mammoth organs rose on scissor-lifts from the orchestra pits of theaters modeled on synagogue architecture.[24] Keyboard operators served as ringmasters of an entire entertainment event. They provided music (and sound effects!) for silent films, but before the lights went down and the projector's arc-lamp leaped to life, the organ was the prow of a social ship. Its pipes bellowed tunes to popular songs. Words appeared on the screen, courtesy of a "magic lantern." Viewers literally "followed the bouncing ball" of light from one projected lyric to the next, sometimes learning English as they sang "Bicycle Built for Two."

The trendy church boasting the latest version of PowerPoint has not discovered anything new, and the traditional church will not likely be led astray by a ninety-year-old flash in the pan. Even the projector's outreach to multiethnic constituencies is old-fashioned. In short . . . *yawn.*

Education. Slideware, in particular, has swept through education, where reading, writing and texts are supreme. Could instructional technology transform a sanctuary into a classroom? Teaching and worship seem closely allied in many religious traditions, so maybe slideware is a natural fit for Scripture, lyrics and sermons. And maybe it is not.

"Power corrupts; PowerPoint corrupts absolutely," screams Yale University's Edward Tufte.[25] This expert in the graphic representation of data argues boldly that slideware is (1) antithetical to learning and (2) shoves out information in a way that disrespects its audience—which is particularly disturbing given this chapter's earlier audience-based definition of worship media.

Theft. To our shame, churches have deserved a reputation for stealing digital materials, sometimes cloaking their larceny behind a misunderstanding of the Berne Convention's fair use provisions.[26] Their theft includes unpaid, uncredited use of visual images and music. The temptation to cut and paste, the pressure of Saturday night deadlines, and the intended outcome of worshipful communication have all been used as excuses for unlawful behavior.

Celebrity and scandal. Technology is laden with the baggage of celebrity and scandal. Evangelists dating back to Aimee Semple McPherson in the 1920s offer object lessons in the cult of personality, when on-air clergy become performers.[27] Though pastors beamed by video to multiple locations may be heirs of noble circuit riders, they may also be mistrusted as entertainers. Of all the worship arts, the moving image presents a special challenge to reputation. Unlike music or sculpture, movies grew up with the sibling of celebrity reporting. The box office success of *War of the Worlds* may be as much a referendum on the private life of Tom Cruise as about a plot to save the planet from alien attackers.[28] I can still hear my grandmother, speaking for a generation of churchgoers, telling me that "a darkened theatre is the devil's workshop."[29]

Congregational passivity. Naysayers dismiss electronic images as passive, imagine themselves pew-potatoes, clocking another hour of screen time in a week already filled with it. Such criticisms may reflect a consumer identity. Christians in particular have long described themselves as outside (even opposed to) the media producing community. Not surprisingly, almost all the meager research on worship media art assumes a consumerist perspective. When people are asked if they like it or are moved by it or whether it is an effective worship channel, the answers typically address the effect of the finished product on congregants who view it—not whether the worship is any more worshipful and accomplishes what worship is supposed to accomplish. Such queries also ignore whether the photographers, editors and worship leaders commune with God while collaborating to plan and conduct worship.

Is it live or . . . ? Musical performers appear to be worshiping *concurrently* with the congregation. Thus, singers in the pew are apt to feel an active (if vicarious) kinship with leaders of live worship that they might not feel with leaders of worship prepared in advance. Because they do not see it made before their eyes, Doubting Thomases in the aisles may be less likely to accept film, multimedia, tapestry, pottery, painting, poetry writing or even prerecorded music and composition as acts of worship, consigning them to the lesser status of artifact or aid.

Lost in digital translation. Over and over, Mark uses the word *immediately* to describe the pace of groupies chasing Jesus from sermon to miracle. So a film or slideware presentation of that Gospel might reasonably be edited with a pace suggesting speed and urgency.[30] But pastors, like most lay consumers of media, are seldom equipped beyond their own personal taste in movies. They cannot coach video editors with even a rudimentary vocabulary of artistic and technical language. Consequently, the use of multimedia frequently becomes a matter of committee preference, molded by commercial and educational norms rather than aesthetic principles and scriptural appropriateness. Only the unspoken demand that church art be

WHAT DID YOU SEE?

When was the last time you saw a movie, TV show or YouTube clip? Why did you watch it? Bored? Curious?

What about the last time you went to worship? What did you expect to see?

Jesus asked the crowds that came to him what they thought they would see. Maybe they wanted to make their own conclusions about the man foretold by John the Baptist. Maybe they had heard rumors. Perhaps it was the only show in town—they were bored.

After asking members of the shuffling crowd about John the Baptist, Jesus compares them to children sitting around the marketplace, bored:

We played the flute for you,
   and you did not dance;
We sang a dirge
   and you did not mourn. (Mt 11:16-17)

Which is more important: how we ourselves prepare for worship, or how much the worship leaders and musicians prepare for the worshipers?

Surely high-tech equipment like digital video, PowerPoint and musical synthesizers can help worshipers to dance and mourn. But why do we want them? Why do we feel that we *need* them? Maybe we're getting increasingly bored in worship because of all the fancy techniques used by mainstream media. We expect and even demand the same level of spectacle. If so, what should we expect to see during real worship?

RONALD A. JOHNSON, GOSHEN COLLEGE

inoffensive exerts more influence.[31] The result is an ongoing reputation of mediocrity from which both the church and its artists have been retreating since the Roman era.[32]

Suspicion and misunderstanding. Sixteenth-century reformers dealt a blow to fitting media worship art by overreacting to concerns about icons and idolatry in the Roman church.[33] Protestants gutted cathedrals, smashed stained glass and toppled statues. During the ensuing centuries Christian artists were not so willing to offer their talents to worship! Still today churches, especially evangelical congregations, mistrust artists and worry that visual art, in particular, will dilute if not corrupt worship. A lot of the evangelical criticism of megachurch worship takes this mistrustful position. Academicians, professionals and businesspersons even today are more likely than painters and sculptors to serve as lay shepherds.

There may be many gifted and experienced multimedia artists sitting in church pews and attending Sunday school each week, but few are bringing the polished art to their local sanctuary. What a sad change from earlier Christian eras when churches were adorned with the best art of the day! Kings and clergy once recruited artists like baseball scouts sniff out Major League pitchers. Worshipers came to expect rich and varied multimedia efforts, telling the gospel story to them in fresco, silk and marble. Indeed, the first model for corporate worship was Bezalel's gallery of sight, texture, movement and fragrance.

RECALLING OLDER VERSIONS

Bezalel. In the nomadic nation of Israel, multisensory multimedia were worship's bone and marrow. Bezalel, among the first people in Scripture described as "filled with the Holy Spirit," was called to execute God's tabernacle blueprints (Ex 25—40).[34] He captained an artisan army of weavers, carvers, smiths, tailors, jewelers and perfumers.[35] They created for their Creator an environment of celebration, mourning, contemplation, repentance and gratitude. The tabernacle was a place of sensual activity, a space set apart for a gathering of grateful, awestruck people. It was not a backdrop for sermons, a collection of visual props supporting verbal proclamation.[36] Instead, the artwork itself constituted the literal centerpiece of God's plan for faithful living.[37]

Drowning in worship media. Tabernacle construction was not without hardship. At one point, Bezalel and his assistant, Oholiab, were overworked. By artists. By art. They had too much going on, and no amount of multitasking was going to save them. Moses actually issued an edict *restricting* artistic activity and donations "because what they already had was more than enough to do all the work" (Ex 36:7). May it be so again some day, Lord.

Local making, local meaning. One of the more unusual aspects of the tabernacle was its covering of dugong hides. The leather's chief virtue was that it was waterproof, not exactly a practical necessity in the desert. But these dugongs were a breed of manatee (a large sea mammal) indigenous to the Red Sea. And worshipers had to "pass through" them as they entered the tabernacle. The contextualized meaning of that decorative art—a reminder of escape from Egypt—could not have been readily unraveled by tribal passersby.

Modern Applications

A church in Southern Georgia prepares a service emphasizing the steadfastness of God. The worship team's digital photographers create slides prominently featuring a huge live oak in the town square. Over the course of the service, congregants come to see the massive trunk, the wide spread of limbs, the languid sweep of Spanish moss, as symbolic of God's unwavering loyalty to his people.

Folks chat at coffee hour, then return home to roasts and hams. As the wheel of the calendar turns, they drive to shoe stores and shuffle to football games, often passing the town's signature oak tree. And when they do, the tree whispers to them slivers of Psalm 51:10 or 1 Peter 5:10.

This horticultural PowerPoint allows a new perspective of Romans 1. God's invisible qualities (in this case, steadfastness) are clearly seen and are understood from what has been made (the oak—and just maybe the digital photography).

Now imagine the same church packaging its presentations for sale via the Internet. A congregation in Ontario buys a CD of images, opens the folder marked "steadfastness," and there beholds the mighty *Quercus virginia,* native to the U.S. Southeast. Like the tabernacle's dugong hides, the spiritual benefit of a Southern live oak is localized. The Ontario Christians may have pretty pictures, but the photos are hollowed of the meanings they possess in Georgia.

Isaiah 60 predicts the restoration of Jerusalem from a catalog of foreign building supplies. A centralized church is not broadcasting its homogenous message outward (one website providing photos to a hundred congregations) so much as it is drawing on local treasures in service to its purpose.

Conclusion

Suggesting a course away from generic, mass-produced graphics, I might seem to be kicking the legs out from under already beleaguered church media makers. But a vision of the unblemished sacrificial lamb may prove instructive. Not only is such an animal near perfect, it is also . . . well . . . a *lamb.* It is a small thing done exceptionally well.

The unblemished lamb means limiting a slideware to five (gender-reconciled, aesthetically beautiful, locally relevant, intergenerationally created) theme slides to offer God for a whole liturgical season—instead of the saccharine eye candy of twenty different backgrounds from anemic stock photos hoping to excite pew

QUESTIONS TO ASK ABOUT USING WORSHIP MEDIA ART

It's five o'clock Friday when you get Sunday's hymn selections and sermon topic. You sit down at your computer, boot up PowerPoint and ask yourself, "Which font did I use last week—Times New Roman or Arial?" If you're in charge of your church's multimedia, you know the routine. Sometimes it helps to step back from the last-minute preparation, take a breath and ask some deeper questions:

- Who is the audience of my church's worship media art—demographically, spiritually or otherwise?
- Is my church's worship media art made corporately? By both genders? By artists, technicians and theologians?
- Do worship leaders allow media makers enough lead time to produce content?
- Is the content relevant to your particular congregation? Appropriately respectful of our denominational or other traditions?
- Is it theologically sound? Artistically beautiful? Technically well executed?
- Is it legal? Does it violate copyright laws?

Okay, these questions are a good start. But how will answers shape the way you and other media artists make the worship art?

BRIAN FULLER, CALVIN COLLEGE

sitters during a single set of praise choruses.

The unblemished lamb means that a representative of the worship planning committee meets with a professional videographer and his or her editor in October to commission a three-minute Advent film for December. The filmmakers donate their expertise. The film becomes a yearly congregational tradition. And everybody still has enough weekend time left to spend with their children.

The unblemished lamb is an ancient symbol of a sensate God. It calls to us through the corridor of history, a "liturgical" hallway etched with catacomb drawings, lit by projectors, stained by colored glass, fragrant with flowers, smoky with incense, worn smooth by the shoes of dancers, echoing with musical instruments and voices, and lined with tables of food. This Lamb invites worship through every available medium—not just those which plug in. Learning to use multisensory media well is itself an act of artful worship for artists and congregations alike.

8

Going Digital with Contemporary Christian Music

STEPHANIE BENNETT

It was 1982. I was waiting excitedly for my fiancé to pick me up so we could drive to a youth camp where our newly formed Christian band—Sound of the Spirit—was booked. Many church leaders thought that rock music's drums were "of the devil," but we had seen God use the steady rock beat and electrifying music to teach, delight and persuade teenagers.

When my fiancé arrived, however, he was frantically fumbling with the car radio, trying to tune in a station playing a song by popular Christian artist Keith Green. I smiled briefly, recalling that we would be singing the same tune in a few hours. But then I, too, heard the horrible news on the radio: Green's plane had crashed. My fiancé and I sat in silence. We had lost an evangelical hero, a real troubadour, maybe even a saint. Green represented what we wanted to be: faithful musicians who played for the glory of God rather than for money, fame and other potentially sinful attitudes that apparently pervaded so-called secular music. In spite of the heartfelt loss, we would carry his bright torch into the expanding contemporary Christian music (CCM) industry.[1] Little did we know what was ahead.

Countercultural Desires

In the late 1960s and early 1970s new singer-songwriters who emerged from the countercultural Jesus Movement saw the established church as largely irrelevant and even hypocritical.[2] Typically clad in hippie-style clothing and performing on streets, in coffee houses, and at a few progressive churches, these Jesus-loving troubadours were not afraid to sing about their faith in youth-relevant language: Green, Honeytree, Chuck Girard (LoveSong), Barry McGuire, the Second Chapter of Acts, Larry Norman (known as the father of Christian Rock) and many others.[3] Later, Phil Keaggy, Rich Mullins and Steven Curtis Chapman similarly would use their gifts for God's glory, each contributing in unique ways to the proliferation of gospel-inspired rock.[4]

Early artists and CCM audiences typically defined Christian music in terms of its lyrics (the message) rather than the musical style or form.[5] They began imagining every style of mainstream music—from folk to heavy metal and eventually rap—as culturally neutral. Christian confessional lyrics (confessing one's faith in Jesus) justified any musical style.[6] Moreover, music ministry meant primarily evangelism, reaching out beyond the tribe.

That limited concept hardly stopped the growth of Jesus music, which began imitating not just the musical styles but also the marketing of mainstream popular music. CCM became big business with its own celebrities, concert tours, radio promotion and retail sales gimmicks. The music arose "to serve the needs

WHAT MAKES MUSIC CHRISTIAN? I KNOW! I KNOW!

Night after night, bluegrass diva Alison Krauss and her band closed concerts with "There Is a Reason." Ron Block's classic song clearly refers to Jesus.[a] However, if you're looking for CDs by Krauss and her band, don't look in the Christian section of a mainstream music store. This is not Christian music, say the powers that be.

Truth is, there are competing definitions of Christian music in a marketplace increasingly governed by legalistic preachers and preachy lawyers. Christian music

- is hymnody. Period.
- is any music that can be used in church worship services—no matter how difficult it is to sing along.
- can be found in all genres—except rock. Strong backbeats are forbidden.
- even includes heavy-metal rock or rap, as long as the lyrics are evangelistic.
- always contains some clear "God talk." Many CCM insiders call this the "Jesus per minute" rule.[b]
- is made by artists who say they are Christians, and their art—in some way—reflects this worldview.

Who's right—if anyone?

U2 front man Bono once told me that Christian music doesn't exist, because it's arrogant for sinful people—he put himself at the top of that list—to sell their music by using a Christian label as a marketing device. The bottom line: music usually gets defined by who sells it. Should evangelicals expect something else?

TERRY MATTINGLY, WASHINGTON JOURNALISM CENTER

[a]See the lyrics at <www.lyricsfind.com/a/alison-krauss/50552.html>.

[b]Terry Mattingly, *Pop Goes Religion: Faith in Popular Culture* (Nashville: W Publishing, 2005), pp. 3-4.

of revival but once the revival was over and the wave of the spirit went flat, the business was in place and had to keep churning out products." It became a "a monster."[7] Still, the industry barreled ahead with its own top-100 charts, record reviews, special dressing room amenities and all the other accoutrements of mainstream music.[8]

Debates about Christian music continue. Switchfoot, a band of five Christian men enjoying mainstream success, questions the whole concept of Christian music. The band's drummer, Chad Butler, says that the label Christian is a "necessary evil" that describes who the music is produced for instead of what it is all about. He explains his perspective:

> I would like to think that the music that I make is best with claws and teeth, instead of being locked up in a cage. As a band we've always been very deliberate in making music for everyone. And we've never changed that. If we're going to define our music it would just be honest music for thinking people. We've always called ourselves a rock band and tried to stay away from anything that would limit our audience. For me, my faith is a really personal, important part of my life, and it's much bigger to me than a musical genre.[9]

From Starving Artists to Sexy Stars

In the early years of CCM, many writers and performers followed the ideal of the honest Bohemian artist who seeks truth rather than social status and economic success. At the time, these artists did not even have radio stations to play their music, whereas radio had already become in the 1960s the primary means of promotion for mainstream artists.[10] As CCM took root, program hosts began developing formulas (formats) for Christian radio.[11]

Sometimes Christian bookstores carried these artists' recordings on cassette tapes or albums, often produced in small, four-track project studios on minimal budgets if not recorded live at concerts. Most shops were mom-and-pop bookstores with critical, conservative views of musical style—even of Southern gospel music.[12] One CCM fan raised on more traditional Southern gospel music remembers at the time asking to hear "real Christian music" instead of the "Jesus rock" that was playing in the store.[13] Jesus artists had to sell their tapes at concerts, coffee houses and a few open-minded churches. Frequently admission was free, but local hosts or musicians typically took love offerings to supplement product sales.[14]

By the late 1970s, however, starving Jesus artists were signing recording, distribution and concert contracts with emerging nonprofit and especially for-profit businesses that specialized in marketing to evangelical youth. Such companies began "cleaning up" artists and their music, making them more acceptable to tribal parents, churches and concert promoters.[15] They also looked for young talent with market potential, hoping to groom such artists for long-term success by stressing CCM artists' ability to evangelize young audiences with popular, gospel-centric lyrics.[16] Companies included Word Records, Benson and Sparrow, along with their artists such as Amy Grant, Michael W. Smith, Whiteheart, DeGarmo and Key, Petra, and scores of others who moved from the smaller venues to begin performing in arenas, stadiums, large churches and multiday camping events such as the Creation Festival, which still draws approximately a hundred thousand attendees each summer.[17]

Before long, much CCM—although less so the praise and worship variety—was musically indistinguishable from mainstream music. Tribal businesses used MTV-styled videos, celebrity posters, elaborate promotional packages, high-priced concert tickets, Jesus junk and other techniques from mainstream marketing. Use of electronic drums, electric guitars, smoke, strobe lights, pyrotechnics and flamboyant costuming (as in the 1980s glam-rock band Stryper) reached its heyday by the mid-1980s to early 1990s. Evangelical stars like Amy Grant and Michael W. Smith reached mainstream audiences but often to the dismay or criticism of others in the tribe. Already in the late 1980s one observer wrote that Christian bands were "getting widespread notice while making music Christians don't understand."[18]

Critics worried that mainstream popularity watered down the gospel.[19] CCM artist Steven John Camp (known as Steve Camp) in 1998 even published a jeremiadlike "Call for Reformation in the Contemporary Christian Music Industry." He called for repentance and urged the industry back to its biblical roots.[20] Yet many parents and tribal leaders disagreed, believing that CCM was at least safer than mainstream music for their children. Many believed CCM would enable them to "resist against a dominant secular society" by making popular music tribal.[21] Meanwhile, the CCM industry kept "churning out products."[22] It was hard to disagree with market success!

In the 1990s, mainstream crossover became less surprising, but Christian artists who "made it" wrestled increasingly with the tensions associated with celebrity, creativity and "the business." An example of this is Sixpence None the Richer's 1998 hit "Kiss Me" that exploded onto the pop music scene. In an interview with *Christianity Today,* Sixpence songwriter and guitarist Matt Slocum discussed the ways this type of megasuccess changed his approach to writing music. "You're not just writing whatever you want. You tend to think a lot more about what people want to hear. There are a lot of people [commenting] from all sides saying, 'This is what we need to sell records' or 'This is what we need to appeal to this fan base.'"[23]

STEVE CAMP NAILS CCM TO THE WALL

Calling the church to return to her first love, reformer Martin Luther in 1517 nailed ninety-five theses to a door of the Roman Catholic church in Wittenberg, Germany. On Reformation Day in 1997, music artist Steve Camp published his own 107 theses calling the contemporary Christian music (CCM) industry to repentance and renewal. One thesis read:

> (31) For if in our worship we pervert His Word, we pervert the truth about God. If in our music we distort His doctrine, we distort a right view of Him. If in our song we misrepresent the Scriptures, we misrepresent the Savior. And if in our ministries we twist His truth, we dishonor His character. (2 Timothy 2:15)[a]

This is a complicated issue. Which CCM songs pervert, distort, misrepresent or twist? No song can capture all of the nuances of complicated doctrines like the Trinity or justification by faith alone, can it?

As a former journalist for *CCM,* I saw many musicians striving to be faithful to God and his Word. They surrendered their gifts to God and selflessly gave up the pursuit of worldly rewards in order to share Christ musically; their music didn't misrepresent. But I also witnessed the ways that some music ministries intentionally twisted God's Word. They sometimes convinced reluctant artists to comply with marketing strategies that seemed to denigrate the integrity of the gospel.

Luther nailed his theses to the church door when he became convinced that the church had lost its way. If Camp is right, the CCM business needs its own reformers now and again. Who should those reformers be? And what should their message be for the current CCM scene?

STEPHANIE BENNETT, PALM BEACH ATLANTIC UNIVERSITY

---

[a]Steven John Camp, "Part Two: The Authority and Sufficiency of Scripture—The Hymnbook of Heaven," in A Call for Reformation in the Contemporary Christian Music Industry, October 31, 1998 <www.worship.com/thesestwo.htm>.

Teaching Tribal Youth

Whether it is spoken, written or sung, reiteration of the metanarrative or the story of God's intervention with humanity plays a primary role in the formation of one's faith. When the message is embedded in the powerful medium of popular music as it is in other expressions of popular culture such as film, television, radio, and literature and drama, the persuasive influence of the message is magnified. It may even be said that music becomes a language through which the Spirit can speak and a means by which tribes can communicate the sacred truths of their history with each other.

HISTORICALLY SPEAKING

Throughout civilization, music has served many formational and communicational purposes, carrying the stories of families and tribes from generation to generation through whatever was the popular medium of the day. Music has long helped people to learn about their culture and, hence, to learn about themselves. Music can help socialize people into a culture or tribe, and CCM's proponents point to the way this music promotes social unity and collective memory.[24] They argue that CCM relevantly instructs evangelicals in their shared identity in the story of God's salvation through Christ, protecting them from mainstream culture's false gods and evil culture.

Supporters say that CCM artist-musicians put to song their own questions, doubts and joys, thereby providing a way for listeners to do the same. Additionally, the music helps broaden the public discussion of issues that Christians face as part of the wider culture. Thanks to CCM, evangelical youth do not have to completely reject popular culture but can find a tribalized version of their own musical style. Youth leaders who condone or celebrate CCM generally assume that all tribal groups share this protective goal.[25]

For stalwart fans of CCM there never seem to be enough ways to experience the music or enough reasons why its expansion is of major significance in the church and in the wider culture.

UNHOLY CCM

At the same time, the broader Christian audience has always included critics who questioned the value of CCM for raising faithful youth. They worry that CCM is not really evangelical but secular or unholy. Why? Because CCM has to water down the gospel in order to attract larger, often mainstream, audiences. Another argument that has been levied is that CCM consists of artistically poor, second-rate imitations of mainstream music that really will not appeal to most youth. Finally, critics offer the long-time concern that CCM itself is part of a sinful music industry that uses the mainstream marketing techniques and celebrity ethos to peddle products. Are these arguments valid?

The latter concern emerges repeatedly in tribal debates over the trend toward crossover music, accusing Christian music as being written and performed for the mainstream market rather than just for the tribe. Perhaps CCM does not water down the religious content of lyrics as much as broaden the context of faith to include more than just loving Jesus and being grateful for salvation—including such issues as dating, depression, unhappiness and the like.[26]

The criticism that CCM is artistically second rate usually comes from evangelicals who see the genre as wrongly insulated from trends in mainstream music.

Some have accused CCM of being inbred and stagnating, forced to conform to the familiar rather than taking risks to create fresh, innovative sound and delivery.[27] Successful tribal and crossover writer-producer-artist Charlie Peacock explains that the narrow, lyrical, confessional definition of CCM "does not allow for the complexity of a Kingdom perspective or the new way to be human that Jesus modeled."[28] Increasingly, the subtle faith in crossover music is evident in mainstream distribution channels; it might even increase the market for CCM by making it easier for nontribal youth to discover CCM artists through iTunes and other sampling services.

> "I repent of ever having recorded one single song, and ever having performed one concert, if my music, and more importantly, my life has not provoked you into Godly jealousy or to sell out more completely to Jesus!"[a]
>
> *KEITH GREEN*
>
> [a]Keith Green, quoted in The Boc <www.theboc.com/freestuff/keithgreen/index.html>.

Yet lyrics still seem to define Christian music for many. Some evangelical leaders continue to argue that there is no such thing as Christian music—only Christian lyrics. They claim that apart from the lyrics a listener would have no way of knowing if a particular song is Christian.[29] Other CCM detractors call for a renaissance of art and creativity, encouraging Christian artist-musicians to be more faithful to the voice God has given them, more original and expansive in their songwriting and performance.[30] Members of the emergent-church movement contend that CCM needs to change from a genre defined strictly by the use of lyrics about Jesus to that which speaks to the full expanse of everyday life among the tribes.[31]

Remaking Identity and Community Through Music

CCM provides some tribal members with "equipment for living" faithfully in society.[32] They resist the dominant, secular society by "taking possession" of mainstream musical styles and changing the lyrics to support their own tribal beliefs.[33] This process of remaking culture for religious purposes is hardly new.

The church has always struggled with musical art and especially the relationship between style and lyrics.[34] Ancient peoples used rhythm and folksong mnemonically to keep track of important events that told the tale of their own tribes.[35] Through music they learned who they were and what was expected of them as active members of their tribe. King David's lyrical poetry (the Psalms) used instruments and the repetition of familiar refrains to help the Hebrews recall, rejoice and revel in their Abrahamic heritage. The gospel has always been carried from generation to generation partly through music, dance and related storytelling. Some of Protestant reformer Martin Luther's greatest hymns, writ-

IF IT AIN'T SOUTHERN, IT AIN'T REAL GOSPEL

White Southern gospel music (SGM). Do you listen to it? Have you heard it? It's one of the most influential Christian musical styles in North America. Bill Gaither's Homecoming videos—peddled on late-night cable TV—helped catapult SGM to international notoriety, along with help from promoters, the National Quartet Convention, Southern gospel radio stations and faithful fans.[a]

Today, groups like Ernie Haase and Signature Sound and Gold City attract large audiences of all ages and denominations, while still exploiting the extremes of male vocal range as the legendary Blackwood Brothers and The Statesmen did fifty years ago. SGM family groups and mixed-gender ensembles gain similar audiences.

SGM has its own Hall of Fame, located at Dollywood (Dolly Parton's Tennessee park). One source says *The Singing News,* SGM's most important fan magazine, is "America's most read Christian music magazine."[b] Take that, you low-ridin' CCMers!

SGM is all over the Internet, including fan sites, concert reviews and blogs. SGM musicians travel Dixie's back roads every weekend, setting up their instruments and singing their hearts out on humble platforms at tiny backwater churches. This is grass-roots entertainment, if not worship.

Lyrics? SGM offers more than a thimble full of core Christian doctrine—after all, its middle name is gospel. Its messages are simple and moving, with little of the subjective psycho-babble sometimes found in CCM. With its roots solidly in poor working-class Southern culture, SGM often reminds fans about the reality of temptation and sin, the necessity of their personal repentance and faith in Jesus Christ, the power of prayers—especially Mama's and Daddy's—and the real presence of a personal Satan, the one who must be overcome daily through Christ's power.

With powerfully crafted lyrics and singable melodies by artists like Mosie Lister, Dottie Rambo, Kyla Rowland and Rodney Griffin, SGM fans are encouraged to face another work week while humming and singing songs with truly memorable lyrics, lyrics with real rhymes, and catchy melodies, the kind you remember the first time you hear them, the kind you start whistling when you leave the church.

SGM's success has provoked discussion about the relationship between ministry and entertainment. SGM's popular groups often set up tables at the back of churches to sell gospel merchandise such as T-shirts, baseball caps, photos, wall hangings, mugs and stickers. Some critics liken this to the situation that Jesus found necessary to clean up in the temple. To many fans though, SGM, not CCM, is the real thing.

MICHAEL GRAVES, LIBERTY UNIVERSITY

---

[a]See news about the performers and their fans at Sogospelnews <http://sogospelnews.com>.

[b]See this description of the magazine at the website for Echo Media: Print Media Experts <www.echo-media .com/mediadetail.asp?IDNUmber=11644>.

ten in the vernacular, offered church music to the laity for the sake of authentic, meaningful worship.[36] The CCM group GLAD even sang a contemporary version of a 1626 hymn. GLAD played versions of "We Praise Thee, O God" in everything from countrified bluegrass to swing-era jazz—Luther might have smiled![37]

Jars of Clay remade psalms and older hymns in jazz, bluegrass and pop. The classic John Newton hymn, "Amazing Grace," has been recorded by artists from Anita Bryant and Judy Collins to Aretha Franklin. In the 1990s, many CCM artists began reclaiming more traditional-sounding music with more confessional lyrics. This made room for an explosion of new praise and worship music and the subgenre of CCM.

Clearly music has always been a dynamic, diverse part of tribal living, contributing in many seemingly paradoxical ways to authentic and fake religious identities, and to strong and weak communities of faith. There has never been a one-way movement toward secular or sacred music; rather, a kind of back-and-forth borrowing of creativity and imitation has occurred.

CCM is virtually inseparable from two musical streams: (1) earlier hymnody used especially in churches and revivals and (2) mainstream popular music styles that owe much to classic rock music and its own origins in blues, Southern gospel and Negro spirituals.[38] Prior to CCM, Southern gospel was American evangelicals' own popular music. For some, it is still the only real Christian music.[39]

Faithfully Singing All Things

Christians are called to be faithful servants of Christ and stewards of the mysteries of God, writes Paul (1 Cor 4:1-2). To the new Christians at Corinth, Paul speaks of the broad call to reconciliation, calling them "ambassadors" of Christ (2 Cor 5:18-20). In music, too, Christians are called to stewardship—i.e., to exercise that creative capacity to reflect God's glory and majesty in all things by serving God and neighbor. Faithful image bearers stay in close fellowship with God, attending faithfully to what the Spirit is saying to the churches about using gifts and talents (Rev 2:29).

Such stewardship includes dialogue and discussion about how to use the arts faithfully, including respecting artistry, authenticity and creative expression. The story of CCM suggests that the power found in creative expression must not be either abandoned to mainstream culture or used mindlessly by the church. Evangelicals have always had to reckon with the fact that God speaks through mainstream music by teaching, delighting and persuading listeners. Moreover, evangelicals' music can speak to mainstream culture; it does not have to be limited to the tribe.

THE MYSTERY, THE MAJESTY, THE MUSIC

"Let a man so consider us, as servants of Christ and stewards of the mysteries of God" (1 Cor 4:1). Music is a special gift for teaching, delighting and persuading. As one of the most powerful and immediate forms of communication, it can convey some of the deepest truths—mysteries—that the nonbeliever may find foolish or irrelevant. Faith is more than logic, more than reason—though it includes both. Music is part of this mystery of faith as word, deed and sentiment beyond human understanding.[40] The affective, emotional aspects of true faith are enormously important as evangelicals gather together to learn and edify one another as well as to praise God. By the miracles of old and new media, the same music is nearly omnipresent in handheld devices and on desktop computers, in cars, and simply in evangelicals' memories.

Why do the strings of a symphony have such ability to bring tears to one's eyes when one listens to a film score? How does the telling of a story set to music evoke such emotion—even passion—from audiences? Humans can recite the scales and understand changes in keys and harmonics, but no one can create the moment when inspiration strikes and beauty emerges to become a new song. The mystery and the majesty of God may be seen and heard in the faithful expression of musical gifts, in ways that reach deeper into the human soul than many other modes of communication.[41] The creation, performance and message can soothe the soul, convince the sinner, praise God and condemn injustice.[42]

STREAMING CCM

Now that digital technologies have made music downloading and file compression possible, the urge to make and share music does not have to be limited to or constrained by market forces. Today's blogs, podcasts, streaming audio files, webcasts and music downloads are twenty-first-century extensions of recording media that helped disseminate CCM in earlier years. These media are enabling those with musical gifts and callings to reach audiences beyond those who traditionally tune into tribal radio and concerts.

Once again, CCM is challenging existing tribal institutions by unleashing musical creativity in the hands of faithful troubadours. Just as Luther returned the music of the church to the people, today creative souls have numerous new outlets to share the music in their hearts. Today it is easier and less expensive to record music on personal computers, to record concerts—legally and illegally—and to distribute the music online rather than through hard media.[43] Social networking sites such as MySpace help musicians reach potential audiences or collaborators, creating new alliances, friendships and companies committed to CCM.[44]

As the opportunities for producing and enjoying CCM are expanding, professional and nonprofessional artists are producing their own versions of musical testimony. Inexpensive recording and editing technologies are leading to new musical collaborations among budding songwriters, singers, producers and instrumentalists who can now work more easily across geographic space. Moreover, critics who disdain or love CCM have new means of telling the world their opinions and finding like-minded souls online.

The Australian artist Rebecca St. James and Beliefnet have partnered to enable her to post devotional pages online; the singer has used her musical gifts and renown as a springboard from which to advance the gospel even as it sells more of her records. By encouraging those who visit her site, St. James is serving tribal and nontribal audiences in the digital environment.[45]

WHY THE DEVIL SHOULD HAVE ALL THE GOOD MUSIC

In 1972, contemporary Christian music (CCM) pioneer Larry Norman asked, "Why should the devil have all the good music?" Since then, the CCM business has cranked out crates of imitation versions of mainstream rock, praise and pop music. Mindlessly following one sales trend after another, the CCM business has left behind a legacy of miffed musicians, crashed crossover attempts and awful albums.

By wrongly defining all mainstream culture as inherently secular (i.e., the playground of the devil), CCM evolved into a lyrical genre of music made merely by and for the tribe. The industry tightly gripped anyone who sang about faith—who belonged to CCM.

This clear-cut Christian versus secular division never worked. Mainstream groups like U2 sang about faith, while some CCMers sang about love, life and politics. Furthermore, executives and producers in the CCM industry tediously tinkered with songs, supposedly making them more acceptable to tribal audiences while irritating artists.

Rather than producing Christian imitations of mainstream fare, the CCM business needs to focus only on contemporary worship music. Such praise music is made for those already saved. It has a distinctive style and distinctive lyrics. It might even be the CCM industry's only lasting contribution to the history of music.

Artists uninterested in worship music should go mainstream, elevating their skills to compete. If they are good enough, they can sing about God there.

Mainstream society should have all the good music. It ought to have a chance to hear high-quality music crafted by gifted Christian artists. It's not going to tune into today's copycat CCM.

PAUL A. CREASMAN, AZUSA PACIFIC UNIVERSITY

Many pages on MySpace and other social networking sites have allowed fans to create a virtual space to share their music. The birth and expansion of YouTube is yet another avenue in which one can experience the concert clips and recording sessions of major and independent CCM artists. Today, independent artists as well as fans have exceedingly more opportunities to detach from the commercial trappings of CCM.[46]

Although crossover marketing, lyrics and style issues still elicit tribal debates, there are probably more musical choices than in any previous era. The problem within the tribe is the same as in mainstream culture: too few people are willing to look beyond the music available on popular music stations or played weekly in church. Instead, tribal members might still spend more money and time rehashing age-old debates about music than locating and supporting new artists. CCM artist Charlie Peacock has chided evangelicals who have "an ocean of possibilities" but settle for "islands of conformity."[47]

CONCLUSION

Many tribal youth still like their parents' and grandparents' sacred music, but North Americans are increasingly divided over musical taste. Rather than grasping the opportunity for greater tribal diversity, evangelicals seem to be using the new technologies like everyone else to pick and choose according to personal taste. Certainly the new possibilities for recording and sharing CCM will help create more customization. This might encase evangelical audiences in even smaller artistic boxes. Or it might create dynamic tribal communities of musical discourse, with growing interaction and creativity across musical and lyrical styles. Isn't that a hopeful thought?

Given the growth of evangelicalism throughout the world, it is probably time for CCM's artists, companies and fans to reach across the boundaries of space and time in order to create fresh versions of old music as well as new music. As pictured in the book of Revelation, the church is multicultural, yet so much CCM seems to be lyrically and stylistically based on largely American, white, middle-class, tribal youth culture. Limiting its use to just one function or one style greatly inhibits the ways music can be used to glorify the Creator.

In the 1980s Keith Green faced the same dilemmas. Those of us who admired him wonder how he would have responded to the growing attempts to make all CCM fit within culturally narrow tribal parameters. Back then we probably held him up in excessive esteem. But we also likely failed to listen adequately to his concerns about the commercial and celebrity aspects of CCM. He rightly reminded us that music is a gift of God that is meant to be received with gladness and used wisely. As stewards of the mysteries of God, our calling is to handle what he gives us responsibly, taking care to nurture, enjoy and uphold the manifest beauty and myriad gifts of a Creator who has lavished his love on us with generosity and great variety, wrapped in a blessedness that is far beyond compare.

9

Praising God with Popular Worship Music

ROBERT H. WOODS JR.

Same church, same sermon. Four very different styles of worship music. Why?

Many North American evangelical churches offer worship-service menus—partly in response to the worship wars (driven by disagreements over musical style)—and partly to reach the unchurched.[1] But does such variety promote self-centered or God-honoring worship? A consumerist mentality? Does it affect how outsiders perceive Christianity? How they perceive evangelicals?

Excitement and energy surround the explosion of popular musical styles in worship. Christian worship music (CWM) has birthed bold experiments—like worship raves[2] and hip-hop churches[3]—and is associated with the emerging-church movement.[4] While most evangelicals call for "sympathetic attention"[5] to CWM, others demand outright rejection. Younger evangelicals, frustrated by the current scene's commercialism, have ushered in a new era of worship as they return to ancient Christian roots and seek authentic worship in vibrant faith communities.

CAPITAL CHRISTIAN CENTER, CALIFORNIA. SUNDAY MORNING.

8:00 a.m. Dodie Skaggs sings "Our Great Savior" at the *traditional* service, accompanied by piano and organ. Pastor Glen Cole, 72, delivers the sermon.

9:30 a.m. Churchgoers at the *classic* service sing along with a ninety-member choir and orchestra. Cole's son Rick, 48, preaches.

11:15 a.m. Guitars blast, lights flash and a man on a platform paints a portrait of Jesus, dazzling *contemporary*-service attendees with occasional back flips between strokes. The younger Cole delivers the same sermon but this time without his jacket and tie.

5:00 p.m. Lights dim and music goes acoustical for the *postmodern* service, creating a college café vibe.[a]

[a]Jennifer Garza, "The Heart of Worship: Traditional Hymns to Today's Praise Music; Churches Are Changing Their Tune to Suit Different Tastes," *Knight Ridder Tribune Business News*, February 2006, p.1.

BORN-AGAIN HIP-HOP WORSHIP?

Can you rap? Flow? Tag? Scratch? If so, you're ready for hip-hop Sunday. This music traveled from the 'hood to the suburbs, then to church sanctuaries—thanks to pastors and musicians who believe that hip-hop can be "spiritually hijacked" for the kingdom of God.[a] Amen?

Places like The House Covenant Church in Chicago, Sanctuary Covenant Church in North Minneapolis, Crossover Community Church in Tampa, and Harlem Hip-Hop praise Jesus with DJs, emcees, graffiti artists, break dancing, rapping, popping, multimedia and spoken word.

Supporters argue that there's nothing new about proclaiming the gospel in vernacular. The apostle Paul and Jesus "did the same."[b] Paul told believers to be all things to all people for the sake of the good news. Critics worry about churches adopting music associated with a lifestyle that glorifies sexism, greed, violence and drug use. How can such alliances be good? But hip-hop worship leaders don't see their worship music as cultural compromise. They're just making the gospel more relevant to people familiar with banks of turntables and synchronized video screens instead of altars and stained glass.

Offering biblical lyrics and confrontational messages about hell, "holy hip-hop" does spread the good news in prisons, urban neighborhoods, church services and concerts.[c] One pastor says he is "not ready to give poetry, creativity and visual expression up to the forces of evil when they can be used for God."[d]

Are you ready to try flow? Or to scratch the whole genre? Why?

PHYLLIS ALSDURF, BETHEL UNIVERSITY

---

[a]Efrem Smith and Phil Jackson, *The Hip-Hop Church: Connecting with the Movement Shaping Our Culture* (Downers Grove, Ill.: InterVarsity Press, 2005), p. 25.

[b]Ibid.

[c]Adrienne S. Gaines, "Get Ready for the Hip-Hop Revolution," *Charisma & Christian Life,* August 2002.

[d]Cathy Lynn Grossman, "Shouting Hip-Hop's Praises," *USA Today,* November 27, 2005 <www.usatoday.com/life/2005-11-27-hip-hop-church_x.htm>.

The Worship Awakening

Today's *worship awakening* includes a dynamic, diverse church music landscape best seen in the popular praise and worship movement, seeker services, the growing Christian worship business and a renaissance of liturgical traditions (such as Episcopalian and Roman Catholic). Jack Hayford, author of the "Majesty" chorus, calls the awakening a "reformation" in worship music.[6] It is driven by "godly pastors and lay leaders trying to be faithful to Scripture and sensitive to the needs of real people."[7]

Jesus Music[8] and the worldwide charismatic movement combined in the 1970s to produce the first praise and worship choruses. Known initially as "Scripture choruses," these short, paraphrased Scripture segments set to pop-styled music found homes in the Sunday worship of neo-Pentecostal and other charismatic churches.[9]

Scriptural lyrics soon gave way to writing a broader range of praise songs expressing one's personal relationship with Jesus. Individual songs from some contemporary Christian artists' albums were included in new hymnal supplements and eventually in mainline hymnals. The Roman Catholic Church's Second Vatican Council ushered in a parallel movement in liturgical churches. The musical style of such groups as the Kingston Trio and the New Christy Minstrels shaped a type of liturgical folk mass.[10]

CWM began replacing traditional hymns in a few churches in the 1980s. By the end of 1990, about a third of all American Protestant churches regularly used popular songs such as "Lord, I Lift Your Name on High" and "Shout to the Lord" either alone or with hymnody.[11] Over 150,000 worship songs are listed on the Christian Copyright Licensing International (CCLI) site, and more than 176,000 churches (130 denominations) hold CCLI licenses.[12]

Today, CWM is the fastest growing form of contemporary Christian music (CCM),[13] complete with its own record labels and concert tours. Evangelicals cannot get enough CWM:

- Worship newsletters and magazines like *Worship Leader* and *Reformed Worship* provide reviews of current CWM, Bible study materials and workshop notices.
- Books about worship are top sellers for Christian publishers.
- Worship studies is one of the fastest growing majors at many Christian colleges.
- Worship music radio networks "praise-cast" twenty-four-hour commercial-free CWM.[14]
- Online clearinghouses feed the worship frenzy with the latest music from Vineyard, Integrity Hosanna, Maranatha, Worship Together and Hillsong.[15]
- Websites provide free worship songs, chord charts and instructional DVDs.[16]
- Blogs, weekly Web columns and discussion boards let participants engage in conversations with artists and worship leaders about the inspiration and writing of new worship music.[17]

In short, CWM is called "vertical music" because songs communicate vertically with God, not primarily horizontally with other people (like mainstream CCM). CWM lyrics focus on the character of God and worshipers' response to him.[18]

WELCOME TO TRADITIONLAND

We baby boomers are getting what we deserve in worship styles. We despised our parents' out-of-date, traditional worship: only one song leader, a massive wooden pulpit stage center, hymn books, singing harmony. All boring, outmoded. So we led the worship wars, overcoming the oldsters and setting up contemporary worship. Now we could really reach the lost. Hallelujah!

We got everybody to sing simple songs in unison, repeatedly. We projected lyrics on large screens at first, then we built boomer-box venues with automated screens that dropped impressively from the ceiling or were built into the brick walls. We replaced the formally dressed song leader with casually attired praise-team members. We added a praise band and dumped the organ and piano in favor of the versatile, jazzy boomer keyboard. We closeted the clunky pulpits so our energetic communicators could dynamically excite and entertain us by wandering around the un-sanctuaries.

One problem: we forgot that contemporary is a moving target. Now we boomers are the oldsters. Our innovations are stodgy traditions. Ungrateful GenXers and younger gadflies don't like our upbeat, brightly lit services.

They prefer more pensive, even mournful worship. They subdue the lights and plant candles all over. We boomers wonder if they're worshiping the devil via new age mediation. Even spookier are their echoing hard floors peppered with signed folding chairs, old guitars and ancient icons on the walls.

Welcome to traditionland, my fellow boomers. You GenXers are next. Get ready to become irrelevant.

Maybe this generation can avoid the inevitable?

KEITH DRURY, INDIANA WESLEYAN UNIVERSITY

The Popularity of Contemporary Praise

Nearly 80 percent of Americans say they prefer contemporary over traditional (hymns) worship music.[19] Why? Many CWM fans believe that it effectively educates children and new believers in basic Christianity. They also contend that CWM's diverse musical styles broaden cultural perspectives by putting worshipers in touch with other ethnic groups and formerly nonreligious styles.[20]

CWM is a catalyst in the spiritual formation of young Christians who value an intimate, one-on-one encounter with God.[21] Setting classic hymns to contemporary styles can also connect listeners—both young and old—to church history and foster appreciation for deep theological reflections. Furthermore, the repetition of songs (usually repeated twice) and phrases in CWM presumably helps worshipers connect emotionally and spiritually with God. Says one worshiper, "The repetition of choruses helps to really stick it not only in my mind, but in my soul."[22]

Given its emotional intensity, CWM generally models active rather than passive congregational participation. In traditional church music, rational content *(logos)* often overshadows emotional experience *(pathos)*. But a worshiper does not have to sing the typical CWM song several times to "plumb the depths of what's going on there meaningwise."[23] Choruses almost immediately connect with singers.

Additionally, fans suggest that CWM draws in the visiting nonbeliever more than traditional hymns. Seeker-sensitive worship experiments have roots in eighteenth-century England,[24] nineteenth-century revivalist camp meetings (Charles G. Finney), and early twentieth-century radio (Aimee Semple McPherson) and TV (Robert Schuller) programs.[25] Since the 1980s churches such as Willow Creek Community Church, Saddleback Community Church, Community Church of Joy and Ginghamsburg United Methodist Church have produced "church for the unchurched." These "seeker services," fueled largely by CWM with positive, inspirational lyrics, provide a culturally comfortable and appealing introductory church experience for many non-Christians.[26]

Finally, CWM helps evangelicals to enjoy worship, including their own expression of faith within services. The music is accessible to musicians who want to participate but do not have the formal training required by traditional compositions. The variety of musical styles is adaptable to just about any instrument, from the harmonica to the French horn. Similarly, worshipers do not need to read musical notation or master complex harmonies to sing along or enjoy the music. CWM is simply "fun" to sing.

WORSHIP LITE

CWM's tribal critics are concerned about the music's aesthetic quality (or beauty) and biblical content (or truth) in the lyrics.

Spectacle and performance. Many traditional church musicians describe CWM as faddish pop worship that mimics the latest popular styles with boring melodies and unoriginal rhythms.[27] Critics often accuse CWM of being merely entertainment, treating worshipers like consumers. Most CWM songs, they argue, are better suited for praise-team solos than congregational singing.[28] Not surprisingly, detractors fear that CWM gives worshipers the worldly spectacle they want rather than the spiritual edification they need. Commercial worship songs may delight congregants while distracting them from the ultimate message.

These critics raise important questions. First, when the musical arts become part of worship, worship might become enjoyable (or beautiful) whether or not the congregants are worshiping in spirit and truth—just as a concert can delight audiences without fostering worship. Second, which instruments are appropriate for worship? When "Amazing Grace" is sung with guitar distortion, pulsating light and a backbeat, does the technomusical packaging change the meaning? Maybe all instruments are not created equally for worship—so much for the harmonica!

Lyrical Wonder Bread. Although CWM's musical style worries critics, the lyrics receive most of the attention. Naysayers contend that the lyrics are too repetitive, lack gender inclusiveness,[29] and quote Scripture from arcane translations that amuse, annoy or confuse worshipers.[30] Many songs reflect pop-culture values such as instant gratification and simply "cut worshipers loose from the full story of God that narrates the history of the world."[31]

As critics point out, much of CWM remains strongly self-referential and me-centered, focusing on what individual worshipers can do for God.[32] Others call it Jesus-is-my-boyfriend music and romantic-pop music. Lyrics such as "To feel the warmth of your embrace" and "I'm desperate for you" are erotically charged and

THE LANGUAGE OF PRAISE SONGS

Many praise songs speak of God as King even though most American citizens today are clueless about kings. Choruses use vague terms like *glorify* and *exalt.* Can you define these? Some songs are repetitive: "I exalt You," sung four times, with one more for the Spirit. For such songs to communicate well, worshipers need to know what the lyrics mean. And they have to sing them meaningfully. Congregants need more than catchy tunes and slick PowerPoint projection.

First, churches can teach about biblical metaphors for God, from king to shepherd. Otherwise worshipers may focus on their own feelings—and misinterpretations—while singing. A worship song "must not be about us." It must point to "the person of Jesus Christ."[a]

Second, perhaps new praise songs, as part of the song itself, could define key terms so churches learn theology as they worship. Worship leaders' mini-sermons preceding the songs may be necessary at times, but often take worshipers out of the moment.

Third, meaningful lyrics solve the issue of meaningless repetition. Scripture's warning against "vain repetitions" implies empty words. But proper repetition—like "Holy, holy, holy"—can "open the worshiper to God . . . with expressions of wonder, love, thanksgiving, lament, penitence, longing, and praise."[b]

Worship music must be relevant and God-centered. It must continually be reclothed in words and metaphors that focus on Jesus Christ. This is a project, not mere projection. How do the worship songs you sing stack up?

SCOTT P. JOHNSON, BETHEL COLLEGE, INDIANA

[a]Sean Gallagher, "Musicians Gather to Reflect on Their Ministry, Worship Together," U.S. News, Catholic News Service (July 16, 2007) <www.catholic.org/national/national_story.php?id=24730>.

[b]Brian Wren, *Praying Twice: The Music and Words of Congregational Song* (Louisville: Westminster John Knox, 2000), p. 202.

may trouble men.[33] A well-respected worship scholar said that "if you can sing it to your spouse or girl/boy friend, forget it!"[34]

In addition, most CWM song lyrics are so short that complex thoughts about God (e.g., the Trinity) cannot be developed adequately.[35] In many cases, songs fail to capture adequately Jesus' pain and suffering on the cross, emphasize defeated sin and gloss over persistent sin in believers' lives, largely ignore corporate confession or repentance, overlook the true cost of discipleship (self-sacrificial living), and pretend that Christians need not persevere in the faith.[36]

In light of such concerns, opponents wonder whether worship music following the pop-song model makes it difficult to communicate authentic truths about God. One critic puts it this way:

> Written, no doubt, within the past 20 years, it is a piece of that resigned sentimentality that is characteristic of "easy listening music." Although pleasant enough, it is spiritual Wonder Bread: It utterly lacks roots, depth, sustenance. It is all right as a starter, to open the heart to prayer. But unless fed by some solid food . . . serious seekers will turn elsewhere.[37]

Dumbing down worship? Many tribal detractors contend that the separate-service (menu) approach actually dumbs down worship for newcomers and fosters an individualistic religion of self-fulfillment.[38] "In an effort to appeal to religious consumers, some churches become like 'Saint Happy's: The Worship Place,' where the slogan is 'Have It Thy Way' while selecting from the overhead menu their preferences for 'Liturgy Lite' or 'Kiddy Kristianity.'"[39] Worship becomes superficial, with nothing deeper for those evangelicals saved long ago.

CONTEMPORARY MUSIC WITH ANCIENT ROOTS

The church has always faced conflicts over contemporary versus secular musical styles in worship, and over concerns about worship becoming mere performance or spectacle. In the Old Testament, the Israelites followed the musical purposes and styles of their pagan neighbors. Music was highly sensory, and many of Israel's songs, including some psalms, were adaptations of pagan tunes.[40] Professional priests performed nearly all temple music. Apart from the occasional *amen* and *alleluia,* the ordinary temple worshiper was largely a spectator.[41] At other times worship was spontaneous and ecstatic, much like many contemporary charismatic worship services.[42]

In the New Testament, the apostle Paul favored diverse material and genres (e.g., psalms, hymns and spiritual songs). His phrase "one another" (Col 3:16) suggests that worship was more than just a Jesus-and-me thing. Singing apparently brought worshipers together in community.

There is no record of instruments being used in worship in the Gospels or

PRAISE THE LORD, YOU PAGAN PLAYERS!

Should non-Christians be allowed to participate in worship bands? One group says "no way." They argue that providing music is a leadership role. How can a church allow nonbelievers to deceive the congregation by pretending to believe what they sing and play? The other side says "you bet." Even nonbelievers are created by God to worship. Moreover, participating in a worship band might lead them to real faith while their talents are being used to bless others. The Spirit can work through them as well as minister to them.

Augustine of Hippo wrote about this problem in his famous book, *On Christian Doctrine,* published about A.D. 400. He said that the gospel is in the *message,* not in the *messenger.* He would rather have a nonbelieving but rhetorically talented person deliver a good sermon than have a verbally inept believer deliver the same quality sermon. Why? Because more listeners would be blessed by the well-delivered sermon.

Yet, in the Old Testament, the temple musicians were Levites: priests (1 Chron 23:5). So, outwardly at least, they were God's people. And to complicate matters even more, consider this: no one really knows who else truly believes in God, down deep.[a] Heartfelt faith is between each person and God. No doubt some Christian worship leaders and pastors are phonies. And there are probably closeted Christians in society who don't want others to know about their faith.

So what should we do about the worship bands? Require participants to take an oath? A spiritual x-ray, perhaps?

DAVID BEDSOLE, SOUTHERN WESLEYAN UNIVERSITY

[a]See Romans 10:9, "If you declare with your mouth, 'Jesus is Lord,' and believe in your heart that God raised him from the dead, you will be saved." The first part is much easier than the second!

Epistles, suggesting that early congregations probably used only vocal music. Perhaps they feared guilt by association since Jews worshiped with the same instruments that Greeks used in their temple orgies.[43] Leaders in the early church had similar attitudes. Clement of Alexandria (ca. 150–ca. 215) said that "one makes noise with cymbals and tympana, one rages and rants with instruments of frenzy . . . the flute belongs to those superstitious men who run to idolatry."[44]

Early Protestant reformers educated worshipers through singing. Martin Luther (1483-1546) taught "theological barbarians" basic theology by devoting Thursday evenings to congregational hymn singing.[45] John Calvin (1509-1564) worried that public worship music would be too seductive and distracting but then sought to improve the "cold tone" in services by commissioning all 150 psalms set to meter with the help of a French poet. Melody lines for Calvin's *Genevan Psalter* (1562) borrowed freely from secular dance songs and bits of Gregorian chant. Because of the dance rhythms embedded in the secular melodies, songs in Calvin's *Psalter* earned the title "Geneva Jiggs."[46]

Church-music history seems to repeat itself. CWM's critics use arguments made two to three hundred years ago. Critics today echo age-old concerns about hymns' extrascriptural lyrics, inelegant scriptural paraphrases, controversial new instruments and melodies borrowed from mainstream culture.[47] The great hymn writer Charles Wesley (1703-1791)—he wrote "Christ the Lord Is Risen Today" and "Hark! the Herald Angels Sing"—was arraigned before a grand jury for the crime of presenting unauthorized compositions in church services![48] And even though Luther did not actually raid taverns for tunes,[49] much music during his time appropriated popular tunes for a higher purpose. The popular song "We Praise Thee, O God, Our Redeemer, Creator," for instance, was set to a rather shocking dance-hall number about a loose-living woman.[50]

FROM PEWS TO PROFITS

Between 1997 and 2002 CWM unit sales doubled. While other genres of Christian music dipped slightly in 2003, CWM thrived, accounting for 11.1 percent of the 47.1 million recordings sold in the Christian music industry. Four of the top-ten bestsellers of 2003 were in the category praise and worship, while "I Can Only Imagine" by MercyMe hit mainstream pop charts.[51]

What spurred the mainstream growth? Star power, aggressive marketing and new avenues of product distribution.

Star power. The majority of praise and worship recordings for years were made live at church services with a worship leader directing the congregation. Recording companies Integrity, Maranatha and Vineyard led in the genre.[52]

In recent years, CWM became part of CCM. Established artists such as Rebecca St. James; Phillips, Craig and Dean; Michael W. Smith; and Third Day sing worship songs at their concerts and release worship records on leading CCM labels.[53] The English CCM group Delirious?—which began as a youth outreach band—released "I Could Sing of Your Love Forever" in 1995. The song has been called a "worship classic."[54] Worship hits from various artists are collected by CCM labels on "ultimate" CD sets.[55] Some mainstream crossover groups like Jars of Clay "go ancient" by setting classical nineteenth-century hymns to fresh, contemporary music. Many new CCM artists sign contracts with worship clauses, obliging them to release a worship album if called upon by the label. For better or worse, CWM has become big business.

Passion (also known as "the 268 Generation") worship conferences—an outreach to postmodern college students—have birthed a new generation of worship artists and bands dedicated to worship.[56] Passion artists produce platinum records, tour the country, lead worship at their home churches and write books on worship. Several high-profile Passion artists include Chris Tomlin,

Matt Redman and David Crowder. Passion's "modern worship"—a phrase that expresses a desire to rise above contemporary and contemporary worship music—resurrects old, even ancient, hymns as a way "to be connected to something bigger."[57]

Marketing and distribution. Before the proliferation of artist-driven worship records, marketing directors at praise-and-worship labels promoted products in ways that did not rely on radio publicity or celebrity artists. They used direct mail to sell recordings to churches and individuals. Maranatha provided music for major conferences/events such as Women of Faith and Promise Keepers, which represented sizable evangelical audiences.[58]

Local retail shops sell most CWM, but the Internet is gaining ground. Church leaders and others can purchase CWM on dozens of websites. EMI Christian Music Group's WorshipTogether.com site, for example, has more than 130,000 registered users and more than 12,000 worship leaders who regularly purchase and download music from the site.[59] CWM artists have personal websites and MySpace/Facebook pages to sell their CDs, promote upcoming tours and communicate with fans. Fans can download legitimate and bootlegged worship concert footage from YouTube.

Unexpected if not strange commercial pairings may blur the lines between the commercial and the sacred. Maranatha did an exclusive ten-CD worship series with Wal-Mart titled Sanctuary, and Target stores provided shelf space for Christian music. The Songs4Worship series, a cooperative venture of Integrity and Time-Life Music, sold extremely well. Songs4Worship spawned Songs4Worship-Devotions, Songs4Worship-Gospel and Songs4Worship-Children.[60]

Integrity's iWORSHIP brand has been somewhat successful with television marketing. The company initially ran ten weeks of commercial spots on national cable outlets including Fox, Court TV, MSNBC, PAX and ABC Family—a model similar to that used for the mainstream Now! That's What I Call Music series. Integrity launched an iWORSHIP tour featuring several well-known worship artists.[61]

In 2002, a Chevrolet marketing campaign sponsored a series of nationwide evangelical rock concerts titled "Chevrolet Presents: Come Together and Worship," described as a "multimedia worship service with an evangelical flair." Popular tribal author Max Lucado preached, and Michael W. Smith and Third Day led music. Lucado and his team turned these concerts into full-scale worship experiences. Mainstream critics lampooned it as "What Would Jesus Drive?"[62]

The impact of a market-driven worship industry on musical preference and practice remains relatively unexplored.[63] CWM's economic bottom line might inadvertently promote certain artists, subject matter and musical styles

THE WORSHIP INDUSTRY'S PROFITS OF PRAISE

Contemporary worship music (CWM) represents $50-million annual retail sales, and millions more from royalties, direct sales, and related conferences and festivals. It is a powerful economic force that inevitably lifts up certain songs and artists and sidelines others.[a]

Evangelicals ought to ask tough questions about the impact of this industry:

- Does the industry call too much attention to worship leaders? Does it unwittingly suggest that an artist's personality is the key for good worship? I'm grateful when I see a worship recording marketed by content rather than the artist's face.
- In what ways might the industry be affecting our understanding of worship? Identify the spiritually necessary components of worship that are unlikely to be promoted by the worship industry. Then celebrate when the industry resists cultural expectations and delivers those same components.
- Does the industry create an entertainment culture in which leading congregational worship is seen as a stepping stone to the higher goal of becoming a recording star?
- Does the industry create a skewed impression of North American worship? While CWM accounts for perhaps half of all songs sung in worship, it represents nearly *all* worship-related advertising. Other music, not supported by publicity, is less likely to be seen as a viable option for many leaders. Over time, could this quietly erode the mosaic of ethnic music in American's congregations?
- Finally, do the industry's economics tend to suggest that financial success is one of the best criteria for evaluating what good worship is?

The lesson? Be discerning. Learn about the industry. Support companies and artists with integrity. Resist the temptation to think that it takes money to worship well.[b]

JOHN D. WITVLIET, CALVIN COLLEGE

---

[a]Pete Ward, *Selling Worship: How What We Sing Has Changed the Church* (Carlisle, U.K.: Paternoster, 2005). Every approach to worship has economic implications. The pipe organ industry, for example, is supported by the twenty-thousand-member American Guild of Organists, an impressive array of pipe organ builders, professional journals, conferences and advertisers.

[b]See, e.g., Camilo José Vergara, *How the Other Half Worships* (New Brunswick, N.J.: Rutgers University Press, 2005).

over others. Artist-oriented marketing strategies may increase sales but also infuse CWM with inappropriate entertainment values. Perhaps aggressive advertising campaigns and commercial pairings increase mainstream visibility while creating a perception of "acceptable" evangelical worship for those outside the tribe.

Gimme That Old-Time Blended Worship

Since Christian worship music always changes, perhaps evangelicals should avoid elevating one style over another. Most traditional worship music stresses theological content, whereas CWM emphasizes self-expression and emotional intimacy with God. But since both are important for authentic worship, they probably are compatible.

Although many seeker churches assume that musical style attracts nonbelievers, research says otherwise. Few megachurch attendees are unchurched.[64] Current seeker services may thus give those outside the tribe the wrong idea that Christianity is primarily about evangelism and only secondarily about worship. In the process, such services may actually narrow the community's appreciation for diverse worship. As the ancient church rightly understood, worship should reflect a basic truth, *lex orandi, lex credendi* (the *way* we sing or pray) is the expression of what we really believe.

One way to address critics' fears and fans' hopes is blended, or convergence, worship associated with the current renaissance in liturgical practices. This "ancient-future" worship combines hymns, psalms and traditional gospel songs with contemporary praise music. Blended worship provides a respect for historic worship and recognition of contemporary styling.[65] For the emerging generations, "authentic worship, blending liturgical and free, ancient and modern, *is* the project, and hymns appear naturally."[66]

Blended worship's musical suitability is judged on its "functional intelligibility"—whether it fulfills the specific and overall purposes of right worship. For example, does the music facilitate congregational participation? Dialogue with God? Such "liturgical fittingness"[67] lets worshipers steer away from defining good worship based on personal preferences or the latest musical fad. And since convergence worship is rooted in biblical sources that draw from the great traditions of the church, it claims to be Catholic, Reformed, evangelical and charismatic.[68]

For such blended worship to work well, however, worshipers must be musically flexible and church leaders must cultivate congregational understanding of biblical worship.[69] At the same time, songwriters and musicians should address the lyrical and musical criticisms noted earlier—such as overly individualistic or me-centered lyrics—while recording labels should support fewer popular artists and select songs that challenge rather than reinforce cultural preferences for one musical style over others. Such partnerships are crucial for a "healthy worship diet."[70] As long as churches do not offer blended worship as a way to accept everyone's personal preferences as equally fitting, they have a chance to avoid reinforcing a consumerist mentality among churchgoers.

The worldwide Taizé student worship movement is influencing blended worship in North America.[71] An ecumenical monastic order founded in 1940, the Taizé community is an important pilgrimage site for many younger evangelicals. Its music uses simple phrases (usually lines from psalms or other Scripture) repeated and often sung in canon.

Other postmodern ministries reinforce Taizé's liturgically oriented, community-driven worship.[72] Such movements—which include Passion—have combined to shape a trend in worship among younger evangelicals characterized by (1) darkness (versus boomers' "bright light worship"); (2) mellowness (versus "upbeat 'happy songs'"); (3) participation (versus "performance"); (4) singing as prayer (versus "music primarily as a means of praise"); and (5) sensory experience (to include all the senses rather than just seeing and hearing).[73]

CONCLUSION

Even though the worship wars might not be as bad as some observers believe,[74] no individual or denomination can completely sidestep the hot debates about worship music. The various types of worship—e.g., traditional, classic, contemporary or postmodern—probably all have elements that are good for authentic worship and others that are problematic. Blended services seem to offer considerable flexibility, but they will not bring about complete peace.

CWM's appeal includes its "rejection of the formalism and uniformity of much of mid-twentieth century Protestant worship," and its "openness to innovation and diversity and its recognition that times have changed: a new day calls for a new way to worship." As the Dutch Calvinist theologian Voetius (1589-1676) put it, *ecclesia reformata sed semper reformanda sicut verbum Deum:* the reformed church is always reforming according to the Word of God. "That goes for worship too."[75]

One writer says that evangelicals should "welcome any worship music that helps churches produce disciples of Jesus Christ" and "banish fears that grip us when familiar music passes away."[76] To this I would add that such "welcoming" must always be done wisely and often self-critically, even at the nearby worship center.

10

Following Pilgrims into Cyberspace

QUENTIN J. SCHULTZE

Harry met Sally—online. Then they married. Soon they divorced. It was like a Christian soap opera. Friends were stunned.

Both were raised in faithful families and nurtured in vibrant churches. Each of them knew other Christians who had met in cyberspace and were still wonderfully wed. Their friends' relationships blossomed once they met in person, with no signs of major trouble.[1] They wondered why their own cyber-courtship failed.

Like other religious tribes, evangelicals are enthusiastically cautious about the Internet. The potential for reaching out, forming relationships and building faith communities seems largely untapped. But will the outcome match evangelicals' hopes for a happy marriage with cyberspace?

ONLINE RELIGION OR RELIGION ONLINE?

Evangelicals' triumphant entry into cyberspace reflects their desires to use new technologies to advance the kingdom of God.[2] Google lists over fourteen million pages using the word *evangelical,* beginning with the Wikipedia entry that demonstrates how difficult it is these days to define the word. Some evangelicals have reached aggressively beyond the evangelical tribe. Few have completely rejected the medium.

Evangelicals are just as active in cyberspace as other Christian groups and Jews. In fact, Catholics, evangelicals and "other Protestant" tribes include about three-quarters of the "heavier" and "heaviest" Internet users.[3]

Evangelicals are active in both "religion online" and "online religion."[4] The former includes using computer networks to exchange information *about* religion—such as information about what someone's own evangelical tribe or other faiths believe and practice. The latter includes practicing religion online (i.e., prayer, Bible study and worship that characterize the doing of religion in the offline world).

The numbers are staggering. Nearly two-thirds of all wired Americans have used the Internet for spiritual or religious purpose. Moreover, these "'online faithful' are devout and they use the Internet for personal spiritual matters more than for traditional religious functions or work related to their places of worship. But their faith-activity online seems to augment their already-strong commitments to their congregations."[5] Online and in-person faith seem to work together in their lives.

HOW AMERICANS USE THE INTERNET FOR RELIGION

- 38 percent of the 128 million Internet users send and receive email with spiritual content.[a]
- 35 percent send or receive online greeting cards related to religious holidays.
- 32 percent go online for news accounts of religious events and affairs.
- 21 percent seek information about how to celebrate religious holidays.
- 17 percent look for information about where they can attend religious services.

[a]Statistics taken from Stewart Hoover, Lynn Schofield Clark and Lee Rainie, "Faith Online: 64% of Wired American Have Used the Internet for Spiritual or Religious Purposes," Reports: Family, Friends & Community, Pew Internet & American Life Project (April 7, 2004), p. 2 <www.pewinternet.org/PPF/r/126/report_display.asp>.

Teaching. Evangelicals' online teaching includes searchable translations of the Old and New Testaments;[6] classical Christian writings, including creeds from nearly every Christian tradition;[7] and databases of Bible commentaries linked to Bible translations and paraphrases. A few evangelicals teach and mentor online via text-chat, email, video-chat and password-protected websites. Seminaries and Christian colleges offer for-credit and noncredit courses, including continuing education.

Pastors and laity blog about living faithfully in contemporary culture. They review films,[8] novels, TV shows, music and even worship services. They publish their churches' sermons in text, audio and video formats; write daily "devotionals" that briefly offer a biblical text and a related "lesson"; stream as well as post recordings of worship services; and share news and information about both tribal activities and developments in the general society that have implications for evangelicals.[9]

Delighting. In addition, evangelicals frequently enjoy witty online interaction and exchange delightful expressions of faith. Blogs demonstrate that evangelicals take pleasure in poking fun at themselves, too. "What should a good sermon be about," asks one website? Answer: "About God and about ten minutes." So much for long-winded preachers!

In spite of their fears about online evils such as pornography, evangelicals like surfing cyberspace for fun as well as spiritual gain. They form networks with friends via Facebook and YouTube, and their Christian and mainstream imitators equip believers to share comics and cartoons with biblical themes,[10] to admit their own faith-related foibles,[11] and to publish online interviews and multimedia clips with evangelical authors and public personalities.[12]

Persuading. Evangelicals also try to persuade online audiences. They post blogs designed to defend and spread their beliefs. Some cyber-evangelicals venture into politics with websites, podcasts and email newsletters aimed at influencing the general public as well as evangelicals on currently controversial and legislative issues. Conservative evangelicals are most likely online to advocate particular interpretations of Scripture and to defend evangelicalism. A few brave souls march into chat rooms to confront skeptics and evangelists of other faiths.

BLOGGING BEYOND THE BOUNDARIES

Web-logging—or blogging—is a popular way for anyone to speak publicly about anything on her or his mind. Got something to say? Just publish it on the Web. Instant fame—if anyone reads it! Should evangelicals follow the trend?

Perhaps blogging is a good way to be salt and light in the larger post-Christian culture. Blogs help evangelicals sidestep mainstream media gatekeepers and address anything, from politics to social issues and entertainment, uncensored. But who is the audience? Like any other tribe, if evangelicals want to gain mainstream readers they have to avoid the Christianese jargon that they take for granted in congregational, denominational and evangelical media.

One positive example is David Brody's political blog, The Brody File.[a] Brody works for the Christian Broadcasting Network but has established a reputation among liberal and conservative politicos for fairness and integrity. "We don't play a gotcha game, and the Democrats know that," Brody says. "There's absolutely no agenda."[b]

Evangelical bloggers will also have to write well—engagingly, excellently, accurately. No preachy prose. No half-baked arguments. No stereotypical evangelical-speak.

C. S. Lewis said that the first step toward the reconversion of a spiritually wayward population was for Christians to become the best writers on any given subject with implicitly and persuasively biblical perspectives. Do most evangelical blogs today meet his standard? Notwithstanding the few blogs like Brody's, most don't. Too many think that just by mouthing off they can convert the world to their perspective. They forget that readers beyond tribal boundaries might be listening in.

ALEX WAINER, PALM BEACH ATLANTIC UNIVERSITY

---

[a]See The Brody File at CBN.com <www.cbn.com/cbnnews/blogs/brodyfile/>.

[b]Howard Kurtz, "From the Local News to a Higher Calling," *Washington Post,* June 11, 2007 <www.washingtonpost.com/wp-dyn/content/article/2007/06/10/AR2007061001335_pf.html>

CYBER-PROMISES

For evangelicals, cyber-media are gifts from God to be used primarily for expanding the kingdom of God on earth in preparation for Jesus' second coming. They use the Internet for evangelism, apologetics and fellowship.

Evangelism within and beyond the tribe. Evangelicals go online primarily for religious gratifications, not for entertainment and information.[13] They use cyberspace to conform themselves to their own religious ideals and expectations—and to evangelize others to be similarly holy. Such holiness always includes necessary assumptions about how to relate their faith to culture—such as what music to listen to, how to vote and whether to view particular movies. In short, they imagine the Internet as a means of ongoing evangelization and reevangelization of people into "Christian culture."

Apologetics—combating false beliefs. Evangelicals also use cyberspace to counter the influence of other religious and secular groups. By spreading the truth, evangelicals hope to combat false teachings,[14] sometimes equating truth with specific positions on political or moral issues. They use blogs, email and social networking websites to challenge secular views on hot topics such as abortion and homosexuality. North American evangelicals generally believe that if they are going to maintain their own, distinctive faith in increasingly multicultural societies where alternative religions emerge and grow, they must leverage the power of every new medium to persuasively defend their own convictions.

Even so, evangelicals do not always agree online about how to interpret Scripture and address specific political and moral issues. Cyberspace reflects the offline world, where people profess belief in Christ but hold opposing political and moral as well as theological views.[15] Online Christian chat can degenerate into uncivil name calling ("liberal," "fundy," "heretic"). When tempers flare, cybersaints do not always act saintly![16]

While defending their view of the faith, some evangelicals end up combating other Christian groups or even people within their own tribe. Probably every theological, biblical or cultural dispute within a denomination produces websites dedicated to opposing forces. In the past, critics of established denominational or megachurch leadership could not easily gain a public hearing. Now they can organize online and publish their own manifestos.

Fellowship. Evangelicals also use the Internet to form stronger faith communities at home and abroad. They believe in the power of faster, more informed and presumably more effective communication within congregations, among parachurch networks of believers, and between churches and distant missionaries. "Computer-communication lines make it a smaller world and speed up missions work. The efficiency is great,"[17] writes one advocate. A Christian music fan says that the medium equips distant fans "to communicate with other fans

THE FIRST CHURCH OF CYBERSPACE

It had to happen. Back in the mid-1990s a guy started a very nontraditional church "with an emphasis on the virtual aspects of our belief system."[a] Huh?

One member of this First Church of Cyberspace (FCoC) speculated that online religion "may ultimately prove to be a metaphor for the myth through which we come ever closer to God and the personal comprehension of God in our time."[b] What does that mean?

But it's a real church. How do we know? Because, as the church's website explains, the FCoC is "legally incorporated" in the state of Florida and is "fully authorized to perform, and has performed, wedding ceremonies, blessings, and babtisms [*sic*]."[c] That reminds me about the cyber-gung-ho guy who wrote me an email asking how to perform the Lord's Supper online. Beam down the bread and wine, Saint Peter.

What about the FcoC's cyber-doctrines? How about this dandy: "Harming yourself isn't a sin, it's just stupid." But apparently this is an eternal church, because the head honcho's "ministry is my [Computerized] Bulletin Board, I think, in fact, that the computer age is the past, present, and future."[d] Makes a lot of virtual sense. For real, dude.

QUENTIN J. SCHULTZE, CALVIN COLLEGE

---

[a]The First Church of Cyberspace home page <www.afn.org/~fcoc/>.

[b]Alan C. Purves, *The Web of Text and the Web of God: An Essay on the Third Information Revolution* (New York: Guilford, 1998), p. 20.

[c]"Frequently Asked Questions About the FCoC," <www.afn.org/~fcoc/fcocfaq.html>.

[d]"Interview with FCoC Founder," September 1993, reprinted from *Cigarette Butts & Coffee Cups* <www.afn.org/~fcoc/interview.html>.

of this genre, something that really couldn't be done unless you knew other fans personally, or were a member of an artists' fan club."[18]

In a controversial report, one Christian pollster-pundit has predicted that tens of millions of Americans will leave their local, physical church in favor of a cyberchurch.[19] Since the same kinds of claims were once made regarding the impact of earlier media such as radio and television, however, this will probably not happen. Instead evangelical tribes will continue using cyberspace partly to enhance local as well as distant fellowship.

FORMING HOLY IDENTITIES

Evangelicals realize, however, that just as cyberspace can strengthen intratribal communication and build faith communities, it can dilute them. The Internet might even be able to infiltrate a tribe more easily and effectively than older, largely one-way mass media. Unlike TV and radio, cyberspace hosts religious cults, antievangelical movements and pornographers who can elicit unholy thoughts, misguided desires and tragic addictions.[20] For all of its benefits, cyberspace also represents declining biblical values, evaporating biblical truth and weakening tribal holiness.[21] The Internet "is organized religion's worst nightmare, a true dogma-killer and heresy-spreader."[22]

Largely because of its highly interactive, decentralized character as a networked rather than a mass medium, the Internet implicitly persuades in both directions, from faith and doubt, doubt to faith—and everything in between. Even as cyberspace equips evangelicals to connect with other believers, it can introduce Christians to pagan ideas, tempting misbehaviors and destructive communities. The medium is a two-edged sword.

In other words, cyberspace is a kind of laboratory for individuals and groups to experiment with self-identities. The Internet "has become a canvas of personal expression, a place to learn and test new ways of being."[23] Particularly for young persons, whose basic beliefs and values are still being formed, the medium "can serve as a space for exploring expressions of religious identity, beliefs and practices."[24] Cyberspace can divide, personalize and even accentuate radical individualism; every user can create a personal religion simply by expressing his or her own views and claiming his or her own version of truth.[25] He or she can surf freely for his or her own "right" faith. On the Internet, "freedom of religious expression rules supreme."[26]

Instead of creating a generic faith community, the Internet might require tribes to discern their distinctive beliefs and practices.[27] Perhaps it will even facilitate schisms within existing tribes as various subtribes organize online. For each religion that has tried to express itself online, other religions have joined cyberspace to challenge existing ones. From this perspective, the Internet looks more and more like a "delivery system for countermovement propaganda," enabling each tribe to oppose other tribes.[28]

One person's blog explains how to "Start Your Own Religion." The writer begins, "I'm thinking of starting my own religion . . . you know, for something to do." She says, "Last semester I took a course called Cults and Religious Controversy . . . [in which] we studied all sorts of different off-the-cuff religious movements. . . . Anyone with a little charisma and a new idea can start one. I've got a surefire formula all figured out."[29]

In addition, some Web surfers are open to traditional religions, including Christianity. "People don't have to make themselves very vulnerable to get online and start searching for answers," observes a leader from the Billy Graham Evangelistic Association.[30] The editor-in-chief of Beliefnet, a high-traffic religious website hosting many different faiths, suggests that the Internet "has a weird combination of anonymity and intimacy. People do open up and they're

THE PRIESTHOOD OF ALL WIKIS

A wiki is an informational website that all users can edit—something like an encyclopedia entry with reader-controlled content. The Hawaiian term means "quick" and is often used alliteratively: "Wiki Wiki," or "Quick Quick." We could say *wiki* means, "Read Read, Edit Edit, Quick Quick!"

The online Wikipedia bills itself as "the free encyclopedia." Nearly any Google search generates Wikipedia results since the gigantic wiki has exploded with postings about everything from World Wrestling Entertainment to Christian alternative rock.

Imagine one worldwide Bible wiki controlled by a church. Imagine that this wiki is the only public place someone could get information about what the Bible says and what it means. Suddenly the Protestant reformer Martin Luther logs in. He's unhappy with some of the online interpretations of Scripture—like comments about church members buying their way out of sins by purchasing indulgences. So he posts alternative ideas like "justification by faith alone" and soon discovers similarly minded gadflies. Himself a priest, Luther nonetheless advocates the "priesthood of all believers" based on the Protestant notion that Jesus Christ is the only mediator between God and Christians.

The result? Hundreds, thousands, eventually tens of thousands of different kinds of Christian denominations with various, often conflicting interpretations of Scripture. Not one Bible wiki but many wikis with *-ism* in their names: Methodism, Calvinism, Lutheranism, evangelicalism, and on and on.

The gain? Freedom from oppressive or misguided authority. The loss? Quick! Quick! Answer right away!

QUENTIN J. SCHULTZE, CALVIN COLLEGE

willing to reveal the turmoil of their spiritual lives to other people they don't know that well."[31]

BLOGGING WITH PAUL

Cyberspace is not a completely new form of communication but an extension of earlier media. We even describe online communication as texting, writing, publishing, mailing, posting and the like. Imagine the apostle Paul writing email rather than manuscript letters. Was he a blogger in his era? His style of writing is probably closer to some of today's blogs than most telegraphic, dispassionate, "objective" newspaper reports![32]

What about multimedia streaming or podcasting? Paul also traveled by boat and foot, delivering his teachings in person to early church leaders. His audiences knew if he smelled, was unkempt and spoke with an accent.

Moreover, long-distance, instantaneous communication is hardly new. Forerunners include electromagnetic induction (inducing an electrical current using magnetic fields, discovered in about 1802), the fax machine (first patented in 1843), wireless radio (ca. 1891), and satellites (1950s). Often what humans think of as an entirely new medium is really just a novel, cost-effective, widely available application of an older technology.

The Web is somewhat like an ancient library. Earliest known libraries in the Western world existed five thousand years ago in ancient Mesopotamia. A library was, like the Web, a repository of writings, sometimes with images. The Latin root *liber* means "to peel," because manuscripts were written on the inner bark peeled off of trees. The great Egyptian library founded in Alexandria about 300 B.C. collected hundreds of thousands of manuscripts, representing a higher percentage of all of the "books" ever published than the Internet today holds of book manuscripts. The scope of current Web holdings and the ease of accessibility are considerably greater than with paper libraries, but the concept of message storage and retrieval is ancient.

Personal pages on social networking websites such as Facebook are like combinations of diaries, personal journals, phone books and posters. Online chat owes much to the telephone (invented in the 1870s), which, like the visit to the neighborhood post office in earlier decades, served the daily desires of people for conversation with friends and family about their lives—and gossip about what is going on in others' lives.[33]

BYTE THE COMPETITION

Generally speaking, evangelical cyber-communicators are not leaders in online innovation. Evangelicals tend to copy mainstream digital media. For instance, after the booming success of social networking sites, evangelicals created "safe" imitations.[34]

The true cyber-innovators are the marketers, especially legitimate retailers (e.g., Amazon), but also pornographers, online casinos and fraudulent spammers. "Business innovates, religion borrows," writes one author-theologian.[35]

Evangelicals generally go along with mainstream ethical practices, too. For example, evangelicals illegally copy and distribute copyrighted files. Illegal file sharing has damaged tribal as well as mainstream music companies. Few born-again teens believe it is wrong to copy and distribute copyrighted songs.[36]

DIGITAL DIRECTIONS

Most of us celebrate new technologies that seem to promise faster, cheaper and easier communication. We like the power to reach out to others, build communities, get helpful information and impress others with our new gadgets. Advertisements for cell phones show smiling, connected users who have got life under their control.[37]

By contrast, a few people look nostalgically to the pretechnological past and hold us accountable for the real benefits of new devices. They question whether humans really do live better, more fulfilling lives today. They might proudly proclaim that they do not have a TV set and would never buy a cell phone or a computer. One Christian environmentalist, also an acclaimed writer, says, "I do not see that computers are bringing us one step nearer to anything that does matter to me: peace, economic justice, ecological health, political honesty, family and community stability, good work."[38]

Neither the overly optimistic fans nor the excessively pessimistic critics of

SHOULD CELL PHONES BE EXCOMMUNICATED?

"Beam me up, Scottie," says *Star Trek* hero Captain Kirk. Almost instantly, a blue-white cylinder surrounds his body, and he disappears into thin air.

While not able to physically transport ourselves, we can mentally teleport to virtual spaces every day using a smaller, personalized technology—cell phones! Beam me up, Verizon—with a photo, please!

Cell phones—and their networks—create "social presence" even when people aren't nearby one another.[a] Like other techno-predecessors—radio, television and the PC—cell phones affect how individuals worldwide experience relationships in time and place. They make many of us perpetually accessible.

At what price? Ringtones interrupt weddings, funerals and worship. Parishioners sheepishly exit prayer gatherings, as if called out by God for something more important. Many evangelicals wonder if cell phones should be regulated, banned or omitted from some activities for the sake of stronger faith communities—even excommunicated from worship services.

The community-minded Amish believe that technologies such as cell phones should not be allowed to weaken home, church and other in-person community activities. Instead, technologies should be used only to enhance such relationships.[b] To them, the individual freedom to call anyone anytime is not as important as the responsibility to commune with friends, family and community.

What would evangelicals lose if they excommunicated their cell phones—at least from church or dinner-time conversation, or when being hospitable to guests? What would they gain? Does *Star Trek*'s futuristic vision of perpetual contact and physical teleportation square with biblical community?

JONATHAN PETTIGREW, PENNSYLVANIA STATE UNIVERSITY

---

[a]Kenneth Gergen, "The Challenge of Absent Presence," in *Perpetual Contact: Mobile Communication, Private Talk, Public Performance,* ed. James Katz and Mark Aakhus (Cambridge: Cambridge University Press, 2002), pp. 227-41.

[b]Brad Igou, "Amish Telephones," *Amish Country News,* 1991 <www.amishnews.com/amisharticles/amishtelephones.htm>.

cyberspace offer a balanced perspective even though there is much truth to their claims. Overly hopeful fans tend to be gullible. For instance, they relay email-based urban legends—such as Charles Darwin's deathbed conversion, the discovery of Noah's ark, Proctor & Gamble's alleged satanic logo, and atheist plots to shut down religious broadcasting.[39] Overly pessimistic critics fail to see the possible benefits for building community, becoming better informed and simply enjoying the newer media as gifts from God.

What is a balanced view of the Internet? First, cyberspace can be used for evangelization, but it might never be as effective as in-person relationship building.[40] Second, even as a social networking medium, cyberspace can foster radical individualism—a kind of create-your-own religion and express-your-own-views mentality.

Third, while the Internet can help build evangelical communities, the resulting tribes can become insular, narrowly focused groups. Much of the Web is made up of consumer-oriented, superficial collections of persons who share narrow interests

YO! GET A LIFE!

Nathan Yoder, an Amish farmer near Grantsville, Maryland, milks cows and drives a horse and buggy. He doesn't own a computer, car or cell phone.

Before you label Yoder a Luddite, consider this: He owns a tractor and uses a landline telephone three walking minutes from his house. He sometimes even pays others to drive his family to visit distant relatives. Such selective use of technology can seem maddeningly inconsistent to outsiders. But it's logical. It grows from a strong theology of the church (Rom 12).

If you wanted to join Yoder's church, you'd have to ask yourself if you would be ready to do the following: (1) get the church's permission before purchasing new technology and (2) give up a device, knowing it would make you less efficient and more dependent on others' assistance. Today these Amish (and New Testament!) spiritual practices of group discernment and mutual aid are lost in most churches. Why? Maybe because the practices foster traditional *inter*dependence over modern independence, community over individuality. Not top American values!

The challenge for MP3-toting evangelicals? Leveraging YouTube, social networking sites and the next new information technology to foster Christian community. Can we have our high-tech media and our community, too?

Nathan Yoder's church lets its members use tractors on hillside fields but only horses on the flatter fields. The horses make for slower work—enough so that Yoder needs help from fellow Amish to harvest on time. Of course, afterwards there's a potluck. Community never tasted so good.

KEVIN MILLER, HUNTINGTON UNIVERSITY

like a particular musical group, church movement, or biblical framework, like end-times predictions regarding the second coming of Christ.

Fourth, while some evangelicals get lost online in the maze of different biblical interpretations and applications, others learn how to discern their Christian faith more fully amid the competing worldviews. The work of local churches in nurturing believers is critically important as young people and adults venture into cyberspace. In addition, perhaps congregations and other Christian institutions should educate believers about using new media wisely.

Fifth, at least a few evangelicals become bold communicators online, willingly sharing their faith with all who ask about it. The same persons might be too shy to do this in person.

Cyberspace is not the ultimate answer to anything—but neither is it the cause of all personal and social ills. The Internet cannot be used easily to seduce young people into occultist religions.[41] Although new religious movements use cyberspace to recruit followers, most people see such movements "as havens for the socially marginal and perhaps even personally deficient individuals."[42] Perhaps evangelicals' confusion about the effects of cyberspace results from not seeing the Internet as both an interpersonal and a mass medium, depending on how it is used.

Clearly Christians evaluate the Internet based on various biblical and theological assumptions.[43] Those who believe in the imminent return of Jesus Christ tend to be more optimistic about online evangelism. Those from holiness traditions are more skeptical about the moral and spiritual value of the online world. Those from peace traditions worry that cyberspace will weaken local community life; they also point to the violent character of so much online communication, where people are quick to speak and fast to put down others but slow to listen. Each tribe highlights opportunities and pitfalls that the other traditions ought to consider as well.[44]

KEY DEFINITION: THE DIGITAL DIVIDE

The phrase "digital divide" refers to the gap between those who have access to cyberspace and those who do not. Sometimes the gap is caused by physical limitations, such as no access to computers or the Internet. But the gap also includes the skills necessary to use cyber-technologies. Many schools around the world lack resources for teaching basic computer skills that the industrialized West takes for granted. The divide is evident in the rich versus poor, urban versus rural, educated versus uneducated, able-bodied versus disabled, and somewhat even in gender differences. Language is also an issue since English dominates cyberspace.[a] For Christians, the digital divide ought to be an important social justice issue.

[a]For a clearer understanding of the digital divide, see "Digital Divide: What It Is and Why It Matters," at DigitalDivide.org, sponsored by Human Interface Technology Laboratory, University of Washington <www.digitaldivide.org/dd/index.html>.

Evangelicals need to recognize that most people in the world do not have access to a computer, let alone to the Internet. Cyberspace's digital divide excludes as many voices as it promotes.[45] Evangelical discourse about the Internet should discern how best to serve specific groups in particular parts of the world—a process scholars call "glocalization."[46]

Even though a church congregation is necessarily local, worshiping in person, there are plenty of worthy uses for cyberspace that do not involve worship. These include forming friendships, mentoring and learning. Although we cannot invite others to dinner online, we can practice hospitality in cyberspace by being welcoming, respectful and available to others.

CONCLUSION

Christians are pilgrims in cyberspace, just as they are in the incarnate world of real bodies. One pilgrim writes, "In a world where reality might be virtual the prime moral and spiritual questions become Who can be trusted? What can be trusted? Is every perception of reality valid or is there a Way through the maze, the matrix, the Web? (If so, bookmark it?)"[47] If only faithfulness were so easy in cyberspace.

So evangelicals, like other tribes, still gather together in local communities of discourse, committing themselves to authentic worship, wise teaching and learning, and mutual edification for the digital road ahead. They use any media that will help them accomplish such worthy goals during their pilgrimage. Another Harry will meet another Sally, hopefully with additional grace to discern God's will in the shadows of high-tech life. As Paul "blogged" to the church at Corinth, we see only vaguely through a dark glass the riddle that we have yet to solve (1 Cor 13).

11

Evangelicals in Theater
Inching Toward Center Stage

PAUL D. PATTON

Betty reluctantly accepted the invitation to be in a community theater production. The director, Betty's friend and neighbor, thought she would be perfect as the grandmother in his new play. She explained teary-eyed that she was honored yet very fearful.

Sixty years earlier she had been invited to enter the prestigious American Academy of Dramatic Arts in New York City, after a college career dominated by life in the theater. But her father argued that she was already over-educated and needed to earn a living. In spite of her friends' encouragement, Betty submitted to her father's demands and buried her theater aspirations.[1]

Soon she became an evangelical and felt even more convinced of her father's wisdom. After all, her tribe provided no models of faithful engagement with the sinful stage. Betty was thankful for being saved from this den of iniquity. It never crossed her mind that she could actually serve faithfully in the theater as a producer, critic or consumer. Even the small, isolated pockets of Christian theater—usually evangelistic or moralistic performances—were off limits. Theater was the devil's playground.

Betty's story might have turned out differently today, where a growing number of evangelical ministers and laity believe that vibrant, engaging worship and living requires greater attention to the artistic and even theatrical aspects of worship and life. In their view, overly instructional, heavy-handed, obnoxiously or simplistically evangelistic worship and tribal expression that do not consider the role of aesthetics cannot delight or reach beyond the tribe. Several trends have contributed to the evangelical tribe's greater engagement in theater.

Behind the Curtain

One trend is the Christ-transforming-culture vision among some evangelicals that challenges excessive separation from mainstream culture. How can evangelicals shape culture if they are not engaged with it? Popular books in the 1970s and 1980s, like Francis Schaeffer's *Art and the Bible,* Frankie Schaeffer's *Addicted to Mediocrity,* Calvin Seerveld's *Rainbows for a Fallen World,* and Hans Rookmaaker's *Art Needs No Justification,* convinced many younger evangelicals to be responsible participants in the arts, rather than opposing art. Such well-received books affirmed evangelicals' emerging work in theater, such as Jeannette Clift George's A. D. Players in Houston and Orlin Corey's Everyman Players.[2]

Moreover, the emergence forty years ago of a tribal counterculture dubbed the Jesus Movement won many youthful hippies to a seemingly more relevant faith in Christ. This movement left a significant mark in the tribe's music and worship styles, generating new recording labels and cultivating fans of Christian contemporary music. These evangelicals were not so quick to accept traditional worship, let alone accept anti-art sentiments within any churches. After all, they also attended movies, mainstream theater and rock music concerts that were increasingly theatrical, multimedia events.

At the same time, mainstream theater was diversifying, beginning in the 1950s. It became increasingly decentralized, expanding from New York City's Broadway to Off Broadway, Off Off Broadway and other vibrant theater capitals on the continent. Theater included alternative performances by and about marginalized ethnic and political groups. Socially marginalized voices—e.g., African American, Hispanic, feminist and gay voices—"celebrated their existence, illustrated their concerns, and challenged the larger culture."[3] In short, mainstream theater became multitribal and even more acceptably and unapologetically evangelistic about bringing the previously marginalized citizens into the mainstream consciousness.

While evangelical congregations slowly introduced theater in worship, parachurch organizations contributed significantly to evangelical engagement. Rather than contending with seemingly over-concerned, anti-art critics within the local tribe, more progressive evangelicals formed theater groups without direct connection to specific church congregations and denominations. They found "new ways to organize what they do, including theater."[4]

Covenant Players, founded in 1963, trained and sent thousands of actors around the world.[5] Colin Harbinson's partnership with Youth with a Mission also significantly contributed to the vision of theatrical possibilities for evangelicals. His play *Toymaker and Son* toured several continents for many years.[6] Christians in Theatre Arts (CITA), started in 1990 at evangelical Malone College, organized an annual National Networking Conference as well as regional gatherings.[7] Its forums cultivated intellectual and aesthetic frameworks for faithfulness and productivity in the arts. The parachurch organization Lillenas Press published scripts for chancel dramas and sermon-starter sketches. It also provided theater-training resources and hosted an annual church drama convention.[8]

A major evangelical movement toward worship-based theater emerged out of Willow Creek Community Church's model of seeker-friendly outreach. As a newer church housed in a theatrical-styled building, and in an attempt to get beyond traditional tribal worship styles, Willow Creek nimbly demonstrated how to integrate drama into worship without worrying about the status quo in other congregations and denominations. The church's order of service included a live, sermon-prompting sketch. Hoping to attract young professionals, however, the church produced remarkably professional sketches, not the typical, amateurish performance that disappoints attendees with higher artistic expectations. Willow Creek avoided under-rehearsed, ineffectively directed, lighted and performed scenes that detracted from the delight as well as the instructional value of the sketches in the context of worship. The church's professional performance standards, as well as its drama-inclusive worship model, spread across the country and demonstrated the possibilities of evangelical excellence and training in theater arts.[9]

Another significant trend contributing to the tribe's engagement in theater has been the growing popularity of art-in-education as a performance medium. Gillette Elvgren, with thousands of productions of his plays throughout the country, became a prolific, pioneering playwright within this genre. Saltworks Theater Company in Pittsburgh, founded in the early 1980s by Elvgren and other colleagues, contracted with the public schools to present "issue" plays for elementary, middle school and high school students. Its entertaining short plays have never been explicitly evangelistic but instead are values-friendly, instructional stories that sensitively address issues such as bullying, addiction and personal character. While some critics might complain that such plays are moralistic, the performances have typically been a well-produced, audience-engaging means of generating discussion about issues that are important for society, not just the church.[10]

Finally, evangelicals have engaged theater for several decades through regional professional theater (at least one full-time staff member) and community theater (volunteer only). Such theaters have been significant contributors to evangelical participation. These have included Lamb's Players Theatre in San Diego, A. D. Players in Houston, Acacia Theatre Company in Milwaukee, Taproot Theatre Company in Seattle, Pacific Theatre in Vancouver and Master Arts Theatre in Grand Rapids. Part of the influence is rooted in their sustained presence as a venue—a place for tribe members to go for nearly thirty years, thereby reinforcing and building upon a new tribal habit of live theater attendance.[11]

HOPING FOR A GOOD SHOW

Evangelical theater has its enthusiastic supporters who seek use of the medium as instruction in worship or for persuasive evangelism outside the tribe. Some assert that there is "no more powerful tool than drama for teaching the gospel."[12] As one fan puts it, humans are a "visual people" who should see as well as hear the gospel. They are apt to affirm the dramatic "sermon starter" in worship as a kind of "acted-out sermon." In this view, the "acted-out story" enlists the congregation's involvement, drawing them to "tune in." It is an accommodation to a culture increasingly "addicted to the visual story medium."[13]

The publishing director of Lillenas Drama says that the "idea of drama in the church is certainly more accepted than it was even just a few short years ago." She believes this developing trend is "exciting news," allowing Christian artists to "find avenues to use their God-given talents to glorify Him and minister to others."[14] Such advocacy often emphasizes theater as a tool for tribal instruction and persuasion. It also tends to underemphasize the importance of delight, thereby allowing the producing artists to avoid assessing whether the performance was good, aesthetically pleasing art or not.

In addition, some tribal proponents suggest that the process of creating theatrical productions can benefit the tribe as a collaborative, culture-engaging activity regardless of the productions' special visual and verbal content. People have to work together for theater to happen. They need to learn self-discipline, consensus building and other interpersonal communication skills. Working together during a demanding, long production schedule is a microcosm of living life in community. For tribal theater, exercising the fruit of the Spirit (Gal 5:22) in a long-term creative endeavor might be a healthy antidote to the contemporary Western culture's worship of efficiency, instant gratification and individualism.

From this perspective, theater is an appropriate, effective context for direct pastoral care. Church members of varying theater experience and talent can be involved in short-term or long-term small-group productions. The pastoral care associated with the process can effectively address the spiritual and relational—not just artistic—needs of the actors and technicians involved. Theatrical engagement thereby parallels the work of the church as a body in which members' "life together"[15] can be applied to building up the Christian community.[16]

Evangelicals who promote theatrical engagement argue that national and regional theaters can reach out beyond the tribe. They worry that tribalism is separation from culture and that evangelicals need to learn how to produce quality, mainstream fare in public venues. They believe that participation as producers, critics and consumers can be salt and light in the broader culture. They also contend that engaging mainstream culture will force evangelicals to join and thus enrich the national discussions about theater and the arts.[17]

DINNER THEATER FOR SINNERS

Were you forced as a child to sit at the "kid's table"—with mismatched utensils, unbreakable plates, and sippy cups—while grownups used china and crystal, cloth napkins, and shiny silverware because they knew how to behave?

Maybe this was like the righteous folks sitting at the exclusive kosher table in Jesus' day. Only the proper things were set, served and said.

Evangelical theater has, for the most part, resembled the "righteous people's table," where attendees try to speak and behave "Christianly" while relegating everyone else to a different location.

The problem? Dining with outsiders, or sinners, is biblical.

Jesus openly shared parables with the poor, criminal and dispossessed. By joining at the sinner's table, Jesus *embodied* the parables for the sake of everyone and gave hope to those who felt unloved, hopeless and condemned. Just as he himself was Word made flesh, he demonstrated and *acted* in concert with his teaching. "Jesus' audacious action hinted that the 'wrong' were as entitled to God's mercy as the 'right' and revealed that Jesus was in dead earnest when he said as much."[a]

Evangelical theater can't remain merely tribal if it wants to be fully faithful to the Great Commission. Why? Because we too are sinners. We get spilled on just as easily as we spill on others. Like Jesus, however, we meet messy sinners where they are at, socially and culturally.

At dinner theater for sinners, we might hear or see something unpleasant, yet that unpleasantness may be truthful. In the process, we might just see ourselves in the faces of the characters on stage. After all, isn't Jesus sitting with all of us at the sinner's table?

DEBRA FREEBERG, CALVIN COLLEGE

[a]Robert E. Webber and Rodney Clapp, *People of the Truth: The Power of the Worshiping Community in the Modern World* (San Francisco: Harper & Row, 1988), p. 45.

Worldly Worries

Evangelical concerns about theater echo the early church's moral criticisms of ancient Roman theater, with its gladiator battles, chariot races, circuses and Greek theatrical fare. Tertullian (155-220) could not imagine theater that would teach, delight and persuade in a holy manner. His *On the Spectacles* (197-202) outlines early Christian defenses of the Roman theater and his critical responses. While Christian fans of theater said the art used people and materials created by God, Tertullian countered, "We must not, then, consider merely by whom all things were made, but by whom they have been perverted." He defended abstinence from theater by quoting Psalm 1:1: "Blessed are those who do not walk in step with the wicked / or stand in the way that sinners take or sit in the company of mockers."[18]

Tertullian argued that both Greek and Roman theater evolved from pagan religious holidays and rituals. Characters Venus and Bacchus, for instance, were "two evil spirits" in "sworn confederacy with each other, as the patrons of drunkenness and lust. . . . That immodesty of gesture and attire which so specially and peculiarly characterizes the stage is consecrated to them."[19] He railed against the vulgar language used in drama, warning Christians that "licentiousness of speech, nay, every idle word, is condemned by God," and then asked, "Why, in the same way, is it right to look on what it is disgraceful to do? How is it that the things which defile a man in going out of his mouth, are not regarded as doing so when they go in at his eyes and ears?—when eyes and ears are the immediate attendants on the spirit."[20]

Augustine (354-430) criticized "theatrical exhibitions" that glorified the shameful acts of the ancient poets and gods.[21] He admitted that such dramatized fiction could "carry him away" and add to his personal "miseries" by "fueling his passions and lusts."[22] Augustine even questioned the usefulness of empathizing with the sufferings of a fictionalized hero, concerned that such empathy might distort the ability to identify and respond to real tragedy. Like Tertullian, he recommended that Roman Christians abstain from the theater.

Perhaps the fiercest critics of the theater were Puritans who sought to create a holy "city upon a hill." It was important to them that their light would not be dulled by the competing distractions and allegiances of theater, which attacked their biblical values and stoic sensibilities.[23] A riot broke out in New York in 1766 as Puritans protested the attempt of a band of traveling actors to open a theater.[24]

Tribal critics today repeat these ancient and Puritan arguments. A seminary president asserts that much of evangelicals' current enthusiasm for stage and screen drama results from their ignorance of the church's historical prohibition. He says that engagement with theatrical culture is the result of baby boomers' unholy embrace of a worldly system and naiveté about how theater communicates and how it shapes the sensibilities.[25]

THE SAME OLD SHOWS

In the middle of the fourth century A.D., a young, North African thespian converted to Christ. Because he acted on the Roman stage, he created controversy in his church. Could he continue as a professional actor? Church leaders demanded that he sever ties with the profession. In order to maintain his calling faithfully, he started an acting school in spite of his pastor's disapproval. Unsure exactly how to respond, the pastor wrote to the bishop, who explained that the actor should give up teaching theater. But the bishop also said that the local congregation should assist him financially during his unemployment. The bishop further offered to employ him if the local church could not afford to do so.[26] One way or the other, the newly converted actor would have to give up practicing and teaching a worldly trade.

This kind of prohibition dominated the church until the middle of the tenth century, when the church's change of heart was remarkably similar to evangelicals' arguments today: drama could be redeemed through performances and reenactments of Bible stories or other stories with biblical themes, as long as these productions taught the faith to parishioners. By the thirteenth century, the Roman Catholic Church permitted theater performances, chancel dramas (again, focusing on Bible stories and biblical themes), to be performed outdoors, beyond the constraints of the sanctuary. This permission provided the intellectual threshold for grasping the sacredness of natural life and, with the progression of

SCARED TO BE CREATIVE?

Evangelicals are created in the Creator's image. Yet some of us nervously flinch, scanning the sky for lightning bolts when we mess with the muse. We feel queasy if we lean against the rock of tradition and sense it shift.

Not surprising. For centuries, churches rarely rewarded (and often punished!) those who pondered, "What if . . . ?" and "Why not . . . ?" (both substantial gateways to creative thinking!)

Unlike God, we cannot create something out of nothing. Our creativity prods fresh associations into new configurations. Still, that requires challenging the status quo. Risky. Tweaking a "Ha!" to dislodge the "Ah!" may become "Aha!" But at what cost?

Suppose you overturned the wrong rock, toyed with significant words (jarred a jot or a tittle) and then lightning *did* strike? Or suppose you offended a weak sister or brother in the faith, even caused someone to stumble? Frightening consequences.

So we must weigh wise discernment against excessive fear of failure or rejection. After all, following Christ is itself precarious business, full of ironic twists—like the meek inheriting the earth and the last being first. Who knows where God's creativity will lead us in life, let alone art? Following Christ is ideal preparation for handling ambiguity, distractions, criticism and reverse thinking—essential tools for breaking barriers to creativity.

(Fill in the blanks)

Try this: What if_________________________? Why not _______________________?

What would our media art look like then?

DARLENE GRAVES, LIBERTY UNIVERSITY

subsequent centuries, the holiness of ordinary topics that could be addressed by the theater.[27]

The new morality plays of the late Middle Ages helped the church to teach, delight and persuade. By the fourteenth century, theater festivals—permitted, but not sponsored by the church—occurred regularly throughout Europe. Community guilds dedicated their talents to presenting religiously themed plays—often reenacted Bible stories—thus reinforcing and celebrating the narratives central to Christian villages' worldview. Morality plays demonstrated the consequences of sin and the irrationality of sinful choices.[28]

INCHING TOWARD CENTER STAGE

Because the historic church generally rejected secular or pagan theater, today's evangelical presence in mainstream theater is probably greater than it has been in centuries. Rather than performing only in churches, evangelicals have formed

DO GOOD CHRISTIAN STORIES NEED HAPPY ENDINGS?

"I'm not going to enjoy this movie," my mother remarked while we were watching *The Prize Winner of Defiance, Ohio.* The film's central character, a struggling wife and mother, had to contend with ten children, poverty and an alcoholic husband. Not exactly *Disney* or *The Cosby Show.*

While *Prize Winner* certainly had upbeat moments, it didn't shy away from showing the family's struggles and sometimes unwise decisions. Although the ending wasn't typical Hollywood happiness, neither did it end in despair and disillusionment. It portrayed the true story of a gifted woman who stayed in a difficult marriage and never wavered in family devotion.

What kind of stories should evangelicals tell? Should the good guys (or girls) always win? Is this realistic? After all, bad things happen to good people, and good people sometimes do bad things. How many Bible stories have something other than Hollywood happy endings?

Evangelical media have long been preachy. The lost become found, sinners turn into saints, or a revival breaks out and a sports team wins the championship. Praise the Lord!

These are good stories, but how will audiences respond if a real-life school bully fails to reform, or if a favorite team loses halfway through the playoffs? Where is the story that portrays how Christians might respond in those situations?

Christians have heart knowledge of some of the most amazing and moving stories in human experience—the good and the bad. Knowing how to tell them well is a key in becoming true artists.

JEN LETHERER, SPRING ARBOR UNIVERSITY

professional groups that stage public plays generally with explicitly or implicitly religious themes.

Theater 315 has enjoyed a vital theatrical presence in New York City as part of the Time Square Ministries, owned and operated by the Salvation Army. Hosting and producing a variety of cogent and accessible plays and musicals, it recently offered *The Great Divorce,* a musical adaptation of C. S. Lewis's book.[29] Also in the nation's theater capital, Lamb's Theater Company produced biblically themed plays and musicals, including the premieres of the musicals *Cotton Patch Gospel* and *Johnny Pye.*[30] San Diego's Lamb's Players Theatre became a multistaffed, professional, nonprofit performing arts theater with a mission "to tell good stories well."[31] Evolved from a 1970s touring company, the Lamb's Players Theatre has one of the largest production budgets of any Christian-affiliated theater in the country.

In Seattle, Taproot Theatre Company[32] provides a full-production schedule of plays and musicals that have delighted audiences for decades. Taproot has maintained a theater-in-education portion of its company, working in schools and community groups in ways similar to Pittsburgh's Saltworks. Houston's A. D. Players produces "plays and programs that uphold human value, offer creativity and promote literacy and education."[33] A full-length season housed in Houston's Grace Theater has hosted more than forty thousand theater guests annually, while the touring company performed before over seventy thousand annually. The theater has offered one of the nation's only salaried internship programs. Milwaukee's Acacia Theatre Company has become the only professional Christian theater company in Wisconsin.[34]

Although each of these theater groups, composed largely of evangelicals, has enjoyed over twenty years of community service, none of them would identify their primary mission as explicitly evangelistic or instructional. As Lamb's Players puts it, the purpose of such theater is to "tell good stories well," to delight more than to persuade. These theaters ensure that mainstream audiences will not be evangelistically assaulted with an altar call, will not have their intelligences insulted by unbelievable conversion stories or unrealistically happy endings. In addition, audiences will not confuse the theatrical experience with a heavy-handed lecture, a play offering possessed by a message that crushes the nuance and imaginativeness of a story under the weight of propositional conviction. In short, these kinds of evangelical excursions into mainstream theater might suggest the tribe's growing aesthetic sophistication. Perhaps evangelicals today more fully comprehend the delicate and complex nature of teaching, delighting and persuading audiences.

At the same time, some evangelicals are reviving the biblical reenactment play or passion plays. For example, Sight and Sound Theatres host over 800,000 guests each year with vast, elaborate sets and dizzying detail. Reenacting epic Bible tales with large casts, professional lighting and costuming, the two theaters in Strasburg, Pennsylvania, have entertained thousands, who come from all over the country to witness the dramatic spectacles. Embracing the instructional and persuasive goals of medieval morality plays, Sight and Sound Theatres seek "to present the Gospel of Jesus Christ and sow the Word of God into the lives of [their] customers, guests, and fellow workers by visualizing and dramatizing the scriptures."[35] Their spectacles do not appeal to everyone, let alone to all evangelicals, but audiences know beforehand the nature and purpose of their productions since the group boldly proclaims its goals.

BACK TO THE PRESENT

The two areas of significant development over the last generation of evangelical engagement in the theater—the increased use of theater in worship and a growing sense of the importance of aesthetic delight—are focusing the tribe's future theatrical engagement. Employing theatrical performances during worship services—as sermon starters and illustrations—is likely to continue even as some churches transfer performances to recorded media. Faithful refinement of the artistic gifts of writing, directing and performing will require continued commitment to artistic critique and training, or the dramatic sketch in worship might become a passing fad in the face of congregants' growing expectations shaped by mainstream media drama.

Also, the tribe will have to learn to tell stories well, not poorly, predictably or stereotypically. Given evangelicals' commitment to the Greatest Story—that three-act structure of creation, corruption and restoration—its storytelling prowess should be more developed. But today much tribal theater is like communist theater in the United States during the Great Depression and World War II, when playwrights were weighed down by Marxist dogma and feared offending the party bosses.[36] With rare exceptions, Marxist plays became elaborate, dramatized tracts lambasting the bourgeois—uninteresting propaganda disguised as stories heavy on instruction and persuasion and weak on narrative delight.

Another dilemma for tribal storytelling is the debate over the use of profanity. Unless the tribe's present and future playwrights are only telling stories of the verbally pristine, they will to have to decide what the protagonist shouts when he accidentally smashes his thumb with a hammer: merely saying "Ouch!" stretches the credulity of the audience beyond its breaking point.[37]

One additional difficulty facing tribal engagement in theater is the tendency to minimize the differences in artistic form between the stage and the screen. As evangelical playwrights seize growing opportunities to record their art for video and film and stream plays for YouTube and the like, they will have to

HOLY SWEARING?

A Christian college theater department chose Author Miller's classic *All My Sons* for a mostly evangelical audience. Opening night came and went without trouble. But later that week the play's director received an angry email complaining about the profane language in Miller's script—a smattering of *damn*s and *hell*s. How could a Christian college produce such a work?!?

One dilemma: deleting words without the permission of the playwright is copyright infringement; it is illegal. Yet speaking the language alienates some of the very audience the producers seek to serve.

Another dilemma: sometimes profane words are part of a culture's everyday language. Writing realistic dialogue then forces the playwright and director to make tough choices. How much is too much profanity? Is it really necessary?

An evangelical artist might put it this way: Can I ever justify using profanity for a sacred purpose? The apostle Paul charges believers to "not let any unwholesome talk come out of [their] mouths" (Eph 4:29).

A third dilemma: What if the words are make-believe, not spoken by real people in real life? Should artists write or perform words that they wouldn't speak in their own lives?

The Old Testament prophets often used profane descriptions to describe ungodly culture. Portions of the books of Ezekiel and Jeremiah are not fit for the pristine boundaries of the church sanctuary but may be entirely appropriate for theater performances. Should we dismiss the prophetic possibilities of a play or other art work because its language wouldn't be appropriate for a Sunday school picnic? If so, Ezekiel and Jeremiah probably wouldn't be invited.

PAUL D. PATTON, SPRING ARBOR UNIVERSITY

remember the lesson learned from this book's early chapters on film and television history—namely, the transfer in form is not automatic. Many successful American playwrights and novelists were failures as screenwriters for this very reason. Evangelical storytellers will have to see the new opportunities for audience development through film and TV and newer online media with guarded enthusiasm, knowing the distinctive characteristics and demands of each form.

Even so, some evangelical thespians have forged ahead in experimenting with newer electronic media. For over a decade, theatrical offerings of Jeannette Clift George's A. D. Players have been available in video formats. *Toymaker and Son* has been broadcast on TV in several countries, including China. Yet, the success of conveying plays written for the stage and transferred to even newer electronic venues, like YouTube, remains to be seen.

In addition to experimenting with electronic venues, evangelical thespians are also cultivating ways to organize themselves in online formats, spawning attempts to build faithful discourse electronically. For instance, members of CITA have opportunities to cultivate discussion, surveys and other forms of research through the organization's online subscription list. Theater professors, artistic directors and playwrights interact electronically with hundreds of colleagues. As another example, Lillenas Publishing makes dramatic materials for church theater troupes available through their website: production suggestions, how-tos and, perhaps most importantly, an online networking forum for participants of varying talent and training levels.

However, so far the evangelical tribe has only begun to take faith-driven artistic risks in storytelling and imaginative development. The tribe will have to learn to embrace a "poetic aesthetic" that "allows for the complex ambiguities of real life."[38] In doing so, evangelicals can wean themselves from the restrictions of a rhetorical aesthetic, a storytelling form requiring the reinforcement of a moral or doctrinal point. The rhetorical aesthetic best serves the sanctuary pulpit, the courtroom and the legislative halls of congressional gatherings, not mainstream theater. Quality mainstream theater is preevangelistic at best, not a replacement for the church's evangelistic efforts and instructional responsibilities.

In this regard, significant signs of encouragement have dotted the tribal landscape. In 1995, Bryan Coley founded Art Within to address the need for developing playwrights and screenwriters.[39] In New York City, the New Works Series of Threads Productions, associated with Redeemer Presbyterian, has committed itself to cultivating promising new scripts.[40] Gillette Elvgren, a gifted writer, director and teacher—and recipient of CITA's Lifetime Achievement Award—has been developing evangelical playwrights at Regent University's graduate school since the early 1990s.

CONCLUSION

Betty's dilemma would probably unfold differently today. Her twenty-first-century father certainly would have had a more difficult time prohibiting his daughter's educational aspirations. More importantly, Betty's subsequent conversion to Christ would have taken place within an emerging evangelical theater scene that provides a myriad of opportunity to explore obedience to Christ as Lord of theater as well as the local congregation. She would have been exposed to a less moralistic tribe, one more aware of biblically informed cultural engagements with the God-given gift of theater, thereby allowing her the opportunity to develop her talent, rather than bury it.

12

Faith-Based Theme Parks and Museums
Multidimensional Media

ANNALEE WARD

Misty-eyed pilgrims watch a bloodied Jesus stumble along the path with a crossbeam tied with rope to his arms, captors lashing him. The music rises as Jesus, nailed to the cross, is hoisted in the air above the emotional crowd.[1] A soloist belts out "Via Dolorosa" while a cloudy sky darkens the mood. The music swells to a majestic "Behold the Lamb." As the narrator proclaims the victory over death, the sun breaks through the clouds and shines on the empty tomb below the cross.

Every afternoon, six days a week from mid-January to Thanksgiving, Jesus is crucified in Orlando, Florida, minutes from Disney World and Universal Studios. "I interviewed Jesus at the Holy Land Experience," I told my coworkers. "He has great hair—looks just like his picture—the Anglo-Saxon one." Not knowing if they should laugh or take offense, they simply stared at me. I quickly explained that the fifteen-acre, $16-million Holy Land Experience (HLE) is part museum, part theme park, part theater—all of it supported by high-tech sights and sounds that define the holy land for visitors who have never been to the real place.

Critics have questioned the founder's motives,[2] the quality of the experience,[3] the particular brand of faith portrayed[4] and the legitimacy of this kind of ministry.[5] The place sounds like something out of *The Simpsons*—Ned Flanders's Praise Land—but the dedicated staff is committed to teaching, delighting and persuading visitors. Les Cheveldayoff, who plays Jesus, says seriously, "I'm here to be used of God . . . to fulfill the role of Christ."

Such living-history experiences are easy targets for jokes. But they are growing in variety and number and often serve as modern-day pilgrimage sites. They offer an odd combination of pious inspiration, tourism, pop culture materialism and even kitsch—cheap, sentimental art. Moreover, they both repel and attract visitors. And they certainly raise questions about the purpose and means in evangelical outreach. The faithful might be inspired but might just as easily be dismayed by the apparent lack of reverence, historical accuracy, appropriateness or artistic quality. Just the same, a Christian theme park can be a cutting-edge, multidimensional means of serving visitors.[6]

ATTRACTIVE PLACES

Holy Land Experience. The HLE describes itself as a living history museum, although it is often referred to as a theme park. The dream began in the 1990s when Marvin J. Rosenthal, a converted Jew and Baptist minister, founded an evangelical outreach ministry to Jews. He wanted an "educational, historical, theatrical, inspirational, and evangelical" experience. If you cannot bring the people on a tour to Israel, he figured, bring the holy land to the people. He hired ITEC Entertainment Corporation, the top-notch designer of Universal Studio's Islands of Adventure.[7]

The more than 200,000 visitors per year to this park encounter lectures on archaeology, shows that bring biblical stories to life, reenactments of rituals, a scale model of Jerusalem in A.D. 66, a film linking ancient Jewish history to Christ and a sophisticated museum experience housing a collection of Scriptures. The park includes the requisite gift shops and food stops such as the Oasis Palms Café, where one might enjoy a Goliath burger or Silas's stew.

Rosenthal sought to develop "a wholesome, family oriented, educational and entertainment facility, where people can come to be encouraged, instructed, and reinforced in their faith."[8] Achieving this goal has not been easy, due to financial concerns.[9] After a battle with the county over taxes and Rosenthal leaving the organization, HLE still needed financial partners to stay afloat. In 2007 the Trinity Broadcasting Network (TBN) took control, hoping to use its broadcasting outlets to boost attendance. As with Universal and Disney parks, HLE symbolizes synergy across practically every medium, from printed materials to video, stage, musical performance and broadcasting.[10]

Other imitation holy lands. Over the years other parks have sprung up claiming to be a holy land.[11] Connecticut's Holy Land U.S.A. drew large crowds in the 1950s through 1970s with its hilltop sign resembling the famous Hollywood icon. All that remains today are faded plywood cutouts and broken statues, but at one time it averaged 44,000 visitors a year.[12] Today a 250-acre Holy Land USA in Virginia takes 25,000 visitors annually on a three-mile wagon ride through Journey Trail to hear and see the gospel in two-dimensional cutouts.[13]

Tierra Santa in Buenos Aires, Argentina, tells biblical stories, primarily from the life of Christ, through mechanical characters and plastic animals. A fifty-foot Christ rises twice every hour at the park endorsed by the Roman Catholic Church. It has drawn over 2.5 million visitors since opening in 1999. One guide explains, "People are trying to seek transcendence, something higher than themselves. They see that the world is so materialistic and come here as an escape."[14] These holy lands often serve as a pilgrimage for the poor.

Eureka Springs. Arkansas's New Holy Land (who wants an old one?!) reenacts the events and sites of Jesus' ministry. Nearby, *The Passion Play* tells the story of Jesus' last week on earth, attracting over seven million people in forty years. Visitors can see the Christ of the Ozarks sixty-seven-foot statue, learn of the origins of the earth in the Museum of Earth History, explore the Center for the Sacred Arts, follow the stations of the cross or meditate in an architecturally significant chapel. The local passion play organization fosters a tourist industry around Christian symbols and stories designed to educate and inspire people in the faith.[15] The Southern location suggests that evangelicals are the major market.

SHOULD CHURCHES HOST HELL HOUSES?

Halloween traditions: trick or treating, costume parties, and haunted houses. These entertainments are not for some evangelicals, who instead host a hell house designed to defy the devil by scaring children into salvation. The more realistic, the better.

And they can be franchised. A Colorado pastor sells $300 "Hell House Outreach Kits"—to over eight hundred churches in every state and eighteen countries so far—complete with a DVD and the possibility of a consultation with the pastor.[a]

Visitors journey through the earthly hell dramatized in seven horrific scenes. Anything goes: from a botched abortion (enacted with bloody meat) to a school shooting, to devil worship complete with a human sacrifice. No topic is off limits if it serves to frighten the faithful straight or convert the wayward to Christ. What fun for All Souls' (or All Saints') Eve!

Do the claimed heavenly ends justify such hellish means? Fans believe that desperate times require desperate measures. Parents and pastors have to compete with mainstream fright fests. Hell houses are just state-of-the-art pop culture, "in-your-face, . . . theatrical stylin'" for an aggressive age.[b] Others argue that such tactics are over-the-top, hyper-manipulative persuasion that denies a person's freedom to choose for or against Christ.[c]

Is there a place for hell houses on All Souls' Day? On any day?

ANNALEE WARD, TRINITY CHRISTIAN COLLEGE

[a]David Casstevens, "Christian Haunted Houses Aim to Scare to Salvation," *Chicago Tribune,* October 29, 2006, p. 4.

[b]See the description of the Hell House Outreach Kit available at New Destiny Christian Center <www.godestiny.org/hell_house/HH_kit.cfm>.

[c]Em Griffin, *The Mind Changers: The Art of Christian Persuasion* (Wheaton, Ill.: Tyndale, 1976).

Creation Museum. Visitors expect a religious museum to offer an educational gaze that objectifies and even reverences a holy object or scene.[16] Near Cincinnati, the Creation Museum, opened in 2007, is a $27-million extravaganza designed to counter natural history museums' secularism with biblical creationism. Here the instruction blends science with a literal biblical reading of human history as only six thousand years old. This "new weapon in a wider 'culture war'"[17] is designed "to equip Christians to defend their faith and to present the gospel."[18] Critics worry that this museum has gone too far—that it is more persuasion or even propaganda than instruction, culminating in an "unorthodox curating."[19]

Still, the place delights children especially, who discover dinosaurs, some roaring as moving heads and tails threaten; a special-effects theater with shaking seats and spraying water; life-size models of Adam and Eve; mineral collections; a model of Noah's ark; over fifty-five videos; and a digital planetarium all held together by an archaeologist's story. Here is a multimedia entertainment mecca offering what *Newsweek* calls "a modern, technologically advanced version of an animated children's Bible."[20] Yet the slick professionalism lends a certain credibility, which is probably what concerns critics who hold other views of how, when, where and why the world was created.[21]

Billy Graham Library. The Billy Graham Center Museum at Wheaton College in Illinois houses many of Graham's papers and artifacts. It also offers an interactive experience to persuade visitors that Graham became one of the most important evangelists of all time and that media evangelism is effective—sometimes stunningly so.

The newer Billy Graham Library near his organization's headquarters in Charlotte, North Carolina, was designed partly by ITEC—which worked on Disneyland and Holy Land Experience. The high-tech tourist destination boasts a child-pleasing animatronic cow, a walk-through crystal cross, multimedia presentations about Graham's evangelistic work, and carefully integrated presentations of the gospel.[22]

Museums, then, are becoming major media venues that persuade as they delight, drawing tribal and mainstream tourists to their increasingly impressive attractions.[23] These attractions employ a variety of media to tell their stories, and they are supported by elaborate websites. They seek to compete for their young people with the costly entertainment venues of the mainstream—venues which are increasing in variety and availability in a globalized market.[24]

AGED ATTRACTIONS

Ancient and medieval theater. Contemporary attractions are rooted in humanity's early performative rituals and storytelling. History shows that humans are attracted to drama and other entertainment, which today includes parklike attrac-

PRECIOUS (OR WASTED) MOMENTS

Precious Moments Chapel, Carthage, Missouri. At the back of the chapel a mural, *Hallelujah Square,* depicts a child being welcomed to heaven by Timmy Angel and surrounded by other dead child angels. Standing at the center of the mural is Jesus Christ.

Visitors hold their babies next to a life-sized Timmy as he wanders the grounds. They shoot keepsake digital videos and photos.[a] For many, Timmy Angel and the chapel are a powerful means to mourn their own lost children. For some critics, an attraction like this seems superficial, sentimental or simply in bad taste.[b] For others it is deeply moving. Who's right?

Like the rest of the population, evangelicals partake of numerous multimedia attractions that connect people with feelings of national pride: watching Lincoln speak in the Hall of Presidents at Disney World; snapping photos of a deadly Confederate infantry assault being repulsed by Union artillery fire at a reenactment of the Battle of Gettysburg; gathering intelligence at the International Spy Museum in Washington, D.C. Do we disparage consumer patriotism with the same dispatch that we criticize multimedia expressions of faith? What makes the secular ones worthily meaningful and the religious ones tackily sentimental—or vice versa?

But perhaps even a few precious moments of meaning can taste sublime. If so, we have to be careful about judging the personal taste of others at meaningful times in their lives.

MARK E. TAYLOR, LOYOLA UNIVERSITY CHICAGO

---

[a]See a description of the Precious Moments Chapel at <www.roadsideamerica.com/attract/MOCARprecious.html>.

[b]Minnesota Public Radio's Savvy Traveler, Cash Peters, includes a stop at the Precious Moments Chapel during a Bad Taste Tour <savvytraveler.publicradio.org/show/features/2000/20000804/badtaste.shtml>.

tions, sports events and museums. As early as 2500 B.C. ancient Egyptians were performing a type of passion play about the death and resurrection of the god Osiris.[25]

The Western world more often traces its theater to the early Greek plays and the Roman games. Much Greek theater, produced between 700 and 500 B.C., was based on myth or history. These productions, which grew more elaborate in both costume and staging, were performed in sacred spaces where the gods were acknowledged.[26]

Romans developed greater variety in their entertainment, all the while centering it on sacred festivals. Much of the entertainment, particularly pantomime, ridiculed Christianity and offended Christians, who became hostile toward drama. By the fifth century, the churches criticized games and spectacles partly because people attended these pagan rituals instead of church.[27] Roman taste eventually deteriorated slowly over time as demand for truly spectacular public entertainment increased. Games included brutal chariot races, gladiator combat and even an enormous sea battle, all staged for entertainment. Eventually circus games and acts were added.[28]

In the Middle Ages, churches incorporated drama into their worship through processionals and pantomimes. Typical plays centered on Easter or Christmas, but by the late Middle Ages they evolved into traveling biblical pageants or cycle plays followed by even more accessible morality plays. Performed in local languages rather than the Mass's Latin, the dramas eventually included ropes and pulleys to simulate flying, achieving a commanding spectacle—the special effects of the day.[29]

Museums, in particular, "stem from the age-old human desires to preserve cultural identity; gain social, political, and economic status; and pursue knowledge."[30] They combine the ancient Greeks' love of history and reverence for the sacred with the Roman desire for entertainment. For Christians, Arkansas's passion play echoes the famous one that has been performed in Oberammergau in Bavaria, Germany, for nearly four hundred years.

Pilgrimages. Fourth-century Christians were fascinated with "the cult of the martyrs and their relics" (bones and other personal items) as well as with holy land topography. This led to the idea of holy places ultimately endorsed by the church.[31] During the Middle Ages, Christians sometimes journeyed to such sacred places, hoping to be healed or at least spiritually blessed by traveling to, as well as being in, such locales. Although today there are fewer Christian pilgrims than tourists, the ideas of spiritual travel and spiritual destinations remain in popular Christian, even evangelical, experience.[32] Perhaps these pilgrims "will continue to seek in tourism all that makes it possible for it to have a stronger influence on believers."[33]

Modern attractions. By the mid-1800s, a form of virtual travel, known as parlor pilgrimage, included cutting-edge media such as "stereopticons, slide shows, scale models, museum displays, [and] world's fair expositions."[34] As early as 1873 there was a scale model of Jerusalem on display at the International Exposition in Vienna, where visitors could experience the holy land without actually going there. The 1893 Chicago World's Fair included "ambitious" holy land exhibits.[35]

At the 1904 Saint Louis World's Fair, a full-sized reproduction of Jerusalem filled eleven acres. Designed to "be a religious educator and witness to the triumph of Christian civilization," the exhibit promised educated guides and inspiring experiences of everything from the Bethlehem manger to the tomb of Jesus, the tabernacle of Moses and the temple where Jesus taught. Foreshadowing some later religious attractions, the exhibit was riddled with consumerism, racism and nationalism couched in a Protestant worldview.[36]

Another related attraction began in 1874 in Chautauqua, New York, where Protestants dedicated a Sunday school assembly to educational self-improvement. The high-end summer camp focused initially on biblical instruction but eventually included the arts, sciences and recreation. One of the founders built a scale model of the holy land called Palestine Park, where a relief map of Palestine is still visible.

Various Chautauquas around the country included biblical dramas and reenactments, holy land photo displays and paintings, ceremonies, models of biblical sites, and lectures[37]—all to nurture faithfulness and satisfy longings for contact with the real holy land. Chautauquans could claim their "rightful Christian inheritance" without leaving America. The holy land belonged to them, creating their sense of "material piety."[38]

More recently, successful TV preacher-entertainers Jim and Tammy Bakker opened Heritage USA. Launched in 1978, within a year it had become one of the top vacation destinations in North America. Straddling the fence between religious and mainstream theme parks, Heritage USA was a safe-haven entertainment mecca with 2,200 acres of North Carolina forest. By 1986 it attracted over six million visitors a year and needed $3 million weekly to stay afloat. A few years later the leadership was rocked by sexual and financial scandals that slowly led to bankruptcy and eventually abandonment of the park in 1997.[39]

Competing with Disney

Smaller venues lack mass appeal, so the latest trend in attractions is *big*. The Holy Land Experience, Creation Museum and Graham Library have invested amounts of money that make mainstream audiences take notice. Other groups have enticed mainstream visitors with family-friendly attractions without overtly religious themes.

Silver Dollar City, Celebration City and Dollywood, for instance, are all owned by Herschend Family Entertainment, whose motto is "All in a manner consistent with Christian values and ethics."[40] These parks fit the mainstream model, offering thrill rides, entertainment and food without religious pitches.[41] Managers know that Southern, Bible Belt culture embraces clean, safe parks. But they also know that something like the gospel music festival at Dollywood is a natural, acceptable expression of that culture that can appeal to nonevangelicals as well. Most visitors probably never realize that evangelical values drive the management.[42]

Praising the Medium and Teaching the Message

The creators and other fans of places like the Holy Land Experience and Creation Museum believe that evangelicals need safe venues that will inspire and

IS DISNEY'S MAGIC FAMILY FRIENDLY?

Christian theme parks such as Orlando's Holy Land Experience offer family-friendly, sanctified alternatives to the vast Disney empire of dreams. Ned Flanders and his family from *The Simpsons* might feel right at home there.

But what about the mainstream versions of the Christian theme parks? Walt Disney conceived of Disneyland as a place where his beloved TV and movie characters and stories could live in a three-dimensional playground. Aren't those family friendly? Who doesn't like Mickey Mouse?! Do these parks present Christians with moral quandaries?

First, can Christians justify spending $1,000 per person for a family extravaganza in sunny Florida? Why not rent a few family films and send the money to missions?

Second, what about the message in Disney's fairy-dust-sprinkled morality tales? Magic in the Disney films has always been a strategic creative choice intended to move across cultural and national boundaries. But should evangelicals immerse themselves in the magic that's a running element of Disney stories? Does the Disney worldview compete with a biblical worldview?

Disney called his first park, Disneyland, "the happiest place on earth," and the many millions who have visited it for generations agree. Disney's parks contain some of the best our culture has to offer in entertainment that, if not clearly Christian, is neither cynical nor debased.

Should discerning evangelical families—that is, those who spend time discussing the content and ideas featured in the products and find a balance outside their Disney diet—receive such mainstream theme parks as delightful gifts of human imagination? If so, perhaps we can wisely enjoy the best of both worlds, Disney's and God's.

ALEX WAINER, PALM BEACH ATLANTIC UNIVERSITY

entertain visitors. Supposedly desperate for "values-based entertainment," evangelicals are the primary markets for a more than $4-billion-a-year religious entertainment industry.[43]

Evangelical supporters of such attractions even hope to persuade outsiders to adopt the faith. They seek to use any means available to spread the gospel, including their own safe spectacle and entertainment.[44] One TV evangelist who created a theme park says that "fishers of men" need "fancy bait."[45] A senior teacher at HLE says that although thrill rides would be unacceptable, anything else "ethical, biblical would be legitimate. If you can get a child to church and get them saved and into the kingdom of God for a piece of bubble gum, then that's a cheap price to pay."[46] One journalist contends that a visitor to the drama at HLE might expect "charmingly cheesy church pageants," but in fact the experience "will surprise you."[47] Fans say HLE is emotional, appealing and even inspiring—not just instructional or persuasive.

Since many parents use vacations to teach their children, these parks often are located along interstate highways and used during holidays, school breaks and summer sojourns. Many of them piggyback on other tourist destinations like Disney, adding teachable stops along the road. The Holy Land Experience raves about its ability to instruct attendees by making the biblical stories real. Visitors speak about the place as a great teaching tool for their children, more attention holding than many church services back home! The Creation Museum teaches with multimedia illustrations and examples—the very media children expect on a vacation.

Scholars believe that Disney has taken its place as a religious site offering symbolic and mythic power. "And because contemporary trends in American religion have created a situation in which nonreligious entities and activities are often used for personal religious (or 'spiritual') ends, Americans (and others) can find in Disney many of the elements they once found exclusively in traditional religion."[48] By using the same media, evangelicals hope to speak truth to a culture steeped in Disney.

But Is the Message Compromised?

Critics worry, however, that by using theme-park methods the message might be compromised. One critic suggests that accommodation to consumer culture "renders the Church ever less able to take a prophetic stand."[49] By focusing on touristy entertainment, these venues might trivialize the core message of tribal faith. Perhaps they can fall into the trap of delighting more than teaching truth, relying on gimmicks and spectacles that fade away when visitors depart.

For example, when creators in Tennessee announced Bible Park U.S.A. in 2007, they stressed that it was going to be a thrill-ride park and that the park would avoid overtly biblical messages that might offend nonbelievers. Creators hoped to present biblical stories as "secular 'history'" narrated by "costumed archeologists as its evangelists."[50]

Others continue to dream of creating such broad-based entertainment meccas, too—at least one of them in England.[51] M. G. "Pat" Robertson of *The 700 Club* announced plans eventually to construct a $60-million park in Israel—a *real* holy land park.[52]

Critics outside evangelical tribes are concerned, too. Historically, Jews have criticized passion plays as potentially anti-Semitic. When the Holy Land Experience opened, it faced protests from Jewish leaders who believed HLE was deceiving the public about its true intentions of converting Jews, especially since the park's creator said profits would be used to evangelize Israeli and American Jews.[53] A local rabbi worried that the park "trivializes the fundamental story of

Christianity by turning its characters into theme-park characters."[54]

Mainstream critics also have cited politicization, especially the tendency of evangelical groups to associate Christianity with nationalistic, right-wing causes. One detractor argued that the Holy Land Experience has promoted a simplistic anti-terrorism, anti-Islam message that "fosters hate among conservative Protestant visitors." She added that the park's apocalyptic theology was naively pro-Israeli without concern for justice for all: "It works to actively destroy Palestinian aspirations for autonomy by spreading anti-Arab and anti-Islamic propaganda among its supporters in the name of supporting Israel."[55] One opponent worried that holy land attractions involved "problematic exclusions and inclusions, effaced histories and privileged scenarios, assemblages of nostalgic desire and fantasy, and embodied interpretations of the 'true' Bible as well as claims to the truly American."[56]

DYNAMIC BUT DANGEROUS

Evangelical forays into theme parks and museums are innovative uses of numerous old and new media. Employing mainstream, market-driven methods opens up new avenues for delightful and truthful interaction with attendees. Still, dangers remain: excessive cost, crass commercialism and confusion of purpose.

Are evangelical attractions beautiful, high-quality places to visit? Some newer attractions are, but historically, they have not been. Few religious theme parks have the Disney budget or aesthetic. Some parks are simply in bad baste—ugly, cheaply built, corny venues. They frequently tend toward sentimental art that will likely appeal only to some visitors who are moved by kitsch. For these tourists, the venues can help them experience and express emotions that they might not have otherwise.[57] Popularity does not make an attraction evil, nor does kitsch render one unworthy of a visit. Cultural elitism can lead to unholy pride and self-righteousness. Excellence can be a goal, but it is not easy to meet in the real world, and navigating that tension is difficult.

Nevertheless, as tourist attractions rooted at least partly in commercial models, these sites risk trivializing the gospel, manipulating attendees' emotions, and deemphasizing the role of sin and evil in a more complete Christian worldview. They also risk overemphasizing the benefits of costly, compared with simple, entertainment. While a tourist mindset brings with it the longing for the authentic sacredness, it also seeks to spend money without teaching about financial stewardship. As the recent attractions have shown, it takes considerable cash flow to remain operational. The price of success is generally high entrance fees,[58] heavy fund raising, seductive gift shops that push tribal messages and cheap trinkets, and temptations to reduce the gospel to nice stories to gain wider appeal.[59]

Many operators desire to use entertainment to teach and persuade, but visitor reaction focuses on emotional inspiration. The draw to sacred space, "geopiety," has "mythic power," while referencing a type of "Christian nostalgia."[60] The goal to inspire is not wrong, but things get muddy when a site wants to persuade and teach. And focusing on entertainment tends to heighten emotional delight at the expense of the message.

Whether it is in an evangelical theme park or experiential museum, the tension between entertainment and ministry will not disappear. Creative and engaging, these expensive ventures draw in the faithful by telling old stories via new media that in person engage all of the senses. Christian stories take on new significance when presented on equal footing with the mainstream parks and museums. But by raising the stakes to compete with flashy quality, big budgets

THE DAY JEREMIAH TOURED A THEME PARK

Rock music fans call Roger Waters (Pink Floyd) a prophet. The media sometimes call corporate leaders or successful entrepreneurs prophets as well. Are they really prophets?

Rabbi Abraham Joshua Heschel says a real biblical prophet "feels fiercely. God has thrust a burden upon his soul, and he is bowed and stunned at man's fierce greed."[a] Fighting greed? Would a theme park give Jeremiah a parking-lot soapbox to criticize greedy people and institutions? What would he say about the SUVs and designer jeans as people are streaming from the lot to the main doors?

Heschel adds that a prophet's words "are often slashing, even horrid—designed to shock rather than to edify."[b] Like Ezekiel's description of Jerusalem's harlotry (Ezek 23), the contemporary prophet's work would not be family friendly. Listen to The Call's second recording, "Modern Romans," which shockingly describes contemporary enslavement. Prophetic? Yes! Easy to swallow? No!

So imagine Jeremiah standing on top of a lemonade stand, angrily shouting at the picture-taking, spiritually lukewarm tourists who just skipped church to celebrate a Sunday together at a Christian theme park. The little children are crying, pleading to go home. Some adults are shouting back at Jeremiah, telling him to clean up his language.

If Rabbi Heschel is even partly right, few of us are in the mood for anything deeply prophetic. It's not likely to be very entertaining, especially when we see the finger pointing at us. And it probably wouldn't be very good for the theme park's business.

PAUL D. PATTON, SPRING ARBOR UNIVERSITY

[a]Abraham Joshua Heschel, *The Prophets* (Peabody, Mass.: Hendrickson, 2007), p. 5.

[b]Ibid., p. 8.

and an entertainment-obsessed mainstream, evangelicals risk losing their authentic and prophetic voice.

CONCLUSION

Back on the streets at the Holy Land Experience, the performance has ended. People wipe their eyes and turn to the ice cream stand. Perhaps they make one last visit to the gift shop for a Roman guard's sword or a cross necklace. Another day of tourism ends. Has it changed a life? Perhaps. Has it helped customers to learn more or increased their faith? Perhaps. Has it distracted tourists from the pains and worries of their lives and the suffering around them? Probably. One thing is certain: as long as the public buys tickets, Jesus will be lashed to the cross.

13

Merchandising Jesus Products

DIANE M. BADZINSKI

The Jesus Is My Homeboy clothing line is worn by celebrities, including pop star Madonna with the female version, Mary Is My Home Girl. One seventeen-year-old, Jordan, saw a photo of the host of MTV's *Punk'd* in Homeboy attire and "wasn't sure what to make of it." What do evangelicals make of it?

No doubt Christian-themed products contribute to the tremendous growth in the religious retailing industry, but they also spur debate within the evangelical tribe.[1] Evangelicals generally like goods that convey faith-related messages, yet wonder whether products with sayings such as "Jesus Is My Homeboy" or "Jesus loves me and my tattoo" cultivate a strong evangelical culture. Do special Christian ringtones and cell-phone carrying cases suggest that evangelicals are obsessed with material consumption? Or that being an evangelical is just another brand of consumerism?

If evangelicals truly believe that all of life must be lived faithfully, they will have to decide not just what to purchase as part of their witness but where and how to shop as well. For instance, most products can be purchased more cheaply online, but should evangelicals perhaps support their neighborhood Christian bookstore—often called mom-and-pop bookstores? (Ironically, an increasing number are owned by corporations.) Ultimately, evangelicals must discern whether what they purchase and where they shop help or hinder the spread of the gospel.

TRASH OR TREASURE?

Christian products include everything from books to music, apparel, plaques and gadgets that carry some Christian-related theme. Christian merchandise is often referred to as a form of kitsch—that is, "any form of popular art or entertainment that is a sentimental, cheaply made trivialization of something else."[2] Qualifiers such as *cheap, frivolous, artistically inferior, dangerous* and *junk* are often used to describe kitsch.

MEMORY MAKERS OR CRASS COMMERCIALISTS?

Cheap rings that turn fingers blue. Tie-dyed T-shirts with Bible verses. Pop posters with paintings of a Caucasian Jesus. These are top sellers at many Christian-themed attractions, where families pick up souvenirs to remember trips.

Americans spend over $703 billion annually on tourism—much of it on merchandise![a] Don't evangelical businesses deserve a slice of the pie? On the other hand, should evangelicals contribute to a culture of trivia?

Christian-themed attractions like the Holy Land Experience or Creation Museum imitate the merchandise mania at mainstream ones. Souvenirs go back at least to the Middle Ages, when Christian pilgrims could return with saints' bones and nails along with wood chips supposedly from Jesus' cross. Today, a consuming pilgrim can purchase a Jesus action figure whose arms rise to bless those who behold it, or a Roman sword to remember the Holy Land Experience. (WWCD, What Would Caesar Do?!)

Souvenirs do prompt memories of places and experiences. Some promise an association with a faith community. Others promote an evangelistic or comforting message—perhaps a "Just as I Am" mug from the Billy Graham Library.

The early church Mass produced and eventually marketed worship items like crucifixes, prayer cards and rosary beads for spiritual development and growth. Should we do the same today—for the sake of memory? Or should evangelicals be different? If so, how?

ANNALEE WARD, TRINITY CHRISTIAN COLLEGE

[a]This statistic is highlighted on the purchasing site for *Tourism Works for America: Travel Industry Snapshots 2007,* published by the Travel Industry Association <www.tia.org/pubs/pubs.asp?PublicationID=33>.

The designations "kitsch" and "Jesus junk" both imply that evangelical products have little or no real artistic or social value, only fleeting market value. Generally only critics use such negative terms. Evangelicals generally use positive phrases such as "Christian art," "Christian jewelry" and "Christian cards" when referring to such merchandise, even though the label Christian might be somewhat deceptive since it is certainly not clear what marks a product as Christian.

Evangelicals must discern whether a particular piece of merchandise is or is not merely Jesus junk—trash or treasure. As one scholar noted, "The Western world is glutted with endless reproductions which are expressions of affluence and waste, bad stewardship and greed. Evangelicals rightly want to be discerning. Too much garbage is, well, too much garbage. It not only clutters, it eventually contaminates. It causes disease. It even kills."[3]

EXPLODING MERCHANDISE

The Christian retailing industry has seen astounding growth since 1980, growing from a $1-billion to over $4.63-billion industry in 2007, with reportedly no end in sight.[4] By 2009 the religious books segment alone will account for $2.91 billion in revenue—a 50 percent increase from 2004.[5] Due to the profitability of Christian-related products, large mainstream outlets such as Wal-Mart and Barnes & Noble as well as online outlets such as eBay and Amazon are snatching larger portions of the Christian retailing market from the smaller Christian bookstores.[6] Although Wal-Mart, for example, has sold Christian books for quite some time, it recently began carrying a full line of faith-based toys—a high-profit item for Christian bookstores.[7]

While the larger mainstream outlets are able to sell popular ticketed items at discount prices, Christian bookstores rely on apparel, framed art and gifts, as well as children's items, for its biggest profits.[8] In 2005, inspirational gifts and merchandise accounted for an estimated $1.9 billion in retail sale, marking an 11.8 percent increase from 2004 and a projected 26.3 percent growth to $2.4 billion by 2010.[9] In fact, only about 25 percent of the sales at Christian stores are from books, with the remaining sales from other Christian-themed merchandise.[10]

Some attribute the explosion in Christian product sales to a spiritual revival in response to the 9/11 terrorist attacks and the war in Iraq.[11] Immediately following these events, evangelical churches saw tremendous short-term growth as people sought answers and considered joining faith-based communities. Christian books and music provided answers and direction, while products such as jewelry and T-shirts symbolized membership in these communities. The popularity of the Christian novel and Hollywood box-office successes—Mel Gibson's *The Passion of the Christ,* for example—also spurred industry growth. And finally, no doubt, a large part of the growth is attributed to the widespread distribution of Christian books and other Christian products in mega-retail and Internet outlets.

PREACHY PRODUCTS

Many evangelicals enthusiastically support the production and consumption of Christian-related merchandise, including the distribution of these products by mega-retail outlets. They believe that Christian products are a wholesome, even evangelistic, alternative to many of the goods flooding the marketplace. As one advocate noted, there is a demand for "God-honoring" toys; just stroll "down a toy aisle in any major retailer, you will see toys and dolls that promote and glorify evil, destruction, lying, [and] cheating."[12] Indeed, there is a need for more God-honoring options, so let the "battle for the toy box" begin.[13]

Fans argue that Christian products are messages that can communicate the gospel, thereby helping to fulfill the Great Commission (Mt 28:18-20). In other words, Christian products are communication tools to persuade as well as teach and delight consumers.

Teaching. Advocates believe that theme-based products can instill ideas and values in children. Holy Huggables—Esther, Moses and Jesus talking dolls—were created out of a father's desire for his daughter to have a doll that reflects his spiritual convictions.[14] Similarly Jay Jay the Jet Plane, so named for his two-year-old son, was created out of a father's passion to influence young children. Jay Jay's adventures are "meant to teach children gentleness, patience and friendship."[15] Prayer Circle Friends, a clone of the Build-A-Bear, are kid-created stuffed animals in which children insert a self-recorded prayer audio chip, presumably teaching the importance of prayer.[16] The Life of Faith dolls, an imitation of the American Girl products, portray ordinary girls in different time periods who have displayed remarkable steps of faith; they teach children the importance of faith.[17] In fact, Messengers of Faith dolls come with a complete set of instructions on how to use the dolls to teach children Bible stories. A motto of the organization One2Believe is to "teach children the Bible one character at a time."[18] No doubt, these toys socialize children into the Christian community.

Even controversial games and shocking merchandise can serve as catalysts for Christian thought and discussion, argue the supporters of such products. The objective of the *Left Behind: Eternal Forces* video game is to kill or convert opposing forces. According to Focus on the Family, the game can stimulate positive, faith-affirming discussion.[19] Of course, this assumes that parents will talk to their children about the game rather than just letting them play it as a Christian alternative to mainstream games. Basically, the game has the potential to teach children about the rapture and its ensuing struggles, although it is not clear exactly how or what they would learn just from playing the game.

Christian merchandise also teaches the importance of community and loyalty among the tribe.[20] Such products brand the purchasers as Christians and advertise to "the world around them that they are Christians."[21] Such products also signal who is and who is not part of the Christian community.[22] Consumers can learn, for instance, to demonstrate their loyalty to particular churches, denominations, evangelical celebrities, music groups and theological perspectives—they can even buy particular Bibles or other products that support their view of the rapture, holiness, etc. These products function symbolically to communicate personal identity, affiliation and beliefs—if not to try to teach those beliefs to others.[23] Cross necklaces and products carrying expressions such as "Jesus Lives" and "He Died for Me" signal a kind of teachable identification with Christ. This function is similar to a concept known as lifestyle branding, defined as "products and services that allow consumers to purchase an emotional attachment to an identity."[24] Witness-wear and other such products serve as an identity marker of one's faith.

Persuading. For many fans, Christian products are tools for sharing faith with

ARE YOU WHAT YOU BUY?

I spotted the following ad in an airport: "You Are What You Buy." It featured an attractive woman blanketed in fashionable garb and accessories. The ad only sought to lure travelers into the airport's shops, but its message summarized our consumption-driven lives.

Are we what we buy? I hope not. But even what evangelicals buy sends a message, and the message can range from unsettling to understandable: materialistic, tasteless, searching for reassurance within a seemingly hostile society, settling for unimaginative knockoffs.

Some evangelical products aim for evangelism by recasting a timeless message in terms that are contemporary, cool: T-shirts proclaiming "Body Piercing Saved My Life." But Christian merchants have done this for decades. Think of posters from the 1970s that borrowed from Coca-Cola: "Jesus Christ: He's the Real Thing."[a]

Every time I walk into an evangelical bookstore it's too easy for me to dismiss much of this stuff as Jesus junk. But someone finds it worth buying. Why else would stores stock it?

Judging others' taste in knickknacks and clothing is not helpful. Still, I wish evangelicals asked pointed questions about the goods they peddle and purchase. Maybe even questions like these:

- What's my motivation for buying? Self-promotion? God-promotion?
- What do these goods say about my view of God?
- What do they say to others about God?

We're not just what we buy. But is that what our purchases say?

RICK JACKSON, SEATTLE PACIFIC UNIVERSITY

[a]For more examples, see Colleen McDannell, *Material Christianity: Religion and Popular Culture in America* (New Haven, Conn.: Yale University Press, 1995).

nonbelievers in culturally relevant ways. They argue that Christian-related products are essential for fulfilling the Great Commission. As one seventeen-year-old expressed it, "I don't want to walk up to anyone with a Bible, but I want to get it across anyway. . . . This [witness-wear] is a way, for teens especially, to show their beliefs. A lot of people will just brush off Jesus, but not if you come to them in a way they can relate to."[25]

Advertisements often capitalize on the ways in which this merchandise is a vehicle for sharing the gospel. The ad for Scripts brand shoes notes how the product is "a great way to share Christ" and have your "feet fitted with the gospel of peace." One ad for a shirt emblazed with the words "Jesus Freak" reads, "From one Jesus Freak to another, it takes one to know one. *Huge witnessing tool!*"[26]

Christian products spur excitement and conviction about one's own faith—even excitement for sharing the faith with others. T-shirts and other witness-wear that display extreme expressions of the Christian faith appeal to the youth. T-shirts saying, "I'll Mosh for Jesus" and "Body Piercing Saved My Life" are brisk sellers among the Christian youth culture.[27] Teens thrive on the extreme—from extreme sports to extreme faith. For teens, "it's all or nothing—do it or die" whether in sports, relationships or faith.[28] Although one may question the appropriateness of the ways in which faith is expressed, few would disagree that it is better to be all out for one's faith than all out for something else.

Delighting. Let's have some fun! After all, "Jesus Saves (especially when He shops at LORD MART!)."[29] No doubt, much merchandise is designed for delight, not deep instruction or effective persuasion. Is that OK?

At MissPoppy.com you can purchase a "Jesus Sports Statue—Football" depicting Jesus completing a "Hail Mary" pass with two tykes at his side. Another product is the rubber Jesus duck for your bath or baptismal; it can be purchased with the "Wash away my sins bubble bath." Why not adorn the dashboard of a car with a bobble-head Jesus? The "Answer Me Jesus" Magic 8 Ball jokingly sees the future: "Ask a question, tip him over, and voilà! YOU know what Jesus would do." Stores and websites sell sport T-shirts and other apparel such as flip-flops, boxer shorts and baseball caps with creative faith expressions. Often witty and clever, sometimes irreverent, such merchandise is meant primarily for fun.

Retail giants—messengers of the gospel. Christian product fans usually see Wal-Mart, eBay, and other retail and Internet giants as welcome partners in the distribution of Christian-related products to mainstream audiences. After Wal-Mart recently allocated shelf space for faith-based toys, supporters urged members of the faith community to seize this opportunity and let their voices be heard by sending the message to other retailers that there is a demand for such products.[30]

Christian retailers surely lose some sales when identical Christian merchandise is sold by larger retail chains in the same area. On the other hand, why shouldn't the larger retailers sell Christian merchandise since Christian retailers peddle "godly" and "family" mainstream products also sold in mainstream stores? Even some owners of small Christian bookstores see the value of mass distribution of Christian materials via retail giants. One owner says, "As a Christian retailer, you're kind of torn because your mission statement, a big part of it, is getting the word of the gospel out. If Wal-Mart is carrying Christian books, is that a bad thing? I'm not sure it is. But obviously, from a business standpoint, it's challenging."[31]

Advocates of Christian merchandise in mega-retail outlets stress that (1) com-

YOGA'S BARE FAITH

Yoga is big business in North America and abroad.[a] Retailers have gone beyond printing images of the Hindu deity Ganesha on stretch pants or mandalas on mat bags. Advertisers are using yoga to market everything from air fresheners and breakfast cereal to lawn food and Korean autos.[b] Even alcohol. An Absolut vodka bottle is balanced upside down on its neck. The ad simply reads "Absolut Yoga."[c]

Traditionalist yogis bristle about such mistreatment of their five-thousand-year-old practice. They reject the commercialization of practices rooted in worldly renunciation and detachment. Are they justified in their criticism?

Marketing the spiritual life may be new to the yoga community, yet it is anything but new to Christianity. Entrepreneurs have long been hawking splinters from the cross and the bones of the saints. WWJD bracelets and Left Behind boxer shorts are just the latest commercial fare.[d]

The yogis' criticism of commercialized religion parallels some evangelicals' fears about Christianized popular culture. Evangelicals rightly ask if Jesus, or at least true faith in him, can be packaged and sold. Yogis question the practice of turning karma, serenity and enlightenment into market commodities. Like ancient Hebrew religion, and later the Christian faith, yoga is grounded in Eastern practices that seem to conflict with Western consumerism.

In spite of their shared Eastern roots, yoga's Hinduism is essentially incompatible with the Christian faith. But they both want to protect the sacredness of their traditions. What are we to make of the fact that two very different religions would share some of the same concerns about commercialized religion?

MARK E. TAYLOR, LOYOLA UNIVERSITY CHICAGO

[a]Julie Schmit, "Big Business Lunges for a Piece of Fat Yoga Profit," *USA Today,* August 30, 2004 <www.usatoday.com/money/companies/2004-08-30-yogabiz_x.htm>.

[b]Megan Lane, "The Tyranny of Yoga" (Oct. 9, 2003) BBC News Online.

[c]This and other ads can be seen in John Philp's documentary *Yoga Inc.*

[d]Ben Witherington, "Accessorizing for Jesus," personal Web log (April 9, 2007) <www.benwitherington.blogspot.com/2007/04/accessorizing-for-jesus_09.html>.

petition is of little threat since such outlets carry a limited range of products, (2) mainstream retailers minister to individuals who would never step into a Christian bookstore, (3) competition will require Christian stores to improve their business practices, and (4) the distribution of Christian products in mainstream retail outlets will ultimately increase the consumer base of the Christian shop by heightening interest in Christian products, driving more consumers into the Christian retail outlets—praise the Lord![32]

JESUS JUNK AND THE GIANTS

Critics of Christian products argue, first, that the sale of these products is "nothing more than an attempt to make money from the gospel," even to "subjugate" the gospel to "financial profits."[33] Jesus junk often subverts or at least waters down the real gospel—in the name of profit.

For instance, the detractors say that Christian products—such as ball caps and T-shirts—with particularly extreme messages hinder the spread of the gospel by inappropriately expressing Christian faith. These products, referred to as "holy paraphernalia," also allegedly hinder the gospel by painting a shallow and incomplete message of Christianity. A shirt with the message "Raise the dead" portrays a staircase leading to a coffin with a hand coming out. A shirt that reads "Don't wait until it's too late" shows an image of a skeleton on its knees. While perhaps a hint of truth—Jesus' triumph over death and the harsh reality of hell, for instance—such expressions tell only part of the gospel message.

Some products, especially Jesus-related merchandise, also stir controversy within the tribe by irreverently portraying Jesus and the Christian faith. From critics' perspective, such mockery is offensive or at least distasteful. Is not Jesus more than "a hip dude" or "the real thing"? The Bible teaches reverence for God, not bringing him down to be "one of the guys." Are consumers making a joke of prayer, for instance, by having a Jesus Magic 8 ball tell them answers to prayer?

Critics ask some tough questions. Are wearers of T-shirts with Christian statements really expressing their faith, or are they embracing the cool, consumerist thing to do? What is the spiritual significance in wearing popular witness-wear?[34] Is the real message in such cases that Jesus is both Savior and a pop icon? That those within the evangelical tribe can embrace Jesus personally while expressing public messages contradictory to the gospel? Does the consumers' image of Jesus shift with the latest clothing and other pop message fads?[35]

Opponents do not want to rule out the possibility that the explosion in the Christian product industry is part of society's obsession with the consumption of material goods. By all accounts, Christians are equating material consumption with "the good life." If, on the other hand, the "good life," according to the gospel, is to strive to be like Jesus,[36] then the consumption of Jesus products fuels an erroneous view of the good life. One critic asks, "How has the historical Christian faith that defeated the Roman empire, changed nations, and transformed the Western world disintegrated to cheap trinkets and religious trash?" He says that evangelicals are the culprits; they purchase products in search of a magic bullet, an easy way out of life's trials and challenges.[37] Might we add, they purchase these products in pursuit of the "good life."

Moreover, critics argue that evangelicals legitimize the consumption of Jesus junk by convincing themselves that they are in pursuit of godly goals. If Christian products are sold on the basis of their ability to sustain a sense of evangelical faith and community, encourage others in the tribe, and propagate the gospel, then purchasing these products becomes legitimate—even if such products cannot really accomplish such deeply spiritual goals. And if the products do not produce buyers' intended effects, the solution is to try buying more of them! Marketers would have evangelicals believe that "thanks to witness wear and other Christian lifestyle products, purchases can have a justified holy purpose. Christian cultural products seem to promise evangelicals that they can consume without being tainted by 'worldliness.'"[38]

Finally, critics worry that Jesus junk marketed to raise money in support of particular organizations further justifies evangelical consumption. For example, C28 (Col 2:8, "not of this world") is a Christian retail store that donates a percentage of all purchases to youth ministries. Kerusso—from the Greek meaning "To herald divine truth as a public crier, to preach the gospel"—claims to be the leading designer and producer of Christian-themed apparel. It sponsors a "Live for Him Red Wristband Project," and 25 cents from each $1.50 wrist band supports Compassion International.[39] The problem, say critics, is not the support of nonprofit groups, but infusing consumption into every aspect of life, even giving. The not-so-subtle message is "Looking good and helping those in need—what a deal."[40]

Retail giants—the other evil. Opponents also argue that the ease and price savings of Internet and mega-store shopping are destroying mom-and-pop Christian bookstores—all in the name of profit, not ministry. Christian bookstores, they say, struggle to sell products that are heavily discounted online and at the big chain stores.[41] Put another way, the big boys get to skim off the profits, while the nearby local bookstores are stuck carrying all kinds of slow-selling stock that the local tribe needs but which is not very profitable.

When it comes to price and quantity, the local Christian bookstores simply cannot compete with the mega-retail and Internet outlets. Many are closing: 244 stores went out of business in 2003, 288 in 2004,[42] and 337 in 2005.[43] One observer warns that Christian bookstores are "in the grip of Goliaths" and struggling to survive.[44]

Owners of Christian bookstores are trying to respond by securing exclusive marketing rights to some of the works of Christian artists. The stores argue on the basis of "loyalty (we made your products a success), ministry (it's more than a business to us), expertise (we can help customers find what they need), and necessity (if the hottest items are available at superstores, especially at a discount, fewer people will shop in our stores)."[45]

MEMORIES OF MERCHANDISE

Although for centuries traditional worship items—crucifixes, religious statues and rosaries—were used by Catholics, religious products marketed primarily to Protestants became a huge economic force during the Industrial Revolution in the early nineteenth century, with such products as Bibles, tracts and a handful of books.[46] These early Christian products were sold by door-to-door salespeople or through catalog orders. The materials were deeply biblical although cheaply made for mass marketing.[47]

As Christian-themed products began appearing in stores in the late-nineteenth and especially through the mid-twentieth centuries, they shared shelf space with nonreligious items in a largely Christian nation. By the end of World War I, however, with rising incomes and the growth of a consumer-based middle class, religious goods were no longer so fashionable and disappeared from store shelves, paving the way for stores specializing in religious goods.[48]

A dramatic increase in the selling of Christian products beyond books occurred in the late 1960s as local Christian bookstores began focusing on more profitable, faster-selling items.[49] Interestingly, for example, in 1967 the Christian Booksellers Association's trade journal advertised only Bibles, but three years later 40 percent of all the advertisements were for items such as cards, jewelry and gifts.[50]

In the 1970s retailers introduced the silver Jesus fish often seen on the backs of cars. This time period also ushered in the height of the countercultural Jesus Movement—a movement of hippie-like evangelicals who produced their own popular music as an alternative to mainstream rock 'n' roll. Hoping to make their own religious art and lives relevant to nonbelievers, they imitated mainstream popular culture in dress, language, communal living, antiestablishment rhetoric and everything else that defined the emerging mainstream youth culture. They readily purchased and displayed goods with slogans such as "Jesus Lives."[51] Since then, new products continue to be marketed: In the late 1990s, more than fifteen million What Would Jesus Do? bracelets were sold worldwide.[52] The week Mel Gibson's film *The Passion of the Christ* opened 75,000 nail pendants were sold.[53]

WHAT A CLONE WE HAVE IN JESUS—ALL OUR SHELVES TO STOCK TODAY!

Christian products are often nothing more than imitations of mainstream merchandise produced and sold by businesses hoping to cash in on popular trends. Focus on the Family's The Last Chance Detectives series is patterned after the Hardy Boys.[54] The Bibleman video and action toys are godly counterparts to Batman. Prayer Circle Friends is a spin on the Build-A-Bear toy idea.[55]

Witness-wear slogans mimic or at least parody mainstream advertising: "Do the Dew." "Jesus is the real thing." "Jesus, is that your final answer?" "Jesus—It's that easy." "Got Jesus?!" Are such parodies fun or plagiarism?[56] Do they communicate real or artificial evangelical faith? Do they enhance mainstream respect for the Christian faith or reduce it? At minimum, mimicking mainstream popular culture tells the world that the Christian retail industry lacks originality, imagination and artistic expression. It is a double-edged sword for the Christian retail industry. Copying market trends brings predictability but often comes at the expense of artistry.[57]

Evangelicals justify such imitation as a means of making the gospel culturally relevant for those outside the tribe. But why does the imitation not work the other way around very often? Why are Christian products not the trendsetters for mainstream copycats? Once a leader in creating art for culture, the church today depends on a mainstream, consumer-based industry where "designers browse malls and trendy secular shops to see what's hot, then create a religious alternative."[58]

SHOULD WE STOP SPENDING FOR THE SAKE OF THE GOSPEL?

Look stylish and donate to charity simultaneously. How? Buy high-end "T-shirts with a Purpose" made by an outfit that donates to charity. Cool?!

Or sell Virtue—"a perfume inspired by Biblical ingredients and marketed as a tool for spiritual attainments." Maybe your church or Christian school could raise funds by peddling this product instead of magazine subscriptions or sub sandwiches. The whole organization could become more virtuous!

Do these kinds of evangelical campaigns promote faith or materialism—or both? Should tribal organizations advocate such campaigns?

Perhaps a growing number of evangelicals are wary of such consumerism. They offer opposing slogans: "The Cult of the Next Thing—Crave and Spend for the Kingdom of Stuff Is Here"; "The Gospel according to Safeway"; "Why the Devil Takes Visa."

What are we to do? We can't maintain a high standard of living without consuming more than we need. But we shouldn't turn the gospel into a consumer cliché. Maybe we can live faithfully by shopping only to satisfy our everyday needs, not for the sake of the gospel. After all, the gospel doesn't need to be bought and sold. The gospel is the gospel. Isn't it?

DIANE M. BADZINSKI, COLORADO CHRISTIAN UNIVERSITY

DISCERNING THE VALUE

Conflicts between fans and critics of Christian products highlight three important tensions: (1) commerce versus ministry, (2) hindering versus helping the spread of the gospel, and (3) poor replicas versus culturally relevant expressions of faith. One strategy for managing these tensions is to critically evaluate the extent to which specific tribal products appropriately and actually serve audiences—whether tribal or mainstream audiences. How effective are Christian products at reaching nonbelievers? At teaching believers? At delighting consumers? In many cases the tribe does not know; the tribe just assumes the products do these things.

A second strategy for managing these tensions is to carefully consider the extent to which Christian products communicate the faith authentically, without distortion or deception or other watering down. What messages are communicated through Jesus junk and other alleged kitsch? One tribal observer says evangelicals should take "the lead ourselves in transforming culture and creating community and meaningful lifestyles in the new social, economic, and technical environment. We need to be demonstrating how faith works in this world of replicas and clones—not just adding to the conundrum by 'repeating ourselves' as we regurgitate clichés instead of living the truth in love."[59]

A third strategy is to develop a set of guidelines for discerning the spiritual worth of particular products. A tribal critic proposes the following guidelines for determining the value, if any, of Christian-related merchandise:[60]

- Does the joining of the holy with the common compromise the message of the cross?
- Does this [product] smack of using the name of Jesus for the sake of profit?
- If it is used as a message for evangelism, will the message be taken seriously based on how it is delivered?
- Do we need to make a "Christian" everything?
- Do you seriously desire to be associated with all of the other Christians who cover their bodies with Jesus junk?

The bottom line is that evangelicals need to discern the worth of Christian products before either consuming or peddling them so that evangelicals do not exchange the "glory of the incorruptible God for an image in the form of corruptible man" (Rom 1:23).

CONCLUSION

Jordan, who was mentioned at the beginning of this chapter, ought to be commended for showing discernment with her remark that she was not sure what to make of the host of MTV's *Punk'd* wearing Jesus Is My Homeboy garb. Jordan may have wondered whether he was displaying his identity with Christ or mocking Christ. Perhaps Jordan was shocked at his irreverence and disrespect for her Savior. Regardless, Jordan's puzzlement suggests a willingness to weigh varying viewpoints prior to rendering a judgment of the appropriateness of the attire.

Perhaps evangelicals will have to recognize that their entire lives—everything they believe, do and say—is part of their witness to the tribe and to the wider world. Perhaps as part of their journey of faith in a media world they need to examine where and how they shop, what they purchase, and what they expect products and services to do for them and for others.

14

Converting Comic Books into Graphic Novels and Digital Cartoons

THOMAS J. CARMODY

Mark became an evangelical through the ministry of a local church and got excited about sharing his faith with classmates. Not raised in a church, however, he knew little about the Bible, even less about theology. He could not imagine himself speaking to others about his faith, especially compared to radio ministers and local pastors he heard frequently. He thought maybe evangelism was not his calling.

Then, while visiting a Christian bookstore, he stumbled upon small, inexpensive, evangelistic comic books. Excited, he purchased a bunch of them and gave some to classmates. His friends often laughed at the biblical messages in the comics but still read them and even swapped them with one other. They even asked him questions about the simple Bible messages in the tracts and about his own faith. He began to realize that he had discovered a familiar, seemingly nonthreatening medium that could lead others to Christ.

Traditionally, critics view comics as "crude, poorly-drawn, semiliterate, cheap, disposable kiddie fare."[1] Fans recognize instead that comics take many forms and sometimes even, like literature, address basic human issues "dear to our hearts: faith, hope, belief, guilt, justice, redemption, ultimate meaning, ultimate evil."[2] Evangelicals, too, are creating and using comics, even exploring how they might be used faithfully in new media to inform, persuade and delight readers.[3]

Foolish Things That Confound the Wise

One major comic book artist, writer and theorist defines comics as "juxtaposed pictorial and other images in deliberate sequence, intended to convey information and/or produce an aesthetic response in the viewer."[4] In other words, comics are sequential art that is not bound by any particular form, style, genre, topic or purpose. They are open narrative conduits that allow artists and writers to present visual stories "in bold and unique ways, for any audience and on any subject they please."[5]

Most North Americans have grown up reading comics, watching Saturday morning cartoons or visiting the local movie theater to view the most recent rendition of their favorite superhero. Their different exposure to comics, however, often leads them to dismiss the medium's power and capacity to communicate. But the fact is that "more people read comics and comic books than any other form of literature on earth."[6] Comics have a kind of universal appeal across age, cultures and even religions.

Evangelicals have discovered the adaptability of comics as a communication medium, particularly because they desire to share their faith with others. Evangelicals typically are the first Christian tribe to embrace established or emerging narrative platforms, and comic books are no exception.

Comic books and tracts. Comic books are "low cost, low tech, long lasting, repeat reading, and already familiar to billions of people."[7] Additionally, they appeal to younger readers or adults who are learning to read or learning a new language. Their simple, entertaining format often aids nonliterate people in becoming literate.[8]

Comic book tracts have been a staple in contemporary evangelical circles for over forty years.[9] These low-cost little comic books usually contain simple illustrations and a basic message designed either to persuade their readers to come to salvation or to teach important moral or religious principles. This visual medium tends not to turn off readers because it seems so entertaining, familiar and unassuming. What harm would it do for someone to read a mere tract? In the reader's mind, this experience is not nearly as threatening as reading the Bible or stepping inside a church. This is why comics and comic books are among the most low profile, inoffensive and prolific methods of spreading the gospel around the world.[10] They have been used extensively by Roman Catholics, mainline Protestants and evangelicals alike.

Japanese artist Nanami Minami has produced for Word of Life Press a number of comic books that teach readers everything from how to understand biblical allusions and expressions found in American films to how to have a happy marriage. She has also written and illustrated an evangelistic comic book that explains her personal conversion while she was an exchange student in the United States.[11]

The United Bible Societies, Africa, produced an easy-to-read comic book in French and Baoulé based on the Gospel of Luke. The book became so popular, especially among youth, that the society planned to translate it for other parts of French-speaking Africa as well.[12] Bible-themed comic books are so effective that United Bible Societies is distributing them to numerous indigenous peoples in their own languages.[13]

Finally, Christians have discovered the delight in using comics and comic books to poke fun at themselves and their religious practices, churches and denominations. Artist John Lawing often poked fun at the idiosyncrasies of both Christian identity and community in the pages of *Christianity Today*.[14] Cartoonist Dave Walker lovingly points out the foibles of his own church life and denomination. At the same time, he hopes to provide a funny way to explain the "inner workings of the church to the outsider."[15]

Graphic novels. One of the most significant advances in the comic book world in the last ten years has been graphic novels. Longer and more detailed in content, artistry, form and binding than traditional comic books, these works once confined to the neighborhood comic bookstore have gone mainstream. Not only have graphic novels found an enthusiastic audience in mainstream media, but they have also found one among evangelicals, some of whom are using graphic novels to evangelize and teach audiences.

Beginning in 2001, Tyndale House Publishers began marketing graphic nov-

WHY WE LOVE AND HATE CARTOONISTS

Cartoons appeal to North Americans. So do cartoonists. When I am introduced to someone in terms of my work as professor or journalist, I get a polite response. When someone finds out I was also a cartoonist for forty years, suddenly I become a worthy conversationalist.

For decades around the turn of the twentieth century, newspaper cartoons appealed to immigrants who might not read English but could figure out the cartoons. They liked to see the political bosses get skewered. Many of us still enjoy a barb aimed at the powers that be, especially when they are doing a lousy job. The hypocritical and foolish actions of Christian leaders are always good cartoon fodder as well.

Those of us who have worked as Christian cartoonists hope that our effectiveness doesn't rest on the illiteracy of our audience. We always wish that our work would influence those who can effect change where needed. We hope our cartoons will be one small step toward advancing Jesus' kingdom. But we usually receive only criticism from readers. Apparently people don't feel strongly enough to applaud when they agree, but they can get mighty angry when they disagree.

As cartooning shifts from India ink and paper to computer-aided illustrating, the basic purposes of cartooning stay the same. What journalist Finley Peter Dunne wrote over a century ago about newspaper, we can say yet today about good cartooning: they're both designed to "comfort the afflicted, and afflict the comfortable." Oddly enough, it sounds like the love-hate job of preaching, too.

So, do you love 'em or hate 'em?

JOHN LAWING, PROFESSOR EMERITUS, REGENT UNIVERSITY

els based on the popular Left Behind book series. These works contain high-quality graphics that stay true to the storyline of the original books and are designed to evangelize young readers who may not be willing or able to read the works in the traditional format.[16]

Head Press Publishing published in the Eye Witness trilogy two graphic novels that vividly portray the passion of Christ and stories from the book of Acts in an updated storyline filled with "archaeological discoveries, kidnappings, and car bombs."[17] The author and publisher of these novels says that his goal is to "not only provide entertainment for existing Christians, but be very enlightening to those who might have never had an interest in exploring Christianity before."[18]

Graphic novels and nonfiction also instruct. Novels such as *I Was an Eighth-Grade Ninja* are coming-of-age stories with classic, even if moralistic, battles of good versus evil. There are also graphic novels that tell and teach the stories of great missionaries and saints and the life of Pope John Paul II.[19] Many Bible-themed novels take their basic storyline directly from the Old and New Testaments and are designed to help readers visualize the great heroes of faith. Graphic novels accomplish this educational goal by "communicating as much through images as through words."[20]

Zondervan, a large evangelical publishing house, released twelve different novels to launch six series of Japanese manga-style works for three different age groups.[21] This publisher recognizes that manga novels are a significant influence on preteen and teen audiences. Zondervan incorporated cutting-edge graphics with new fictional storylines and familiar stories from the Bible in the hope of teaching, delighting and persuading audiences—as well as turning a profit.[22]

One of the hottest graphic novels in the mainstream media was written by a former evangelical university art student. Doug TenNapel's unusual *Creature Tech* is "heartfelt, touching in a strange way, and serious about concepts like faith and family without being preachy or corny."[23] TenNapel seeks to infuse the topics of "sin, redemption, politics and science into his plots."[24] He believes that many Christians want to take the easy way out when it comes to producing and understanding any type of graphic or visual art. TenNapel claims that "Christians are going to have to learn that art isn't automatically good if it's made by Christians. And Hollywood will have to learn that art isn't automatically bad if it's made by Christians."[25]

Comics and the digital age. Aware of the growth of digital technology and the Internet, many evangelicals have embraced high-tech producers and distribution channels for comics as well as other art forms. They see new media—from cell phones to iPods and laptop computers—as ways that comics may be accessed, ordered, transmitted and created.[26]

For instance, digital comic book tracts still follow the sequential art form that

WILL GRAPHIC NOVELS REDEEM COMICS?

Buying a comic book used to lead dedicated fans to questionable stores to purchase low-budget tales about their favorite superhero's cosmic struggle with evil. In the 1950s some adults even worried that communists were using comics to indoctrinate youth, whereas most youth sought adventure and an imaginative outlet.[a]

Today, comics are legit—just check any mainstream bookstore's classy display of graphic novels. They're hot. They sell—big time. They are like old-fashioned comic books but longer and with more complex and mature storylines. They're also bound like books rather than magazines.

Now tribal publishers and bookstores have hopped on board. But are they just capitalizing on sales trends? Or hoping to spread the gospel beyond the tribe through the artful interplay of text and comic illustrations?

Nonbelievers do read graphic novels. Mainstream schools are using them even to reach reluctant readers.[b] It's become a mass medium of sorts.

When William Eisner popularized the phrase "graphic novel" in the late 1970s, he envisioned a literary art form that could explore serious themes differently than what was possible merely with prose.[c] Today these novels include everything from funny and entertaining stories to dark and serious ones.

These are not like squeaky-clean Christian romance novels! Some graphic novels do explore basic philosophical questions about life. Will Christian writers and publishers use the medium to address questions about God? If so, will mainstream as well as tribal readers buy gospel-inspired versions?

STEPHANIE D. DAVIS, SPRING ARBOR UNIVERSITY

---

[a]Charles Temple, Mariam Martinez and Junko Yokota, eds., *Children's Books in Children's Hands: An Introduction to Their Literature* (Boston: Pearson, 2006), p. 6.

[b]Phillip Crawford, "A Novel Approach: Using Graphic Novels to Attract Reluctant Readers and Promote Literacy," *Library Media Connection* 22, no. 5 (2004): 26-29.

[c]Lorena O'English, J. Gregory Matthews and Elizabeth Blakesley Lindsay, "Graphic Novels in Academic Libraries: From *Maus* to Manga and Beyond," *The Journal of Academic Librarianship* 32, no. 3 (2006): 173-82.

is the foundation of any comic book, but they may also include music, photographs, or digitally enhanced or created images combined with text.[27] Since they are digital, they do not have to be purchased and handed directly to a person; rather, they can be downloaded and emailed to anyone at anytime.[28] Sharing a religious comic book tract with someone on the other side of the world or just across the street is as easy as clicking a mouse.[29] At least one website is designed to help evangelicals who desire to draw comics but are intimidated by digital technology. The site provides information to assist individuals to use the digital programs such as Flash and Shockwave to create animated cartoons.[30]

Comics in the digital age promote a kind of democratic, decentralized communications movement—a movement that is neither hierarchical nor formal but popular—with many loosely connected members across cultures and geography. New graphic computer programs enable even those who are not talented artists to create comics, while the Internet provides an opportunity to reach an international audience without the need for a publisher or agent. No longer are Christian fans of comic books limited to just reading about their favorite biblical superheroes; they can now create their own characters and stories to teach biblical principles, persuade audiences to follow Christ, and delight readers and listeners with new comic stories.

Supporters and Detractors Are More Than Comical

Evangelical fans are convinced that comics and comic books can contribute to the church and be relevant to the human condition by

- presenting evangelistic messages at home and overseas
- teaching biblical precepts through storylines taken from the Bible or adapted from the lives of Christian missionaries, saints and leaders
- reaching an audience that is predisposed to respond to vivid visual images
- helping members of a specific tribe to become more humble by poking fun at themselves
- aiding nonliterate people to learn to read

Fans point to examples of each of these uses of the medium. Often they know from their own experiences that what the general public sometimes dismisses as a secondary, ineffective medium can take on a very important role in the life of individuals, small groups of advocates and even broader cultural movements, including religious ones. People do get into this medium just as much as they get into books and movies.

Mainstream comics are remarkably open to people of faith, unlike some of the other mass media. Consider the gentle, sometimes openly Christian messages presented by Charles Schulz in his *Peanuts* comic strips, or the occasionally dramatically evangelistic and theo-pointed presentations by Johnny Hart in his *B.C.* and *Wizard of Id* comic strips. The socially and politically astute work of Pulitzer Prize-winning cartoonist Doug Marlette similarly demonstrates that Christian artists can gain influential positions in mainstream media through the art of comics.[31]

Despite evangelicals' general acceptance of comics and comic books, however, tribal critics continue to express concerns. Some decry the artistic merit of many Christian cartoonists, claiming that their illustrations are substandard

MY LIFE AS A WACKY WEB CARTOONIST DEPICTING THE DEVIL

For twelve years I have created an online cartoon, *Reverend Fun,* usually five times weekly, in color, with captions.[a]

I like ludicrous cartoons that throw off readers and make them laugh or think. Like two children playing cards on the grass: "I'll trade you two Billy Grahams for your Oral Roberts." Or a pastor at the pulpit who says while pointing to the side: "Before we take an offering I have a couple of announcements . . . First of all, I wanted to present the new church ATM."

I depict the devil as a cutesy idiot rather than the usual, ghoulish Satan. Why take the devil seriously? He's basically a dummy who lives a preposterous lie. But my pixie devils with comical horns do elicit email from upset readers who want a monstrous Satan.

I don't write *Reverend Fun* explicitly to evangelize. If I did, who'd read it? Yet I get email from atheists and agnostics who like the cartoon. One atheist magazine even interviewed me because it appreciated the fact that I didn't sugarcoat Christianity.[b] The Rev. got them thinking about faith—even asking me questions about it. On their website they published a *Reverend Fun* cartoon depicting an open coffin with a guy standing over it saying, "Poor ol' atheist Joe . . . All dressed up, and nowhere to go." Wild!

I also get notes from Christians who use *Reverend Fun* to generate religious discussions with nonbelievers. The Gospel Communications Network, which launched and hosts the cartoon, even published two books of *Reverend Fun* comics.

People respond differently to religious humor. Visit my website and let me know what you think about *Reverend Fun.*

DENNIS HENGEVELD (REV. FUN), GOSPEL COMMUNICATIONS NETWORK

[a]See my website at <www.reverendfun.com/>.

[b]"Reverend Fun, the Interview," Freethunk! <freethunk.net/reverend-fun/reverend-fun-interview.php>.

and their storylines lack imagination, while others complain that comics and comic books do not reflect the sacredness required to properly communicate biblical truth.[32]

Such criticisms do not appear to be valid from at least a marketing perspective. Evangelical publishers go to considerable effort and cost to produce quality products that can teach, delight and persuade their target audiences. They know, too, that consumer expectations are high because most evangelical fans are familiar with high-quality mainstream productions. Additionally, they probably realize that sequential, art-like comic books have been an important method of communicating sacred truth throughout Christian history.

Comics in Church

Sequential art, which many believe is the foundation of all comics and comic books, has long been part of the arts in Christianity.[33] Throughout history, a majority of the church's members and potential converts could not read. Visually oriented, relatively simple, chronological art has been a significant part of the church's efforts to teach, delight and persuade for over a thousand years—long before the printed word.

The stations of the cross. The stations of the cross or way of the cross is essentially a presentation of sequential art in stations or graphic, comic-like frames that mark important events in the passion of Christ.[34] The stations present various biblical and tradition-derived events in the final hours of Jesus' life on earth as a visual tool to aid Christians in remembering and meditating on the passion. These events cover Jesus' condemnation by Pilate to his entombment in Joseph of Arimathea's crypt.

Often portrayed in sculpture, paintings, stained glass or other media, the various station frames have been recreated (and thus reinterpreted by new artists) in probably hundreds of thousands if not millions of church grounds and buildings around the world. Roman Catholics and some Protestant tribes walk to each of the stations sequentially, prayerfully, meditatively, recalling the sacrifice of Christ for the sins of humanity. In some of the larger cathedrals, where congregants in the back could not see and could barely hear the Mass occurring at the front, the stations depicted on the walls and windows gave participants an opportunity to recall the death and resurrection of Christ before participating in the paschal banquet (the Eucharist). Mel Gibson's *The Passion of the Christ* film was essentially his filmic interpretation of the stations.

The bronze doors. One of the most famous artworks in the world is a group of gilded bronze doors dating from the fourteenth to the mid-fifteenth century, found in a church in Florence, Italy. These doors created during the Renaissance consist of twenty-eight rectangular panels in sequence, depicting scenes from the Bible. Each panel is designed to be read separately, starting at the upper left corner like a page of a book.[35] In an area where the majority of the Catholic people were illiterate at the time, these sequentially portrayed images allowed everyone present to visualize some of the stories of Christianity.

Stained-glass windows. Some of the most stunning, evocative sequential art anywhere in the world exists in the many stained-glass windows adorning Europe's medieval and Renaissance cathedrals. Just as in comics, many of these windows are visual representations of Bible stories or the lives of saints; they were created primarily to teach aspects of the Christian faith. While such stained glass "was undoubtedly valued for its contribution to the beauty, sanctity and richness of the church building, it was also employed as an effective means of communication, and a comprehensible means of instruction to the faithful worshiper."[36] When these cathedrals were constructed, most of the local population was illiterate, so it was helpful to use pictorial language as illustrated by the stained-glass windows to instruct the faithful in Christian truths.[37] In a sense, many churches' stained-glass windows are like beautiful, religious comic books that aid devotion and learning as well as offer aesthetic delight.

Nineteenth-century published works. In North America between the 1820s and the beginning of the twentieth century, the publication and distribution of biblically themed graphic works probably reached their height. Since literacy was more widespread in this country during the nineteenth century than in medieval or Renaissance Europe, evangelistic Christians turned to the printing press and the graphic artist rather than the sculptor or painter to mass produce visual messages.

During this time, the American Tract Society and the American Sunday School Union developed a large number of graphic tracts, books and beginning readers. These sequential artistic works were designed to teach readers how to lead moral lives by abstaining from various vices, and to persuade with evangelistic messages directed at anyone who was not an active church member.[38] These inexpensively mass-produced text-and-image booklets became the forerunners of today's modern comic book tracts and graphic novels. Oddly enough, even mainstream comics and comic books owe much to the legacy of the Bible tract. As we see later, mainstream comics' storylines frequently focus on the human condition and often raise the same basic issues addressed by Scripture.

MUST SUPERHEROES BE EVANGELICAL?

Some of the most popular comic books containing powerful religious themes or storylines are produced by mainstream media. Many comic books released by such mammoth media players as Marvel Comics (the home of Spider-Man, X-Men and the Fantastic Four) and DC Comics (the home of Superman, Batman and Wonder Woman) tell mythic stories in which characters are engaged in the universal battle between good and evil. These narratives richly address justice, self-sacrifice, guilt, repentance and redemption. Some are moralistic, but most are remarkably nuanced and intellectually challenging.

The stories presented in comic book form usually contain implicit or explicit theological issues.[39] Stan Lee, creator of Spider-Man and many other superheroes, wrote that he "wasn't consciously trying to inject religious themes" into his stories, but it is obvious that "religious and mythological themes are dramatically intertwined in comic books."[40]

For instance, a character like Superman provides a wonderful springboard to discuss many of the biblical and theological attributes of Christ.[41] The Man of

Steel is loving, self-sacrificing, kind, compassionate, patient, gentle and faithful. He seeks justice for the poor, the oppressed and the hurting. Superman is a Christ figure, not Jesus Christ, the Holy Spirit or the Creator; yet it is hard to imagine Western culture accepting these kinds of comic book heroes without an underlying notion of ultimate, personal goodness, namely, God. In fact, Superman's weakness (kryptonite) suggests that he is not omnipotent or omnipresent like Christ; Superman's weaknesses are distinctly human and point to the fallenness of humankind.[42]

In spite of having superpowers or heightened human abilities, the majority of the characters in mainstream comic books are presented as truly human. These characters often struggle with relational problems, financial difficulties, physical disabilities, gender bias and difficulties encountered as a result of racial and ethnic stereotyping. They may be superheroes, but they are far from perfect beings, certainly not gods. For instance, Peter Parker (Spider-Man) is always having relational problems with his girlfriend, Mary Jane, and he is perpetually short of money because he only works as a freelance photographer for the local newspaper.

Moreover, Superman's goodness enables readers to imagine how they might be more like him, so the readers are open to being "evangelized" into such virtue. Clearly superheroes do teach, delight and persuade especially younger readers how to live in the service of others, even though human beings do not have as much power as the heroes. Though some people may denounce using mainstream superheroes as role models when discussing the Christian faith and its saints, "if we disqualify a character from having Christ-like aspects solely because he does not act exactly like Christ, then we cut ourselves off from many opportunities to point out Christ in fictional characters that attract the attention of people who need him."[43]

On the other hand, detractors complain that this medium overall is filled with too much violence as well as with immorally clad superheroes who accomplish feats that only God could undertake. One response to this concern is that "the stories that move us are the ones we most need to hear about to be whole. So in some crazy way, these stories filled with violence and people in skintight leotards draw us closer to the sacred, and inspire us in our own quest to do good."[44]

Likewise, biblical characters themselves are often immoral people who certainly lived in violent, wicked times. Comics and comic books do use excessive, unnecessarily violent, and erotic depictions at times, just as do other media. Still, even when these books are graphically sexual and violent, they are relatively unrealistic still shots, not more realistic moving-image media. Perhaps comics and comic books affect readers more (at least more than moving-image media) on the basis of what the reader brings to the pages (personal experience and imagination and discernment) than on what the pages bring to the reader (the mere images and words on the page).

Comic books are also one of the few mainstream media in which a reader may actually come to know and learn about the religious perspectives and affiliations of many its major characters:[45]

- Clark Kent, and his alter ego Superman, is Methodist.
- Bruce Wayne, and his alter ego Batman, is either an Episcopalian or Roman Catholic.
- Peter Parker, and his alter ego Spider-Man, is Protestant.
- Kurt Wagner, and his alter ego Nightcrawler, is Roman Catholic.
- Anna Marie, and her alter ego Rogue, is Southern Baptist.
- Matt Murdock, and his alter ego Daredevil, is Roman Catholic.

SHOULD A CHRISTIAN COMIC BOOK ALWAYS PORTRAY THE TRUTH?

But can there be too much honesty when it comes to telling Bible stories in visual media? Mark Carpenter directs Dust Press, which creates comics based on Bible stories. He believes that these stories should be portrayed honestly, even when they involve violence.

His goal? Honesty. Tell it like it is—no sanitized, safe stories. No simplistic resolutions. As Carpenter puts it, "We ask the questions but we don't resolve them."[a] God's in charge. But terrible things do happen in these stories.

The story that turned him on to depicting the Bible visually is the parable of the good Samaritan. The road in that parable was probably about thirty inches wide, a real haven for scoundrels who could quickly jump out and attack travelers. Carpenter imagined telling that story as it looked and felt for the beaten man and the Samaritan who risked his life to help. A great cartoonist, Carpenter concluded, should not simply entertain through storytelling, but "tell it as it is—the politics, the geography, the culture."[b]

Carpenter hears most criticism from parents, not younger readers. Parents ask him where the "joy of the Lord" is in his comics. He replies that he seeks to be honest about each story: "If we are dishonest, if we hold things back from children, they discover that later and there's a backlash. 'You weren't honest with me.' 'You didn't trust me.' 'You didn't empower me to deal with that.' Bye, goodbye, and they're gone. So on behalf of the church-at-large we need to be honest." Sometimes graphically so.

TOM CARMODY, VANGUARD UNIVERSITY

[a]Mark Carpenter, interview by the author, tape recording, Costa Mesa, California, August 23, 2007.

[b]Ibid. Dust Press has even produced comics on engaging stories like Elijah and the prophets of Baal.

Comic books do not emphasize these tribal connections, but they nevertheless use them to help explain aspects of a character's life, including motivation, and to develop some plotlines. It is unimaginable that TV shows and feature movies would so consistently tie major heroes to faith traditions. There is a freedom in comic books that resists the mainstream media pressure to secularize content.

Not all mainstream comic book characters are evangelical or even Christian. Yet their heroes, storyline and themes tend to address a worldview rather than just seek to entertain. This is why both evangelicals and nonevangelicals often find the medium intellectually if not theologically appealing. These stories often are like literature or more serious films that address the human condition, even if their artistic sensibilities are significantly different. Comic books do not pretend to be fine art or stained-glass depictions of the saints, but they do establish scenarios that are frequently worthy of serious discussion by members of religious tribes.

Conclusion

Evangelical fans recognize that comic books can often act as discussion starters to begin religious conversations with Christian and non-Christian friends.[46] Comics and comic books are and have always been literature for the masses—and this is probably what interests (and worries) so many people about them. They are inexpensive to produce, hard to keep from being distributed, and potentially subversive to the powers that be. As evangelical fans point out, though, Jesus Christ was and is subversive. The gospel is revolutionary, sometimes even for the church! So individuals and small groups of people have taken up the medium throughout history to spread their messages as well as have a bit of fun. Today evangelicals like Mark, mentioned in this chapter's introduction, hot off the sawdust trail, see real potential in this medium even as critics worry about who will seize the medium in the digital age.

15

Evangelicals' Quest to Find God's Place in Games

KEVIN SCHUT

Shortly after graduating from college, my wife and I taught at a West African school for missionary families. One day I engaged seventh-graders in a discussion about role-playing games (RPGs) like Dungeons & Dragons (D&D). "Are they really evil?" students asked. "Well," I replied carefully, "Some people can kind of get too involved. But I've played them a lot, and I believe that you're not in any danger if you play moderately and if you can separate fantasy from reality."

The next day one student's father, a school administrator, called me into his office and kindly but firmly explained that I was wrong. Playing games like D&D involved evil spirits, he warned. They are not innocent pastimes. Was he right?

Enter the Dragon

RPGs emerged in the late 1960s as gamers in the war-gaming subculture shifted from using generic miniatures to playing make-believe characters in imaginary worlds.[1] In these games, players create fantastic heroes or villains—such as Tolkienesque wizards, flying heroes and vampires. Game referees (often called game masters or dungeon masters) tell players what is happening in the imaginary world, and the players respond by explaining what their characters attempt to do. Actions are resolved according to the game rules and referees' decisions.

The notoriety of D&D, the first commercially successful RPG, stemmed partly from several well-documented cases of suicide. Parents blamed D&D for destabilizing their children, and both mainstream and tribal evangelical media publicized these stories. Public anti-gaming campaigns also accused D&D of promoting occult activities,[2] such as performing gestures and reciting magical incantations.[3] Game fans (including Christians) aggressively countered these charges, accusing the anti-game campaigners of fabricating evidence, misrepresenting events and blowing potential problems out of proportion.[4] Even though the public flap subsided in the early 1990s, some evangelicals still believe that such games promote the occult.[5]

Ironically, a more recent evangelical movement argues that RPGs and other games can be God's tools if used persuasively for evangelism or to instruct children in biblical values. These opposing views shape how the tribe responds to the growth of a huge, global gaming industry—primarily, although not exclusively, based on the sale of digital games (games for both personal computers and video game consoles like the Xbox 360).[6]

However, evangelical fans and critics alike often miss some bigger points. First, like all forms of culture, games can carry sin and grace, and promote evil and good. Second, like all media, games are capable of teaching, persuading and delighting. Too much emphasis on teaching and persuading is likely to stifle the creative possibilities of gaming. Finally, thinking clearly about games means looking at more than game content—it means considering the strengths and weaknesses of the medium as a whole.

KEY DEFINITION

Role-playing games merge storytelling with game rules, creating a powerful mix of drama and competition.

Mixed Games

North American culture includes an enormous universe of games: board games, card games, social games like RPGs, and computer or video games. In this chapter, the term *game* refers to *all* of these kinds of games, whereas specific types of games are referred to by their format or medium, such as *digital* games, *board* games or RPGs. Differences are obvious: a standard card game looks and sounds vastly different from a cinematic video game. Nevertheless, there are significant similarities and connections between different game types: they all involve play structured by rules, and many gamers like to play multiple kinds of games.[7]

Evangelicals are deeply involved in all types of games. In addition to playing and making mainstream games, some of them support an explicitly tribal gaming industry. Evangelical groups review games, provide information about mainstream and tribal games, discuss games online and in print, and sometimes publicly attack gamers and games in both political and cultural arenas.

Gamers gain delight, instruction and skill. Like mainstream fans, evangelicals justify games primarily as fun to make and play. A Christian game company says that "a game should not only have good content but should be fun to play. It is our wish that the games you buy from us will bring hours of enjoyment and laughter to your family or play group."[8]

Moreover, some evangelicals cite mainstream studies documenting educational benefits of digital games, such as greater hand-eye coordination[9] and intellectual growth.[10] One youth pastor notes that video games teach multitasking.[11] In addition, evangelicals sometimes argue that games can teach tribal values and beliefs, even "enlighten believers and nonbelievers concerning God's truths by providing entertainment that is rich with Christian content. These productions must be highly entertaining and engaging in order to create 'teachable moments.'"[12]

Tribal and mainstream enthusiasts further claim that gaming teaches or at least facilitates positive social skills, such as friendship—especially playing massively multiplayer online games (usually called MMOGs). Evangelical computer and video gamers often join game-playing guilds or clans that function like a combination of a family, a military unit, a sports team and a social club—if not a youth group.[13] The evangelical players guild (or gaming community) known as the Men of God International has created a military hierarchy with twenty-two ranks based on factors like length of membership and service to the community.[14] Other tribal guilds, including Fans for Christ and the Christian Gamers Alliance, have formed around the online discussion of digital games and RPGs.[15] The Christian Gamers' Guild says that "players are interacting with each other, sharing time together and getting to know each other, sometimes to a depth of understanding that few pursuits encourage. At the same time, they are creating the social interactions of their characters, experimenting with questions of how people relate to each other."[16]

Another justification for gaming is what I call "the Inklings defense." J. R. R. Tolkien, a devout Catholic and writer of *The Lord of the Rings*, argued that fantasy stories create make-believe worlds or "secondary realities" which can help readers to understand the good and bad within our own world.[17] Author and Christian apologist C. S. Lewis likewise contended that myth (foundational stories about human beings, their nature and their place in the world) can connect people with spiritual reality even if the stories themselves are not literally true.[18] As a tribal RPG enthusiast puts it, "I find that one of the most beautiful parts of D&D is the chance to stretch the imagination. A player can imagine other worlds, mystical creatures, endless seas, magnificent cities and more. When we were children we imagined things like this, at least I would say most of us did. Isn't our imagination a gift from God?"[19]

Finally, evangelical fans have increasingly viewed games as evangelistic tools. They have used MMOGs as virtual or imaginary places for witnessing to mainstream gamers. The Spirit of Elijah gaming guild, for instance, aims to "bring the light of Jesus to [the MMOG] Guild Wars."[20] Many evangelical guilds post a plan for salvation on their websites. In "Confessions of a Dungeons & Dragons Addict,"[21] an RPG fan discusses how his involvement with his gaming groups has helped him lead some players to a saving relationship with Christ.

Critics worry about false teachings, bad behavior and susceptible gamers. Tribal critics seem to be louder and more common than tribal fans—especially regarding digital games. Sex and violence seem to be their greatest concerns. They worry that game violence is potentially worse than TV or film violence because players *enact* repugnant and antisocial behavior instead of just watching it. *Christianity Today* writes, "Good teachers know three things that contribute to effective learning: active participation, rehearsing behavioral sequences rather than discrete acts, and repetition, repetition, repetition. Video games employ all three."[22] Opponents also blast the mainstream game The Sims and its sequel for allowing, and perhaps promoting, extramarital sex and homosexual behavior.[23]

Evangelicals' broader and long-standing concern, however, seems to be that

IS FANTASY FOR EVANGELICALS?

Quick! Name the most popular movie series of recent years. I'll give you a hint: a ring. Short guys with big feet. How about in the last thirty years? Think "May the Force be with you."

What do films like *Lord of the Rings* and *Star Wars* have in common? Myth and legend. Symbols of the divine and supernatural. Magic. Make-believe.

Why do we enjoy such stories? Maybe fantasy worlds with religious themes offer "apotheosis"—"the meeting with the god."[a] C. S. Lewis called it "passing into beauty."[b] Could fantastical films thereby give us insight into the real world we inhabit?

The otherworldly storytelling in these films should ring true for most evangelicals. Christianity is fantastic faith in the unseen God. And evangelicals put their faith in someone who is supernatural, Jesus Christ. Plus, there are plenty of biblical parallels: elves are like angels; magic like miracles; Frodo like Christ; Vader like Satan. Good triumphs over evil in the end.

So why should evangelicals fear fantasy? Perhaps fantasy can bring some viewers frighteningly close to the dark side. Or perhaps evangelicals fear imaginative storytelling. Wizards in gray robes and evil lords in black masks can look strange, even dangerous.

Viewers today need discernment and savvy to understand how fantasy works and to distinguish between it and spiritual reality. Frodo and Vader provide opportunities for us to look past "what something is" to "what something stands for."

JENNIFER LETHERER, SPRING ARBOR UNIVERSITY

[a]Joseph Campbell, *The Hero with a Thousand Faces* (Princeton, N.J.: Princeton University Press, 1973), p. 149.

[b]C. S. Lewis, *The Weight of Glory* (San Francisco: HarperSanFrancisco, 2001), p. 42.

games take players' minds off of God and godly things.[24] In their view, games can foster an overly competitive attitude out of tune with Christian neighborliness. "No one gets a high score by receiving unmerited mercy,"[25] writes one detractor. A tribal magazine editor criticizes Rockstar Games (maker of *Grand Theft Auto*) for encoding a bankrupt worldview into its games: "Others exist only to make us feel good. After that, dispose of them."[26] Writers in tribal magazines share anecdotes about children acting antisocially and obsessively because of supposedly occult-inspired imagery and narratives of many of the Pokémon creatures.[27] A few evangelicals still argue that a standard deck of playing cards is based on occult traditions and includes coded satanic messages.[28]

Tribal critics assume that digital games especially can subtly seduce players into false beliefs and destructive behaviors. One critic says of The Sims, "I played for seven hours straight at my first sitting. I hardly stopped to eat or empty my own bladder (and mind you, I was eight months pregnant at the time)." We "run the risk that playing god will seem preferable to being ourselves. . . . [We can] become so busy trying to save our virtual realities that we scarcely notice Creation itself is groaning."[29] Sociologist Michael Jindra says that games' enticing "alternative universes" are ultimately isolating and addictive.[30] Such arguments echo the worries of a chess-loving pastor who confessed in a seventeenth-century tract on the morality of gaming: "When I have done with it, it hath not done with me."[31] The "low-cost or no-cost failure [of games] can encourage young people to try everything once," contends a contemporary critic. "Life, however, doesn't always offer second chances."[32]

WHEN THE GAMES BEGAN

Games were common and apparently widely played in practically all eras,[33] although early Christian authors did not write much about them. The apostle Paul is certainly aware of sports, which he uses for analogies (1 Cor 9:24-27). However, the early church's concerns about games likely referred to the bloody arenas where so many Christians were martyred, and not to everyday gaming among friends, usually in their homes.

Contemporary assumptions about the good and bad of gaming arose in the medieval and early modern period. Recorded sermons and treatises attacked the evils of gambling (games of chance), the slothfulness attributed to gaming and the potentially addictive nature of games.[34] Many listed games with objectionable behaviors. Pastor John Northbrooke's 1577 book title covers the landscape: *A Treatise Against Dicing, Dancing, Plays, and Interludes: With Other Idle Pastimes.*[35] The lesson seemed to be keep working and avoid leisure.

Other earlier Christians praised the nobility of chess, talked about games as God's gift of entertainment, and wrote about gaming rules and strategies. In the

ALTERNATIVE UNIVERSES—FOR BETTER OR WORSE?

Some argue that digital virtual worlds of MMOGs create "alternative universes," such as those in EverQuest, World of Warcraft and the various Sims. One non-gaming virtual world, Second Life, is used for both educational and recreational (sometimes deviant) purposes. It has even generated its own virtual economy (whose currency can be traded for real-world dollars), which compares to the size of the economies of small countries.

In some ways, the desire to enter into another world may be evidence of humans' status as sojourners here on earth, our sense that we really belong someplace else—"heaven is my home." But are human excursions into virtual universes only innocent, temporary distractions—perhaps merely necessary escapes from the real, stressful world? Or are these journeys into unreality evidence of humans' yearning for a better life and world to inhabit?

Consider that some of these alternative universes are utopian and others dystopian or apocalyptic. For many players, these games may meet, for better or worse, some kind of spiritual need for a meaningful vision of the future. Maybe these virtual worlds simply fulfill base human desires for power and control. In the case of MMOGs, they might be ways of connecting socially with others while remaining in control.

Christian communities supposedly allow for deeper face-to-face relationships, which include leaving oneself open and vulnerable to others. Is something lacking in such faith communities that creates believers' own desires to seek out better worlds? How can Christian communities and MMOGs coexist—if at all?

MICHAEL JINDRA, SPRING ARBOR UNIVERSITY

thirteenth century, King Alfonso X of Portugal wrote in the preface to *Libro de Juegos* (Book of Games): "Because God wanted that man have every manner of happiness, in himself naturally, so that he could suffer the cares and troubles when they came to them, therefore men sought out many ways that they could have this happiness completely. Wherefore they found and made many types of play and pieces with which to delight themselves."[36]

Recent Tribal Divisions

Tribal fans and critics of gaming have increasingly sounded like earlier tribal observers of popular novels and movies. The rise of RPGs and digital games in the late 1970s and early 1980s elicited two irreconcilable perspectives toward gaming: *outright rejection* and *loving adoption.*

About the time that concerns over D&D were fading in mainstream media, a public panic emerged over video games. Although mainstream critique of digital game violence dates back at least to the 1970s,[37] public outrage really took off in the early 1990s, largely due to the release of Mortal Kombat, a top-selling combat game that allowed victorious players to perform gruesome, photo-realistic mutilations on fallen enemies.[38] In 1999, reports said that two students who shot classmates and staff at Columbine High School in Littleton, Colorado, fanatically played the first-person shooter game Doom.[39] Media reported concerns about Manhunt, a savage game in which the player takes on the role of a murderer, and the infamous 2005 *Grand Theft Auto: San Andreas* "hot coffee" controversy, caused by a hidden pornographic mini-game that could be unlocked by anyone with the right software (which, of course, was promptly posted on the Internet).[40] Evangelical groups often led such public outcries, angrily denouncing the moral depravity of the digital-game industry and pressing for government legislation and reforms, primarily aimed at protecting children.[41]

Meanwhile, tribal fans of gaming started playing[42] and making their own games. DragonRaid, a Christian RPG, first appeared in 1984.[43] Christian trivia games appeared in the wake of the Trivial Pursuit craze.[44] When the Nintendo NES conquered living rooms around North America, developer Wisdom Tree produced games like Bible Adventures for it.[45] Cactus Tree Game Design began publishing "wholesome" card and board games in the early 1990s.[46] The evangelical digital-gaming industry grew enough to support establishing an annual Christian Game Developers Conference. While this tribal game industry is still tiny in comparison to the enormous global games industry, it is now large enough to warrant attention in mainstream publications like *Wired*.[47]

IF YOU CAN'T PLAY 'EM, MAKE 'EM YOURSELF

Most evangelical game producers sell or distribute relatively simple, instructional, kid-oriented board games,[48] trivia computer games, and arcade-style or puzzle computer games. Often they are spun off of prominent Christian television or radio shows written for children, such as the Adventures in Odyssey or VeggieTales series.[49]

Tribal companies typically have not tried to compete with highly glamorized mainstream games, especially the highly masculine, action-oriented combat and strategy digital games. This started to change a little around 2000 with a tribal first-person-shooter game, *Catechumen*.[50] Rather than running through strange dungeons plastering demon guts against the wall, the Christian evangelist character uses blasts from his Sword of the Spirit to convert murderous pagan Roman soldiers into kneeling, praying penitents. In the sequel, *Ominous Horizons,* the player goes on a paladin's quest to recover bits of the first Gutenberg Bible. A more recent release is the less militant *Axys: Truth-Seeker,* a low-quality imitation of mainstream games like Nintendo's Zelda series.

Left Behind: Eternal Forces (2006) became the first explicitly evangelical action game to try to cross over into the mainstream market with sizable production and promotion budgets. In this real-time strategy game based on the Left Behind novel series, the player controls a faction called the Tribulation Force (the post-rapture church), and spends the game gathering resources, constructing buildings, building units, and trying to either conquer or defend territory, all on a running clock (thus real-time). The forces of God fight the evil Global Community Peacekeepers for the souls of citizens. While the player's Tribulation Force creates evangelists and musicians who convert people by raising their "spirit level," evil forces try to reduce that spirit level with the help of evil recruiters, rock stars and activists. The game drips with tribal language and features between-level essays about topics like abortion and creationism while playing contemporary Christian music (with a "buy" link). Because the Christian side can build military units capable of killing enemies, both mainstream and some tribal critics publicly took issue with the game, generating a firestorm of controversy resulting in considerable news coverage. Critics included conservative *and* left-leaning Christian groups.[51] While some of the criticism was overblown,[52] the game clearly showcased a militant brand of evangelicalism.

Take a Mainstream Turn

The tribal gaming industry is small, so it is not surprising some evangelicals work—mostly unnoticed—in mainstream game writing, design, development, production and distribution.[53] The role of their faith in the highly collaborative industry is likely limited, especially in major digital-game-production corporations, since individuals have specialized roles in large teams. Some evangelicals avoid working for companies producing morally offensive games, but even in other companies the day-to-day business interactions do not present clear opportunities to shape the creative end product.[54] One evangelical sees his role as a "gatekeeper of the studio" who has "been raised up by God to be an influence with the people I hire."[55]

More visible are evangelical gaming guilds and clans as well as review publications and websites.[56] Focus on the Family's *Plugged In,* for instance, evaluates high-profile, mainstream digital games. A few tribal websites are dedicated almost exclusively to computer- and video-game news and review.[57] The influence of these groups on mainstream companies or evangelical developers is impossible to measure, but given the challenges of successfully marketing and selling a game, most publishers go out of their way to generate buzz with their core market.

A few Christians have achieved significant success within the mainstream industry. Lutheran Sid Meier is one of the most prolific and widely respected game-makers in the industry, producing superstar hits like Civilization and Sid

Meier's Pirates.[58] The animator and artist Doug TenNapel, creative force behind cult classics The Neverhood and Earthworm Jim, talks openly about his faith and work.[59]

Robyn and Rand Miller, evangelical creators of the 1993 mainstream blockbuster Myst started the project after producing some nonviolent children's games.[60] Myst challenged the industry's belief at the time that only action games could succeed, launching a peaceful exploration game set in a beautiful fantasy world depicted in ground-breaking graphics that are still impressive. A player has to piece together a mystery by traveling through this imaginary space and solving puzzles. One of the bestselling PC games of all time,[61] Myst did not spawn a host of industry copycats,[62] and its creators have not achieved the same success again, but it remains a remarkable accomplishment.

GAMING FOR GOOD AND BAD

Games are quite varied. Fans and critics alike can find something about them to compliment and condemn. Obvious issues include unnecessary violence and unhealthy representations of sexuality. An enormous array of games promotes potentially unhealthy power fantasies—a kind of lording over others.[63] But these concerns hardly exhaust the widening landscape of contemporary gaming.

Unfortunately, tribal and mainstream critics are frequently misinformed as well as alarmist. Their attacks on RPGs, for example, sometimes seem ignorant of the basic rules of play, and they often twist the material which they *have* seen.[64] Even well-researched criticisms generally overlook the broad range of game genres, each one offering different playing experiences. In addition, detractors fail to study how the games are actually used—the range of possibilities for play. Even the most notorious games, while clearly not suitable for everyone, can provide mature players with a freedom to discern and practice moral choice. Game players of all ages need to consider not just what others tell them about games but also how they use particular games and the ways that such games seem to be affecting them personally and collectively (both positively *and* negatively).

A moralistic veneer. Many evangelicals believe that the way to redeem gaming is to remove offensive material to ensure that the game teaches and persuades what the tribe already believes. But is a clean veneer an adequate measure of what it means to produce a Christian game? For one thing, the moral nature of a game is often more than surface deep. A conquest game that features holy people spouting pious phrases and fighting spirit warfare instead of gun battles might be light on gore, but it is still a conquest game within a worldview that assumes people should lord it over others. For another, a moralistic veneer rarely produces fresh, powerful, uplifting or challenging stories. Bad voice acting, poor graphics, predictable narratives and poorly constructed gameplay—none of which are uncommon in clean evangelical digital games—are not likely to delight most tribal and mainstream users. If games cannot engage and delight, they will be poor teachers and persuaders as well. Most Christian games are morally safe but terribly bland.

Goodness beyond Bible stories and tribal jargon. Evangelicals recognize that sin corrupts everything, including mainstream *and* Christian culture. But they sometimes forget that God can be present in all media and forms of communication—not just in tribal fare.[65] Although they have a place, the use of obviously tribal language and overtly biblical stories should not be the measure of a game's quality. Doug TenNapel says that if "you're a Christian, and the good stuff is in you already . . . [y]ou don't have to set out to make a Christian thing. Try being

DIARY OF A VIDEO GAME ADDICT

As video games get more realistic, alluring and pervasive, reports of addiction multiply. Are they credible?

In 2007, the highly respected American Medical Association hotly debated whether video game addiction should be classified as a disorder alongside bipolar disorders or schizophrenia! The AMA says up to five million Americans are addicted.[a] There are special youth camps for addicts and several websites address the topic.[b]

Christians have long asked important questions about possible addiction, especially in the context of loving God and neighbor:

- Does it negatively affect your relationships with others and God?
- Is it the thing you most look forward to in life—your idol?
- Does it affect your health, job or grades?
- Is it your escape from responsibilities or just short-term relaxation?
- Is your identity or self-worth connected with the activity?

Warnings have been issued about limiting TV by keeping it out of bedrooms and away from children under two years of age. Do video games deserve similar warnings? To limit play, some families refuse to buy consoles (e.g., PlayStation, Xbox). Others restrict the amount of play time.

Are these reasonable concerns and approaches to the problem? Should we even worry about gaming if it is a gift from God to be enjoyed? Or can it become an unhealthy, central focus in our lives?

MICHAEL JINDRA, SPRING ARBOR UNIVERSITY

[a]Mohamed K. Khan, "Report of the Council on Science and Public Health," Report No. 12-A-07 <www.ama-assn.org/ama1/pub/upload/mm/467/csaph12a07.doc>.

[b]See, e.g., On-Line Gamers Anonymous (OLGA and OLG-Anon), <http://olganonboard.org>.

brutally honest about the things you really love and hate and give them a voice with characters. See where it goes. It may not be great, but it will be honest . . . and there's a greatness in honesty that for some reason most Christian entertainment can't ever manage to get . . . across."[66]

Three aspects of creative gaming. Every medium has its own strengths and weaknesses. Digital games, for instance, provide easy access to interactive entertainment and sensory stimulation. This is partly why computer and video games are both a potentially dangerous distraction (for addiction, self-absorption or aggression) and a powerful tool for teaching, being creative and socializing people.[67]

Three potentially positive features distinguish games from other media. First, games are system toys. Chess, Pictionary, hopscotch and *Pac-man* all are interactive systems of rules. They demonstrate that human beings are creative, playful systematizers who like to invent rules and try them out. Second, with a few exceptions, games are social as well as individual practices. Gamers create communities and form friendships by giving people reasons to gather and talk.[68] Third, some games, especially RPGs, can create interactive, imaginary worlds worthy of reflection and decision making. Unlike literary and cinematic media, digital games and RPGs (and to a lesser extent, some board and card games) allow players to travel interactively through imaginary worlds, touch them, hear from them and talk within them. By contrast, many media are much more one-way transmitters of worldviews that do not provide nearly as much opportunity for players to design their own experiences and make their own conclusions.

A call to produce, play and evaluate games. An evangelical approach to gaming needs to start with the fact that gaming is a God-given potential. As stewards of God's world, human beings have the opportunity to create quality games that are not artistically inferior, games that teach and delight well and sometimes even persuade believers and nonbelievers alike. *Myst's* creators rightly bucked the trend of violent gaming but not by substituting spirit attacks for destructive weapons. Rather, they created a game that had enormous creativity, originality, artistic excellence and integrity. *Myst* was (and is) a good game, with not an ounce of Scripture or explicitly religious veneer.

Evangelicals will not be able to advance the quality of gaming in church and society unless they develop critical criteria that avoid simple, moralistic concerns. They will need to discern the shape of the virtual worlds they play in—someone constructed these worlds, and these places have ideas and values built into them. Players also need to be responsible stewards about their use of their gaming time; unlimited gaming, no matter how good the games, can negatively affect real-world relationships and responsibilities.

PLAYING GAMES WITH OURSELVES

Does fantasy gaming get between you and others—even God? Many evangelicals who have participated in Neil Anderson's Steps to Freedom in Christ program believe so.

Anderson's step two explains how people try to escape from reality by daydreaming, watching TV, going to movies, listening to music, taking drugs and alcohol, and playing computer and video games.[a] In effect, we lie to others and even ourselves by living in a fantasy world while our real life falls apart.

Sometimes the fantasy life can become preferable to real life. A friend quit role-playing games because it became a gateway to living a sexualized second life that he kept hidden from friends and family. He resided in a fantasy world, as if it didn't affect his real relationships.

Maybe gaming can even distract us from God. Can we get so involved in a fantasy world that we live as if God doesn't matter, or exist?

A different friend returned to role-playing games after giving them up for years. This time he invited his three sons to participate. He was in his second year at a local seminary, on his way to becoming a pastor, and used gaming as a way to socialize with family and friends.

One step toward staying connected is gaming in moderation. If we spend too much time gaming, we play out fantasy games with our own lives instead of on the computer. We act selfishly without considering family, friends and God. We play games with ourselves and others.

BILL WIARDA, MADISON SQUARE CHURCH, MICHIGAN

---

[a]Neil Anderson, *The Steps to Freedom in Christ* (Ventura, Calif.: Gospel Light, 2004), pp. 6-9.

CONCLUSION

Evangelicals' concerns about gaming will continue partly because the human desire for play is irrepressible, and partly because a giant worldwide industry is tirelessly expanding its audience and profits. In fact, MMOGs alone will likely become a major fixture of our culture, perhaps with profound but uncertain consequences.

What should I have told the parents or the school administrator in West Africa who condemned RPGs? I guess this chapter would have been an appropriate response! Christians are not called to blindly celebrate the world of gaming, but neither are they called to sweepingly condemn it. Rather, God calls gamers of all stripes to intelligently engage this expanding facet of worldwide culture.

16

Advertising
Fueling a Passion for Consumption

TERRI LYNN CORNWELL

Tired of "empty and unfulfilling relationships"? Visit the United Methodist Church (UMC). So said a mainstream newspaper ad as part of a $20-million UMC campaign called "Open hearts, Open minds, Open doors," designed to increase awareness of the denomination and its programs for all ages.[1]

But why would your life lack passion? Maybe you're consuming the wrong products and services. Time to *consume* the *right* product: the gospel. Where? The UMC, of course.[2]

Not to be outdone, an evangelical congregation in Indiana designed a local campaign in which provocative pictures on a billboard contained a website linked to "an artsy mini-movie with shots of a seedy motel and a man sunk in morning-after regret,"[3] followed by the church's logo.

As Christians adopt mainstream advertising, mainstream marketers are skillfully surpassing the efforts of evangelicals and mainline denominations. U2's Bono,[4] for example, elicited the help of the advertising industry with his Red Campaign, which asked private companies to create products featuring that color. Forty percent of the profits made on these products were sent to organizations working to eradicate poverty and disease in Africa.[5]

Marketing creates backlashes, too. The Red Campaign's expenses relative to donations drew concern from nonprofit watchdogs, social-cause marketing experts and ad executives.[6] Evangelicals asked the questions: Does "buying Red" lead Christians to become more materialistic—buying unneeded things? Does tribal advertising promote a distorted prosperity gospel designed to persuade believers that wealth and health are all they need?[7]

Promoting Heavenly Products

The twentieth century might be called the Golden Age of Advertising. Ads are basically (1) enticements to buy, use or believe something; (2) identifiers of the advertiser; and (3) presentations in a particular, paid medium (e.g., buying space in a paper or time on TV). A T-shirt with a logo is not an ad, although it is promotional. An advertiser-placed banner on the *New York Times* website hawking the latest Dell computer is an ad. Over the past century, such ads supported the tremendous growth of magazines, newspapers, radio and television; most satellite TV channels; and the burgeoning Internet, which includes ads in online banners, pop-ups (!*&%$) and virals—ads meant to be transmitted online from one person to another.[8] A few media—such as *Mad* magazine, public television stations and nonprofit evangelical radio stations—grew without advertising revenues.

KEY DEFINITION

Integrated marketing communication (IMC) includes advertising and other tools used to persuade.

Advertising (the *process* of creating and using advertisements, not the paid ads themselves) is rarely used alone. Instead, advertising is part of *integrated marketing communication* (IMC), which includes a coordinated group of communication tools used to persuade people to believe or do something. Usually IMC aims to convince people to purchase a product or service, but more and more IMC is used for nonprofit purposes, such as persuading people to vote or encouraging them to join a charitable organization. IMC tools are part of the traditional marketing mix, known as the four *p*'s of marketing—product, price, place and promotion.[9]

Gospel product and target. The Methodists' ad (the right *promotion*) about gaining deeper relationships by finding the gospel (the right *product*) was designed to be in the right *place* (the classifieds) and to offer readers the right product *price* (free—since sins are fully paid for). Evangelicals use all the media available to advertisers, from newspapers and magazines to radio, television and the Internet to reach their target audiences, which range from *seekers*—individuals with spiritual interests who do not have a church affiliation—to regular church attendees familiar with the gospel to lay leaders and pastors. In *The Purpose-Driven Church,* successful megachurch pastor Rick Warren describes a hierarchy of targets from the "unchurched" to "regular attenders" to "members" to "maturing members" and finally to "lay ministers."[10]

Like Warren's Saddleback Church, other evangelical congregations use a variety of media and strategies. Some of them advertise locally their own showings of the popular VeggieTales children's videos to attract the attention of unchurched parents and persuade them to attend a church. The South Baton Rouge Church of Christ hosts "bridge events," where church members bring friends, and regular church activities are advertised on posters and flyers enticing the visitors to become more involved.[11]

Mission organizations' basic product is often the feeling of doing good in a fallen world by supporting a worthy cause. Audiences are encouraged to volunteer and contribute funds to help the less fortunate. Prominent examples include TV commercials or Internet banner ads[12] asking individuals to sponsor impoverished children around the world. When the plea is emotional, advertising can be extremely effective. Other examples of nonevangelistic evangelical advertising include the following:

- magazine ads for everything from church pews to Christian colleges and seminaries
- newspaper ads with the time and place of worship
- radio, TV, billboard and online ads creating denominational awareness
- special promotional advertising like T-shirts used by numerous youth mission programs[13]
- direct marketing (junk mail) soliciting financial contributions to parachurch ministries

Some evangelical IMC campaigns build a ministry's *brand equity,* the "assets that add to the value assigned to a product" in the minds of consumers.[14] The greater the equity, the stronger the brand image.

Branding. The process of *branding*[15] is essential to an effective IMC program. Large evangelical churches, in particular, use this process to help increase membership, create a distinct image of the church in the minds of individuals (the church's *brand*), and ensure that members actively support the programs of the church and remain members for a lifetime *(brand loyalty).*

Marketers often use the phrase "brand loyalty continuum" to describe this process: Consumers move from *brand awareness* ("I know there is a church on the corner of Fourth and Main") to *brand acceptance* ("That church does good things in the community") to *brand preference* ("My choice of a worship place is the church on the corner of Fourth and Main, but I will try other churches, too) to *brand loyalty* ("I can't miss Sunday services at the church at Fourth and Main, and I will give time, talent and money to that church"). This is "beginning branding," and most churches are already doing this intuitively.

Every medium that mainstream and tribal advertisers use can support the organization's brand. For-profit organizations have used coordinated branding techniques for many years, and nonprofit organizations are following suit. A basic rule for nonprofits in the digital age is to "brand your organization effectively online" because "your website is a 24/7 storefront for your organization."[16] This is partly why so many seeker-oriented megachurches launch major websites with everything from sermon podcasts to location maps and mission statements—all designed with clean graphics and peppered with photos of smiling members.

Branding requires evocative storytelling as well as visual imaging (logos)[17] and pithy slogans.[18] Every Christian college, for instance, has a history that is part of its story. So do the faculty, and these may or may not support the official story that the college tells in its ads, brochures and website. Branding is partly an attempt to tell particular stories about specific goods and services or organizations—stories with their own, organizationally approved plots and characters.

When these stories are continually reinforced and "treated as truths in everyday interactions," the brand gains power.[19] Strengthening the brand involves moving the consumer from a simple, rational understanding of the product's benefits to an emotional bonding with the product, to experiencing how the brand reflects an important aspect of the culture. Once a brand becomes cultural, it has the potential to become iconic, like Coca-Cola or Harley David-

WHAT'S AN EVANGELICAL BRAND?

What describes a truly evangelical brand? Trustworthy? Family-friendly? Socially active? Make your own list. Compare it with others' lists. How much do you agree? If evangelicals are going to practice advertising and branding, then they had better agree on the essential values for an evangelical brand.

But even if you can identify common values, how do you connect them to a wider audience, rather than just to others in the tribe? That question matters because advertisers rarely persuade rationally: "Our product is proven to whiten your shirts." Instead, they associate products with target audiences' existing values. In North America, those values might include material success, sexiness, fame, patriotism and rugged individualism.

That's why some pick-up truck commercials splash the American flag in the background even if the vehicles are made in Canada or guzzle gas. Soft drink companies pay sexy supermodels to drink their product. Credit card companies hire celebrities to hawk their products. Unfortunately, it doesn't matter if the product has anything to do with its image, as long as the association attracts consumers.[a]

When evangelicals embrace branding, whose values dominate? What associations drive the message? Self-sacrifice? Health and wealth? Justice? Political ideology? How can a countercultural faith, which challenges the powers and principalities of the day, ever become a successful brand? How can branding *not* sanitize Jesus and distort the call to pick up our crosses and follow him?

Reexamine your list of qualities for the evangelical brand. What values are there, and where do they come from?

RICK JACKSON, SEATTLE PACIFIC UNIVERSITY

[a]For more on the association principle, see Richard Campbell, Christopher Martin and Bettina Fabos, *Media and Culture,* 6th ed. (New York: Bedford/St. Martins, 2008), pp. 405-6.

son. This is "advanced branding," and it often takes on a life of its own, beyond the control of the organization.

Ideas, philosophies and individuals, too, can have positive or negative brand images. The Republican and Democratic parties are distinguishable brands. Nazism is a horrifically negative brand except in the eyes of some neo-Nazi groups. Billy Graham connotes a positive brand of evangelists (rational or *mind-share branding*). Many individuals' high regard for Graham fosters such an affective connection *(emotional branding)* that his American influence *(cultural branding)* establishes an evangelical if not religious icon *(iconic branding)*.[20] Even Jesus Christ has a kind of brand image based not just on the story of his life as outlined in Scripture but also on the stories that others tell about him and the actions of his followers.

Churches with high brand equity derived from emotional or even cultural branding include Willow Creek Community Church in Illinois. Many persons from other American and Canadian evangelical churches easily recognize the Willow Creek brand of videos, dramas and music now available in publications and online. Likewise, Virginia's Thomas Road Baptist Church (TRBC), founded by the late Jerry Falwell, achieved high brand equity in its region as well as nationally through its extensive TV presence. In the cases of Willow Creek and TRBC, however, public notoriety elicits criticisms from those who have heard stories personally or in the media that lead them to think negatively about the churches. Again, things like word of mouth, critical blogs and mainstream news coverage affect brand equity and are not easily altered.

Not surprising, then, the relationship between the church and advertising, particularly its obsession with branding, is "uneasy,"[21] and there are numerous fans as well as critics of the idea of merging the two.

"Purpose-Driven" Advertising Fuels Gospel Passion

Evangelical advertising instructs, delights and persuades audiences—sometimes all at once.

Teaching. The simplest church advertising informs audiences about the time and place of worship, directions to the church and perhaps the church's personality: "informal worship," "caring community," "seeker-friendly." TRBC has used phrases like "complete ministries for all ages" and "dynamic music ministry" to appeal to those within an hour's drive from the church. The *Purpose-Driven Church* model suggests creating a composite profile of a church's target audience, such as "Saddleback Sam." Other evangelical ads give people information vital to their everyday lives. *Focus on the Family* knew that many in its target audience watched ABC-TV's *Supernanny* program[22] and purchased TV ads during the time that program was aired.

ON CHRISTIANS' SENSE OF HUMOR—OR LACK THEREOF

I wrote a seemingly funny classified ad for *Christianity Today (CT)* that elicited more protest mail than anything in the magazine's history. No kidding!

The short ad said in part, "Nominations for Antichrist now being sought . . ."

I learned that Christians can be sensitive to humor. One Christian's joke can be many others' blasphemy. In fact, a pastor's website now seriously gives "The Antichrist for-a-Day Award" to someone who has "shown himself (or herself) (un)worthy by particularly odious acts or comments, especially against Christians, or the Bible, or God, and Jesus Christ the savior of all."[a] Glad he wasn't granting that award when *CT* published my ad!

Christians enjoy lively humor but are unsure where to place the boundaries, especially in matters of faith. Some Christians err on the safe-chuckle side (like those mildly amusing church signs). Afraid to test the comedic waters, they use extra-safe humor that's not very funny or insightful. Other believers push the limits and do sometimes offend. *CT* may well place me in that category!?

But biblical humor is sometimes crude and earthy, often satirical and even sardonic. For example, Paul tells the legalists who believe that circumcision is necessary for Gentiles' salvation that they should go all the way and castrate themselves. Sounds like something a stage comic would say—though with cruder language.

Maybe cartooning requires Christian freedom to step over the line of offense occasionally, just to know where the line actually is for most people. When laughter gives way to pure anger, the cartoonist may have crossed that elusive boundary.

JOHN LAWING, PROFESSOR EMERITUS, REGENT UNIVERSITY

[a]Douglas Cox, "The Antichrist for-a-Day Award" <www.sentex.net/~tcc/antichr.html>.

Delighting. Evangelicals have used humor effectively to delight audiences. "I believe in Jesus; I just don't like organized religion," quipped Saddleback Sam. A direct mail response to Sam added, "Then you will like Saddleback. We're *disorganized* religion."[23] Even simple ads on bumper stickers can be a source of pleasure: "America, Bless God," "Don't Drive Faster than Your Guardian Angel Can Fly,"[24] or "Imperfect? You'll Fit Right In!" the slogan for the United Methodist Church's CrossRoad Church in Florida.[25]

One of the newest outlets for advertising is product placement[26] in electronic games—advergaming—or even the creation of an online game which in itself is a form of advertisement. So far few evangelicals have ventured into the costly realm of placing ads in mainstream games, but Christian video games themselves are a growing market. There is even a Christian Game Developers Conference with an appropriate logo: a cross with controller buttons.[27]

Persuading. Persuasion is at the heart of evangelical communication because encouraging people to make a commitment to live faithfully is critical to the tribe's mission. Most church advertising attempts to alter behavior by encouraging people to attend church, at the very least. The United Methodist ads instead aimed to change the image many nonbelievers have of organized religion or a particular denomination. Where ads have run, Methodists report a 6 percent increase in wor-

CAN IMAGES PERSUADE DOUBTERS?

Words can persuade, but so can images, and especially in today's highly visual culture. Unfortunately, many evangelicals don't get it.

Consider the case of Dan Brown's highly popular novel, *The Da Vinci Code.* Brown's fiction boldly questioned the deity of Christ. Evangelicals furiously responded with books, websites, blogs and DVDs defending the validity of the Bible's Gospel accounts.[a]

Ironically, evangelicals missed the primary basis for Brown's argument: his interpretation of a painting by Leonardo da Vinci. *The Last Supper,* he claimed, showed that Mary Magdalene was Jesus' wife and that she had his child. On the basis of his interpretation of the painting, Brown argued that the church has violently suppressed this truth for centuries.[b]

Why didn't evangelicals question Brown's use of the painting to make his case? Why did they use texts to disprove Brown's essentially visual argument? Perhaps evangelicals' inability to persuade with images goes back at least to the Reformation, when the printing press put the Bible into the hands and before the eyes of all literate people. The Reformation made many Christians into people of the Book, a community of words and texts.

Today advertisers and filmmakers freely admit their intention to persuade audiences with their images. Meanwhile, evangelicals pretend that only words matter. Out of sight, out of mind?

Jesus certainly was and is "the Word." But Jesus is also the Word "made flesh." He "appeared" to his disciples and others. He drew in the sand and left believers with the legacy of the bread and the wine—visual sacraments meant to remind us repeatedly who and whose we are.

Images can help persuade doubters. Just ask Dan Brown.

MARK E. TAYLOR, LOYOLA UNIVERSITY CHICAGO

---

[a]See e.g., Darrell L. Bock, *Breaking the Da Vinci Code: Answers to the Questions Everyone's Asking* (Nashville: Thomas Nelson, 2004); Hank Hanegraaff and Paul Maier, *The Da Vinci Code: Fact or Fiction?* (Carol Stream, Ill.: Tyndale, 2004); and Ben Witherington III, *The Gospel Code: Novel Claims About Jesus, Mary Magdalene and Da Vinci* (Downers Grove, Ill.: InterVarsity Press, 2004).

[b]Consider the rhetorical structure of Teabing's argument as it develops in chapters 55-61 of *The Da Vinci Code.*

ship attendance during Lent, Advent and back-to-school time with the hope that the messages will also "steer viewers toward a better way of life."[28]

No matter how "purpose-driven" evangelical advertising becomes, however, two aspects of communication are generally beyond its control. First, consumers create their own *buzz* through word-of-mouth or viral communications. With enough buzz, the publicity reaches a *tipping point* where products, ideas or even membership in a particular church reach a point beyond control of the original source.[29] Second, the Holy Spirit trumps any IMC campaign, no matter how holy the marketers!

Excess Passion

Advertising receives its share of witty criticism from within and without the tribe: "50 percent of an advertising budget is effective, but no one knows which 50 percent." "Only 6 percent of individuals come to a church based on its advertising."[30] "Advertising is Robin Hood in reverse, helping the rich get richer while the poor get poorer."

The excess of materialism. Perhaps the biggest criticism is that advertising draws people into materialism, where only riches matter. Because advertising fuels the capitalistic system, it helps individuals accumulate excessive wealth. Some argue that current figures on the disparities in household income provide the best example of the excess that American capitalism and its "advertising rhetoric" have created.[31] Should evangelicals deeply desire material things, whether large, fancy church buildings or the latest religious jewelry or Christian paraphernalia? If church ads focus only on facilities, grounds and products, for instance, critics could rightly argue that evangelical advertising just reinforces the selfish ways of the secular world.

The excess of the profession. Critics also challenge advertisers for enticing its young people into jobs where they face numerous pitfalls as they attempt to sell products and ideas that may be physically and even spiritually injurious to consumers. What about beer advertising (drunkenness) or donut advertising (gluttony)? Should prescription drugs be advertised directly to consumers? Should Saturday-morning TV advertisers peddle products to evangelical youth—to any youth? Is it good for a Christian college to teach advertising techniques?

If mainstream advertising experts cannot monitor their tactics, how will evangelical college graduates, hoping to be successful in the profession, be able to do otherwise? And even if Christian advertising professionals stick to promoting only church-related issues, they may rely on excess. "Is your sex life a bore? A chore? . . . Why does it seem like everyone else is having all the fun?" asked the Granger Community Church mini-movie ad. While this ad campaign increased attendance 70 percent at the church on one particular Sunday,[32] critics could easily point to the excess of those in charge of the advertising.

The excess of emotion. Critics challenge advertising from both a secular moral perspective and a biblical perspective for manipulating audiences' emotions. Because advertising frequently uses emotional appeals (such as fear and envy), it seems to bypass reason. Some critics believe that such advertising unethically demeans a fundamental human attribute (reason), thus making people less than human. From a biblical perspective, excessively emotional appeals may deny the image of God in all human beings. Perhaps advertising tactics should be judged according to the degree to which they undermine the human capacity for rational decisions, constrict free choice among alternatives and foster largely selfish in-

CHURCH SIGNS: FRIENDS OR FOES?

Every time I pass a church marquee flashing a cute slogan or clever adage, I wonder who comes up with these things:

"Got time to play golf? You have time to go to church."
"Fight truth decay. Study the BIBLE."
"Got Jesus?"
"Open Sundays."
"How will you spend eternity: smoking or nonsmoking?"

When I see these, I imagine an office where hundreds of such slogans are generated a week. When there is enough for a book, the slogans are bound, shrink-wrapped and shipped to pastors looking to add a little sizzle to their sermons and signs.

We live in a market-driven economy, and the consumer-is-king mentality seems to have bled into churches. Pastors feel they have no choice but to keep up. I wonder, though, if faith can really be distilled down to clichés. Do such cutesy sayings really arouse curiosity about the church, let alone God? Or do they just cheapen the gospel?

The other day, I saw a man working on a church sign in the rain, his Mercedes idling. All I could make out was the word *divorced. Great,* I thought, *that's the pastor, or maybe just some guy with five extra minutes, pronouncing judgment on the world in the name of God.* I drove by, shaking my head.

When I drove by later, this is what the sign said:

Paul Smith,
Divorced
I Rest My Case at
The Foot of the Cross

What I thought was a slogan turned out to be a confession. And I wept only a little.

DAVID BEDSOLE, SOUTHERN WESLEYAN UNIVERSITY

terests.[33] "You could be the miracle a child like this is waiting for," read the copy under a poignant photo of a child on the Christian Children's Fund website, the top "sponsored link" found after a Google search.[34] Effective ad copy or excessive emotion?

Mere excess. Finally, critics decry tasteless, inappropriate, offensive and simply mindless advertising. "Jesus Loves Osama," read the sign outside Australian churches in early 2007, referring to Osama Bin Laden, the terrorist mastermind of the 9/11 airplane attacks in New York City and Washington, D.C. These signs, along with a quote from Jesus' Sermon on the Mount telling followers to "love your enemies and pray for those who persecute you" (Mt 5:44), were hung by Anglican and Baptist churches and "outraged families of Bali bomb victims."[35] Were they tasteless? Offensive? What kind of image did they create of the local Christian community?

Ancient Persuasion—A Noble Profession

From Moses to Paul, persuasion has always been at the heart of God's plan, and persuasion is also at the heart of advertising.[36] The fall from grace created a gap between the way the world is (*sinful,* especially unjust and filled with conflict) and the way that God intended it to be (*saved,* especially for eternal peace and justice among people and between people and God—what the Old Testament writers called *shalom*). To move people toward shalom, God-followers practice persuasion, a gift that enables faithful human beings by grace to bring ultimate love and hope to those who need it.

In the last centuries before Christ and the first few centuries after his resurrection, however, public persuasion became one of the most ignoble professions. Taken over largely by well-trained but highly unethical rhetoricians (public persuaders), rhetoric was similar to much advertising and IMC today. When Augustine of Hippo (354-430) became a Christian late in the fourth century, he gave up his successful career as a secular rhetorician. Augustine's speaking style at the time was admired by his contemporaries, who were accustomed to associating eloquent Latin oratory with insincerity. Augustine himself even records that he was ashamed of the lies and flattery that filled his discourse.[37] Rhetoricians did not have to believe what they said. They were like word prostitutes who used their gifts for anyone else's satisfaction. To counteract these prostitutes, Augustine said Christian teachers should not abandon oratory, but use the art to fight injustice and error, keeping in mind that wisdom is more important that eloquence.[38]

Augustine taught that the God-given purpose of public communication is to serve one's audience as one's neighbor. The person who should be served, ultimately speaking, is the needy audience member, not the persuader or others. God is served when communicators love their audiences as their neighbors. The great ancient Greek rhetorician Aristotle said rhetoric/persuasion is using all methods (sounds like IMC!) at one's disposal to effectively persuade others. As Augustine taught, and as the church taught for many centuries after his death, without the right motive such all-embracing persuasion is ethically inadequate for those called to love God and their neighbor (audience) as themselves.

CONVERTING TO CONSUMERISM

Almost from its origins, the United States loved public discourse, advocacy newspapers, political debates and certainly sermons—undoubtedly the most-practiced art of persuasion in North America. During the nineteenth century, when production was moving from the home to the factory and Americans were just beginning to learn the "art of consumption," revivalism helped fuel the "sanctification of choice."[39] The personal decision for Christ—the conversion—was easily adapted to a propensity toward conversion to new products, brands and experiences, "creating a congenial cultural climate for the rise of national advertising."[40]

Individual Christians were also influential in spreading the gospel of advertising. Coca-Cola magnate Asa G. Candler, a devout Methodist, touted his product with the zeal of an evangelist and even ended sales meetings by having the group sing "Onward, Christian Soldiers."[41] The founder of the once-popular Wanamaker Department Store was a lifelong Presbyterian and friend of evangelist Dwight L. Moody. Wanamaker led the trend of marketing the Christian holidays of Christmas and Easter with elaborate displays in his Philadelphia store.

Advertising soon became what one historian called "the rhetoric of democracy."[42] It's hard to imagine a modern, industrial democracy without open public discourse, without commercial persuasion, without advertising. By the early years of the twentieth century, North American advertising had invaded every area of life. Christian tribes, especially evangelicals, adopted mainstream marketing techniques to "sell" the gospel and increasingly to peddle various Christian products, from music to books and even wallpaper with Bible verses on it. Evangelicals contribute to more than sixteen thousand exposures to commercial messages, symbols and reminders that each American alone sees daily.[43]

BALANCED CONSUMER DIETS

"Our humanity is diminished when we have no mission bigger than ourselves," argues U2's Bono.[44] These missions might be good or bad: Hitler and his expert propagandists had a grand mission to exterminate the Jews and dominate the world. For evangelicals the good mission is *the* mission: gratefully serving a loving God who persuades people daily to join the kingdom of God. All evangelical

THE CAT AND MOUSE GO EYEBALLING

Consumers have eyeballs. Advertisers want them. So the sport is keeping advertisers from getting them. It's a cat-and-mouse game of eyeballing.

Savvy consumers fast forward through recorded commercials, install pop-up blockers and ignore banner ads. They create audio playlists rather than suffering through radio commercials. Mice 3. Cat 0.

Meanwhile, advertisers begin sending text messages and even videos to hand-held devices. One service sends a Bible verse to your phone for about twenty cents daily.[a] But what ads will accompany Scripture? Cat possibly 1. Mice, beware.

Google buys YouTube for $1.6 billion. First it runs dinky ads on the site. Then it includes "less intrusive" ads as "overlays" on the bottom 20 percent of the screen during particular videos. Fewer than 10 percent of users close overlays, and click-through rates are five to ten times a typical standard display ad.[b] Cat 1. Mice 0.

"Bringing ads to clips turns what has been a huge platform without economics into a platform with a lot of economics," notes one ad-overlay customer.[c] Perhaps such advertisers realize that the overlays could become more entertaining than the underlying videos. Cats everywhere. Mice everywhere.

The sheer number of videos on YouTube—five to six million per month[d]—makes it difficult for an individual to "capture eyeballs" for any purpose, let alone to present the gospel. And would a commercial overlay be appropriate for an evangelistic video? Cats and mice confused.

Tune in next week for the ongoing saga. We want your eyeballs to sell to needy advertisers.

TERRI LYNN CORNWELL, LIBERTY UNIVERSITY

---

[a]Stephanie Simon, "God's Call Comes by Cell Phone: Bible Verses on a Blackberry, Sermons on an MP3; An Explosion in Digitalized Spirituality Is Making True Believers of Online E-vangelists," *Los Angeles Times,* May 16, 2006.

[b]Abbey Klaassen, "YouTube's Monetization Plan: Overlay Ads That Aren't Intrusive," *Advertising Age,* August 21, 2007.

[c]Quoted in Jefferson Graham, "Google Plans Ad 'Overlays' for Some YouTube Videos," *USA Today*, August 21, 2007 <www.usatoday.com/tech/techinvestor/corporatenews/2007-08-21-you-tube-ads_N.htm>.

[d]YouTube does not share many statistics, but *Wall Street Journal* writer Lee Gomes pieced together information by conducting a "scrape" of YouTube's Web site (a legal way of gathering bits of information from a Web site and piecing them together). In July 2006, there were 5.1 million videos on YouTube and more than 6 million a month later. Lee Gomes, "Will All of Us Get Our 15 Minutes on a YouTube Video?" *Wall Street Journal Online,* August 30, 2006 <http://online.wsj.com/public/article_print/SB115689298168048904f92aczYTICtKrTSiZ8vumR3eZCI_20070830.html>.

choices about advertising have to be seen ultimately in these terms as part of the largest, greatest, most mind-boggling mission of all times and places. Only then can evangelicals avoid mere advertising.

In 1997 the Vatican released its Ethics in Advertising report, one of the few explicitly Christian documents on this topic.[45] It offered a balanced discussion of the benefits and potential harm of advertising to society. The report admitted that advertising is a necessary part of today's world economy and can be a useful tool for sustaining honest and ethically responsible competition. It explained that advertising provides consumers with important information, contributes to market efficiency and creates new jobs; it noted that religious institutions can use advertising to communicate their messages of faith. Advertising can uplift and inspire people and motivate them to act in ways that benefit themselves and others, and it can even "brighten lives simply by being witty, tasteful and entertaining."[46]

On the other hand, the Vatican reminded humans that advertising can also harm. It can ignore various needs of certain segments of the population, stereotype individuals, and even move people to do evil deeds that are self-destructive or destructive to society. The report warned that advertising should not perpetuate a life of "having" rather than "being," nor should it use the practice of branding to move people to act on the basis of "irrational motives."[47]

While the Vatican recognized that the use of branding strategy has a greater potential for misuse than many other advertising strategies, it suggested a worthy solution:

> The Church looks with favor on the growth of man's productive capacity, and also on the ever widening network of relationships and exchanges between persons and social groups. . . . From this point of view she encourages advertising, which can become a wholesome and efficacious instrument for reciprocal help among men.[48]

Protestants, too, have argued that since humans bear the image of God (Gen 1:26-28), public communicators should strive to be conscious and reflective of the impact of their messages. Because our potential for developing this capacity depends on other people, we have ethical obligations to behave rationally ourselves, help others to act rationally, and communicate truthfully.[49]

From this perspective, the "drink Pepsi and people will love you" ads are unethical. Pairing a sexy Cindy Crawford with a can of Pepsi as the reason to buy Pepsi bypasses rational processes, as do car ads that stress power and domination ("BMW, the ultimate driving machine"; "Mercedes—move up").[50] Such advertising is unethical not just because it uses emotional appeals, but because it demeans a fundamental human attribute and makes people less than human.[51]

CONCLUSION

Mainstream media's Red Campaign shows us how advertising and marketing can be used for social causes, such as persuading people to combat poverty and disease in Africa by "buying Red." Similarly, the United Methodist Church has recruited more members by emphasizing its "open hearts, minds, and doors," while mission organizations like World Vision, with its savvy use of technology,[52] have gained attention and support for its worthy programs.

But mainstream and evangelical advertisers must act responsibly when working in such a powerful medium; they clearly have the skills to encourage irresponsible thoughts, values, beliefs and actions. Ultimately, the apostle Paul's guidelines point the way to right practices: morality (refrain from gratuitous sex, violence, profanity; protect innocent children; combat materialism), truthfulness (state truthful messages and be true to your audience as your neighbor), and beauty (delight audiences with well-crafted, pleasant, fun, and attractive messages). Above all, believers are to worship the Creator, not the creation.[53]

We should, as Gary Scott Smith stresses, "strive to redesign economic and social life, including the practices of advertising, the meaning of work, patterns of consumption, and attitudes toward possessions, in accordance with the biblical ideals of justice, shalom, and compassion."[54] Evangelicals, whether creating advertising to teach, delight, and persuade or consuming advertising for the same purposes, should seize this kind of vision for a God-given gift meant for a fallen world.

17

Promoting Public Relations in a New-Media Environment

PETER A. KERR

When some megachurches cancelled Sunday Christmas services to give overworked staff much-needed family time,[1] a few unhappy churchgoers spoke to reporters. Suddenly these churches were roundly criticized in print, broadcast and online media.

A handful of congregations engaged the press, hoping to get their side of the story to the bewildered public. They released messages on family values, how a building is not the essence of a church, and how Christmas is really about celebrating the birth of a Savior and not just about a church service. Other churches ignored the news reports, hoping the bad publicity would just go away.

One Kentucky church took a middle ground, releasing to the media a short rationale for its decision. Unsatisfied, journalists wrote many critical articles, often quoting outraged Christians.[2] In a mid-December sermon, the Kentucky pastor said that on Christmas day "every home chimney would be a steeple" as church members would hold worship services at home. He admitted he was "deeply saddened by the knee-jerk response of the Christian community as a whole to give the benefit of the doubt to the media and not a church or a Christian brother. I'm still troubled that more Christians did not stand up for us. Can you see or begin to see that the devil is stirring the pot on this?"[3] He cited Jesus' silence during his trial to justify his own decision not to fully engage the modern press.

Was this the best response to bad publicity? Should this pastor and many others have given interviews to the news media rather than responding to critics only in sermons? Whether they like it or not, evangelicals face public scrutiny for their actions as both individuals and institutions. Like mainstream businesses and governments, they are increasingly pulled into public controversies reported and sometimes even created by traditional and online media. Evangelicals are realizing that they cannot control their own public identities by silence and that restricting communication to their own tribe has limited benefits.

CHURCH CONFLICTS ARE BIG NEWS—WHEN THEY INVOLVE SEX

Mainstream news media love church scandals. Consider these audience-generating beauties:

- TV preacher Jimmy Bakker resigned in 1987 after reports of him having sex with a church secretary—and a related payoff to silence her.
- Televangelist Jimmy Swaggart in 1988 tearfully told his audience, "I have sinned against You, my Lord."[a] His denomination defrocked him for his lack of repentance, reportedly over relations with a female prostitute.
- Pastor Ted Haggard, leader of the National Association of Evangelicals, resigned in 2006 following reports of his homosexual activities and drug use with a male prostitute.

While such memorable sex scandals gain headlines, they are relatively rare as far as church-related crises go.[b] The most common church crisis? Take a guess. Answer: conflict among members. Less sexy, indeed. Next on the list after conflict among members: disputes between a member and the congregation or staff, followed by battles over worship music and worship styles.

The news media amplify church-related sex scandals, while congregations are much more likely to suffer from internal fights among people who can't or won't work out their disagreements peacefully. Sex makes the news, while infighting festers in the pews.

What kind of crisis merits mainstream or tribal news coverage? Which type most tarnishes the image of the church in society?

MICHAEL SMITH, CAMPBELL UNIVERSITY

[a]Jimmy Swaggart, "Apology Sermon," delivered February 21, 1988, reprinted from J. M. Giuliano, *Thrice Born* (Macon, Ga.: Mercer University Press, 1999), American Rhetoric: Online Speech Bank <www .americanrhetoric.com/speeches/jswaggartapologysermon.html>.

[b]Eilene Wollslager, Karen Legg and John Keeler, "A Typology of Crisis Communication in the Local Church," paper presented at Campbell University Faith and Communication Conference, Campbell University, Buies Creek, North Carolina, May 19, 2007.

Evangelicals are starting to see public relations (PR) as part of their cultural engagement strategy, affecting everything from evangelism and attendance to community relations. Failure to embrace PR as a necessary part of public communications[4] leads to diminishing impact upon society and news coverage only when Christians squabble with each other.[5]

The Power of PR

PR has many definitions,[6] but nearly all of them agree that it involves *fostering positive relationships with audiences ("publics") both inside and outside an organization.* For a few practitioners this has included deception and mere image making—often referred to in politics as spin doctoring. Such tactics fail in the long term because the goal of PR involves building and preserving a relationship and a lasting reputation, guiding what comes to mind when people hear, think or read about an organization.

Christian practitioners must define PR not only in terms of image or reputation but in terms of truth. They must be mindful of "speaking the truth in love" (Eph 4:15), conversing with each other and the media in ways that are "full of grace" and "seasoned with salt" (Col 4:6), always guided by values above profit. PR requires appropriate persuasion—never manipulation or deception that can ruin relationships.

For example, the church described in the introduction needed not only to explain why its decision to cancel Christmas worship services was appropriate but also to persuade evangelicals (and possibly the media)[7] that it had made a wise decision. While the media played up the controversy, churches should have been using the publicity to tell the Christmas story to the world rather than shrinking from the limelight.

When controversy is not the news peg selling the story, PR often gains audiences by using creative promotions, attractive materials and well-crafted messages. Practitioners disseminate information within a religious organization via attention-grabbing flyers, periodicals, email and message boards, communicating with external media by monitoring the press/blogs, writing press releases and editorials, updating websites and marketing publications, and interfacing with local community members and governments. In most churches all these duties, along with marketing and publicity, naturally fall on the senior pastor. Larger churches and other ministries are now commonly using volunteers or hiring PR and design specialists for these tasks.

The majority of Christians practice PR not in churches or ministries but in businesses, PR agencies, universities and government. These jobs are ideal for serving both society and God's kingdom. Often businesses are finding that it is the PR folks who hold them accountable for their own promises and policies because PR practitioners are directly accountable to interested publics. A strong moral influence in PR could stymie many business scandals by informing organizations of their own codes of ethics and holding them to their own standards. Christian practitioners can also influence ethics statements that describe a business's core values and may even be in positions to direct company donations to worthy causes.

Often PR professionals keep a close watch on the news, monitoring it for their clients. This intense effort to stay abreast of current information puts them in outstanding positions to understand culture and influence it by writing editorials and passing their findings to pastors and other Christian activists.

Many Christian organizations use internal PR tools but often maintain a turtle mentality about external press. These evangelicals prefer to shrink into their shells rather than attract mainstream reporters to tribal events, worrying that the media are too liberal, too corrupt, too ungodly or too biased for balanced

MINISTRY PR

- Proactively inviting the media to tribal activities ranging from service at local food banks to disaster relief efforts.[a]
- Responding to media requests with well-designed, targeted messages to defend their reputations, and their Savior's reputation, and to foster cooperation with like-minded constituencies.
- Partnering with journalists to become sources of information on specific topics and assisting them to find interview candidates from the congregation/organization.[b]
- Establishing better methods to connect congregations with worthwhile tribal resources such as prayer chains, books, magazines and websites.
- Raising donations and recruiting volunteers via media.
- Communicating an evangelical worldview through media such as films,[c] weekly or monthly newspapers,[d] and websites.[e]
- Fostering two-way communication with all publics—from other tribes to mainstream and tribal media—in order to provide honest, caring responses to all concerns and criticisms before they become divisive.
- Keeping a pulse on an organization's internal health by arranging focus groups and informal discussions as well as conducting valid polls and surveys on demographics, biblical knowledge, church opinion, etc.

---

[a]Susan Moyer, ed., *Katrina: Stories of Rescue, Recovery and Rebuilding in the Eye of the Storm* (Champaign, Ill.: Spotlight, 2005), discusses the religious response. For more on the Christian response, see the activities of the Evangelical Free Church of America <www.efca.org/katrina/> and others <www.christianitytoday.com/ct/special/katrina.html>.

[b]Debra Childers, interview by author, Louisville, Kentucky, March 23, 2007. Director of Media Relations at Southeast Christian Church near Louisville, Childers is often asked to find sources from certain demographic groups (such as people with disabilities or war experience) and befriends members of the media by inviting them to church Easter plays, etc. One Nebraska pastor told the local paper that he was interested in commenting on moral topics and was rewarded with a monthly "philosophy corner" section. Stephen Kerr, interview by author, Broken Bow, Nebraska, June 21, 2001.

[c]The football film *Facing the Giants,* produced by Sherwood Baptist Church in Albany, Georgia, played nationally in over one thousand theaters and grossed over $10 million. See "Facing the Giants," The Numbers: Box Office Date, Move Stars, Idle Speculation <http://the-numbers.com/movies/2006/FCGNT.php>.

[d]Many megachurches have their own periodicals or provide content to a company that produces their newspapers and sells advertisements to cover printing costs.

[e]Bryan Sims, interview by author, Lexington, Kentucky, April 25, 2007. Spiritual Leadership, Inc., is partnering with the Lexington Leadership Foundation in Kentucky to create a pilot website that it hopes will become a model for every city. The website is expected to link Christians across the city, assisting them with finding a church, or even a Bible study near them if their church does not offer one, disseminating prayer needs and praises, and even allowing Christians from one church to get involved in ministries at another church.

coverage. Because these leaders assume they will never achieve positive press, they refuse to try. When they are forced into the spotlight by a crisis or scandal, their inexperience leads to the realization of their worst fears about garnering poor coverage.

Other evangelicals feel ignoring mainstream news media only ensures other voices will have more influence. Choosing to brave the battles and knowing that often even bad publicity can produce good results, they learn about PR or hire practitioners to proactively shape the public's perception of their organizations

FIGHT OR FLIGHT?

Facing opposition from the media, Christians traditionally fight (develop a combative mentality) or turn tail and run, abandoning all media coverage. Is there a middle ground?

How about playing by the rules and putting forethought into media encounters? What might that include? Here are three simple things to get started:

1. *Talking the talk.* This includes using the industry standard Associated Press writing style and studying other resources to understand message development and how a typical media encounter differs from a normal conversation.[a]
2. *Getting off the bench.* Initiative is key. Don't wait for the press to sniff out bad news; instead, become more transparent and proactive. Christians have always devoted resources to defend biblical truth and key principles of faith from outside attack, but they are starting to put resources toward PR to ensure enduring delivery mechanisms for those messages. For example, Christians influence millions by being interviewed on such popular shows as the *Oprah Winfrey Show* and *Larry King Live.*[b] The John 3:16 signs at sporting events are being replaced by testimonies of Christian athletes from almost every professional sport.
3. *Developing a tough hide.* The media will always report negative events, but thick skin can weather the storms and result in people seeing Christ and his church in a new light.

Instead of obeying the fight or flight impulse, many evangelicals are learning how to interact better with the press and the public—building bridges toward conversion.

PETER KERR, ASBURY COLLEGE

[a]Resources for this training could involve someone in your church who does PR, or you could use self-help resources such as Ronald Smith, *Strategic Planning for Public Relations,* 2nd ed. (Mahwah, N.J.: Erlbaum, 2005), p. 2; Sally Stewart, *Media Training 101* (Hoboken, N.J.: Wiley & Sons, 2004); Carole Howard and Wilma Mathews, *On Deadline* (Long Groves, Ill.: Waveland, 2000); Barbara Digs-Brown, *The PR Style Guide,* 2nd ed. (Belmont, Calif.: Wadsworth, 2007).

[b]Debra Childers, interview by author, Louisville, Kentucky, March 23, 2007.

and faith. Techno-savvy students may be especially capable of volunteering at these organizations to assist with PR.

Cultural Glue

Protestant Christianity provided much of the cultural glue that bound early American society together, shaping the language and creating common values, culture and identity.[8] As Alexis de Tocqueville wrote in his 1830s classic *Democracy in America*,[9] religion provided the "habits of the heart" which softened the human tendency toward radical individualism and self-interest in a free society. The Bible was often the primary textbook in schools,[10] infusing morality into both family and civic life.

By contrast, today the "local church appears to be among entities that have little or no influence on society."[11] The mainstream media provide the cultural glue in Western society, molding the language and dominating conversations. Mass media teach, delight and persuade Americans, telling the formational stories that influence personal morality and self-image, create national identity, and foster a public faith in "American values" such as relativism and radical individual rights.[12] Television and movies vie with religion not only for people's time but also for their hearts and souls.

Therefore, well-practiced, highly ethical PR has become an important means of competing with other voices by injecting evangelical viewpoints into the public square, and is essential for maintaining strong relations with the other people and institutions that shape society. "Without our strategic involvement in the culture-shaping arenas of art, entertainment, the media, education, and the like, this nation simply cannot be the great and glorious society it once was."[13]

THE BENEFITS OF CHRISTIAN PR

- Less public misunderstanding and antipathy toward evangelicals and their organizations, with commensurate improved reputation in society.
- Friendlier and more effective interactions with local communities and governments.
- Better-informed evangelicals who positively affect culture.
- Greater understanding of tribal needs and issues through improved communication among evangelical organizations and their constituents.

Businesses recognized long ago that journalists tend to be cynical because edgy reporting attracts audiences. PR practitioners who understand journalists can properly word their organization's perspective so as to overcome this negative bias and generate stories that better approach reality. Proponents of PR feel that using the news media without extensive forethought, or refusing to engage the press, will fail to get messages to the public and forfeits the opportunity to shape society.

POTENTIAL PITFALLS

Corrupting influence. Tribal critics are quick to point out that active engagement with the media carries risks. The business practices of PR might corrupt evangelical institutions, which should be committed to values beyond competition, self-interest and profit. Churches, in particular, are living organisms rather than mere organizations; the trend toward church management—e.g., CEOs, CFOs, PR directors, flow charts and spreadsheets—could corrupt congregations to the detriment of biblical standards such as mutual accountability, love and turning the other cheek.

Misallocation of resources. Some feel PR is too resource-intensive for the often unpredictable results. Short-term PR blitzes and half-baked retaliations against liberal media usually do little good. Leaders who are hypersensitive to legitimate criticism may be tempted to a less than Christian response as they engage media who are often jaded from the disproportionate coverage of ministry scandals and unaware of the monumental sacrifices many ministers make everyday. Many tribal leaders recall times when they or their organizations were unfairly represented in mainstream media, so they are inherently gun-shy and understandably pessimistic about improving media relations. The value of using new media such as blogs and online videos is even more uncertain, although critics appear quicker to use them.

In truth, nearly every organization has been covered negatively by journalists; the problem is hardly just bias against religion. To some extent the very nature of news is conflict. One of the primary reasons Christians have fled from media engagement is that they expect perfect coverage and praise from every story. This contrasts with most mainstream organizations, which are ready to break into their version of the Hallelujah Chorus if the coverage is just balanced. Some evangelicals see negative news and question if it is worth the time and effort to try to make it more positive. Why not just cut and run, using the resources for missions or helping the poor?

Political entanglement. More moderate evangelical critics also worry that PR sidetracks ministry by embroiling tribal organizations in political battles. They warn that PR and mass media practices will never replace face-to-face evangelization,[14] no matter how positive the news coverage. Few will be converted by reading positive news stories or listening to more complimentary podcasts about a tribal organization. Moreover, excessive involvement in political discourse can interfere with evangelical ministry. In tune with a fairly traditional tribal perspective, the evangelical authors of *Blinded by Might*,[15] one of whom is a major mainstream news columnist, argue that evangelicals ought to stay out of political battles and instead evangelize the lost.

While these critics agree that the media shape public debate and that evangelicals should be involved personally in politics, they worry that evangelical leaders and organizations might become excessively entangled, creating the impression that the church is essentially a political rather than a spiritual institution.[16] At the same time, however, they say little about the new media that make it much easier for critics to publish online the half-truths and innuendo that discredit evangelicals in public life. Such criticism undoubtedly affects mainstream views of evangelicals and evangelical institutions, and in the long run negatively affects evangelization.

Mediating Reality for God

Perhaps the closest parallel to a press agent in the Old Testament (OT) was Aaron. When Moses complained that he lacked eloquence, God replied, "What

IS BAD NEWS BAD?

Why do evangelicals cancel their newspaper subscriptions or stop watching CNN? One reason is all the bad news. Shouldn't we stick with good news? Maybe we could if we lived in a good world.

There are times when God calls his followers to call it like it is. Ezekiel, like a good reporter, spelled out devastation so awful that "every heart will melt and every hand go limp" (Ezek 21:7). It nearly got the messenger killed.

So what are evangelicals to do when mainstream media accurately report a prominent pastor being fired for frequenting a male prostitute? Or that an evangelical parachurch leader has ripped off believers with get-rich-quick schemes?

We could get angry at the paper—or at our leaders. We could also claim news bias! Or we could ask ourselves why tribal media weren't first to report those stories. Evangelicals who won't admit bad news about themselves only invite investigative reporting by those with no grasp of faith. We ask to be misunderstood.

And truth be told, we relish bad news—if it is about those who persecute us. King David did. But the larger pattern in Scripture is that when God or his followers bring bad news, there's something deeper to be learned by it—maybe life-changing. And good news often follows bad news in God's economy.

At its best, news reports the truth that matters. Maybe we need more Ezekiels in the bad-news business.

MICHAEL A. LONGINOW, BIOLA UNIVERSITY

about your brother, Aaron the Levite? I know he can speak well. He is already on his way to meet you, and his heart will be glad when he sees you. You shall speak to him and put words in his mouth; I will help both of you speak and will teach you what to do. He will speak to the people for you, and it will be as if he were your mouth and as if you were God to him" (Ex 4:14-16). While other OT texts are also positive toward oration, such as Proverbs 16:21 advising that "gracious words promote instruction," the OT is also replete with admonishments against slick and deceptive speech.

Similarly, in the New Testament (NT), James cautions Christians to be "slow to speak" (Jas 1:19) and even likens the tongue to an untamable fire (Jas 3:6, 8). However, the importance of public opinion is also acknowledged, as Paul calls diverse believers to live in harmony so that those outside the church will be ashamed to unfairly criticize congregations.[17] Concerned about how his followers would represent him, Jesus prayed for Christian unity "so that the world may believe" (Jn 17:21). Some even see John the Baptist as Jesus' promoter and believe Jesus was "a master of publicity and public relations" because he advocated letting "your light shine before men" and engaged in PR by polling his disciples, asking, "Who do people say I am?" (Mk 8:27).[18] The entire NT can be seen as an ancient form of publicity designed to persuade audiences to follow Jesus.

Spinning information, peddling unnecessary or damaging products and services, coercing audiences, gossiping about people and institutions, playing one group against another—these and many other poor communications practices fall far short of the Bible's mandate of humble, compassionate truth telling. Christians are called to speak the truth in love (Eph 4:15), not merely to be honest or to advocate for the right causes. Perhaps the "best way to counter our image problem is to follow the path of the early church: to avoid behavior that betrays disunity and contentiousness, and to devote ourselves to care for the weak and underprivileged. And to be brutally honest about the church's own failings."[19]

Both good and bad publicity were important aspects of Christianity's rise to the status of an official world religion.

> The combined energies of several media channels and devices—the public displays of martyrdom, the vociferous and colorful competition among heresies within Christianity, the aggressive mission of the Church, and the flow of communication in its worldwide organizational web, as well as the imperial edicts for and against Christians—all these contributed to the victory Christianity gained over its pagan competitors in the marketplace of religion.[20]

This was also the case during the Reformation, as Martin Luther dutifully wrote numerous essays criticizing some of the practices of the Roman Catholic Church while biblically justifying his own positions.[21] Luther's sometimes bombastic disputes with Roman Catholic prelates and theologians undoubtedly ensured that

Luther's and other reformers' messages were heard, if not universally accepted.

Christian Origins of Modern PR

In many ways evangelical movements and social concern in the nineteenth century can be seen as the precursors of modern media publicity and thus PR. In America this includes evangelists such as Dwight Moody and Charles Finney, who participated in the Second Great Awakening, drawing huge crowds and prompting many conversions. Finney alone reportedly led more than 500,000 to Jesus Christ. Finney's controversial innovations included choirs, allowing women to pray in public, an "anxious bench" up front for sinners who needed extra conviction, and delivering impromptu sermons.[22]

JESUS' UNUSUAL PR

Jesus instructs his followers in the Sermon on the Mount to let their lights shine so all "may see your good deeds and glorify your Father in heaven" (Mt 5:16). Later, Jesus says that works of charity should be performed *in secret* as the right hand should not know what the left hand is doing (Mt 6:2-4).

So, how do evangelicals let their works shine while keeping them hidden? Is this a contradiction or paradox? What might it say about public relations?

First, Jesus boldly announced his kingdom program. He held a press conference and announced that he was appointed to proclaim the good news, release the captives, heal blindness and free the oppressed (Lk 4:18-21). Press reports were mixed (Lk 4:29). Did he understand the audience?

Second, Jesus simply did what he announced. He shared the good news of the kingdom, released, healed, and restored people to wholeness and health. He enacted his proclamation, sometimes quietly asking others not to tell about his good works. To the parents of a resurrected daughter, for example, he says to not broadcast what he has done (Lk 8:56). Why would he do that?

Jesus' motivation wasn't self-promotion. He did God-promotion, Father-promotion and eventually Spirit-promotion. He kept his work secret even while reports spread like a fire.

Jesus represented his organization—the kingdom of God—by the way he lived, without slickly designed campaigns, photo ops or positive spin. He was who he was. He did what he proclaimed. He followed through on promises. All for the glory of God.

In Jesus' PR, even most who heard his stories did not understand. Yet those who opened up and listened and observed him did receive the message. Jesus' secret message thereby changed the world. What kind of PR was that?

ELIZABETH W. McLAUGHLIN, BETHEL COLLEGE, INDIANA

Many of these evangelists' sermons were published in books and newspapers, and their tours were heralded with flyers, posters and other marketing materials that led to newspaper coverage. Revivalists often championed social causes such as the abolition of slavery and the prohibition of alcohol consumption.[23] In the process, itinerant preachers created a Christian camp-meeting culture that regularly drew huge crowds to hear the preaching and enjoy the music and sensational sites of conversion. Some thought all the commotion was worth emulating for a profit, and thus the traveling circus was born.[24] Phineas T. Barnum created the "greatest show on earth" in 1871 and became the father of press agentry in America.[25]

PR really took hold in America during the world wars, as government leaders sought to gain public support for the United States' involvement in the conflicts. Both founders of modern PR—Ivy Lee and Edward L. Bernays—worked first in government and then for corporations.[26] Although some church activity may have been a precursor to modern PR, it eventually lagged behind corporate and governmental uses.

PROMOTING FAITH

A growing number of ministries employ public relations to market stories and combat negative mainstream publicity about God and the faith. This preevangelism function of PR is vital, as the battlefield of the hearts and minds of unbelievers is currently assaulted by a constant bombardment of messages from the mass media that declare Christianity to be a stale, ignorant and hypocritical religion. These negative claims act as barriers for interpersonal conversations that could lead to conversions. While portraying the positive aspects of faith in old and new media may be important for fostering conversions, using media is certainly an appropriate expression of evangelical zeal for the name of the Lord and desiring his name to be glorified and held in respect.

Getting stories into the news that put faith in a positive light may be easier than expected because journalists are always searching for positive stories to counterbalance their natural tendency to herald negative events.[27] Evangelicals have the opportunity to tell their stories, such as the ways that they serve the local community, assist the poor and protect the environment. If just one or two stories a month won coverage on local TV news and local media websites, it would go a long way toward improving the reputation of the church and the desirability of accepting Christ as Savior.

One pastor and social activist in Washington state developed a strong public voice by building relationships with journalists. "I believe in working the media," he said. "I have done it so long that they now call me. I suppose I get at least one media call virtually every week to comment on some aspect of the news." While not all coverage has been positive, much of it allowed him to present his perspectives fairly to the public. "I have noticed that as our congregation and influence has grown, the newspaper coverage has gotten generally better."[28]

This pastor also advocates publicly for local organizations that strive to protect the unborn and underprivileged. The groups use flyers, email distribution lists, websites, press releases, and word of mouth to get out vital information and build alliances. "I have had a few people on the edges of the media try to take me out for political reasons with very slanted coverage, but generally the mainstream media has been good," he said.[29]

The media relations director at a large church in Louisville, Kentucky, says, "The media professionals in my community are collaborative, respectful, and fair-minded. As I look around at the walls covered with articles, I can say we have received more than fair coverage. Our job is not just to react, but we must engage the media and encourage relationships with all media outlets in our communities."[30]

One organization that has been particularly active in PR is the Salvation Army, which has branded its somewhat militaristic name to be synonymous with careful and effective use of donations. Organized with PR functions at the local and regional levels, the Salvation Army even has a secretary of PR at its headquarters in London, England. Exemplifying a gracious Christian attitude, the organization has been careful not to become overly critical of groups that have tried to ban its volunteers from street corners and shopping malls during the holiday season.[31]

Large-scale PR campaigns sometimes seem to have impact, but the precise results are difficult to evaluate. For instance, PR helped get voters out for the 2004 elections, using the hot-button issue of homosexual marriage to convince evangelicals to go to the polls to elect conservative politicians.[32] The Southern Baptist Convention (SBC), concerned about immoral content in Disney movies and its offering of marital benefits for homosexual partners, coordinated a large-scale campaign to boycott Disney in the 1990s.[33] The precise impact of both endeavors is difficult to determine and would have to take into account any backlash effects (such as people perceiving the SBC to be moralistic or self-righteous).

Many examples of successful PR efforts exist, including when a Christian public watchdog group conducted a widespread information campaign that included emails and public statements to stop Wal-Mart from giving financial support to homosexual advocacy groups. Wal-Mart desisted, and announced that it did not wish to enter into the culture wars.[34]

Preparing to Meet the Media

Whereas the Roman Catholic Church has hierarchical leadership, extensive official doctrine and its own elaborate communications system,[35] Protestants lack a unified voice.[36] Because Protestant groups are a patchwork of practices, people and perspectives, media covering them can pick and choose whatever Christian perspective they desire. This leads to stories that almost invariably reflect only one, narrow, often seemingly hypocritical or militant perspective, though occasionally a mainline Protestant group will be used to morally justify a journalist's own liberal viewpoint.[37] The result is that the general public sees Protestantism as a source of social conflict, not as a solution to social or moral and spiritual problems.

Evangelicals need to be prepared to make their voices count during times of such conflict and one-sided media coverage. Some groups might even have a positive media campaign "always at the ready, to initiate at exactly the right moment—not to build attendance, but to build the truth."[38]

At a minimum, evangelical institutions need to develop crisis communication plans. When I led the media relations team of about thirty PR practitioners in Washington, D.C., that handled Ronald Reagan's state funeral, we had a two-hundred-page plan, and we still had to work hard to stay ahead of the media frenzy and fast-paced changes. A recent study suggests churches in particular are largely unprepared.[39] It further reports that most crises stem from personal conflicts and styles of music/worship, though there also are larger issues that arise. Churches and ministries should have plans for how to respond during crisis events that could range from a child being abducted from Sunday school to various types of leader misconduct.

Crisis communication plans should include a clear chain of command for decisions, contact data of all members and pertinent government agencies, and a system for communicating to all key constituencies (the tribal organization, media, local community, headquarters/denomination, etc.). Though every incident has unique features, normally an organization should release all potentially negative information to mainstream and tribal media as soon as possible. Otherwise journalists will eventually discover and report the information bit by bit, thereby progressively reducing the public credibility of the organization, which will invariably appear to be hiding information. Of all groups in society, Christians should practice transparency the most, being first to admit their mistakes[40] and striving to be charitable to one another and to those outside the tribe. The fruits of the Spirit[41] should serve as the measure of conduct.[42]

CONCLUSION

PR is an important means of teaching and persuading society about evangelicalism. If tribal leaders will dedicate themselves to learning the trade, possibly even taking classes or seminars on PR, many will be able to deftly use the media to

FREEDOM OF THE PRESS AND SPEECH—FOR EVANGELICALS?

Who gets to speak for a religious institution such as a Christian college? Administrators? Students? Anyone on campus?

When I was president of a Christian university, a student once wrote an anti-Semitic article in the campus paper. Local Jews rightly protested. They also pointed out that our library contained an academic journal that denied that the Holocaust occurred. We had egg on our faces!

We responded by inviting key Jewish leaders to campus. We admitted our mistakes. Some journalism students were unhappy—they championed freedom of the press. But now was the time to make amends. Our candor and humor helped us make new friendships with the Jewish community.

Later campus leaders created a bureaucratic hierarchy to control internal and external communication. Students and faculty weren't allowed to speak to the press. The school hired savvy professionals to frame controversies, spin stories and keep the institution from looking bad in the media. We gained a more polished image in the media but lost a sense of community, of sinners seeking imperfectly together to become like saints.

In his university debate club, renowned Christian theologian and apologist C. S. Lewis argued that the weakest and most ignorant among us should be allowed to speak.[a] Then, as a community we can see where we err, where we need instruction, how fallible we are. Maybe this is the biblical PR model—truthful images without hypocrisy. After all, Jesus entrusted his message to ignorant, foolish, sinful disciples. He recruited people who lied, misspoke, sinned creatively and even betrayed him.

What if one of today's slick PR agents had edited the sacred Scriptures to improve the church's public image? Would any of us be able to recognize the true church today?

TERRY LINDVALL, VIRGINIA WESLEYAN UNIVERSITY

[a]C. S. Lewis, "The Founding of the Oxford Socratic Club," in *God in the Dock: Essays on Theology and Ethics*, ed. Walter Hooper (Grand Rapids: Eerdmans, 1970), p. 128.

tell the good stories of Christ and what he is doing through his body on earth today. This does not have to take the form of self-promotion but can be Jesus-promotion, an activity every Christian should prayerfully perform.

Hiding like a turtle and deceiving like the biblical serpent are not options for evangelicals. Instead, the first step is to ask hard questions like "What is our image in the community? How can people find out about us? What can we do that will show the community a glimpse of God's love in action?" Providing answers to these questions and establishing PR messages and means may help to reverse the ways that the Christian community has "effectively served as the scapegoat or whipping boy for the mass media for several decades. The standard criticism will ring hollow; the typical caricatures of Christian people will vanish as the skeptics and critics recognize a wave of change through which true love for others has replaced hypocrisy and infighting."[43]

Benjamin Franklin once cautioned, "Never argue with a man who buys ink by the barrel." This is still somewhat true, but today's digital media can better distribute the ink; evangelicals can employ PR to avoid arguing, while still providing input into culture. Evangelicals have an opportunity to tell their stories through the mainstream media gatekeepers or by using podcasts, websites, emails, blogs, etc.—if they have the talent, experience and vision to do so well. This promotion must be accompanied by loving action, which will always be the best PR move.

While churches can close their doors at Christmas, they can no longer close their eyes to public opinion. The public is forming its opinions, and evangelicals themselves are consuming culture through media. Modern PR techniques can be adapted for evangelical use, just as evangelicals have successfully used other communication media, in order to best be salt and light for our culture. As evangelical theologian Carl Henry once wrote, "Instead of allowing the media to crowd out the Mediator, the claim of the Mediator must be affirmed upon and through the media."[44]

18

Internationalizing Evangelical Media

ROBERT S. FORTNER

Pentecostalism emerged in Uganda in the 1970s when members of the dominant Anglican tradition of the Church of Uganda, frustrated with the church's apparent lack of biblical commitment, left for more orthodox Pentecostal churches. But by the mid-2000s, Ugandan Pentecostal churches faced crises involving sex and money—similar to their American Pentecostal counterparts. Sex-related accusations included adultery, rape and sodomy. Financial accusations involved fleecing and selling blessings to donors, who had to seed contributions in order to receive their own financial harvest. On top of these charges, a preacher was caught importing a personal electronic device that would allow him to send electrical charges to congregants, convincing hopefuls that the preacher was anointed!

Red Pepper, Uganda's leading tabloid, wrote that the media had "reported cases of homosexuality, extortion and using electric shock gadgets to con worshippers. The public has also become increasingly critical of the methods pastors in some Pentecostal churches use to extract money from their followers."[1] Pentecostal churches were "rated among the organizations with highest incomes in the country," according to Uganda's NGO Board (a federal agency).[2]

Apparently the gadget pastor's inspiration came from American Benny Hinn, who had attracted forty thousand people to a healing rally in Kampala. Hinn's ability to slay people in the Spirit—in which they fall backwards—likely inspired imitators, even those who needed electrical assistance.

The Ugandan scandal, in particular, illustrates the negative impact of American-based mass media efforts in other countries. Negative effects seem to dominate the media landscape. The wholesale import of such programs has contributed not only to scandal but to Muslim-Christian tensions in Nigeria,[3] the rapid growth of Pentecostalism in Africa,[4] the rise of Islamic televangelism (which uses many of the same techniques pioneered by Western Christian televangelists),[5] the close connection between evangelicals and the State of Israel that makes Arabs equate Christianity with Zionism,[6] and the creation of crusades by televangelists in many countries of Africa and Asia, such as the Festival of Blessings crusade in India run by Benny Hinn in 2005. More broadly, however, the practice of Christianity globally and the use of communications media within non-American contexts also have their own, regional dynamics.

LATIN AMERICA

Roman Catholicism has long been dominant in Latin America. Throughout the twentieth century, some Latin American Catholics called for social justice, developed liberation theology, and flirted with populism and left-wing politics—including communism.[7] But among interior tribes and many urban *mestizos* (those of mixed indigenous and non-indigenous ancestry), there has also been significant Cristo-paganism, a veneer of Catholic ritual layered on traditional beliefs. This Christian patina led many evangelicals to object to Catholics' syn-

A POST-NETWORK MONUMENT TO BABEL?

Before the rise of radio and TV networks from the 1930s to the 1950s, there were no powerful national or international media. There were smaller communities of discourse organized around different groups' interests in particular periodicals and books. Evangelicals, too, had their book publishers and tribal magazines—like denominational magazines on home coffee tables.

TV networks eventually created national audiences through widely viewed early sitcoms like *Leave it to Beaver* and dramas such as *Gunsmoke* along with national newscasts and sports events. By unifying Americans' media habits, the networks created a modern Tower of Babel—like the biblical city that spoke one language and worked together to build a tower into the heavens (Gen 11:1).

So what's happening in the era of YouTube videos, blogs, and millions of other websites? We're living in increasingly narrow networks of virtual communication and community. Some—like those organized around cell phones and instant messaging—can connect existing families and peer groups.

But at the same time, other new networks actually divorce us from family, neighborhood and congregation. We spend hours chatting online with distant people we'll never meet in person. We surf the Web without talking with anyone. We sit in one room all day without ever communicating in person with anyone. In some strange way, we can live outside of our bodies, bouncing around cyberspace, visiting places and people.

In the twentieth century, Americans were a multitribal nation that had raised a network tower in Babel. Now our little networks might be a monument to a crumbling Babel.

RONALD A. JOHNSON, GOSHEN COLLEGE

cretism and to call for revival.[8] From about 1970 to 2000, evangelicalism spread rapidly throughout the region. Although some of this growth could be traced to the arrival of United States–based televangelism, most of it has come from missionaries on the ground, especially among the poorer segments of society, and from indigenous use of electronic media.[9]

Latin America's private-sector broadcasting enabled evangelicals to deliver the Word easily via media. For instance, Quito's HCJB World Radio began back in 1931,[10] becoming the first Protestant evangelical international radio operation the same year that Radio Vatican started.[11] Local AM and FM stations developed across Latin America, many of them owned by the Catholic and, later, Protestant churches, as well as by private entrepreneurs with religious sensibilities. These radio and later TV stations provided local access to both North American and home-grown media preachers.

In addition, the massive movement of people from south to north, either to avoid political instability or to escape poverty, exposed many Latin Americans to evangelical U.S. churches. With the development of transportation and communications technologies, and the close ties that these made possible with their societies of origin, the Protestant charismatic religious experiences encountered in the north were easily transplanted.[12]

Latin Americans learned that evangelicals' charismatic authority could be measured quantitatively by "the size of congregation attracted, number of countries visited, money raised, sinners converted—and in this context mediated messages are of particular value because they can reach so many people across such great distances." So the power of the charismatic movement appeared to depend partly on its spatial bias—its ability to become "demonstrably diffused to so many contexts and people."[13]

AFRICA

Among the similarities and differences between African and Latin American evangelical experiences, five are especially obvious. First, Latin America was colonized largely by two Roman Catholic countries, Spain and Portugal, while Africa was colonized by many countries, both Roman Catholic (Belgium, France, Portugal and Spain) and Protestant (Great Britain, Germany and the Netherlands).

Second, Africa has no common language, whereas in Latin America Spanish and Portuguese are the lingua franca. Many Africans speak three or more tribal languages in addition to their national or trade language.[14] This slows down Christians' ability to create media programs that can appeal across the continent and requires more Bible translation work.

Third, Africa was under colonial rule far longer than most Latin American countries, facilitating national radio monopolies. TV is still restricted largely to main cities, while radio is vital, along with mobile phones. Consequently, televangelism grew slowly, as did Christian radio until the 1990s.

Fourth, African Christianity clashes significantly with Islam; North Africa is largely Muslim and sub-Saharan Africa largely Christian, with significant Islamic populations in border-state countries such as Ethiopia, Nigeria, Uganda and Kenya.

Finally, the existence of Islam in North Africa has meant that Christian missionaries are not able to proselytize openly in many countries. They are restricted to tent-making work as teachers, doctors, nurses and other service professions—witnesses rather than evangelists.

Similarities between the two continents include widespread poverty; lack of education; extensive barrios, or slums, on the outskirts of most large cities, such as Rio de Janeiro, La Paz, Nairobi and Johannesburg; and underdeveloped infrastructure, especially in rural areas, that denies people access to transportation, electricity, clean water, medical care and schools. The lack of rural infrastructure, in turn, makes amenity-rich cities magnets for rural populations, who then come to populate the barrios and slums of the cities.

Nevertheless, developments in media use, including privately owned or church-owned radio stations, the growth of televangelism (both imported and indigenous), and the spread of Pentecostalism, have all reached sub-Saharan Africa. Privately owned Christian radio stations have also begun operating in Sudan.

Both Roman Catholic and Protestant missionaries have been active in Africa since the nineteenth century.[15] Both started schools and hospitals in their respective spheres of influence and were tied closely to colonial interests. Missionaries were protected by colonial authorities and were seen as part of the civilization process. They also had little regard for each other, and where both were active, the invective flowed freely.[16] Once African countries began to achieve independence in the 1950s and after (the greatest number achieving independence in the 1960s), missionaries stayed on, translating Scripture into tribal languages, evangelizing, planting churches, and engaging in humanitarian and educational activities. African priests and pastors were trained and gradually took over the reins of indigenous churches.

In addition to churches tied closely to Rome (Catholic) and Westminster (Anglican), American-based denominations (Presbyterians, Baptists, Nazarenes, Methodists, etc.) also established themselves.[17] In the 1970s Pentecostal churches were established, most of them independent of direct foreign connections, although many African pastors received their training in Western Bible schools or seminaries, or began their work with little to no training, inspired by the Western Pentecostal movement.

The poverty of Africa, exacerbated by conflict and corruption, has kept most churches (outside the white churches of South Africa) relatively poor.[18] Therefore, Africa is a base of operation for many secular and evangelically based Christian relief organizations, such as the Luke Society, World Vision, Compassion International and denomination-based groups. They, along with parachurch organizations such as Feba Radio, HCJB, Trans World Radio and Adventist World Radio, have addressed a variety of problems, including disease (HIV/AIDS, malaria, river blindness, polio, etc.), sanitation (digging wells, installing latrines, providing preventive health information), deforestation (through such projects as TWR's solar cooker distribution), and education (through educational radio programs and training workshops). All these activities are inspired by evangelistic commitments, although many of them have no obvious evangelistic intent.

But indigenous groups have fostered most of the amazing church growth on the continent. As elsewhere, Christianity has actually been "moving toward supernaturalism and neo-orthodoxy, and in many ways toward the ancient world view expressed in the New Testament: a vision of Jesus as the embodiment of divine power, who overcomes the evil forces that inflict calamity and sickness upon the human race."[19] This distinctive "Third Church" is part of the revolution occurring in Africa, Asia and Latin America, which is far more sweeping in its implications than any current shifts in North American religion, whether Catholic or Protestant. There is increasing tension between what one might call a liberal Northern Reformation and the surging Southern religious revolution, which one might equate with the Counter-Reformation, the internal Catholic reforms that took place at the same time as the Reformation—although in references to the past and the present the term "Counter-Reformation" misleadingly implies a simple reaction instead of a social and spiritual explosion. No matter what the terminology, however, an enormous rift seems inevitable.[20]

Asia

Asia hosts three of the most populous countries in the world (China, India and Indonesia), which offer particular evangelistic challenges. China is officially closed to all foreign missionaries and officially only allows people to belong to government-sanctioned churches.[21] For Christians, this means membership in the Three-Self Patriotic Church (a reference to the Trinity).

Indonesia is the most populous Muslim nation in the world and, along with Malaysia, is officially an Islamic state. North Korea is officially an atheist state. And India, while it has a significant number of Christians (largely in the south), also has militantly anti-Christian and anti-Muslim political parties. There are various other restrictions on Christians in Asian countries such as Burma (Myanmar), which excludes Christian missionary work; Thailand, which more passively resists such work; and Vietnam and Laos, which actively persecute Christians. Pakistan, too, is a dangerous place for Christians to practice or proselytize openly because of the presence of active and ultraconservative Muslims.[22]

Despite the difficulties, Christianity often thrives. The Philippines has a majority Christian population. South Korea's population is one-third Christian; Seoul hosts the largest Pentecostal Christian church in the world, with over 800,000 members.[23] South Korea is the second-largest source of missionaries after the United States.[24] Its Christians target some of the most difficult places in the world to evangelize, joining Western missionaries in over 160 countries where they "have become known for aggressively going to—and sometimes being expelled from—the hardest-to-evangelize corners of the world. Their actions are at odds with the foreign policy of South Korea's government, which is trying to rein them in here and elsewhere."[25]

Given the difficulties of evangelizing in closed or restricted countries, much of the non-indigenous evangelism is via media, including radio, terrestrial and satellite TV, print, and the Internet. Despite the closed nature of many Asian societies, there have been some spectacular successes in bypassing the restrictions and sometimes evangelizing successfully.[26]

The number of Catholics and Protestants in China, for instance, might be closer to 80,000 than the official figure of 21,000. Certainly Christianity has grown staggeringly since 1979, when China began relaxing the fierce restrictions on religious activity imposed during the Cultural Revolution of the 1960s.[27] The Christian broadcaster FEBC played a "major role" in sustaining Christianity during the Cultural Revolution even though "many people were sent to labor camp if caught listening to foreign broadcasts."[28] The "vast majority of China's Protestant house church Christians . . . are deeply pro-American and determined to evangelize the Muslim world, something Americans generally have been too frightened to do with much boldness."[29] By 2007 *Asia Times Online* claimed that 10,000 Chinese were becoming Christian each day. "China may be for the 21st century what Europe was during the 8th-11th centuries, and America has been for the past 200 years: the natural ground for mass evangelization."[30]

New Burmese Christians among the Karen people have been giving up their ancestral spirits. Christianity apparently gives believers "access to the outside world and removes the limitations of the local spirits, while the Bible represents the ultimate truth and is set against the religion of the dominant ethnic group."[31]

In contrast to Western individualism, Asian's corporate culture generates clusters of new believers, with entire families or even villages choosing to embrace the faith, often as a result of the decision of the "head man."[32] Similarly, in the far Western highlands of Papua, New Guinea, where various hill tribes began to adopt Christianity in the late 1970s, the "big men" allowed young people to study in a Bible school, then permitted these youth to introduce what they had learned into Urapmin life.[33] This charismatic Christianity was thus introduced by indigenous people, not outsiders.[34]

In other cases, however, external influences have been critical. For instance, among the lu Mien and Hmong of the Vietnam highlands, entire villages have embraced the Christian faith as a result of radio broadcasts.

The Middle East

Evangelism is the most complex and difficult in the Middle East. This area includes not only the roots of the three great monotheistic religions (Christianity, Islam and Judaism) but the scenes of intense Western-Islamic conflicts, Jewish-Islamic clashes, and a unique evangelistic dynamic based on dispensationalist interpretations of the role of Jerusalem and Israel in the end times. Although evangelists and others declare that their primary objective in the area is preaching the gospel or saving souls, there are also underlying political and messianic motives.[35]

The Middle East and North Africa are largely Arab peoples, along with Jews (especially in Israel), Christians (especially in Lebanon and Egypt), Turks (in both Turkey and Cyprus) and Greek Cypriots. Filipinos and other Asians are guest workers, so evangelists use various languages along with Arabic—itself a cluster of languages or dialects. The Arabic of the Gulf states is different from that of Egypt and North Africa. Arabic cultures differ as well. The cultures of North Africa, or of the Bedouin (a nomadic people), differ from those of the Gulf or Iraq. There are extremely conservative versions of Islam (such as Wahabism in Saudi Arabia), and quite modern (or progressive) forms, such as that of Qatar or the United Arab Emirates. Although the basic expectations (the Five Pillars) of Islam are the same, the faith is practiced according to tribal, political and ideological differences from area to area.

Christian missionary activity has been active arguably since at least the time of the Crusades. In modern history, missions work in this region has taken many forms. Christian missionary workers first established printing presses in the Middle East;[36] set up hospitals and clinics; provided education; and served as engineers, technicians, management consultants and in many other occupations as witnesses or tent-makers.[37] There are evangelistically driven publishing missions (Arab World Ministries), radio and TV stations (Feba and TWR), satellite TV channels (SAT-7), relief organizations (World Vision), and Internet ministries <www.arabicbible.com>.[38]

The most difficult issue for Middle Eastern evangelism is Zionism.[39] Several ministries built a radio and TV station in Southern Lebanon in 1979 that was so

GOING NATIVE IN A GLOBAL MEDIA MARKET

While many North Americans dislike tribal broadcasting, elsewhere programs often receive a warmer reception—especially when they are locally produced. In some Islamic countries, for example, several million people view weekly Christian movies, biblical dramas, cartoons and youth-oriented programs. Native shows include the weekly Egyptian-made *One Hour Youth* and *TV Majellah,* a magazine-style show produced in Lebanon. When produced by Arabs, much satellite-delivered programming positively portrays Christianity.[a]

The newer broadcast mission model gives power to indigenous people to manage their own media ministries. HCJB Global calls this "radio planting."[b] By identifying native partners who share a vision for radio outreach, providing equipment, and giving technical expertise and mentorship, the ministry plants self-sustaining radio stations staffed by nationals. Such international media ministries become partners for interpersonal ministry.[c]

Churches are producing indigenous programs, too. In South Korea, where 26 percent of the population is Christian, some churches have their own studios to produce video content for cell phones and the Web.[d]

Some native broadcasts receive funding from Western denominations and mission groups that use media to inform and mobilize believers. The Assemblies of God World Missions produces monthly DVD programming for member churches,[e] while the Christian & Missionary Alliance produces video news reports, a video magazine, video podcasts and a video blog.[f]

Grassroots activism and media savvy have captured the imaginations of Christian young adults in the West and various mission fields. Young media producers understand how significant a role media and the Internet can play, mobilizing the faithful to support international evangelism and social action. As long as this support allows native partners to manage their own media efforts, positive portrayals of Christianity are likely to continue.

KATHY BRUNER, TAYLOR UNIVERSITY

[a]Learn about Christian broadcasting in the Middle East at <www.sat7.org>.

[b]Learn about HCJB Global at <www.hcjb.org/mass_media/radio/radio_planting.html>.

[c]"Media and Technology: The Rainbow, the Ark & the Cross," Lausanne Occasional Paper No. 48, 2004 Forum for World Evangelization, hosted by the Lausanne Committee for World Evangelization, Pattaya, Thailand, September 29 to October 5, 2004.

[d]Jonathan Petersen, "Mobile, Glocal & Evangelism," *Lausanne World Pulse,* June 2007 <www.lausanneworldpulse.com/worldreports/735?pg=3>.

[e]Learn about the AGWM Communications program at <http://wmm.ag.org/>.

[f]Learn about Alliance Video at <www.cmalliance.org/resources/av/av.jsp>.

obviously pro-Israel that the indigenous churches (such as the Coptics in Egypt) saw it more as a threat and provoker of conflict than a tool of outreach.[40] Arabs fear that Christianity is too closely tied to Israel, or that American Christians are Zionist, partly because of the biblical interpretations this ministry broadcasts.[41]

Europe

People commonly speak of "post-Christian Europe," with its empty cathedrals and pews throughout Western Europe.[42] These people remember that the area was once "the global center of Christianity," and its millions of missionaries "traveled to other continents to spread their faith by establishing schools and churches."[43] But the United Kingdom has fallen to third place as the source of missionaries only because of the rise of South Korean evangelistic work. Even in Albania, an atheistic country that officially outlawed God, many citizens "have resumed spiritual practices with a faith strengthened by the years of suppression. At the same time, new practices and beliefs are being planted by a wave of foreign missionaries and money, making this tiny Adriatic country a remarkable example of the globalization of religion."[44]

European religious conflicts are also significant. Eastern and Central European nations persistently held that each was "endowed with a traditional, predominant faith, which formed an element of its past greatness and deserves to be rebuilt." Moreover, they believed that particular religious minorities threatened their national interests—especially faiths of imperial neighbors. In Poland, for instance, the "Roman Catholic Church was popularly associated with patriotic values, whereas the loyalty of Orthodox and Lutheran Christians was historically assumed to be suspect."[45] Suspicion lingers between the northern Protestant countries, such as the Netherlands, Germany, and Scandinavia, and the southern Catholic countries (France, Spain, Portugal and Italy), and between Eastern (Orthodox) and Western (Catholic) Christendom. Faith and nationality support each other, especially in Eastern European areas like the Balkans, making proselytism seem suspiciously like an invitation to ethnic assimilation.[46]

Europeans tend to devalue religion and to see it as a danger to the continent's consolidation and cooperation. They recall the Hundred Years War and World War I, a conflict between Christian nations that decimated a generation in the carnage of trench warfare. They remember the troubles of Northern Ireland and the hatred that flared in the Balkans. Finally, they have witnessed terrorism based in fanatical Islam. Media and nonmedia evangelism have to address suspicions based on all these factors, along with the consequent indifference, or hostility, to the gospel.[47]

Pan-Global Evangelism

Many Christian evangelistic efforts cross regional boundaries. These include Bible translation organizations such as Wycliffe; international radio organizations such as AWR, HCJB, Feba Radio, FEBC and TWR; program producers that cooperate with these broadcasters, paying for airtime or for the salaries of producers, or both (the Christian Reformed Church's *Back to God Hour, Words of Hope, Back to the Bible, Through the Bible* and many others); international television ministries such as CBN WorldReach; Bible distributors like the World Bible League or the Gideons; crusade organizations (such as the Billy Graham, Morris Cerullo or Luis Palau groups); campus ministries (Campus Crusade, InterVarsity, Navigators, Young Life, YWAM); business organizations (CBMC, International Fellowship of Christian Businessmen, Harvest Evangelism); drama and art organizations (Youth for Christ); and various Jesus film projects (Jesus Film Mission Trips, The Jesus Film Project, Jesus Film Harvest Partners).

Both Trans World Radio and Feba/FEBC broadcast in more than 160 languages each;[48] CBN International claims as its mission to "see 500 million people brought to faith in Jesus Christ" through means of the mass media;[49] and the Jesus Film Project claims that the 1979 film has been seen 5.6 billion times (including repeat viewings), translated into over one thousand languages and shown in 229 countries.[50] Also, many Protestant denominations have extensive missionary activities abroad. Southern Baptists, Nazarenes, Assemblies of God, Churches of God, Anglicans, Orthodox Presbyterians, Reformed Christians (CRC, RCA), and independent churches, such as Mars Hill Bible Church in Grand Rapids, Michigan; Willow Creek Community Church near Chicago; Southern California's Saddleback Community Church; and Mariners' Church all sponsor missionary work from within their own congregations.[51]

In addition, there are numerous indigenously produced clones of United States–pioneered evangelistic programs. Many U.S. radio organizations provide scripts to indigenous producers to use in making their own radio programs. CBN's *700 Club* has been copied in several countries using the same format seen in the North America but using indigenous hosts, and in many cases the activities of the United States–based organization (especially of *The 700 Club*'s Pat Robertson) are carried on them with sometimes controversial results.[52] The Trinity Broadcasting Network's (TBN) international broadcasts have elicited anti-TBN websites highlighting its "heresy."[53] Many North American and British media mission organizations have also accepted affiliate organizations in other countries that raise funds for their work (especially Australia, New Zealand, Germany, Norway, Sweden and South Africa).[54]

There are also dozens, if not hundreds, of websites aimed at international evangelization. Most of these are affiliated with organizations that have already been mentioned, but there are also independent websites not affiliated with any of these traditional media organizations. For instance, Internet Evangelism,[55] Jesus2020.com, WhoisJesus-really.com, godlovestheworld.com and the umbrella site GlobalMediaOutreach.com all aim to evangelize internationally via the Web in English and other languages.[56] Such sites, however, are only available (or

WORLDLY WORSHIP MUSIC

As praise and worship composer Peter Moen explains, "When I arrived in the Philippines for the first time, we had all the press and cameras. It was a huge deal, and I remember thinking, Why are these people here? I had never toured there—but guess what? The songs had toured there."[a]

Major North American praise and worship labels realize the potential of going global. Integrity Music operates out of Singapore, London and Australia; Vineyard Music out of Brazil, New Zealand, South Africa, Holland, Germany, the U.K., Scandinavia and India. Native-language recordings of Western music produce profits.[b]

But what's the price of North American influence on worldwide worship?

Westerners connect worship music with entertainment. Worship artists, even writers, become celebrities. *Christianity Today*'s website features the top worship albums of the year under the heading "Entertainment." Many North American students don't see incongruity, but most international students are puzzled.

Much contemporary North American worship is "seeker-sensitive." It focuses on instant meaning ("Liturgy Lite")[c] often disconnected from historical Christianity, which requires some understanding of the faith and meaning of the various parts of worship. Generally speaking, praise and worship music is theologically thin, doctrinally weak.

Ironically, recent worship renewal among some younger North American evangelicals embraces "world music." For instance, they sing repetitive Taizé choruses from France. These evangelicals are calling for worship music that promotes unity within and among multicultural congregations.

Perhaps North American praise and worship music will eventually give way to world music.

ROBERT H. WOODS JR., SPRING ARBOR UNIVERSITY

[a]Deborah E. Price, "Praise and Worship Genre Blessed with Global Growth," *Billboard* 115, no. 7 (2003): 1.

[b]Ibid.

[c]Marva Dawn, "Worship Is Not a Matter of Taste," *Creator* 21 (November 1999): 5-9.

useful) to the minority of people in the world with Internet access or even more exclusively broadband access. Mobile (cell) phones in developing countries are beginning to be as ubiquitous as radio; these phones have resulted in evangelistic strategies using SMS (simple message system).[57] The American Tract Society also has a website for sending evangelistic tracts from the Web to a cell phone.[58]

Conclusion

Evangelicals' different understandings of missionary work underlie some in-

GET YOUR MOJO WORKIN' IN LOCAL NEWS

Media call them mobile journalists, or mojos. They hit the road with laptops and audio and video equipment to feed written stories and video continuously to their local newspaper and its websites.

Why? Partly to save papers, now read by only 30 percent of the population. But mojos also demonstrate a renewed interest in local news, called hyperlocalism. Papers are attending to little league baseball games, citizens' personal achievements and other down-home stories.

Get this: The hyperlocal *Daily Record* in Dunn, North Carolina, reaches 100 percent of the population. Years ago the paper's founder began asking everyone in the community to contribute news, even reports of birthdays, out-of-town guests, Sunday sermons and other topics of everyday conversation. Boring stuff? Maybe to some, but the community feels a sense of participation in the news. As the editor tells locals, "If you can get us the information, we'll do our best to publish it."[a] Imitators call this approach "me media."[b]

The easiest way to create hyperlocal news is to allow online story submissions and to add Web-based publication supported by advertising. In other words, the paper version is supplemented with online text, video, audio and perhaps even blogs. Some bloggers can even serve "as a self-anointed Fifth Estate" watching "over abuse of power in the media themselves."[c]

In a sense, hyperlocalism parallels the church as a worldwide, catholic body of all believers but with neighborhood parishes that care for the community.

MICHAEL RAY SMITH, CAMPBELL UNIVERSITY

---

[a]Lisa Farmer, personal communication, June 26, 2007.

[b]John J. Cassidy, "Me Media: How Hanging Out on the Internet Became Big Business," *New Yorker,* May 15, 2006, pp. 50-59.

[c]David Demers, *History and Future of Mass Media: An Integrated Perspective* (Cresskill, N.J.: Hampton, 2007).

terchurch tensions. Sometimes evangelical tribes see "God's gift of salvation as coming exclusively through one's own church; seeing the task of mission as exclusively concerned with social matters or exclusively with spiritual matters, rather than in a wholistic way."[59]

There is not one entity engaged in worldwide evangelism. Rather, missionaries include Baptists, Pentecostals, Presbyterians, liberals and conservatives alike, Roman Catholics, Orthodox, and sects such as the Mormons and Jehovah's Witnesses, all claiming to represent the "one Holy and apostolic church" and the "one true" path to salvation. Mixed in with denominations, charismatic pastors, and evangelists are radio and TV ministries, Bible societies, tentmakers, educators, translators, and tract publishers, as well as organizations such as Campus Crusade, TEAM, Brother Andrew, and individual church members and independent church missionary committees that fund ad hoc projects around the world. Imagine what it must be like to be on the receiving end of all these efforts! How can local groups make sense out of the conflicting priorities and claims? It must often sound like Pentecostal cacophony rather than spiritual unity.

19

Energizing Media Ethics

MARK FACKLER

The following are three short lessons in tribal media ethics.

1. *The National Courier*—a one-time national tribal newspaper—wanted a story about the establishment of the proposed Billy Graham Center at Wheaton College. Centers like this are rare for evangelicals, so the story would play prominently in the newly-founded *Courier,* and it would be puffy good news.

Yet conflict is everywhere, especially when money and prestige are at stake. The conflict in this story concerned private homeowners facing Wheaton's Blanchard Hall along College Avenue. The college needed that land for the center, but one owner, also an employee at the college, did not want to sell. College officials told the reporter that this holdout was simply seeking more "of the Lord's money" than her home was worth, although they declined to comment on the meaning of *repercussions,* a word passed to this employee by her supervisor while on the job. The published story told of great expectations, but the land-purchase conflict dropped out. A subeditor told the reporter that the risks to the advertising stream would not permit investigations at that time. The employee sold her house, quit her job and went into counseling. The center was built. A lesson in tribal reportage.

2. A newbie writer signed his first contract with a tribal publishing house. His book sold out its first and second printing and went into a third. But no postal delivery in all that time included the writer's long-awaited first-ever royalty check. He began to sniff around. Indeed, other contractors with the same company were likewise deprived. The author and his cowriter determined that the only way to collect was to show up at the publisher's office until the long overdue check was presented. This they did, and thus they reckoned their books on the book. A lesson in tribal business.

3. A professor at a well-known tribal college received a call from the head of the Evangelical Press Association (EPA)—the tribal equivalent to the Society of Professional Journalists. The Zondervan Corporation (a major tribal book house)

CAN EVANGELICALS BE OBJECTIVE JOURNALISTS?

Many people think that evangelical reporters don't have a prayer of a chance of being objective. They say evangelical reporting is tribal propaganda, not journalistic truth. But can *any* journalist be objective?

Since the 1920s North American journalists have sought to be neutral, unbiased, totally open-minded—i.e., objective. In fact, all reporters—including evangelicals—do have beliefs that guide the way they live, work and report the news. This professional doctrine of reporting assumes that the *method,* not the *journalist,* is objective:[a]

1. Never add anything that was not there.

2. Never deceive the audience.

3. Be as transparent as possible about your methods and motives.

4. Rely on your own original reporting.

5. Exercise humility.

Truthfulness, transparency, honesty, humility . . . sounds almost biblical. Shouldn't this lay to rest the idea that biblical faith and journalistic objectivity are incompatible? If anything, evangelicals might be better equipped to doggedly pursue the facts. They believe in objective truth, right?

Yet many Christian journalists still see an invisible line between who they are as objective Christians and who they are as objective journalists.[b] They assume that biblical truth and journalistic truth cannot be the same. So they report only to the tribe, creating a Christian news ghetto.

Perhaps evangelicals ought to think about objectivity more as a method to follow than as a quality of character. This might reduce the apparent conflict between biblical and journalistic truth telling. Maybe the most virtuous, Christ-like persons will also be the best journalists—the most honest, truthful and humble.

PHYLLIS ALSDURF, BETHEL UNIVERSITY

---

[a]Bill Kovach and Tom Rosenstiel, *The Elements of Journalism: What Newspeople Should Know and the Public Should Expect* (New York: Three Rivers, 2001), pp. 74, 78.

[b]John Schmalzbauer, *People of Faith: Religious Conviction in American Journalism and Higher Education* (Ithaca, N.Y.: Cornell University Press, 2003).

had lodged a formal ethics complaint against *World Magazine* (the closest tribal equivalent to *Time* or *Newsweek*) over *World*'s coverage of the gender language issue in the New International Version of the Bible (the tribe's most respected translation, owned in part by Zondervan). The complaint specified violations of EPA's code of ethics. The professor joined two others, also appointed by EPA's CEO, to determine the merits of the complaint. Their report cited *World* as guilty in part, not guilty in part. The report was never made public after *World* (an EPA member) lodged *its* complaint on the complaint to the EPA director and his board. A lesson in tribal accountability.

These and other stories in this chapter are part of the subtext of this book's effort to tell the tale of evangelical media. Each verifies that moral quandaries abound, no matter the tribe or good intentions. While tribal media seek to transform the world for Christ, they invariably suffer some of the same moral lapses, mixed motives and selfish intentions evident in mainstream media. Greed, force of will, self-preservation and image play important, if not decisive, roles. Yet this moral—and immoral—subtext rarely surfaces in evangelical media's coverage of *themselves.* Instead, mainstream media deliver the bad news to the public, including tribal moral defenses and justifications for actions that seemingly are not appropriate for followers of Christ.

TRIBAL MORALITY

Christians and Jews have thought about moral obligation throughout their interlinked histories. While biblical Hebrew had no word equivalent to *virtue,*[1] the Old Testament (OT) includes virtuous and not so virtuous characters, blessings from God and judgments for sin, and prophets who for the most part tried, often as single voices in an oppositional culture, to carry the Word of the Lord to their contemporaries, and through Scripture, to us in the twenty-first century.

Clearly, moral accountability was *present* to the life of each member of the covenant community. No day was lived apart from that accountability. They interwove political might, personal virtue and God's sovereignty through the tribal history.[2] But the story of the covenant is jagged at best. OT morality is founded on the Ten Commandments, anchored in grace, yet violated by everyone. Heroes are polluted and priests politically tainted. God wants goodness, but in the end God himself rescues us from a heap of badness.

In the New Testament Gospels, the power of the cosmos meets the humility of Messiah Jesus, whose greatest act is submission to God's will in a tortuous death, and whose resurrection demonstrates that grace will win against all adversaries. Moral victory does not come by way of empire but by weakness, meekness, mournfulness and a thirst for goodness (Mic 5:1-12).

The epistles, too, do not offer systematic theorizing about the moral life or integrated instructions on how to act. Instead, they roam through a vision of moral life that definitively excludes "individual decision-making by appeal to the deductions of universal reason" and focuses instead on "faithful obedience in the light of tradition and revelation."[3] The apostle Paul tells one church after another how to act in their time and place, but today's tribes have to wrestle with applying his instructions or principles.

Nevertheless, the moral center of the Christian story for all tribes is hope and grace in union with the Triune God. Only the moral periphery of Christendom is contested. For those who ponder the institutions of mass media and communications, those contested areas include truth telling and promise keeping, virtue and privacy, and sometimes the very purpose—or *telos*—of moral communication.

GUIDING LIGHTS

Augustine (354-430) says in *The City of God* that good can be done for many reasons, yet the pride which dominates doing good negates any moral quality to it.[4] Only good done humbly counts as moral goodness. Furthermore, members of the tribe cannot do any good themselves, under their own power or will. As the apostle Paul said, the mind can be willing but the flesh is weak! Only Jesus Christ was and is morally perfect. As soon as we imagine ourselves to be wonderfully moral creatures, pride has taken over our hearts and infected our minds. We arrogantly play God, to paraphrase Augustine.

Imagine this: a religion that says "be good" and then admits that we cannot pull it off! "Thus Christian ethics is distinguished in form and content from every other form of ethical belief."[5] We have to learn to love from one another, largely by doing it. We have to struggle together with how and when to speak up, to protect others' privacy, to quit our jobs because we are being asked to communicate intolerable messages in downright evil ways.

Moreover, we learn moral wisdom within the church not just by talking among ourselves, worshiping, praying, and studying Scripture but by listening to the wise voices of the tribe's past, both modern and ancient: to tradition, to history, to the ancient minds and hearts who frequently understood Scripture and life better than we do. Is there really *any* new communication dilemma under the sun? Created by God, human beings have always taught, delighted and persuaded one another—and invariably for good and for bad.

From Roman Catholics comes *Veritatis Splendor* (1993),[6] a remarkable document that says again what Christians have thought throughout the ages. Real freedom is not listening or speaking or writing or texting at will but instead *communication*—potentially available to all—that leads people by faith and reason to discover the truth of God. To disconnect freedom from God's Word—and thus from God's commands and God's grace—leads to the false but widely held notion that all we need is personal freedom. Free speech and freedom of the press might be necessary for human flourishing, but they are not morally sufficient. Down deep, we all know that pure freedom is a concept which simply does not exist.

Cicero's (106-143) cardinal virtues of prudence, justice, courage and temperance all provide valuable insight for thoughtful people bent on understanding morality and its complexities.[7] We would also do well to consider the wisdom of Aquinas (1225-1274) on natural law,[8] Martin Luther (1483-1546) on the early

Reformation's rejection of virtue ethics,[9] and George Lindbeck's contemporary thinking on the cultural-linguistic theory of morality in which "patterns of experience" and "holding of beliefs" constitute a vocabulary for making sense of experience.[10] Well-known ethicist Clifford Christians says that we humans are created as relational or social beings who commune with one another (and with God) and therefore must look beyond our personal desires and decisions to public ethics.[11] To come full circle, loving ourselves is not enough; our communication has to demonstrate our love of God and neighbor, too.

MORAL MEDIA LIFE

The stories in this book about tribal media demonstrate that many evangelicals want to persuade tribal outsiders to align with Jesus of Nazareth, to trust fully for their futures in the death-conquering evidence of his resurrection. This mission is called *evangelism*—spreading the Good News. It comes directly from Jesus, and no outsiders are excluded from it, regardless of how offensive or inappropriate the persuasion may appear to those from other tribes (Mt 28:18-20).

In spite of the centrality of the tribe's evangelistic mission, however, evangelical media practitioners are not free to persuade by any means. Indeed, the right means is through the exercise of virtues, especially the theological virtues: faith, hope and love.

Coercion and the image of God in all humans. Nor are tribal persuaders permitted to conduct their mission under *coercion*—under force or bodily threat—in spite of the fact that the Christian church historically did this time and time again. Why do so many nonbelievers, or believers in other gods, bring up the Crusades, the nine or so evangelistic military conflicts waged by Christians largely against Muslims between about 1000 and 1300? Because outsiders must be permitted to say no to the message, to decline, refuse, abstain—indeed, to challenge it with rhetorical might.[12] Why? Because every human being is created in the image and likeness of God and thereby deserves to be treated respectfully.[13] Some of Jesus' harshest criticism of religious persons involved their disrespectful, unloving, self-righteous, even coercive persuasion.

Truth telling and promise keeping. If there is a moral priority or first principle for the content of faithful communication, it must be telling the truth in love. Lying disrupts social life, destroys trust and breaks relationships. Even liars do not wish to be lied to! To lie is to lose a social good as valuable and necessary as clean air and safe water.[14] But no one, within or outside the tribe, can tell "all the truth." The truth is always bigger than human beings, often more complicated and convoluted than we can fathom. We live in the middle of relational messes, broken media and mixed-bag ministries that we can hardly understand, let alone communicate about fully to others. So we need to get

WHEN FAITH, TRUTH AND LOYALTY COLLIDE

A Christian reporter landed the religion beat at a major U.S. newspaper full of hope that he could improve religion coverage in the mainstream media. Fast forward eight years: The reporter is dismayed by scandal, exploitation, abuse—all in the name of God. He loses his faith.[a]

Journalism requires a commitment to truth, no matter where it leads. The pursuit of truth—above personal beliefs or philosophies—sets the best journalists apart. But what happens when your search for truth collides with loyalty to your faith or to your tribe's perceived interests?

Some argue that journalists are free agents, responsible mainly to the profession and readers. As a journalist, your internal censor can't be loyalty to any particular group. Sure, strained or broken relationships with family and friends may result,[b] but that's the nature of the craft.

Christian journalists may well be seen as betrayers of their faith when their central moral commitment collides with the agendas of their tribe. But if all truth is God's truth, then how can the journalistic pursuit of truth be contrary to faith?

One reporter wrote, "If the reporters have any integrity at all, it is they who suffer, caught between two allegiances."[c] Christian journalists are no different; they can suffer when caught between their craft and their tribe. And if one journalist loses his faith, who bears the responsibility? The journalist? Or those who can't discern between faithfulness to truth and to themselves?

RICK JACKSON, SEATTLE PACIFIC UNIVERSITY

---

[a]William Lobdell, "Religion Beat Became a Test of Faith," *Los Angeles Times,* July 21, 2007.

[b]Samuel G. Freedman, *Letters to a Young Journalist* (New York: Basic Books, 2006), p. 34.

[c]Jeff Schmalz, quoted in Freedman, *Letters,* p. 36.

beyond the unreasonable standard that the tribe knows and can communicate all the truth about everything.

But *lying*—intentionally deceiving others—cannot be allowed if the evangelistic mission of Jesus practiced by tribal media is to have integrity and receptivity in public, let alone in church. Liars—including benders, spin doctors and image cosmetologists—are increasingly common in tribal circles. Helping someone to speak the truth well is one thing. Helping them to pull the wool over the eyes of the tribe or wider society is something else. Nothing in Christian revelation or tradition justifies such poor esteem for the truth. Yet it goes on daily within the tribe—much more than this book has admitted or had the space to develop.

Virtue orientation. The moral insight that evangelicals need as followers of Jesus includes *purposes* (teleology), *duties* (deontology) and *virtues* (areteology). Cicero established the cardinal virtues, while Aquinas is cited as the first (after Paul) to expound the theological virtues of faith, hope and love. What virtues ought evangelical media practitioners develop in response to today's growing cynicism, materialism and "do-what-works" mentality that typifies Western culture?[15]

Evangelicals should instruct, delight and persuade. But when and how do we connect these purposes to the underlying purpose of loving God, neighbor and self? Phrases like "crossover media," "secular art" and even "Christian entertainment" do not get us very far. We have to broaden the discussion, to ask ourselves what kinds of persons and communities we are called to be. What is a loving Bible-themed park producer, entertainer or publicist? How would we identify someone as a blogger whose hope is truly in Christ, not in his or her own clever prose or forceful ego? What do many of the videos on YouTube suggest about the moral character of the persons who post them for others to enjoy?

Here is the rub: evangelicals cannot begin to get a handle on their virtue orientation without comparing the stories of their own lives with those of believers in other times and places. Virtue development for evangelicals is tricky business, given the looming sin of pride, which waits like an asp to poison the soul of the virtuously strong. The tribe needs bloggers, videographers, novelists, essayists,

THE DAY MY BOOK WAS BANNED

My evangelical publisher called to say he had a big problem with one of my books. Errors? No. Heresy? No. What, then? An evangelical celebrity of sorts was publicly telling people that my book would lead some Christians to watch devilish films with antibiblical themes. Huh?

Allegedly, I was encouraging people to see *Tootsie,* which promotes cross-dressing; *Dead Poet's Society,* which encourages adolescent suicide; and *The Color Purple,* which displays lesbianism. In short, my book purportedly was putting hearts and minds and probably salvation at risk for readers who might be psychologically damaged or cast into hell by seeing such demented, anti-Christian films.

Wow! I had no idea that I had such power! I thought about the likely controversy, the media attention, the wonderful *sales* potential with this kind of brouhaha. Experts say that bad publicity is better than no publicity when it comes to book sales and movie revenues. Maybe I could get Dustin Hoffman or Robin Williams or Oprah Winfrey to give me a piece of their royalties from the heretical movies. Real opportunity! My mind worked overtime.

What should I do? Fight—or at least fight fair? Take on the critic? Challenge the publisher? Turn the other cheek?

I chose the latter. Soon the publisher recalled and then burned every copy of my book. What's the moral?

QUENTIN J. SCHULTZE, CALVIN COLLEGE

columnists and reporters who can cast the tales that help us to see ourselves as we really are, in the light of truth. The tribe does not need more empty promises about "winning the world to Christ" with the latest high-tech magic. Instead of scrutinizing its own past communication, the tribe often moves ahead to the latest medium. The proper evangelistic mission runs full speed ahead while the virtue orientation slips behind. Soon, means seem to justify ends.

Our lives, and our virtue orientation, develop holistically, not just via the media. Often, evangelicals who are the biggest media critics suffer from one major flaw: they focus on big-picture media evangelization campaigns while missing the logs in their own eyes. They simply do not see the problems in their own, local, everyday, virtue-deprived lives. They want to mend the world with the gospel story without tending to the stories of their own organizations, neighborhoods and congregations. They forget that virtue is not learned primarily in books or on websites but in everyday relationships framed around work, play, family, worship and the like.

In real life, interpersonal and mass communication meet. In this complex interaction we become the kinds of persons who are worthy or unworthy of telling the world to listen to us, watch our productions, read our materials and visit our places. Distinctively Christian virtues such as selfless love—*agape*—rarely have been part of the media ethics of any contemporary tribes even though Augustine reminded the church sixteen hundred years ago that communicators are called to love their audiences as their neighbors. At least some scholars are now interested in the full range of virtues related to media practice.[16]

Telos, *purpose, direction—where love and justice meet.* The *telos* (ultimate purpose or end) of the evangelical project requires moral reflection. Tribal media do not become more ethical merely by doing more. They have to think about what, and especially why, they are doing it, and even more about the ultimate purpose they have in mind. Believing in sin as well as grace, evangelicals must be what theologian Reinhold Niebuhr called "Christian realists."[17] Evangelicals should rightly aim to love their audiences. But in the midst of a messed-up world they also have to seek *justice*—to give people what they deserve, what God would have them gain, what shows respect for the image of God in all people.

How can we reconcile the fact that so many tribal media proclaim the love of Jesus Christ but rarely speak up for the poor, homeless and exploited in society? Don't the suffering deserve a voice—just as Jesus gave them a voice in his time on earth? Does it make sense for evangelicals to spend millions on evangelistic media campaigns when the person down the street is going hungry and no one at the nearby church or at city hall knows about it? What about evangelical media operators who do not pay their staff a living wage yet hammer away incessantly about moral decline in society and the need for generous donors to keep their programs coming?

Lutheran pastor and writer Dietrich Bonhoeffer was imprisoned during World War II for plotting to kill Adolf Hitler, and was hanged just before the end of the war in one of Hitler's last petty acts of revenge. During his years in prison, however, Bonhoeffer pastored his German guards and authored some of the most compelling Christian works of the twentieth century—books like *The Cost of Discipleship*. Living in a cell, restricted from access to most mass media, yet full of love and seeking justice, he implored believers to avoid "cheap grace" and seek the fullest possible justice for all people. Bonhoeffer spoke up in spite of the cost. He became one of the most moving examples of the range to which love and justice conflict and interact in a broken world.[18] Unless evangelicals embrace love and justice together, they, too, will testify to cheap grace no matter how impressive their media productions.

AFRICAN GRACE ON THE WEB

A college student from West Africa was quoted in a Christian college newspaper story, but the quote carried tones of nastiness and pettiness. Kwame said it, but he wasn't proud of his words. Shamefaced, he approached the editor to request that the quote be deleted from the story. Denied. To delete one quote would lead to all such quotes appearing only on approval of the person quoted. The editor might have rehearsed John Wayne's line from *The Comancheros:* "Words are what men live by, words they say and mean." Kwame's rancid quote was published.

Then, following customary practice, the "news of the week" went onto the paper's website. Now the world, including Kwame's own faraway family, could find Kwame's words on the Internet and laugh at his dimwitted comments. So also could prospective employers or graduate school committees. Forever, those words would hang in the ether.

"Please," he asked again, "delete me! I've paid. I've learned!" Request accepted. A lesson in tribal mercy.

MARK FACKLER, CALVIN COLLEGE

ETHICAL SUGGESTIONS FOR MEDIA USERS AND PRODUCERS

I am neither priest nor prophet, and not necessarily a good or nice person either. But to leave without a few directed pieces of unsolicited advice is to chicken out (old term)—to be one of the beastly lazies (really old term; see Tit 1:12).

Moral rules alone will not rescue evangelical media from their shortcomings, but public codes of ethics point the way to greater integrity and ensure at least some accountability. The tribe needs to grapple with rules that would help it know when it is disrespecting audiences, manipulating theme park attendees or merely entertaining worshipers. A code of ethics can help even if it is not a solution. Unfortunately, too many codes are image-making, not real, ethics—like telling advertisers to tell the truth without indicating what it means to lie about a product or service.

CYBERSPACE, EXPLOITATION AND SOCIAL TATTOOS

The website was called May Madness. Modeled after the brackets of the NCCA college basketball championships, it was a contest to select the "hottest" woman at a Christian university. Information about each of the "contestants" appeared on the site, including photos of the women taken from their Facebook and MySpace pages. The photos ranged from staid portraits to cheeky or revealing poses. As word of the contest spread on campus, so did outrage against the organizers. Within days the site came down.

This case reveals much about cyberspace, where actions once limited to personal networks move into public ones. The apparent freedom of cyber-transparency carries a price: a loss of control over one's privacy. And control matters because "privacy protects us from being misdefined and judged out of context in a world of short attention spans."[a]

Even though the women who posted their pictures on social networking sites willingly yielded some privacy, they never sought to be exploited by the organizers of May Madness. But the harsh reality of cyberspace is that once those images went online, the women had no control over how others viewed, used or misdefined them.

Exploitation is only one risk. Potential employers search the Facebook and MySpace pages of job applicants, and words and images that once felt like harmless fun turn into personality-defining liabilities. Like a tattoo on a person's arm, these cyber-revelations can turn into social tattoos that are nearly impossible to erase.

RICK JACKSON, SEATTLE PACIFIC UNIVERSITY

[a]Jeffrey Rosen, *The Unwanted Gaze: The Destruction of Privacy in America* (New York: Random House, 2000), p. 8.

Codes need adequate and wise enforcement or they will not gain the public's, let alone the tribe's, respect. Enforcement cannot be left to the volunteer boards of directors of ministries and publishing houses who have vested interests in keeping codes general enough to be meaningless. Too many tribal media boards are composed of individuals with huge stakes in public image. Instead, boards and directors need a corps of wise, external leaders who will speak up and hold the media accountable. Years ago the renowned journalist-philosopher Walter Lippmann called for a council of the wise to monitor the actions of American newspapers.[19] His idea was roundly criticized and rarely approached, partly because it seemed so elitist. Of course, the mainstream media felt that they should monitor themselves. So much for *public* accountability.

Evangelicals are part of a heritage of mutual accountability extending back to ancient Israel, and even before that to the beginning of human life before God the Creator. Churches are meant by God's design to be communities of accountability, not collections of individual communicators who say whatever they think. Boards of directors of every media should be pleading for input from wise and humble Christians who are alert to the "way the world works" but also tuned to the virtues of God-focused purposes and methods.

In addition to using ethical codes as agreed-upon public standards, tribal media must continue promoting virtue among their ranks—especially learning and relearning what it means as communicators to "act justly and to love mercy and to walk humbly" with God (Mic 6:8). There is no end point to this project. Solomon, wise as he was reputed to be, is evidence enough for the need to keep on learning. The virtues to be cultivated, explored, practiced and honored have nothing at all to do with becoming a celebrity, winning awards, racking up more donations, boosting page views, primping for the camera or successfully mimicking contemporary media style. Fortunately, virtue need not be invented. Our inventory is full. But virtue must be interpreted and played out for its logic to be displayed.

Finally, evangelicals have to address their purpose honestly and humbly. The main mission of evangelization is not the whole story. No evangelism is possible without the ineffable action of grace, which cannot be circumscribed by media strategies. Rather, the end point in media must be the same as the end point in every human effort expended under the eye of the Triune God: God's own renown and magnificence, a song in the face of grace, awe confronted by the Word, and the simple response of gratitude for the covenant promise. Here again, instruction and delight are just as important as persuasion; in fact, it is impossible to fully separate the three purposes. God-glorifying communication extends beyond the bounds of such simple categories. Every Christian impulse toward mission should have this ultimate end: persons in community praising God. For this, tribal media need a theology of (shalom-based) culture and a theology of (love/justice-based) cultural transformation, not merely a new technology.

Leadership is action based on wisdom. Christians of every era are called to tell the truth in all that they say, via all media, with their entire lives. When evangelicals take up this multimedia task, however imperfectly, they glorify God by enlarging the world's understanding of Jesus' divine aid, and they increase the scope and depth of the Spirit-led covenant community. This kind of leadership is truly ethical. It looks beyond the mediated idols of our age, such as profit, image and survival. All media—caught in the matrix of technique, money, prestige and divine calling—are important channels of blessings to a hard-of-hearing world. Here and there, moments of truth and breakthroughs of artistry are evident. The chapters in this book speak of them. The integrity and draw of the Christian message lie with those entrepreneurs.

20

Considering a Catholic View of Evangelical Media

PAUL A. SOUKUP, S.J.

Several years ago, the *National Catholic Reporter* carried a story warning readers about the popular Left Behind series of Christian apocalyptic novels. Writers in *The Living Light*, a quarterly publication of the United States Conference of Catholic bishops' Department of Education, point out to their readers that the series denies a number of Catholic teachings and is both subtly and overtly anti-Catholic.[1] While the staff of the bishops' Department of Education probably wanted to prepare teachers for questions from their students who read the Left Behind series, the charge of anti-Catholicism in evangelical discourse was not new.

At the same time, evangelicals and Catholics have found common cause in the United States, working together to defend life at all its stages, to support marriage and family life, and to imbue the culture with religious values. Why, then, the mutual suspicion? What role, if any, do older and newer media play in stereotypes or misunderstandings?

The Catholic and the evangelical traditions of Christianity share wide areas of agreement: not only the values noted above but also the acceptance of the centrality of Christ, a devotion to the Word of God revealed in the Bible, and, less centrally but more relevant to the question, a movement from the margins of U.S. society toward the center. For Catholics, this occurred slowly over the last hundred years, with a defining moment usually credited to the election of John F. Kennedy in 1961 as the first Catholic U.S. president. Catholics today appear in all areas of society. For evangelicals, this movement toward the mainstream is still taking place with ongoing public misunderstanding and criticism not unlike that which Catholics faced a century earlier.

Being Outsiders Together

Groups who perceive themselves as outsiders use a "rhetoric of opposition" that defines themselves as different from others.[2] Such rhetoric, even when addressed outside the group, has the more important function of speaking to the group and reinforcing group identity. From this perspective, both an older Catholic rhetoric and the traditional evangelical one will share at least this characteristic. As is clear in so many evangelical media, the evangelical tribe often defines its identity in terms of us versus them, with them being all of those outside the tribe.

When nonevangelicals tune into many tribal broadcasts or visit tribal websites, they get the impression that they are outsiders who need to be saved or morally or politically converted to one or another cause. It seems to outsiders that evangelicals are indeed tribal—not in the Native American sense but in the sense of seeing themselves as different from and, sometimes, superior to other groups in society—including other Christian groups. Even the way that some evangelical media use the word *Christian* to include only born-again evangelicals contributes to this kind of exclusivism. Evangelicals generally use the phrase "Christian bookstore" to distinguish such shops not just from mainstream bookstores like Barnes & Noble but from Catholic ones as well.

In other words, evangelicals' public rhetoric can easily lead to charges that they are biased, exclusive and even negatively anti-this or anti-that (anti-just-about-everything except themselves, according to some mainstream critics). In the religious realm, this rhetoric of opposition focuses not on similarities of belief with other groups—even other Christian groups—but on particular differences in biblical interpretation, while at the same time ruling out any other interpretation and sometimes the very principle of interpretation itself (as if evangelicals do not interpret Scripture but somehow know exactly what Scripture means).

This dependence on a rhetoric of opposition might also explain why so many aspects of contemporary evangelical communication resemble past (and sometimes present) communication practices in the Catholic Church. Both groups place a premium on communicating internally and externally. Both have established a fairly comprehensive network of print materials (books, magazines, newspapers, bulletins and so on). Both have religious bookstores to support those materials. Both have experimented with and established broadcast ministries. Both explore the use of new communication technologies and have growing, impressive online presences. Both seek to direct the consumption of communication materials by members of their groups, telling them what to consume and what not to consume. Both openly acknowledge the impact of communication media on society and question how the religious community should respond. Both can become defensive in the face of mainstream culture that seems at times to threaten its values, beliefs and institutions. Because of this, both seek to meet all the communication needs of their tribes.

This attitude toward communication as being critical for identity, community and reaching outside the tribe is so deeply evangelical and Catholic that the affinities can become oddly humorous. A Catholic leader quipped that, after the establishment of a Catholic school system, Catholic hospital system, Catholic insurance groups, Catholic News Service and Catholic communications, the next logical step would be a Catholic highway system! If that sounds strange, consider the story in chapter one of this book about one of this book's editors flying to a Christian Booksellers Convention with a woman who was in the Christian (evangelical!) wallpaper business.

So the irony, from a communications perspective, is that both evangelicals and Catholics sometimes long for (or seem to feel more comfortable with) a religious ghetto, where they can practice their respective approaches to Christian faithfulness in peace. Even though both groups are evangelical in the sense of reaching out to make converts, they also find great comfort within the tribe. It is also likely that both tribes spend more of their formal communications dollars on intratribal messaging than on extratribal messaging. The Catholic Periodical Literature Index includes over 170 periodicals.[3] The largest Protestant group, Southern Baptists, indexes thirty to forty titles yearly in the Southern Baptist Periodical Index.[4] Nearly all of these periodicals serve the tribe instead of focusing on converting outsiders.

THE POPE CELEBRATES CYBERSPACE

The Vatican, which now has one of the largest websites of historical Christian documents as well as contemporary papal pronouncements, began archiving paper materials over a millennium ago. On World Communications Day in 1989, Pope John Paul II said,

> Surely we must be grateful for the new technology which enables us to store information in vast man-made artificial memories, thus providing wide and instant access to the knowledge which is our human heritage, to the Church's teaching and tradition, the words of Sacred Scripture, the counsels of the great masters of spirituality, the history and traditions of the local churches, of religious orders and lay institutes, and to the ideas and experiences of initiators and innovators whose insights bear constant witness to the faithful presence in our midst of a loving Father who brings out of His treasure new things and old.[a]

[a]Pope John Paul II, "The Church Must Learn to Cope with Computer Culture," Eternal Word Television Network, May 27, 1989 <www.ewtn.com/library/PAPALDOC/JP2COMPU.HTM>.

WHY THE EVANGELICALS BEAT THE MAINLINE MEDIA

To many people in many cultures, the most dramatic symbol of modernity[a] is mass communications, especially electronic. To many Americans, the mainline churches most openly embrace modernity. Supposedly, mainline denominations are the most progressive. In theory, they would have been the media pioneers and leaders in the use of radio, television, movies and the Internet.

Not at all. In open competition in North America or anywhere else, the more conservative religious groups—evangelicals included—outpace the more moderate, liberal and modernist ones. If those conservatives were typed as otherworldly and the mainline churches as this-worldly, both groups' use of mass media challenge the stereotypes. Evangelical media efforts seem to be more fully *in* the world.

Why did the conservatives, once cruelly dismissed as "red-neck," "hillbilly," "holy roller," "backwoods" and "rube" from the Bible Belt(s) become technologically sophisticated and programmatically adept at holding audiences, while the mainline, with few exceptions, made few efforts to build media and gather audiences?

One thing the mainline has wanted to do is keep its dignity, shunning the overt worldliness of show-business approaches to spreading the gospel and entertaining the faithful. I recall the Reverend Claude Evans, then campus pastor at Southern Methodist University, making national headlines and being pictured "dancing"—locking elbows and spinning is all that it amounted to—in the aisle of the campus chapel. His colleagues and supporters sneered. I recall radio humorist and mainline Presbyterian Stan Freberg doing some very respectable but creative "go-to-church" radio commercials. He was lambasted not by conservatives but by liberals. Undignified.

The apostle Paul's "being all things to all people" gets quoted in situations like this. Why not entertain, if that's what audiences want? With some notable exceptions, the mainline churches don't try to be and do all things. Why?

Maybe most mainline denominations have the heritage of church establishment in their bones: Episcopalians in England, Congregationalists in New England, Presbyterians in Scotland, Reformed in central Europe, Lutherans in Germany and Scandinavia. The Methodists (carrying the Anglican genes) came closest to breaking the mold in the late nineteenth century but chose to grow more staid in the late twentieth century. And establishments—when they are established—do not have to enter the marketplace and compete. So when they become post-establishment (something they realized later in the century), it's too late to get new habits and learn new tricks.

In these respects, I compare mainline Christian groups to the noble Greeks when the restless Romans ruled the empire. The Greeks had philosophy, true art, great history, fine literature and left-over temples, but power had shifted. They looked down on the law-making and military Romans and their barbarian neighbors from their lofty perch, while the former outsiders, in effect saying "to hell with dignity," got in there and competed. Whether all the moves of either were truly congruent with their gospel messages is for others to decide. If the gospel calls for pragmatism, we know who won: the conservatives, who determined what worked—and therefore what was deemed to be true.

MARTIN E. MARTY, FAIRFAX M. CONE DISTINGUISHED SERVICE PROFESSOR EMERITUS, UNIVERSITY OF CHICAGO

---

[a]*Modernity* includes human belief in rationality and progress, often equated with belief in scientific ways of discovering truth and technological means of ushering in progress.

Communicating Beyond the Tribe

When a religious group values its identity, it is not always sure how to communicate beyond its own tribal borders, for fear of losing its identity in the process. Both Catholics and evangelicals have struggled to find a culturally accepted mode of expression. They wonder how to use newspapers, radio programming, TV, music, worship media, the Internet and so on. Should they merely imitate the media forms of the wider culture, or should they develop a distinctively tribal format? Should they stand apart from the culture in which they live, or should they seek an accommodation? It might surprise some evangelicals to discover that Catholics are similarly concerned about remaining *in* without becoming *of* the world! This is partly why Catholics have been much slower to make worship more contemporary, even with guitar Masses and the charismatic movement that swept through some Catholic circles in the 1960s to the 1980s.

North American Catholics, as members of immigrant minority communities often facing discrimination, have wrestled with these questions for years. The parallel is not perfect, but some evangelical groups from lower socioeconomic groups today still face similar discrimination or at least elitist criticism. For instance, some of the televangelists are pummeled by TV talk show hosts and newspaper columnists who love to make fun of the evangelical celebrities' ostentatious clothing, freshly coiffed hairstyles, gaudy furniture, Southern accents and taste in country-style music. Even the term *fundamentalist* is used by some mainline media to put down seemingly unlikable or culturally awkward evangelicals.

This kind of cultural tension might be worsened by most evangelical tribes' lack of a clearly defined leadership structure. The impression one gets from mainstream media is that evangelicals are led by entrepreneurial, independent, charismatic (in the secular sense) pastors and preachers, the best known of whom have founded megachurches or begun television ministries. As the various chapters in this book show, each communication medium embraced by evangelicals depends somewhat on a few powerful leaders who have shaped those ministries. Moreover, these leaders and their ministries tend to be criticized not just by mainstream media but even by some evangelicals themselves. Evangelicals have replaced one pope with many popes. High-ranking religious leaders are lightning rods for criticism in any tradition but especially for mainstream media for whom the leaders symbolize all that is wrong with a religion more than what is right with it—with few North American exceptions such as Billy Graham.

Again from an outsider perspective, it seems clear that evangelical structures of charismatic leadership and independent churches lead to competing interpretations of the evangelical *tradition*—even if some evangelicals do not like to use the word because it seems to put rote ways of doing things above Scripture. There is an evangelical tradition that can be traced back to late-nineteenth-century revivalism, before that to the Great Awakenings, even earlier to the Reformation, and to the early church. The fact that so many evangelicals do not seem to be aware of their own theological and church traditions—along with the fact that evangelicals normally are quick to welcome new members who bring a theology and an understanding of Christianity formed outside of the evangelical tradition—leads to ongoing conflict and confusion within the evangelical tribe. The transition from minority group to established group requires self-confidence and the ability to balance the competing interests and creative expressions of the group. This becomes more difficult since the evangelical community consists not just of one local church but of a wide association of churches. The message to outsiders is that evangelicals cannot even agree among themselves, let alone with outsiders.

The Catholic Church dealt with these sorts of tensions by appealing to a long theological tradition and a hierarchical governing structure rooted in that tradition. Here, then, is one area of significant difference between the evangelical and Catholic approaches to communication. The Catholic Church has a mechanism in place to plan for and coordinate communication, however imperfectly. It has accepted methods both to criticize its communication structures and efforts and to act on that critique. It also has a structure that allows a given individual or group to speak for the entire body—both to speak within the tribe and to speak outside the tribe. This is the Catholic Church's "integrated marketing plan"—to borrow a marketing phrase used in chapter sixteen of this book—that catches the overall concept if not the spirit of such controlled communication.

THEOLOGICAL DIFFERENCES IN COMMUNICATION

Other differences between the Catholic and many evangelical approaches to communication stem largely from theology. Historically rooted in Reformation theology, many evangelical communities arise from the Free Church tradition and reject any kind of centralizing organization. Insisting on the primacy and truth of the Bible, the evangelical tradition stresses biblical literalism. Focusing on commitment to Jesus as Savior, the tradition highlights individual conversion and an ongoing relationship with the Lord. Each of these key aspects has consequences for communication, media use and media study.

What evangelicals might see as market-driven, dynamic communication, Catholics often see as overlapping and sometimes competitive or even contradictory communication efforts. Evangelicals seem to be competing with themselves! The Reformation roots of this theology can also have the unfortunate side effect of a lack of attention to the wider history of Christianity. Many times, thought and research about Christian communication jumps from Augustine to the post-Reformation period as if no Christian communicators existed in the medieval and pre-Reformation period. Yet as the authors have mentioned in this volume, those were critically important times for the creation, collection and spread of manuscripts—the early "network" era long before the creation of the movable-type printing press. There was also significant work on oral communication, including preaching, and on worship itself as communication—singing, prayer, sacraments and all. Why wouldn't evangelicals using PowerPoint today in worship dip into the wisdom behind the use of stained-glass windows and other nonverbal communication from many centuries ago?

All Christian groups interpret the Bible. Important evangelical beliefs, such as the rapture (whose centrality in the Left Behind series prompted those questions by the Catholic Department of Education) arise from particular nineteenth-century interpretations of biblical texts, interpretations not shared by other Christian groups. Evangelicals' focus on biblical literalism leads to their emphasis on a sender-message-receiver model and a practical failure to incorporate studies that stress the role of the audience in interpreting, resisting and shaping messages. Ironically, evangelicals also focus on sin, which surely must affect how people interpret Scripture and other messages.

The ahistorical tendency of this theology can sometimes lead to a lack of appreciation of how communication technology shapes not only faith expression but faith itself. But today we must more consciously attend to both the challenges and the opportunities presented by communication technology. In the sixteenth century, Luther and the other reformers made extensive use of the printing press, and many scholars and historians credit it with adding power and range to the Reformation.[5] In addition to the external effects of the printing press—the availability and distribution of materials (especially the Bible), the forms of writing and polemic, and so on—the printing press also fostered widespread literacy, which in time "restructures consciousness."[6] Writing leads to greater interiority and personal responsibility.[7] The Reformed churches, with their greater emphasis on Bible reading than in the Catholic tradition, stress much more than Catholics the interior and personal relationship with Jesus Christ, whereas the more orally based Catholicism focuses on community, ritual and group identity as members of the body of Christ.

The Oral Turn

These historical accidents of communication technology shape the evangelical experience. Today, as communication forms manifest a secondary orality (i.e., oral presentations based on written texts[8]), people's consciousness again undergoes a restructuring. In addition to the benefits of literacy, people have more experience of orality, in radio, television, film, telephony and so on. No surprise, then,[9] that ritual and multimedia community events have become greater parts of evangelical worship. Megachurches simply would not happen in a print-Bible-only world. But that also means that the personal response to Jesus Christ and the purely bibliocentric experience of religion will subtly change.[10]

This has two consequences. First, evangelical communities (and indeed all Christian churches) must pay more attention to audience-reception studies. How do people negotiate meaning and create meanings from the multitude of communication materials available to them? The "media, culture, and religion" perspective[11] argues that religious groups need to pay much more attention to what people actually do in their construction of religious meaning than they have in the past. Even the most devout church member will assemble coherent (at least to them) religious meaning from biblical, ecclesial and popular culture.

Second, an important opportunity and challenge for evangelical communication lies in "materializing religion."[12] Every religious faith must have its physical form: "Religious beliefs are embedded and embodied within myriad physical forms proclaiming and affirming adherence to this spiritual way, that credo and that line of theological argument. Articles of faith of the mental and constitutional sort are complemented by articles of faith of the material and sensory sort."[13] Religious belief needs physical expression. No surprise that statues and stained glass, distinct architecture and vesture, music styles and rituals mark out Catholic churches. No surprise, either, that evangelical churches now seek out material forms to manifest their faith: books, music, television, radio, Internet sites, public relations, films—all the communication media discussed here seek to "materialize" evangelical belief. In other words, evangelicals seek to develop a consistent aesthetic.

Scholars acknowledge that contemporary society has split aesthetics from religion. They also emphasize the importance of art and artistic expression to religious belief and practice.[14] In this view every religion has a distinctive aesthetic. Easier to recognize through historical study (the Lutheranism of Bach's music, the Methodism of Wesleyan hymnody, the Catholicism of Gregorian chant, to cite only musical examples), a religious aesthetic grows from the religious traditions, especially of Christianity.

A Catholic Aesthetic

Richard A. Blake finds such an aesthetic in the work of Catholic film directors, whether or not they maintained their church allegiance and practice. For him, this "indelible Catholic imagination" grows from a theological grounding and informs all their subsequent creative expression. His exposition of the workings of a religious aesthetic shows how religion or theology interacts with artistic expression. To illustrate his thesis, he first describes key characteristics of Catholic theology:

> Catholic theologians . . . tend to stress God's presence in the world, and thus for them the material universe is "somewhat like God." Catholics thus find analogy a useful means to arrive at knowledge of God, who, as processed through the analogical imagination, is something like human experience of the material world. . . . In contrast, Protestant theologians, in many of their classic works, tend to stress God's absence from the world. God is known in rare moments of self-revelation, such as the unique event of the person of Jesus Christ. A theology that stresses the absence of God must be understood in terms of a dialectical imagination: God is completely other.[15]

Blake then describes how these different theological starting points will lead to different aesthetic expressions:

> In the Catholic imagination, if God is perceived as present and active in the material world, it makes perfect sense to celebrate that presence by decorating churches with statues, paintings, and stained glass. But if God is absent, then a more austere form of church design better reflects the human condition: life in this present material world is bleak, but a better life is coming. In addition, since Catholics consider the community sacred because of God's presence here and now, Catholics will tend to stress moral and doctrinal conformity, which defines and supports the community, while Protestants will be more comfortable with private interpretation of Scripture or dogma.[16]

How, then, does a Catholic theological aesthetic take shape? Blake suggests three key elements together with six theological footprints or signs.[17] First, a Catholic aesthetic will stress *sacramentality* (that is, the principle that God chooses to use the physical world as a means of self-communication). Objects and experiences can take on spiritual significance and even supernatural value.

To quote Gerard Manley Hopkins's poetic expression, "The world is charged with the grandeur of God."[18]

Second, a Catholic aesthetic manifests *mediation*. People, events and things function as mediators "between God and God's activity in the world."[19] God is a multimedia communicator! Just as Christ is the mediator between God and man, so is the body of Christ.

Third, a Catholic aesthetic both *builds on and builds up communion*—Catholics belong to a group because they belong to the body of Christ. Redemption occurs not alone but as a member of that body. Solidarity is an essential virtue, the one true tribalism.

Blake then offers more concrete manifestations of this aesthetic: "Catholics love saints"; "Catholics love the physical"; "Catholics love the sacramental"; "Catholics love devotional activities"; "Catholics love mentoring"; "Catholics love conscience"; "Catholics love narratives of moral growth"; and "Catholics love the ordinary."[20] Each of these, he argues, helps to locate and identify a specific Catholic imagination or aesthetic. The importance of his argument lies not so much in what he offers as evidence but in his recognition that any given theological tradition within Christianity will have particular marks of creative expression.

An Evangelical Aesthetic

What about distinctively evangelical communication? Because I write from outside the tribe, I hesitate to offer even an outline of an evangelical aesthetic. However, if we examine only the theological threads of evangelical life already noted, we can see some consequences in the materials of communication. The centrality of the Bible and its literal interpretation suggest that an evangelical aesthetic will emphasize words and reliance on textual approaches (in songs, sermons, Internet sites and so on). Similarly, one would expect an aesthetic of illustration (stories with a point) and commentary (in books and magazines). Films would have some measure of a didactic (teaching) aesthetic, with stories connected to the Bible.

The self-identity of the evangelical communities as free churches leads to an aesthetic of individualism, not only in a preference for characters who stand alone against the crowd but for an individual spirit of critique. Works created by some tribes within the evangelical community may not find acceptance among others. This spirit of self-reliance may also interact with what Max Weber identified as the spirit of capitalism, leading to an aesthetic of work and reward, and of entrepreneurship.[21]

Conclusion

Like Catholic communication before it, evangelical media and communication seek a cultural role, both in the church and within the larger society. Moving from a more insular position, defined by opposition, into the mainstream, the group must now define itself by a particular aesthetic. In other words, evangelicals have to know who they are as a people, even how they understand ultimate reality, and how that reality is to be communicated. They cannot do this in a vacuum, without knowing their history and the various strands of theology and piety that have shaped their history as part of the larger church. Evangelical media and their creators have an opportunity to play an important role in the ongoing theological identity of the community. As communication practices change, so will self-understanding—not only in the larger society but also in the church.

21

Looking with a Jew at Evangelical Popular Culture

MARK I. PINSKY

New Testament–based popular culture is largely irrelevant to most North American Jews, except when it offends, such as in the case of Mel Gibson's *The Passion of the Christ.* Then some Jews quickly object to the way their biblical forebearers are portrayed: evil, sinister Messiah-rejecters. Typically the result is cross-faith squabbling among mainline Protestants, Catholics, evangelicals and Jews over the art's message.

But even heated conflicts provide opportunities for furthering mutual understanding. A prominent rabbi told his synagogue he was "trying to see the movie *The Passion* through the eyes of our Christian neighbors," and how the controversy and the criticism of the film have caused more harm than good. "It's important for us to try to understand how Christians see this film, and how potentially hurtful it is for Jews to be attacking the central story of Christianity, for asking them to adjust their perspective on what is so central, so important to their faith."[1]

Jews, like Christians, can use *The Passion* to examine their faith. As a well-known rabbi suggested, "The best response that we in the Jewish community can have to this film is to educate our children more about the Jewish perspective," including "the Jewish historical understanding of that time, our understanding of Jesus, the Jewish notion of the Messiah."[2] Misunderstanding goes both ways. "I think that while most Christians don't understand the Jewish perspective, most Jews do not understand the Christian one, either," offered another rabbi.[3]

Being Jewish in Judeo-Christian Culture

Does the hyphenated concept of a Judeo-Christian tradition define the cultural core of contemporary American society? Probably. The idea of a "unified Judeo-Christian tradition" is just over one hundred years old. But where does the Judeo part end and the Christian begin? Even more muddled is that gray area where the two traditions may overlap.[4]

I was raised in a Conservative, observant Jewish home in the southern New Jersey suburbs, in a family of four that watched *Leave It to Beaver* together. I voraciously consumed popular culture even as I moved to North Carolina in 1965 to attend Duke University—where I first read the New Testament (NT). Twenty years later I moved from Durham to Southern California, where I specialized in covering religious broadcasting for the *Los Angeles Times* in Orange County, home of Robert Schuller's *Hour of Power* and the Trinity Broadcasting Network (TBN). A decade later, in 1995, I became religion writer for the *Orlando Sentinel* and since then have been immersed in the world of Sunbelt evangelicalism and its relationship to popular culture. I have written three books examining religion in secular animated television comedies and film, as well as evangelical popular culture. Without irony, I can say that some of my best friends are evangelicals, and my reporting leads me to church more often than a lot of Christians.

I have seen that when evangelicals base their work on the Hebrew Bible (which Christians refer to as the Old Testament [OT]), friction sometimes emerges. Church historian Martin E. Marty is amused "to see how many stories like Noah, Samson, Gideon, and other derring-do are featured in our warrior culture, and I think Christians tend to do so more than Jews."[5] Jews often assume a special interest in their Scripture, and they can be either generous or touchy about the way in which it is used by others. "I don't see it as Jewish tradition being hijacked by Christian genres of popular culture but rather that they are repackaged—a little watered down maybe—but I support the notion of faith-based programming," says one Orthodox rabbi.[6]

The animated feature *The Prince of Egypt,* based on the book of Exodus, was a mainstream production from a Hollywood studio, DreamWorks SKG, led by three Jews—filmmaker Steven Spielberg, music mogul David Geffen and Disney veteran Jeffrey Katzenberg. With Michael Eisner, Katzenberg is credited with the second golden age of animation at Disney with blockbuster classics like *The Little Mermaid, Beauty and the Beast, Aladdin* and *The Lion King. The Prince of Egypt* was Katzenberg's first major project at DreamWorks.

Katzenberg, a committed, synagogue-attending Jew, made extensive efforts to consult Jewish, Christian, and Muslim scholars and leaders throughout the production process of *The Prince of Egypt,* incorporating many of their suggestions and addressing their criticisms in the final version. As a result, many Christian pastors across the country adopted the film, preaching sermons based on it and organizing group screenings.

Do evangelical filmmakers consult Jewish scholars and leaders? I doubt it. Why? There may be some resentment over the widespread perception that Jews already have a stranglehold on Hollywood. But for Christians, the problem may not so much be exclusion or insensitivity or arrogance as the fact that many evangelicals assume that they are the majority. If they do not interact with Jews regularly, they might not even think about consulting with Jews when using OT source material. This, I think, is a loss to both sides, as interfaith dialogue can be critical to the excellence of the final product.

JEWS VIEW VEGGIETALES

Bible college dropouts Phil Vischer and Mike Nawrocki, creators of the VeggieTales series of computer-generated morality tales, realized that wit and good writing could help them compete with the big studios. They also understood the two-track formula of successful children's animation: comedic images and songs for children; witty jokes and cultural references for adults watching with them. Their company, Big Idea, managed to escape the tribal market and crossed over to mainstream audiences, from Target stores to NBC-TV and Telemundo, where the show drew about a million viewers a week in early airings.

VeggieTales drew on numerous OT stories, including David and Goliath; Joshua; and Shadrach, Meshach and Abednego. "We made the rule early on that we wouldn't portray Jesus as a vegetable," Vischer explained. "That eliminated most of the stories from the NT. Virtually everything else is letters and correspondence. All the big, cinematic stories are in the OT, so that's where we spent most of our time."[7] Sometimes, the VeggieTales versions are removed from the context of the Bible—perhaps to desanctify them and allow them to be funnier. They are then plopped down in some silly setting, often recognizable only to parents (or grandparents) raised on commercial television. The DVD *Moe & the Big Exit*, for example, was based on the Exodus, like DreamWorks' *Prince of Egypt*. In the VeggieTales version, the story is a sequel to the *The Ballad of Little Joe*. That DVD is the story of Joseph and his brothers, set in the Old West and in turn loosely based on the popular western TV show *Bonanza*, which featured Michael Landon (a Jew, later responsible for *Highway to Heaven*) as the youngest son.

Like many of the episodes, *Moe & the Big Exit*—based on TV's *Lone Ranger*—began with the major series characters, Larry the Cucumber and Bob the Tomato, serving as hosts, reading a letter from a young fan who has a problem, in this case a girl who feels powerless. At the conclusion, Larry and Bob explain that "God's Word is for everyone." The words of Psalm 28:7 flash on the screen: "The Lord is my strength and my shield; my heart trusts in him, and I am helped." The message is simple and repetitive. "God can give you the strength to do what he asks," Bob says. "If you let God be your strength and follow his directions, you'll be amazed at what he can do through you." At least one rabbi "found the biblical link a little dubious and confusing." He added that "creators, who should be commended for introducing faith-based storylines, may be better served concentrating on regular biblical storylines that push ethical morality and family values. We need this also."[8]

The book of Jonah, with its theme of returning to God and the nature of divine mercy, is read on Yom Kippur, the Day of Repentance, which concludes the Jewish High Holy Days. Vischer and Nawrocki, to some degree inspired by elements of the Disney classic *Pinocchio,* chose Jonah as the subject of their first, full-length $15-million VeggieTales feature. The movie earned $25.5 million in U.S. theaters in 2002,[9] but combined production and marketing costs ultimately resulted in a restructuring of the company and change of ownership.

This version of the Bible story is told in its biblical period, as a story within a story, recounted by the comic "Pirates who don't do anything" to a group of young vegetables whose trip to a youth rock concert has been delayed by an accident. The point of the story that the cranky youngsters are told at the outset is about compassion: "When you see someone who needs help and you wanna help 'em."

Jonah goes into the sea and the storm ceases, but soon the ominously familiar chords of the *Jaws* movie theme are heard. Swallowed by the big fish, Jonah sits on the deck of one of several wooden ships in the cavernous stomach and finally gets the message. "I might as well face it," he says. "God gave me a job to do and I disobeyed him. I ran the other way. I've done something terrible, and now I'm getting what I deserve. I'm going to die in this whale." Or not. An angelic gospel choir of apparently African American vegetables appears to sing a raucous hymn called "God of Second Chances." However, as with the earlier image of Jonah with his scroll, the choir robes with stiff shoulders give the singers the shapes of crosses. As they sing, cutaway shots of the wooden masts of the other marooned ships provide a scene of more crosses.

"Yes, folks assumed the choir robes in Jonah represented crosses," Vischer said. "To the best of my knowledge, this was not intentional symbolism. I believe the designer was simply trying to give the simple veggies 'shoulders' to give the animators a little more to work with in animation." Vischer added, "As for the ship's masts in the belly of the whale, those were intentional Christian symbols. Jesus interpreted Jonah's three days in a whale as a symbolic precursor to his own three days in the grave." Vischer explained that the text "refers to Jonah calling out to God from *sheol,*" which in Hebrew means "grave" or "underworld." His production designer "wanted the interior of the whale to bring to mind a graveyard, which, as a Christian artist, implied crosses." These interpretations "are very prevalent in Christian commentaries," Nawrocki added.[10]

By and large, evangelicals fairly treat the OT for mainstream audiences. NT references are subtle and rarely heavy handed. Anyone but a Jewish religion reporter or a rabbi might not notice them at all. Vischer explained that he and Nawrocki "study the Bible very carefully. We'll figure out the key plot points, the key themes, and set them aside as sacred—cannot be messed with." The rest, he says, they have fun with. "My own retellings of stories were so simple and basic that I usually just worked off the biblical text," Vischer said. "Mike got a little more elaborate with his work on Jonah and researched various commentaries for background information."[11]

Nawrocki consulted Jewish sources on this and other episodes. "I know I've read rabbis on the Internet," he said, in particular when he and Vischer did their version of the less-well-known story of Ruth and Boaz. "It was obvious to me that the writers had really done their homework and tried to capture the essence of the story," said one rabbi, who was untroubled by the Christian symbolism in *Jonah*. "It seemed a better fit than the Exodus in *Moe*."[12]

Although they have done many OT stories, VeggieTales has been especially successful with smaller stories, like the book of Esther, one of the shorter ones in the canon, appearing just before Job. Esther is set in exile from Judea, in Persia, and is unique in that neither the word *God* nor *Lord* appears in the Hebrew text. By today's standards of gender equality and egalitarian marriages, it is retrograde. Its precipitating conceit is an act of wifely defiance by the queen of Persia, Vashti, which leads to her banishment or execution, depending on which Talmudic interpretation you accept. The king decrees that "all the women will respect their husbands, from the least to the greatest . . . that every man should be ruler over his own household" (Esther 1:20-22). Her successor is chosen in a royal beauty contest, and the result is a mixed marriage, between a pagan king and a Jewish maiden.

While there are no specific references to Jews—characters talk about "our people" or "our family"—the cartoon version relies on some Christian and apocryphal versions of the scroll, adding numerous references to God and the Lord. "I bow to no one but God and my king," Mordecai tells the infuriated Haman. "We try to bring God into all our stories, even if he isn't mentioned explicitly in the source material," Vischer said. "Esther and Mordecai, as pious Jews, would have had that assumption of God and Providence, and recognized their place in God's will," said Nawrocki. The soundtrack at times sounds like traditional klezmer music (a distinctive Jewish folk style which originated in Eastern Europe and was often performed by small bands at weddings).

As in Jonah, costumes on tall, narrow characters form what appear to be a cross, in this case Esther's shoulder pads. She is reluctant to be a heroine, like the biblical figure. "You never need to be afraid to do what is right," Mordecai tells her early in the cartoon, when she does not want to join the royal beauty pageant. Later, she questions why she is obligated to risk her life to save her people.

Mordecai says, "God must have a reason, Esther. Perhaps he put you here for such a time as this. . . . You never have to be afraid to do what's right. I'll pray for you. We'll all pray for you." Convinced, Esther sings, "There is nothing I can't face when God is on my side." The narrator explains, "Sometimes God has plans so big only he can see them." Here at least some rabbis were impressed. "I thought the VeggieTales on Jonah was, on the whole, quite good," said one rabbi. "I was impressed with their correct definition of a prophet being a messenger from God, and *not* someone who 'sees the future.' I thought that some of the humor was puerile [childish] but that the message and the content were very good. I found that the point came across without hitting me over the head."[13] Another rabbi remarked, "I enjoyed the [Esther] episode," he said, "but I was surprised that the Jews were not mentioned at all."[14]

Evangelical Sensitivities for Jewish Audiences

Some evangelicals urge caution when adapting stories from the OT. "Those of us who wish to portray characters from the Hebrew Bible share a responsibility to interpret those characters and their stories accurately," said a seminary professor. "Too often, we have been guilty of reading NT theology back into the OT at the expense of careful exegesis and sound interpretive method. While Christians may certainly recognize the fulfillment of specific prophecies regarding the person and work of the Messiah (e.g., Mic 5:2, among many) in the NT, we must be diligent not to impose a convenient Christological interpretation on an OT passage whose context has nothing to do with messianic issues (e.g., the allegorical interpretation that links the lovers' relationship in the Song of Solomon with the relationship between Christ and His church)."[15] He adds that the best resources for understanding Hebrew texts in their cultural and historical contexts are often Jewish.

Still, evangelicals have their own views of the OT based on their reading of the NT. This kind of reading of Hebrew Scripture offends some Jews, especially when Jewish converts offer it publicly. For instance, a converted Jew who founded the $15-million Holy Land Experience theme park in Orlando aimed to inform Christians of the Jewish roots of their faith and to convert Jews in North America and Israel to Christianity.[16] When the park opened in 2001, the issue of targeting Jews for evangelism became a heated issue, locally and nationally, and the founder vociferously defended his view that the Jewish people did not have sole custody of the OT. However, over time the controversy waned as he assured people that the primary objective of Holy Land was to educate, enlighten and, to some degree, entertain. When the founder left, however, messianic literature and most ritual objects from the park's three bookstores disappeared. It seemed that the park was shoring up its primary market, evangelical believers, and forgoing Jewish evangelism.

ACTING JEWISH—*AND* CHRISTIAN

Sometimes Jews make appearances in commercial television series or movies with an overtly (if watered down) Christian construct. Comedian (and Jew) Richard Lewis played a rabbi on the WB network's *7th Heaven*. His character's daughter marries one of the sons of the show's main character, a mainline Protestant minister. "It's Judaism 101 as the Camdens learn about Shabbat, circumcision, conversion and Jewish baby-naming practices," wrote Jewishjournal.com. The show's creator, Brenda Hampton, a mainline Protestant who also created *Mad About You* (which featured another Jewish-Christian interfaith couple), said she used Lewis and the romance because "I thought at this point in our history it might be nice to include people of other faiths on the show." Jews would probably not be offended, she said, since "We never use the word, 'Jesus.' We try to be as harmless as possible."[17]

Touched by an Angel was another popular show produced by evangelicals. The theme of the series was redemption, and at the conclusion of most episodes a white dove flew across the screen, symbolizing the presence of the Holy Spirit. However, the episode entitled "Bar Mitzvah" told the story of three generations of Jewish men. The grandfather was a once-devout man who rejected his faith after a stroke and fought his way back to health through force of will. (This role was played by film icon Kirk Douglas, a Jew who had suffered a stroke in real life.) The patriarch's son, who immersed himself in his tradition's spirituality, developed a terminal brain tumor. A boy, preparing for his bar mitzvah, was torn between the religious values of his father and those of his grandfather.

Concerned that the story be told with sensitivity, the Christian producers called on two other Jews, Allen Estrin and Rabbi Joseph Telushkin, to write the episode. Telushkin asked Douglas to take the part: "When he sent me the script," Douglas said, "I liked it very much. And I enjoyed doing it. . . . I like *[Touched by an Angel]* because it's one of the shows that try to deal with spirituality and not any specific religion. And I applaud that."[18] In this case, however, the episode concludes with the grandfather convincing the boy to proceed with his bar mitzvah, joining him in the pulpit to read the Torah. And when the episode ended, the show's trademark, the dove, did *not* fly.

CONCLUSION

Who owns popular culture? Christians? Catholics? Jews? Evangelicals? Corporations? Who controls it? Who *should* control it? The market economy controls American popular culture, as it does much of the rest of our lives. In that context, however, there is a tradition of American religious pluralism, a civic assumption which requires a certain amount of mutual respect and sensitivity. Within the practical constraints of capitalism, popular culture should be pluralistic, reflecting our increasingly heterogeneous culture itself. That should go equally for the evangelical tribe and my own tribe in Hollywood.

Arguably, the best-known evangelical on North American TV is Ned Flanders, Homer Simpson's next-door neighbor, created and developed for the most part by avowedly non-Christians—including several Jews—on *The Simpsons* writing staff. Notwithstanding, many discerning Christians have come to see Ned as a positive, if sometimes silly and overzealous, role model.[19]

Evangelicals will have to decide for themselves whether they are treated fairly by Jews, just as Jews will have to discern the spirits that animate evangelical interpretations of the Hebrew Bible. There are no Judeo-Christians to provide the final say. Given the increasing role of non-Christian, non-Jewish faiths in America, such a contrived person would hardly suit the future, anyway. Events like the brouhaha over Gibson's *The Passion* can be divisive, but they can also lead theists, deists and atheists to consider anew how they portray one another, even how they view one another in their hearts. As the great Jewish sage Maimonides advises, "There is no doubt that every man who ennobles his soul with excellent morals and wisdom based on faith in God [whether Jewish or non-Jewish] certainly belongs to the men of the world to come [Heaven]."

Conclusion

Being Fairly Self-Critical About Evangelical Media

QUENTIN J. SCHULTZE
AND ROBERT H. WOODS JR.

The conversations in this book are over, but the conversations in our lives continue. We suspect that most readers were grateful, disappointed, bewildered or inspired—perhaps all at the same time! The same responses colored the conversations when most of the authors assembled to talk about their contributions to this volume.

The authors graciously accepted the risky challenge "to speak the truth in love" about evangelical media. There is always some pain in self-criticism. Part of the pain comes from admitting that evangelicals sometimes do not have the media figured out and make mistakes. Evangelicals' personal and tribal identities are closely tied to the media they use, the media celebrities they admire and the artists they appreciate. Even the very idea of criticizing evangelical media seems to be disloyal to the tribe.

But there is no single tribe of evangelicals. The various fans and critics highlighted in this volume reflect evangelicals' own diversity of views on mainstream and tribal media. Constructive criticism from one tribe can look like knee-jerk disloyalty to another. Clearly, evangelicals find their unity in Christ, not in their divergent opinions about popular culture or new media. In fact, being a faithful evangelical media critic in North America is a balancing act. On one side is praise for outstanding evangelical media efforts—creative, authentic, virtuous and the like. On the other side is blame for poorly done, propagandistic, even unbiblical media efforts. Both can be accurate assessments.

The conversations in this volume suggest a few important conclusions.

Evangelicals are predictable. They respond conventionally to new media. First, they praise the new opportunities to spread the gospel. They see God at work in emerging innovations. They rave positively about the evangelistic potential. They love to raise money to launch new media projects. Just as predictably, however, evangelicals' excessive optimism sometimes leads them to be poor stewards of such resources. They naively think that just by using media they will have a positive impact on church and culture—as if how they use the media is unimportant. Someone once joked that exaggeration is one of evangelicals' special gifts.

At the same time, various evangelicals predictably rant against so-called secular uses of new media. They protest loudly against immoral content, especially the big three—sex, violence and offensive language. They warn believers to stay away from new media forms and secular producers, rallying the tribe to live "separate and apart" from such unholy media. Moreover, some of the most vehement critics fail to examine the very media and artists that they condemn. Eventually, as an accommodation to the new media, critics support pro-Christian or family-friendly content and create their own parallel forms of Christian entertainment. In some cases, these imitations make bold attempts to compete with mainstream offerings.

A third group observes the actions of the champions and critics, listens carefully and takes notes. These critical friends of evangelical media do not deny that the church should evangelize and edify, but they avoid placing the church in opposition to the world. Instead, they see the church in dialogue with the world's cultures. Such critical friends recommend caution in all media engagements but see the potential to renew media forms for the sake of Christ.

Evangelicals avoid self-criticism about tribal media. Evangelicals are often quick to criticize mainstream media but not their own tribal media. They tend to shun self-criticism while hurling insults at nonconformists even within their own ranks. Innovative evangelical media artists do sometimes receive more criticism from the tribe than from mainstream audiences. In addition, occasionally evangelicals who question the efforts of a popular media ministry (Who can contest the idea of ministry!) themselves become the victims of harsh and often unfair condemnation. Nevertheless, there is no sustained, broadly evangelical community discourse about media.

Evangelical media generally lack originality. Although Christians historically were among the most creative artists, writers and dramatists, today's North American evangelicals rarely lead the way in mainstream culture. It is disheartening to consider how rarely evangelical media are truly cutting-edge productions. Serious evangelical films sometimes are merely laughable—so artistically bad that they function as comedy to many believers. Many evangelical websites are amateurish designs with sloppy prose and silly graphics. The advertisements on evangelical websites and in evangelical periodicals frequently look like garish posters for B-grade science fiction films. What about the sets used on some evangelical TV programs—or the hairdos and costumes? Without being cultural elitists, we can probably conclude that evangelical productions tend to suffer from a lack of artistic quality.

Evangelical media feast on the flock. Despite their good intentions to reach beyond the tribe, few evangelical media appeal to readers, viewers or listeners beyond the in-group. In fact, these media derive their support from the tribe. Tribal audiences keep them going financially. Without tribal support, most evangelical media would cease operation. This is good for keeping the flock connected, but not for getting beyond the flock. Perhaps the most significant impact of evangelical media has been to make various tribes more internally cohesive with shared identities and common understandings of who they are and how they should relate to mainstream culture. Consuming evangelical media is like listening in on a conversation within one or another tribal group with a shared view of reality.

Evangelicals express narrow concerns about media morality. Most evangelical media and evangelical critics of mainstream media view the world from a relatively narrow frame of moral reference. Sex, violence and offensive language hardly represent the range of moral issues in society, let alone Jesus' own moral concerns. So while evangelical media and media critics complain about nudity or curse words in books or on television, they somehow seem to ignore other issues along the way. What about the media's promotion of racial and gender stereotypes? What about consumerism? Why don't evangelical media seem very concerned about poverty or other social injustice? Of course there are exceptions, as mentioned in this book. But the overall perspective in evangelical conversations about media is quite narrow. In short, evangelical media seem to lack a biblical-prophetic voice that can cut through religiosity and moralism to get to the roots of the problems in the church and society—roots like greed, indifference, self-righteousness, nationalistic idolatry and spiritual fakery. Instead they get worked up about the latest, isolated news reports about media immorality. Then evangelicals, however valid their concerns, generate publicity for the very media that they are criticizing. As the saying goes in mainstream media, "Bad publicity is better than no publicity."

Evangelical media lack ethnic diversity. Although North American evangelicals include many ethnic groups and races, most evangelical audiences hardly know it. Even more than their mainstream counterparts, evangelical media are owned and operated primarily by white Anglo-Saxons. This volume correspondingly says very little about African American, Hispanic and Asian media. Why is this? Well, maybe because few of the authors in this book represented these ethnic groups. Programming and media personalities listed by an African American colleague of ours were not familiar to many of our authors. Or maybe it is because many African Americans, Hispanics and Asians do not use *evangelical* to identify themselves or their Christian media efforts. We do not know for sure, but we don't expect it to last. A large part of the growth of evangelicalism in North America is among Hispanic and Asian populations. We fully expect that evangelical entrepreneurs within these groups will increasingly launch media, as is already happening among Hispanics in some major cities.

Evangelicals share mainstream society's focus on technology over stewardship. As hopeful evangelicals employ older and newer media, they think about the power of communications rather than the cost. Supposedly newer media are better than previous ones. And mass media are more influential than interpersonal ones. The result is evangelicals' significant investments in media campaigns and productions.

Rarely do evangelicals take stock of the role of media in their personal, family, community and church lives. What happens, for instance, when each family member has a personal TV, a computer, a radio and an iPod? Which media products do family members then have in common to enjoy, discuss and discern? Similarly, how much time do congregational members spend in fellowship, prayer, education, worship and community service? No matter how valuable particular media content might be for evangelicals, the issues of time and cost come into play. Spending time and money on some media can reduce the positive benefits of other forms of communication.

So where should evangelicals go from here? The future of evangelical media in North America depends on at least six responses. We suggest that evangelicals should attempt to do the following:

Develop informed, critical stances regarding new and older media. The tribe needs media champions but also media critics who really understand the increasingly complex media landscape. These critics ought not to be mere naysayers, but should be well-informed, balanced observers. Like Old Testament prophets, they need to show evangelicals how the tribe is falling short of its own goals and where it is ignoring the negative impact on itself as well a society. Evangelicals need to know when their own emperors are not wearing any clothes!

Offer timely and well-deserved praise. Instead of being just critics, however, evangelicals need to give thanks to members of the tribe who are using media faithfully. Sometimes it will be obvious when evangelicals create remarkably worthwhile media content for large audiences. Just as important to the future of evangelical media are the imaginative, grass-roots efforts of bloggers, church media artists, youth group projects and the like. Similarly, is it too much to expect churches to support talented members who plan to study media in college or work for mainstream media?

Think outside the tribal box. As many chapters in this volume make clear, evangelical media tend to beget similar evangelical media and yet more clones. The tribe tends to limit its imagination. Perhaps evangelicals worry that they will be criticized for being too avant-garde. Or maybe they worry just about offending sisters and brothers in Christ. These are legitimate concerns. But the new-media landscape also provides opportunities to try new genres and technologies without having to raise enormous funds and practice poor stewardship. After all, many younger evangelicals are already experimenting with new media forms, using their personal video cameras, Web-design software, computer audio-editing systems and desktop publishing technology to produce media content. Besides, we live in a time when more young people get their theology from films or weekly television programs than from Sunday sermons. Can we really afford *not* to think outside the box?

Consider how non-Christian audiences will receive the content. In the age of YouTube, blogs, digital photography and file sharing, it is increasingly difficult to keep any media messages within a tribe. Evangelicals' cultural bubbles are bursting, letting messages flow into and out of their formerly close-knit tribes. Practically every media message that evangelicals produce has the potential to become a mainstream PR issue. So evangelicals should increasingly consider how their messages will be received by mainstream audiences, even other religious groups. Perhaps more than ever, evangelicals will be judged by what they are actually doing as well as by what they profess. And the gap between doing and professing will be broadcast by critics within and outside the tribe. Moralistic and politicized messages, for instance, can become boomerangs when moralistic evangelicals fall from grace and when evangelical political movements fall flat.

Reach out to the margins. Jesus repeatedly spoke of the marginalized in society—the poor, weak, broken and dispossessed. More than that, Jesus spoke *for* them. He was not nearly so interested in representing the religious establishment, including the religious celebrities of his own day. One can wonder how Jesus would feel about today's evangelical media stars across the various channels, from books to broadcasts. What would evangelical media say to church and society if they welcomed the stories of the people who are living on the margins of social respectability? We do not know for sure. But one thing is clear: the current evangelical emphasis on clean-cut, upper-middle-class, photogenic, super-positive-thinking, know-it-all media celebrities gives a gilded view of social reality and truncates the gospel.

We hope that our critical comments in this concluding chapter are offset at least somewhat by our suggestions for the future. We do not aim to condemn evangelical media efforts. Depending on the situation, we describe ourselves as champions, critics or critical friends. And we wrestle daily with the same questions our students and colleagues wrestle with, whether we are teaching, writing or creating our own media.

But we have to be honest about what works, what fails and why—just as the authors of the various chapters have called us to do. We also have to take stock of the current state of evangelical efforts in the emerging media landscape. In order to move ahead wisely, we have to look back critically, then look inside ourselves humbly. We have to consider the logs in our own eyes. While we do so, let's remember that the point of being self-critical about ourselves and evangelical media is to "test them all; hold on to what is good" (1 Thess 5:21), and "in all things grow up into him who is the head, that is, Christ" (Eph 4:15).

So, are we headed "back to the future" in the next twenty years, or will the future of evangelical media be less predictable? Will evangelical media be characterized by tribal and mainstream critics alike as cutting edge, creative, prophetic, culturally diverse and socially responsible when the next edition of this book is published? Time will tell. So will the many conversations that occur between now and then. Let the conversations continue!

Contributors

Phyllis Alsdurf is a journalism professor and director of the Johnson Center for Journalism and Communication at Bethel University in Saint Paul, Minnesota. She and her husband enjoy time at their north-woods cabin with their boxer, Stella, in tow.

Diane M. Badzinski chairs the Department of Communication at Colorado Christian University. One of her favorite research projects is media portrayals of faith families.

David Bedsole teaches rhetoric, writing and communication at Southern Wesleyan University. He also writes poetry, songs and rambling, polemical blogs when not hanging out with his wife and their dogs, Shiloh and Quintilian.

Stephanie Bennett teaches communication at Palm Beach Atlantic University and is a devotee of the work of French philosopher and social theorist Jacques Ellul. Having worked as a journalist since the 1980s, she still enjoys writing about music, media and the beauty of life lived in the fellowship of Christ.

Kathy Bruner teaches media at Taylor University and is especially interested in the intersections of faith and culture. She began writing and producing shows in her family's driveway in the third grade and still freelances as a producer/writer.

Randall Bytwerk teaches communication at Calvin College and has written three books on totalitarian propaganda. He enjoys backpacking, screwball comedies and practical jokes.

Thomas J. Carmody chairs and teaches in the Department of Communication at Vanguard University of Southern California. He enjoys perusing used bookstores and discussing everything from nineteenth-century sermons to modern graphic novels and comic books.

Clifford G. Christians directs the Ph.D. in communications and the B.S. in media studies programs at the University of Illinois, Urbana-Champaign. He is working on universals in media ethics.

Terri Lynn Cornwell teaches communication at Liberty University. She served as a legislative director in the U.S. Congress and currently researches advertising, public relations and international adoption. In her earlier, carefree years, she flew her own airplane and was actually persuaded to skydive—twice!

Paul A. Creasman teaches media theory, criticism and production at Azusa Pacific University. He reminds people that *Mere Christianity* and *Hitchhiker's Guide to the Galaxy* (both highly complex philosophical treatises) began as radio programs.

Stephanie D. Davis serves as education/instructional librarian at Spring Arbor University, where she teaches children's literature. She peruses children's sections of bookstores and reads graphic novels.

Keith Drury teaches practical ministry at Indiana Wesleyan University, where he started the worship major and served as its first full-time professor. His books include *The Wonder of Worship—Why We Worship the Way We Do* (Wesleyan, 2002). In summers he backpacks with students and has completed the Appalachian Trail and Pacific Crest Trail.

Mark Fackler teaches communication ethics and law at Calvin College. He is a high school baseball umpire, so, in the spring at least, he always gets it right.

Robert S. Fortner is director of the Media Research Institute and professor of communication arts and sciences at Calvin College. He researches the use of media for missions and develops solutions to humanitarian crises and military conflict, especially in the developing world.

Debra Freeberg teaches theater and communication at Calvin College. She has directed over forty productions; written plays for children, the church and the legitimate stage; and led seminars and faculty development workshops. Stockholm is one of her favorite cities.

Brian Fuller left the mountains of North Carolina to teach media production at Calvin College. His recent films include *FutureWorship 1.0,* chronicling church use of multimedia throughout the United States, and *The Hope of the Quechua,* a documentary about community-development initiatives in Ecuador.

Darlene Graves is a professor of communication at Liberty University. Her seminars and research areas include the creative process, leadership, the arts and faith development, and the role of women in Southern gospel music.

Michael P. Graves teaches communication at Liberty University and studies early Quaker preaching, visual rhetoric and popular culture. His recent award-winning, coedited book is *More Than Precious Memories: The Rhetoric of Southern Gospel Music* (2005).

Dennis "Max" Hengeveld, also known as Rev. Fun, has published two cartoon books *(Reverend Fun . . . Offline* and *Reverend Fun's Has Anybody Seen My Locust?).* He lives in Silicon Valley and enjoys irreverent fun.

Rick Jackson teaches journalism, media law and communication ethics at Seattle Pacific University. He is a former newspaper copy editor and religion reporter.

Michael Jindra teaches sociology and anthropology at Spring Arbor University. His first publication on the "religiousness" of Star Trek fans set into motion his interest in how people use popular culture.

Ronald A. Johnson teaches HD production at Goshen College and produces projects distributed through DVD, the Web and the area public TV station. As homeschoolers, he and his wife explore the worlds of classical ballet and piano with their daughters and jazz fusion drumming and classic cars with their sons.

Scott P. Johnson administers and teaches in the communication department at Bethel College, Mishawaka, Indiana. Coming from backgrounds in music, theater and Catholicism, he is interested in these as they intersect with communication in worship.

Peter A. Kerr teaches communications at Asbury College; led media relations in Washington, D.C., during the Ronald Reagan State Funeral; and is founder of KerrComm (Kerrcommunications.com). He enjoys traveling around the world with his family, reading theology and physics, and helping to transform churches with Spiritual Leadership, Inc.

Larry Lake teaches writing and ethnobotany at Messiah College, and has conducted anthropological research in West New Guinea, where his parents were missionaries. He has recently completed a book on the life and adventures of the wealthy American scientist Richard Archbold, who used seaplanes to explore the interior of New Guinea in the 1930s.

John Lawing is professor emeritus in journalism at Regent University in Virginia Beach, Virginia, where he taught for twenty-five years. For twenty-one years he served as reporter, editor, columnist, art director and cartoonist for publications such as *Christianity Today* and the *Christian Herald.* His cartoons have appeared in the *New York Times, Time* and the *Saturday Evening Post,* among others.

Jennifer Letherer is affiliate faculty at Spring Arbor University and cofounder of Mapreader Productions, L.L.C. She has never been beaten at Star Wars Trivial Pursuit, and wishes she could find someone to play the Turner Classic Movies edition of *Scene It?* with her.

Terry Lindvall is the C. S. Lewis Professor of Communication and Christian Thought at Virginia Wesleyan College, author of *Sanctuary Cinema* (2007) and other works, and has been spotted wearing knickers to Octoberfest celebrations.

Michael A. Longinow chairs Biola University's journalism department and has written five chapters in anthologies on journalism history, religion, and evangelical cultures. He reported for dailies in Illinois and Georgia, covering civil rights, the courts, schools and politics at the city, state and national levels.

Elizabeth McLaughlin teaches communication at Bethel College, Indiana. She researches public relations, visual rhetoric and the ways women express the image of God through their symbolic actions. A recreational fencer, she collects swords and considers it the perfect antidote to a mid-life crisis.

Martin E. Marty is Fairfax M. Cone Distinguished Service Professor Emeritus, University of Chicago, pastor, columnist and author of over fifty books.

Terry Mattingly directs the Washington Journalism Center at the Council for Christian Colleges and Universities and for twenty years has written the weekly "On Religion" column for the Scripps Howard News Service. He leads the GetReligion.org website, which evaluates the mainstream media's coverage of religion news. He is the author of *Pop Goes Religion: Faith in Popular Culture* (2005).

Kevin D. Miller teaches communication at Huntington University and is a former associate editor at *Christianity Today* magazine. His interest in the intersection of culture, religion and communication consummated in his marriage to Lydia, a Russian-speaking woman.

Paul Mouw teaches mass media at Judson College after three decades in religious book publishing. His own books include *Toolbox for Video Storytelling: How to Write and Produce Your Missionary Video* (2002).

Paul D. Patton teaches theater and popular culture at Spring Arbor University, where his play, *The Celebrity*, was recently published by Heuer. He is also the founder of Trinity House, a Detroit-area arts venue.

Jonathan Pettigrew is working on a Ph.D. in communication at Penn State University. He studied the role of cell phones in relationships but learned more about the topic through his concurrent dating, engagement and marriage.

Mark I. Pinsky, religion writer for the *Orlando Sentinel,* is author of *A Jew Among the Evangelicals: A Guide for the Perplexed* (2006). He considers looking for religious content in cartoons mixing business with pleasure.

William D. Romanowski teaches film studies at Calvin College and is the author of *Eyes Wide Open: Looking for God in Popular Culture* (2001). He has worked as a musical and dramatic performer.

Andrew Quicke teaches film and television at Regent University and writes books about broadcasting and film. A former current-affairs producer for BBC-TV in London, he has lived and worked in Bangkok and Jerusalem. He and his wife have a second home in Tuscany, Italy.

Quentin J. Schultze is the Arthur H. DeKruyter Chair and the executive director of the Gainey Institute for Faith and Communication at Calvin College. His many books include *Christianity and the Media in America: Toward a Democratic Accommodation* (2003). He is an avid birder.

Kevin Schut teaches media studies at Trinity Western University. His research focuses on computer games, technology, faith and culture.

Kathleen Osbeck Sindorf teaches media, public relations and advertising at Cornerstone University, Michigan. She cohosted *The 700 Club,* covered Asia as the Christian Broadcasting Network's senior international correspondent, and was vice president of communication for Precept Ministries International. She also loves nonverbal communication and is an avid scuba diver.

Michael Ray Smith, a professor at Campbell University, is author of *Feature-Writing.Net* (2005), a guide to getting published, and *The Jesus Newspaper* (2002), an examination of a mainstream newspaper that used Christian principles in its content. He's more likely to quote Homer Simpson than Homer's Odyssey.

Paul A. Soukup, S.J., teaches communication at Santa Clara University and researches communication and theology, including multimedia translations of the Bible. His books include *Out of Eden: 7 Ways God Restores Blocked Communication* (2006).

Scott Tanis started on air in Christian radio at the age of twelve. He loves to travel and has been to Egypt and Jordan for the preproduction of a video series about the exodus of the Israelites.

Mark E. Taylor teaches communication studies at Loyola University Chicago and is a physical therapist, Master's swimmer and yoga practitioner. He enjoys surfing the ocean as well as the Net.

Alex Wainer teaches media and film at Palm Beach Atlantic University. He has contributed articles to Prison Fellowship's Breakpoint publications, which examine faith and popular culture.

Annalee Ward teaches communication at Trinity Christian College and is author of *Mouse Morality: The Rhetoric of Disney Animated Film* (2001). She loves educational travel, media and preaching—sometimes mixed together.

Ken Waters teaches journalism at Pepperdine University and has authored several book chapters and academic articles on the history and function of Christian magazines. He is a former international journalist and PR director for World Vision.

Bill Wiarda is the communications manager at an urban, multicultural congregation in Grand Rapids, Michigan. He has been gaming since the early 1990s and has recently explored ways to bring God into his games and gaming-related relationships.

John D. Witvliet directs the Calvin Institute of Christian Worship and teaches at both Calvin College and Calvin Theological Seminary. His books include *Worship Seeking Understanding: Windows into Christian Practice* (2003).

Robert Woods teaches communication in B.A. and M.A. programs at Spring Arbor University. His books include *The Message in the Music: Studying Contemporary Worship Music* (2007) and *Media Ethics: Cases and Moral Reasoning* (2004). He has played guitar in a church worship team.

Notes

Foreword

[1]The word *numinous* comes from the Latin *numen*, "deity." See Rudolf Otto, *The Idea of the Holy: An Inquiry into the Non-rational Factor in the Idea of the Divine and Its Relation to the Rational*, trans. John W. Harvey, 2nd ed. (New York: Oxford University Press, 1958), p. 5.

Introduction

[1]Cicero *The Orations of Marcus Tullius Cicero* 4.11[1].

Chapter 1: Getting the Conversation Going About Media and Culture

[1]We are intentionally ambiguous about the meaning of *evangelical* because evangelicals themselves do not agree completely on what makes one an evangelical. We assume that evangelicals are Christians with a relatively conservative view of the Bible as the Word of God who believe in the necessity of personal conversion or salvation.

[2]There is no single, agreed-upon Christian perspective on popular culture, let alone on particular artifacts like a worship song or a comic-book series. For a sense of the range of Christian—including evangelical—views, see Philip J. Rossi and Paul A. Soukup, S.J., eds., *Mass Media and the Moral Imagination* (Kansas City, Mo.: Sheed & Ward, 1994); Jay Newman, *Religion vs. Television* (Westport, Conn.: Praeger, 1996); Richard J. Mouw, *Consulting the Faithful: What Christian Intellectuals Can Learn from Popular Culture* (Grand Rapids: Eerdmans, 1994); William D. Romanowski, *Pop Culture Wars: Religion & the Role of Entertainment in American Life* (Downers Grove, Ill.: InterVarsity Press, 1996); Craig Detweiler and Barry Taylor, *A Matrix of Meanings: Finding God in Pop Culture* (Grand Rapids: Baker, 2003); Colleen McDannell, *Material Christianity: Religion and Popular Culture in America* (New Haven, Conn.: Yale University Press, 1995); Rodney Clapp, *Border Crossings: Christian Trespasses on Popular Culture and Public Affairs* (Grand Rapids: Brazos, 2000); John Wiley Nelson, *Your God Is Alive and Well and Appearing in Popular Culture* (Philadelphia: Westminster, 1976); Richard J. Mouw, *He Shines in All That's Fair: Culture and Common Grace* (Grand Rapids: Eerdmans, 2001); Steve Turner, *Imagine: A Vision for Christians in the Arts* (Downers Grove, Ill.: InterVarsity Press, 2001); Richard Winter, *Still Bored in a Culture of Entertainment* (Downers Grove, Ill.: InterVarsity Press, 2002); Kenneth A. Myers, *All God's Children and Blue Suede Shoes: Christians and Popular Culture* (Westchester, Ill.: Crossway, 1989); William D. Romanowski, *Eyes Wide Open: Looking for God in Popular Culture*, rev. and exp. ed. (Grand Rapids: Brazos, 2007); and Andrew M. Greeley, *God in Popular Culture* (Chicago: Thomas More, 1988). Quentin J. Schultze discusses the various ways that Christians have tried to understand popular culture, especially television, in chap. 5 of *Christianity and the Mass Media in America: Toward a Democratic Accommodation* (East Lansing: Michigan State University Press, 2003).

[3]We are using the term *tribe* anthropologically to refer to cultures or especially subcultures. In one

sense, American evangelicals are a tribe within Christianity; other Christian tribes might include Roman Catholics and mainline Protestants. In another sense, evangelicals themselves are divided into tribes, including denominations.

[4]See Richard H. Niebuhr, *Christ and Culture* (New York: Harper and Row, 1951). For a critical update on the Christ-and-culture perspective, see Craig A. Carter, *Rethinking Christ and Culture: A Post-Christendom Perspective* (Grand Rapids: Brazos, 2007).

[5]One radio exception is the Catholic Channel on the Sirius Satellite Radio network. There is also a scattering of Catholic radio stations across the United States. Cable and satellite TV include the conservative Eternal Word Television Network (EWTN).

Chapter 2: Looking Beyond Radio for Listeners

[1]As noted in chap. 1, Christian radio is dominated by evangelicals. Thus, this chapter will focus on how the evangelical tribe uses radio. Also see Quentin J. Schultze, "The Invisible Medium, Evangelical Radio," in *American Evangelicals and the Mass Media,* ed. Quentin Schultze (Grand Rapids: Academie Books, 1990), pp. 171-95; Quentin J. Schultze, "Evangelical Radio and the Rise of the Electronic Church, 1921-1948," *Journal of Broadcasting and Electronic Media* 32 (Summer 1988): 289-306; Mark Ward Sr., *Air of Salvation* (Grand Rapids: Baker Books, 1994); J. Elwin Wright, *The Old Fashioned Revival Hour and the Broadcasters* (Boston: Fellowship Press, 1940); and Bob Lochte, *Christian Radio: The Growth of a Mainstream Broadcasting Force* (Jefferson, N.C.: McFarland, 2006).

[2]Arbitron, "American Radio Listening Trends—Format Trends" <http://wargod.arbitron.com/scripts/ndb/fmttrends2.asp>. In winter 2007, the music-based Contemporary Christian format captured a 1.0 share and the Bible-teaching religious format captured a .5 share among all listeners across all times of the day. "Share" is the percentage of the listening audience hearing a particular station at the time of measurement. For example, if a city has one million people in it, and all one million people were listening to any radio station at the time of measurement, a 1.5 share means fifteen thousand listeners were listening to that particular station. *Radio Today: How America Listens to Radio,* Arbitron, 2007, p. 59 <www.arbitron.com/downloads/radiotoday07.pdf>, estimates the audience for CCM radio to be a generous 2.4 share, an increase from 1.8 in 2002. Lochte (*Christian Radio*, p. 14) claims that Christian radio garners a 5.2 share, but this figure is based on data from all religious formats, not just evangelical formats. Data on podcast and webstream listening are very limited, so the figures noted above reflect broadcast radio listening only.

[3]Arbitron, "Format Trends." Between 1998 and 2007, the national audience for the Contemporary Christian format grew from a .3 share to a 1.0 share. In the same time frame, the national audience for the religious format (preaching and teaching programs) fell from a 1.0 share to .5 share. The increase in listeners to the contemporary Christian format may result from an increase in the number of stations playing that format over the same time period.

[4]Clark Greer and Tim Phipps, "Non-Commercial Radio Stations and the Web," *Journal of Radio Studies* 10 (2003): 17-18. See also *Radio Today: How America Listens to Radio,* Arbitron, 2005, p. 51 <www.arbitron.com/downloads/radiotoday05.pdf>.

[5]Arbitron, "American Radio Listening Trends—Audience Composition" <wargod.arbitron.com/scripts/ndb/audience2.asp>. See also *Radio Today 2007,* p. 59.

[6]Stephen D. Perry and Raymond L. Carroll, "Subgenre Radio Formats: The Case of Music-Intensive Religious Stations," *Journal of Radio Studies* 3 (1995-1996): 53. See also George Barna, *The Barna Report: 1992-1993: America Renews Its Search for God* (Ventura, Calif.: Regal, 1992), p. 105. Barna identified in the early 1990s the trend that continues today—young evangelicals tend not to tune in to evangelical radio.

[7]Madison Trammel, "Making Airwaves," *Christianity Today,* February 2007, p. 28. Salem's major-market presence distinguishes it from other evangelical radio networks. The K-Love network owns more stations than Salem but operates in fewer major markets.

[8]W. Terry Whalin, "Salem Impact: Two Men Influencing Their Culture," *Wireless Age,* May/June/July 1996, pp. 24, 26.

[9]*Radio Today 2007,* p. 59.

[10]Anna Wilde Mathews, "Ever More Popular, This Radio Preacher Actually Died in '88," *Wall Street Journal,* December 19, 2002.

[11]In 2007, there were fifty-four religious radio stations available through iTunes. Nine of them were also available on terrestrial radio. The rest were stations that stream exclusively online.

[12]Sandra K. Chambers, "Our Love Is Loud," *Charisma and Christian Life,* February 2003, p. 55..

[13]Jay Howard and John Streck, *Apostles of Rock: The Splintered World of CCM* (Lexington: University of Kentucky Press, 1999), p. 65.

[14]Stephen D. Perry and Jennifer L. Tofanelli, "Testifications: Analysis of Meaning in CCM Radio Station Feedback," paper presented at the annual meeting of the National Communication Association, Chicago, November 4-7, 1999.

[15]Margaret Bendroth, "Fundamentalism and the Media, 1930–1990," in *Religion and Mass Media: Audience and Adaptations,* ed. Daniel Stout and Judith Buddenbaum (Thousand Oaks, Calif.: Sage, 1996), p. 76.

[16]Howard and Streck, *Apostles of Rock,* pp. 78-83.

[17]Paul A. Creasman, "Sanctified Entertainment: Contemporary Christian Music Radio," *Religious Broadcasting,* April 1996, pp. 26-30.

[18]Robert H. Woods Jr., "CCM Radio: A Uses and Gratifications Analysis" (Ph.D. diss., Regent University, 1999), p. 264.

[19]Ward, *Air of Salvation,* p. 29.

[20]Ibid., p. 26.

[21]Tona J. Hangen, *Redeeming the Dial: Radio, Religion, and Popular Culture in America* (Chapel Hill: University of North Carolina Press, 2002), p. 152.

[22]Perry and Carroll, "Subgenre Radio Formats," p. 49.

[23]Dick Jenkins and Wes Ward, "CCM and Teaching/Talk Programmers Agree! Stay on Mission with the Great Commission," *NRB Magazine,* September 2004, pp. 25–27.

[24]Jim Pennington, "Christian Radio: Breaking out of the Gospel Ghetto," *Christianity Today,* June 29, 1979, p. 32.

[25]Studies estimate that Fuller's audience exceeded twenty million listeners weekly. Philip Goff, "'We Have Heard the Joyful Sound': Charles E. Fuller's Radio Broadcast and the Rise of Modern Evangelicalism," *Religion and American Culture* 9 (1999): 67.

[26]William Martin, "The God Hucksters of Radio," *The Atlantic,* June 1970, p. 51.

[27]Clifford G. Christians, "Redemptive Media as the Evangelical's Cultural Task," in *American Evangelicals and the Mass Media,* ed. Quentin J. Schultze (Grand Rapids: Academie Books, 1990), p. 331.

[28]Quentin J. Schultze and William D. Romanowski, "Praising God in Opryland," *Reformed Journal* 39, no. 11 (1989): 11.

[29]Carole Flake, *Redemptorama: Culture, Politics, and the New Evangelicalism* (New York: Penguin, 1984), p. 182.

[30]Matt Seward and Duncan Dodds, "Christian Music Radio: Out of the Closet and into the Spotlight," *Religious Broadcasting,* February 1993, p. 77.

[31]James Long, "Can't Buy Me Ministry," *Christianity Today,* May 20, 1996, p. 22.

[32]Paul Baker, *CCM: Where It Came from, What It Is, Where It Is Going* (Westchester, Ill.: Crossway, 1985), p. 45. See also Howard and Streck, *Apostles of Rock,* pp. 31-36, for more objections to rock music as a form of CCM.

[33]Laurie P. Cohen, "Battle Stations: Radio Evangelist Finds a Deft Way to Expand While Muscling NPR," *Wall Street Journal,* August 14, 2001.

[34]Marshall McLuhan, *Understanding Media: The Extensions of Man* (Cambridge, Mass.: MIT Press, 1994), pp. 3, 7.

[35]Ralph Martin, *Worship in the Early Church* (Grand Rapids: Eerdmans, 1964), pp. 24-7.

[36]Early radio researchers predicted that radio was so good at communicating the gospel across space (for example, out of the church and into the home) that parishioners would stop attending church. This fear continued into the late twentieth century with little evidence that evangelical broadcasting diminished physical church attendance. See Paul F. Lazarsfeld and Frank N. Stanton, *Radio Research 1941* (New York: Duell, Sloan, and Pearce, 1941), pp. 290-92; and Ben Armstrong, *The Electric Church* (Nashville: Thomas Nelson, 1979), p. 17.

[37]Robert S. Fortner, "The Church and the Debate over Radio: 1919-1949," in *Media and Religion in American History,* ed. William David Sloan (Northport, Ala.: Vision, 2000), p. 235.

[38]Mark I. Pinsky, *A Jew Among the Evangelicals: A Guide for the Perplexed* (Louisville: Westminster John Knox Press, 2006), p. 122.

[39]Susan J. Douglas, *Listening In: Radio and the American Imagination* (New York: Random House, 1999), p. 40.

[40]Ellen Barry, "Katrina's Aftermath: A Lifeline Sent by Airwave," *Los Angeles Times,* September 10, 2005; James Rainey, "New Orleans DJ Puts Hope in Heavy Rotation," *Los Angeles Times,* November 28, 2005.

[41]Seward and Dodds, "Christian Music Radio," p. 74.

[42]"Southern California's KYMS Sold," *The CCM Update* 9, no. 25 (1995): 1-2.

[43]Arbitron, "Format Trends."

[44]Arbitron, "Audience Composition." Seventy percent of the audience for the Adult Standards format is sixty-five and older.

[45]Arbitron, "Format Trends."

Chapter 3: Thinking Outside the Tribal TV Box

[1]Tim Scott, interview by author, telephone conference call, Upland, Indiana, March 7, 2007.

[2]The Barna Group, "More People Use Christian Media Than Attend Church," Barna Updates (March 14, 2005) <www.barna.org/FlexPage.aspx?Page=BarnaUpdate&BarnaUpdateID=184>. Also see Robert Abelman and Stewart M. Hoover, eds., *Religious Television: Controversies and Conclusions* (Westport, Conn.: Greenwood/Ablex, 1990); Hal Erickson, *Religious Radio and Television in the United States, 1921-1991: The Programs and Personalities* (Jefferson, N.C.: McFarland, 1992); Heather Hendershot, *Shaking the World for Jesus: Media and Conservative Evangelical Culture* (Chicago, Ill.: University of Chicago Press, 2004); Gregor T. Goethals, *The Electronic Golden Calf: Images, Religion and the Making of Meaning* (Cambridge, Mass.: Cowley, 1990); Shane Hipps, *The Hidden Power of Electronic Culture* (Grand Rapids: Zondervan, 2006); Quentin J. Schultze, *Televangelism and American Culture: The Business of Popular Religion* (Grand Rapids: Baker Books, 1991); and Michael Suman, ed., *Religion and Prime Time Television* (Westport, Conn.: Praeger, 1997).

[3]"Microphone Missionary," *Time,* April 14, 1952, pp. 18, 20.

[4]Pope Paul VI, "On Evangelization in the Modern World: Apostolic Exhortation *Evangelii Nuntiandi,*" (Washington, D.C.: Publications Office, United States Catholic Conference, 1976). Pope

Benedict XVI advocated that media programming in general should communicate "what is the ultimate foundation and meaning of human, personal and social existence," and contribute to "the propagation of all that is good and true." See "Pope Benedict: Media Must Be Responsible, Protagonist of Truth, Not Self-serving, Profit-driven," Catholic News Agency (January 24, 2006) <www.catholicnewsagency.com/new.php?n=5820>.

[5]See also Michael S. Horton's discussion of the church's relationship to culture in "How the Kingdom Comes," *Christianity Today*, January 2006, p. 2 <www.christianvisionproject.com/2006/01/how_the_kingdom_comes.html>.

[6]See, e.g., the description of the television program *Aspiring Women* on the Total Living Network website at <www.tln.com/program/aw/about_show.html>.

[7]Kevin Downey, "Jesus Is My Homeboy," *Broadcasting & Cable*, July 29, 2006 <www.broadcasting cable.com/article/CA6357457.html>.

[8]Quentin J. Schultze, *Redeeming Television* (Downers Grove, Ill.: InterVarsity Press, 1992), p. 21.

[9]Barna Group, "More People Use Christian Media."

[10]Quentin J. Schultze, *Christianity and the Mass Media in America: Toward a Democratic Accommodation* (East Lansing: Michigan State University Press, 2003), p. 50.

[11]Frank Wright, "Written Testimony of Frank Wright, Ph.D., President and CEO, National Religious Broadcasters (NRB) Submitted to the Federal Communications Commission as Part of Public Hearings Held in El Segundo, California," October 3, 2006.

[12]James Careless, "Leap of Faith," Trinity Broadcasting Network Announcements, WDC Media <www.tbn.org/index.php/7.html?nid=201>.

[13]See Frank Wright, "By All Means," *NRB*, June 2004, p. 4.

[14]Glenn Plummer, "The Seventh Millennial Dawn," *NRB*, January 2000, p. 4.

[15]Mariah Blake, "Stations of the Cross: How Evangelical Christians Are Creating an Alternative Universe of Faith-based News," *Columbia Journalism Review* 3 (May/June 2005) <http://cjrarchives.org/issues/2005/3/blake-evangelist.asp>.

[16]Jeanne F. Hunter, "'Godcasts' Spread Word on the Web," *USA Today*, March 16, 2006 <www.usatoday.com/tech/news/2006-03-16-godcasts_x.htm>.

[17]Blake, "Stations of the Cross," p. 39.

[18]Ibid., p. 35. Blake is quoting Frank Wright, President and CEO, National Religious Broadcasters, the trade organization for religious broadcasters.

[19]Christian Television Network, "Christian Television Network's Philosophy" <www.ctnonline.com/about04.html>.

[20]Wright, "Written Testimony," p. 3.

[21]Malcolm Muggeridge, *Christ and the Media* (Grand Rapids: Eerdmans, 1977), p. 30.

[22]For a discussion of the health-and-wealth gospel, see Quentin J. Schultze, *Televangelism and American Culture* (Grand Rapids: Baker Books, 1991), p. 134. The reference to "cheap grace" comes from Dietrich Bonhoeffer, *The Cost of Discipleship* (New York: Macmillan, 1963), p. 45.

[23]Quentin J. Schultze, "TV and Evangelism: Unequally Yoked?" in *The Agony of Deceit*, ed. Michael Horton (Chicago: Moody Press, 1990). See also Hipps, *Hidden Power of Electronic Culture*.

[24]Stewart M. Hoover, *Mass Media Religion: The Social Sources of the Electronic Church* (Newbury Park, N.Y.: Sage, 1988), p. 178. For historical perspective on conservative Protestantism's changing attitudes toward political involvement, see Alan Wolfe, *The Transformation of American Religion* (New York: Free Press, 2003), pp. 111-17.

[25]Jerry Falwell, "'Global Warming' Fooling the Faithful," WorldNetDaily Commentary (February 24, 2007) <www.worldnetdaily.com/news/article.asp?ARTICLE_ID=54413>.

[26]Barna Group, "More People Use Christian Media."

[27]Randall Balmer, "Still Wrestling with the Devil," *Christianity Today,* March 2, 1998, pp. 30-36.

[28]Schultze, *Televangelism and American Culture,* pp. 193-96; Goethals, *Electronic Golden Calf,* pp. 170-71.

[29]"January '07: The 50 Most Influential Christians in America," *The Church Report,* January 2007 <www.thechurchreport.com/mag_article.php?mid=875&mname=January>.

[30]See The Barna Group, "Billy Graham Tops Religious Leaders," The Barna Update (February 19, 2007) <www.barna.org/FlexPage.aspx?Page=BarnaUpdate&BarnaUpdateID=265>. For a comparative look at mainstream perceptions of evangelicals, see *Time* magazine's "The 25 Most Influential Evangelicals in America," a list that paints evangelicals with a broader stroke than does *The Church Report,* so that a smaller percentage are television celebrities. See David Van Biema et al., "Evangelicals in America," *Time,* February 7, 2005 <www.time.com/time/covers/1101050207/>.

[31]Larry Martz, *Ministry of Greed: The Inside Story of the Televangelists and Their Holy Wars* (New York: Weidenfeld & Nicolson, 1988), pp. 42-58.

[32]Barna Group, "More People Use Christian Media." For example, televangelist Robert Tilton's website fuels the critics' fire when it explains the hardship of making a financial vow: "Vowing is one of the best ways to stretch your faith—but only when your vow goes beyond your natural resources or abilities. I don't need much faith to vow $100 if I have $2,000 in a savings account. But, if I don't even have a savings account and can barely pay my bills, then a $100 vow will stretch my faith indeed." Robert Tilton, "What Is a Vow?" Success N Life <www.successinlife.tv/vowing .html>.

[33]For more on how this fundraising model began, see a discussion of religious radio history in Schultze, *Christianity and the Mass Media in America,* pp. 139-74; and Erickson, *Religious Radio and Television,* pp. 10-17.

[34]For more discussion of this creative stranglehold, see Schultze, *Redeeming Television;* and William D. Romanowski, *Eyes Wide Open: Looking for God in Popular Culture,* rev. and exp. ed. (Grand Rapids: Brazos, 2007), pp. 27-42. Romanowski says the problem is not that Christians use popular art for evangelism, exhortation or discipleship, but that those "confessional" purposes become the *only* legitimate reasons for Christian involvement with media and the arts.

[35]Schultze, *Televangelism and American Culture,* pp. 183-93.

[36]Barna Group, "More People Use Christian Media." See also Barry Litman and Elizabeth Bain, "The Viewership of Religious Television Programming: A Multidisciplinary Analysis of Televangelism," *Review of Religious Research,* 30, no. 4 (1989): 329-43; and Janice Peck, *The Gods of Televangelism: The Crisis of Meaning and the Appeal of Religious Television* (Cresskill, N.J.: Hampton, 1993), p. 140.

[37]Barna Group, "More People Use Christian Media."

[38]"Poll: America's Evangelicals More and More Mainstream but Insecure," *Religion and Ethics Newsweekly,* April 13, 2004 <www.pbs.org/wnet/religionandethics/week733/release.html>.

[39]The Life Today website describes the economics of professional evangelism at <www.lifetoday .org/site/PageServer?pagename=out_fivein05>.

[40]Barna Group, "More People Use Christian Media."

[41]Richard G. Tansey and Fred S. Kleiner, eds., *Gardner's Art Through the Ages,* 10th ed. (Fort Worth: Harcourt Brace College, 1996), 1:302-3.

[42]Martin Luther, quoted in Roger S. Gottlieb, ed., *The Oxford Handbook of Religion and Ecology* (New York: Oxford University Press, 2006), p. 117.

[43]Mark Ward, *Air of Salvation: The Story of Christian Broadcasting* (Manassas, Va.: National Religious Broadcasters, 1994), pp. 81-83.

[44]Ibid., p. 84.

[45]Robert E. Webber, *The Younger Evangelicals: Facing the Challenges of the New World* (Grand Rapids: Baker Books, 2002), provides an overview of the emerging church movement, which, among other things, attempts to recapture imagery in worship, encourage progress in contemporary Christian visual arts, and engages in informed criticism of mainstream visual arts and media. See also Eddie Gibbs and Ryan K. Bolger, *Emerging Churches: Creating Christian Community in Postmodern Cultures* (Grand Rapids: Baker Academic, 2005), pp. 20, 70-71, 173-90.

[46]Michael Medved, "Hollywood Makes Room for Religion," in *Religion and Prime Time Television*, ed. Michael Suman (Westport, Conn.: Praeger, 1997), pp. 111-16. Medved notes the growth of Inter-Mission, the Los Angeles Film Studies Center and MasterMedia International, and an even more dramatic increase in religious activity among Jewish industry professionals. In addition to these organizations, I would add Actor's Co-op, Media Fellowship International, Act One, the Hollywood Prayer Network, Catholics in Media Associates and others now loosely tied through HollywoodConnect.com.

[47]Amber Nasrulla, "God's Entourage: How Private Faith Is Going Public Among the African American Elite of Hollywood," *Los Angeles Times*, October 22, 2006.

[48]Thomas Skill, James D. Robinson, John S. Lyons and David Larson, "The Portrayal of Religion and Spirituality on Fictional Network Television," *Review of Religious Research* 35, no. 3 (1994): 251-67.

[49]Judith M. Buddenbaum, "Reflections on Culture Wars: Churches, Communication Content, and Consequences," in *Religion and Primetime Television*, ed. Michael Suman (Westport, Conn.: Praeger, 1997), pp. 47-59. Buddenbaum reports on the results of her 1994 survey of Christian church leaders concerning religious portrayals in mainstream media.

[50]"TBS Unveils Extensive African-American Targeted Marketing Campaign to Launch New Comedy Series Tyler Perry's 'House of Payne,'" *Black Talent News*, May 31, 2007 < http://www.blackprwire.com/display-news.asp?id=3114>.

[51]Nasrulla, "God's Entourage."

[52]"Mission Statement," Inspiration Network <www.inspiration.net/popups/about.cfm>.

[53]Chris Busch, "For a Religious Program, Are Religious Stations and Networks Better, or Are Secular Stations and Nets?" weblog posting on Phil Cooke, The Change Revolution (August 2, 2007) <www.philcooke.com/media_buying>.

[54]This impact has precedent in religious broadcasting. See Bradley E. Schultz, "The Effects of Digital Environments on Religious Television Stations," *Journal of Communication and Religion* 23, no. 1 (2000): 50-71. The author interviews Quentin J. Schultze, who draws a parallel to the early days of radio when some ministries could not afford government-mandated upgrades.

[55]John Eggerton, "NRB Reluctantly Opposes à la Carte," *Broadcasting & Cable*, August 12, 2004 <www.freepress.net/news/print.php?id=4302>. Ironically, religious broadcasters support the concept of à la carte cable because it would allow consumers to screen out objectionable content. However, without "must-carry" regulations that would require cable companies to carry broadcast stations and leased-access cable programmers, "NRB [National Religious Broadcasters] program producers and broadcasters would be reduced to economic inviability" because they would not be selected as part of many consumers' channel lineups.

[56]Deborah Bothum, "Media Companies Preparing for 2010," Media 2010: The Consumer Takes Control, *Variety*, MPEG video <www.variety.com/index.asp?layout=vision&taxid=23363&elementid=2140029644>. The video features Deborah Bothun, U.S. Advisory Leader for Entertainment, Media and Communications for consulting firm Pricewaterhouse Coopers, making recommendations for media executives.

[57]Ray Richmond, "Thinking Outside the Box," *The Hollywood Reporter*, October 12, 2006, p. S-1.

[58]Many ministries have understandably shied away from product advertisement. Advertising soap or toilet paper during a ministry program seems incongruous, if not tacky.

[59]Bothum, "Media Companies."

[60]Schultz, "The Effects of Digital Environments."

[61]Clive Thompson, "The See-Through CEO," *Wired,* April 2007, pp. 135-39.

[62]Lev Grossman, "Power to the People," *Time,* January 1, 2007, pp. 42-58. See also Jeff Howe, "Your Web, Your Way," *Time,* January 1, 2007, pp. 60-61.

[63]Nearly 80 percent of adults eighteen to twenty-nine use the Internet, compared with just 60 percent for those ages fifty to sixty-four. Lee Rainie et al., "4 Internet: The Mainstreaming of Online Life," Pew Internet and American Life Project, <www.pewinternet.org/pdfs/internet_status_2005.pdf>, p. 61.

[64]Mainstream networks are scrambling to figure out how to monetize new media. In 2006, the Television Academy awarded the first Primetime Emmy for content distributed through broadband only. See Richmond, "Thinking Outside the Box," p. S-1.

[65]Warren Littlefield, "Content Remains TV's King, but Technology Is Its Queen," *The Hollywood Reporter,* October 12, 2006, p. 11. See also Elena Malykhina, "YouTube Mobilizes," *Information Week,* December 4, 2006, p. 20.

[66]One noteworthy example is the Nooma series featuring Pastor Rob Bell of Mars Hill Bible Church in Grand Rapids, Michigan. He is the on-camera talent for a series of provocative film shorts. Bell's weekly sermons are available free as podcasts. "Filmanthrophy" is the trend for wealthy individuals or groups to create documentary media in support of particular causes. See, for example, the work of companies like Participant Productions at <www.participantproductions.com/films/>.

[67]A sampling of film festivals includes the 168 Hour Film Project, the Damah Film Festival, the Redemptive Film Festival, and the Heartland Truly Moving Pictures organization and Heartland Film Festival. Bluefish TV, Barna Films and Worship House Media are just three of the many companies and clearinghouses offering creative resources for use in teaching, preaching, discipleship and group study.

[68]Edward C. Baig, "Will Consumers Tune in to a Tiny TV in Their Hand?" *USA Today,* August 17, 2006 <www.usatoday.com/money/industries/technology/2006-08-17-mobile-tv_x.htm>.

[69]"Snack Attack," *Wired,* March 2007, pp. 125-35.

[70]Goethals, *Electronic Golden Calf,* p. 179.

Chapter 4: Moving from Film to Digital Movies

[1]Kevin Jackson, ed., *Schrader on Schrader and Other Writings* (Boston: Faber and Faber, 1990), pp. 8-15, 136.

[2]Basic book sources on evangelicals and film include Roy M. Anker, *Catching Light: Looking for God in the Movies* (Grand Rapids: Eerdmans, 2004); Peter Fraser, *Images of the Passion* (Westport, Conn.: Praeger, 1998); Robert K. Johnston, *Reel Spirituality: Theology and Film in Dialogue,* 2nd ed. (Grand Rapids: Baker Academic, 2006); William D. Romanowski, *Eyes Wide Open: Looking for God in Popular Culture,* rev. & exp. ed. (Grand Rapids: Brazos, 2007); Bryan P. Stone, *Faith & Film: Theological Themes at the Cinema* (Saint Louis: Chalice, 2000).

[3]James K. Friedrich, *National Council of Churches Broadcasting and Film Commission* (Green Lake, Wis.: Fourth International Christian Film Workshop, 1947), Billy Graham Center Archives, 327, Wheaton College, Ill.

[4]Herbert A. Jump, *The Religious Possibilities of the Motion Picture* (New Britain, Conn.: South Congregational Church, 1911).

[5]*City of the Bees*, DVD, directed by Irwin Moon (1962; Chicago, Ill., Moody Publishers: 2004);

Red River of Life, DVD, directed by Irwin Moon (1957; Chicago, Ill.: Moody Publishers, 2004). Both of these films demonstrate the kinship between Christian faith and "true science"—an early intelligent design concept—keying on Isaiah 41:20 that "people may see and know . . . and understand."

[6]Stephen Dine Young, "Movies as Equipment for Living: A Developmental Analysis of the Importance of Film in Everyday Life," *Critical Studies in Media Communication* 17, no. 4 (2000): 460. See also Kenneth Burke, "Literature as Equipment for Living," in his *The Philosophy of Literary Form: Studies in Symbolic Action* (Berkeley: University of California Press, 1957), pp. 253-62.

[7]Statistics from Jesus Film Project website <www.jesusfilm.org/aboutus/index.html>.

[8]John Gilman, *Freedom Cry* (Virginia Beach, Va.: Dayspring International, 2004), p. 11; see also John Gilman, *They're Killing an Innocent Man: The Cry of Those Who Have Never Heard* (Virginia Beach, Va.: Dayspring International, 1991).

[9]Lois Blewett, *Twenty Years Under God: Proclaiming the Gospel of Jesus Christ to the World* (Minneapolis: WorldWide Publications, 1970), p. 513.

[10]See, e.g., <www.movieministry.com/>; <www.christiancinema.com/>; <www.MovieGuide.com/>; <www.hollywoodjesus.com/>; <www.pluggedonline.com/review/>. These sites recommend and interpret films for their audiences.

[11]See Henry James Forman, *Our Movie Made Children* (New York: Macmillan, 1933), p. 179; and Terry Lindvall, *The Silents of God: Selected Issues and Documents in Silent American Film and Religion* (Lanham, Md.: Scarecrow, 2001), pp. 7-9.

[12]Charles M. Sheldon, "In His Steps Today: What Would Jesus Do with the Drama?" *Christian Herald,* December 4, 1920, pp. 1247-48.

[13]Terry Lindvall, *Sanctuary Cinema: Origins of the Christian Film Industry* (New York: New York University Press, 2007).

[14]A. W. Tozer, *The Menace of the Religious Movie* (Wisconsin Rapids, Wis: Rapids Christian Press, n.d.); and Gordon Lindsay, *Should Christians Attend the Movies?* (Dallas: Voice of Hearing, 1964).

[15]U. E. Harding, *Movie Mad America* (Grand Rapids: Zondervan, 1942), p. 13; Dr. John J. Wick, *What's Wrong with the Movies* (Grand Rapids: Zondervan, 1940); Lester F. Sumrall, *Worshippers of the Silver Screen* (Grand Rapids: Zondervan, 1940); and Robert L. Sumner, *Hollywood Cesspool* (Grand Rapids: Zondervan, 1955).

[16]Ted Baehr and Pat Boone, *The Culture-Wise Family: Upholding Christian Values in a Mass Media World* (Ventura, Calif.: Regal, 2007); K. L. Billingsley, *The Seductive Image: A Christian Critique of the World of Film* (Westchester, Ill.: Crossway, 1989); Brian Godawa, *Hollywood Worldviews* (Downers Grove, Ill.: InterVarsity Press, 2002).

[17]Robert K. Johnston, *Reel Spirituality: Theology and Film in Dialogue,* 2nd ed. (Grand Rapids: Baker Academic, 2006); William D. Romanowski, *Pop Culture Wars: Religion and the Role of Entertainment in American Life* (Downers Grove, Ill.: InterVarsity Press, 1996).

[18]Michael Medved, *Hollywood vs. America* (Grand Rapids: Zondervan, 1992).

[19]A quantitative analysis of *Christianity Today*'s treatment of 123 films from 1956 to 1985 found that the number of film reviews increased exponentially, particularly in the number of reviews of mainstream motion pictures whose main subjects were not religious. Paul C. Stevens, "The Christian in the MGM Lion's Den: A Content Analysis of Changing Evangelical Attitudes Toward Motion Pictures in 'Christianity Today' Film Reviews from 1956 to 1985" (master's thesis, Regent University, 1989).

[20]Dann Halem, "Onward Christian Movies," *Premiere,* March 2004, p. 3 <www.premiere.com/movienews/1504/onward-christian-movies-page3.html/>.

[21]Ibid.

[22]Augustine, *On Christian Doctrine* (Indianapolis: Bobbs-Merrill, 1958), p. 75.

[23]John of Damascus, *On the Divine Images* (Crestwood, N.Y.: SVS Press, 2002).

[24]Bonaventure, *Liber III Sententiarum* 3, dist. 9, art. 1, ques. 2, in *Opera theologica selecta,* trans. Frati Quarrachi-Firenze (Florence, Italy: Florence Press, 1941), p. 194.

[25]Thomas Aquinas similarly wrote that images can facilitate "the instruction of the unlettered, who might learn from them as if from books"; impress upon believers the "mystery of the Incarnation and the examples of the saints"; and "excite the emotions which are more effectively aroused by things seen than by things heard." *Commentarium super libros sententiarum: Commentum in librum* 3, dist. 9, art. 2, ques. 2.

[26]Gregory the Great, *Liber IX, Epistola LII Ad Secundinum* in Patrologia latina 77, cols. 990-91, quoted in David Freedberg, *The Power of Images: Studies in the History and Theory of Response* (Chicago: University of Chicago Press, 1991), p. 470. Dionysius Areopagiticus also emphasized how meditation is enabled by the cult of images, "We are led up, as far as possible, through visible images to a contemplation of the divine." *De ecclesia hierarchia* 1.2, trans. Ernst Kitzinger, Patrologia graeca 3, col. 373 (New York: Cambridge University Press, 1952), pp. 137-38.

[27]David Morgan, *Protestants and Pictures* (New York: Oxford University Press, 1999).

[28]Robert H. Woods Jr., Michael C. Jindra and Jason D. Baker, "The Audience Responds to The Passion," in *Re-Viewing the Passion: Mel Gibson's Film and Its Critics,* ed. S. Brent Plate (New York: Palgrave Macmillan, 2004), pp. 163-80.

[29]Devin Leonard, "The Passion of Philip Anschutz," *Fortune,* April 18, 2006 <http://money.cnn.com/2006/04/17/magazines/fortune/waldenmedia_fortune_050106/>.

Chapter 5: Pursuing New Periodicals in Print and Online

[1]J. D. Keeler, J. D. Tarpley and Michael Smith, "The *National Courier,* News and Religious Ideology," in *Media and Religion in American History,* ed. W. David Sloan (Northport, Ill.: Vision Press, 2000), p. 281. For more on the *National Courier* saga, see Ken Waters, "Christian Journalism's Finest Hour? An Analysis of the Failure of the *National Courier* and Inspiration," *Journalism History* 20 (1994): 55-65.

[2]David Wimbish, telephone interview by the author, April 7, 1994.

[3]W. Howard Norton, "An Annotated Bibliography of Religious Journalism" (master's thesis, University of Indiana, 1971), p. 25.

[4]Ken Waters, "Vibrant but Invisible: A Study of Contemporary Religious Periodicals," *Journalism & Mass Communication Quarterly* 78, no. 2 (2001): 313.

[5]Charles Austin, "The History and Role of the Protestant Press," in *Reporting Religion: Facts and Faith,* ed. B. J. Hubbard (Sonoma, Calif.: Polebridge, 1990), p. 110.

[6]Martin E. Marty, "Protestantism," in *The Religious Press in America,* ed. Martin E. Marty et al. (New York: Holt, Rinehart and Winston, 1963), p. 36.

[7]See, e.g., David Abrahamson, *Magazine-Made America: The Cultural Transformation of the Postwar Periodical* (Cresskill, N.J.: Hampton, 1996); Charles P. Daly, Patrick Henry and Ellen Ryder, *The Magazine Publishing Industry* (Boston: Allyn & Bacon, 1997); and Carolyn Kitch, *Pages from the Past: History & Memory in American Magazines* (Chapel Hill: University of North Carolina Press, 2005).

[8]Waters, "Vibrant but Invisible," p. 313.

[9]Bobby Ross Jr., "Virginia Tech Massacre Challenges Young Campus Minister," *Christian Chronicle,* June 1, 2007 <www.christianchronicle.org/modules.php?name=News&file=article&sid=703>.

[10]Waters, "Vibrant but Invisible," p. 313.

[11]*The Wittenburg Door* can be accessed at <www.wittenburgdoor.com/>.

[12]Cameron Strang, telephone interview by author, June 12, 2007.

[13]Ibid.

[14]Quentin J. Schultze, *Christianity and the Mass Media in America: Toward a Democratic Accommodation* (East Lansing: Michigan State University Press, 2003), p. 92.

[15]Ibid., p. 99.

[16]Ibid.

[17]See, e.g., Phyllis Alsdurf, "Christianity Today and Late Twentieth-Century Evangelicalism" (Ph.D. diss., University of Minnesota, 2004); Dennis P. Hollinger, *Individualism and Social Ethics: An Evangelical Syncretism* (Lanham, Md.: University Press of America, 1983); and Linda-Marie Delloff et al., *A Century of 'The Century'* (Grand Rapids: Eerdmans, 1984).

[18]Jim Wallis, *Revive Us Again: A Sojourner's Story* (Nashville: Abingdon, 1983).

[19]For more information, see the Sojourner's website announcement of the debate at <http://sojo.net/index.cfm?action=action.P07&item=pentecost07_candidates_forum>.

[20]See, e.g., Austin, "History and Role of the Protestant Press"; Marty, "Protestantism"; Marvin Olasky, *Telling the Truth: How to Revitalize Christian Journalism* (Wheaton, Ill.: Crossway, 1996); Will H. Norton, "An Annotated Bibliography of Religious Journalism" (master's thesis, Indiana University, 1971).

[21] Austin, "History and Role of the Protestant Press," p. 112.

[22]Martin E. Marty, interview by author, April 24, 2000.

[23]Gaylord Albaugh, *History and Annotated Bibliography of American Religious Periodicals and Newspapers Established from 1730 to 1830* (Worcester, Mass.: American Antiquarian Society, 1994).

[24]P. Mark Fackler and Charles H. Lippy, eds., *Popular Religious Magazines of the United States* (Westport, Conn.: Greenwood, 1995), p. xi.

[25]Roberta Moore, "Development of Protestant Journalism in the United States, 1743-1850" (Ph.D. diss., Syracuse University, 1968), p. 19.

[26]Frederick Detweiler, *The Negro Press in America* (Chicago: University of Chicago Press, 1922), p. 43.

[27]Moore, "Development of Protestant Journalism," p. 8.

[28]See Teresa Lueck, "Women's Moral Reform Periodicals of the 19th Century: A Cultural Feminist Analysis of the Advocate," *American Journalism* 16 (1999): 37-52.

[29]See David Paul Nord, "The Evangelical Origins of the Mass Media in America, 1815-1835," *Journalism Monographs*, no. 88 (1984).

[30]Olasky, *Telling the Truth*, p. 166.

[31]See, for instance, James Sutter, *Journalists Who Made History* (Minneapolis: Oliver, 1998), pp. 15-28.

[32]Olasky, *Telling the Truth*, p. 272.

[33]Martin E. Marty, *Modern American Religion: The Noise of Conflict, 1919-1941* (Chicago: University of Chicago Press, 1991), p. 188.

[34]See Mark G. Toulouse, "*Christianity Today* and American Public Life: A Case Study," *Journal of Church and State* 35 (Spring 1993): 241-84.

[35]Martin E. Marty, "Not of This World . . . but Like It," *Christian Century*, June 1, 1998, p. 663.

[36]From the mission statement on the *Sports Spectrum* homepage <www.sportsspectrum.com/about.html>.

[37]The OOZE <www.theooze.com>, Emergent Village <www.emergentvillage.org> and *Next-Wave* <www.the-next-wave.org>.

[38]Jamie Buckingham, "With Tears in Our Eyes," *National Courier*, September 16, 1977, p. 18.

Chapter 6: Publishing Books for the Tribe and Beyond

[1]"Vivendi's Purchase of Houghton-Mifflin Will Make It One of Top Four Companies in U.S. Education Market," *Electronic Education Report* 8 (June 6, 2001): 1; Bill McConnell, "Taking on Goliath," *Broadcasting and Cable,* June 19, 2000, p. 14; Jonathan Karp, "Conglomerates: A Good Thing for Books," *Media Studies Journal* 10 (Spring 1996): 123.

[2]Raya Kuzyk, "Brave New Genre: The Religious Partners with the Secular in a Singular 21st Century Friendship," *Library Journal* 131 (May 2006): 8-12. The Christian Booksellers Association (CBA) and the Evangelical Christian Publishers Association (ECPA) categorize their bestsellers into biblical studies, Christian living, church and ministry, fiction, general interest, inspirational and theology. Under Christian living, the top listings in mid-2007 were books on prayer, courage in the face of life obstacles, marital communication and vocational direction.

[3]Josh Getlin and K. Connie Kang, "Left Behind? Not This Book Series," *Los Angeles Times,* April 3, 2007. Best-selling author T. D. Jakes, pastor of a multi-ethnic Dallas megachurch, hosted a nationally syndicated TV program and appeared (as himself) in a film about abused women. Other celebrity pastors whose books catapulted to top billing include Max Lucado, Joel Osteen, Rob Bell and Rick Warren. Warren's 2005 book *The Purpose-Driven Life: What on Earth Am I Here For?* sold over 25,000,000 copies, making it one of the biggest-selling hardbacks in U.S. publishing history. By 2007 it sold alongside an audio version and a life journal, in camouflage cover, and with such companion items as a devotional by Warren, a music CD and video.

[4]Christian Classics Ethereal Library can be accessed at <www.ccel.org>. The Digital Christian Library can be accessed at <www.thedcl.org>.

[5]Maryanne Murray Buechner, "Don't Call It Vanity Press," *Time,* May 3, 2007 <www.time.com/time/magazine/article/0,9171,1617545,00.html>. See also <www.xulonpress.com>.

[6]Quentin J. Schultze, "Going Digital: Will the Internet Have as Much Influence as the Printing Press?" *The Christian Century,* January 31, 2001, pp. 16-21.

[7]Appeared in the list of "June 2007 Top 50 Bestsellers" at <www.cbaonline.org/nm/BSLs.htm>.

[8]Daniel Radosh, "The Good Book Business: Why Publishers Love the Bible," *The New Yorker,* December 18, 2006 <www.newyorker.com/archive/2006/12/18/061218fa_fact1>.

[9]Allison Kennedy, "Best Seller, Students, Local Clergy Weigh in on Their Favorite Versions of the Bible," *Columbus Ledger-Enquirer,* April 16, 2007.

[10]A few specialty Bibles include *Life Recovery Bible, Woman Thou Art Loosed! Edition, Revolve New Testament, Grace for the Moment Bible* and *True Images Bible for Teen Girls.*

[11]The religious children's book market alone represents $70 million in sales out of an estimated $1.1 billion total market for children. James Arndorfer, "Religious Publishers Tap into Children's Crusade," *Advertising Age,* March 7, 2005, p. 53.

[12]Dawn Baumgartner Vaughan, "What Do Teens Think They Know About Religion? Notre Dame Project Uses 3,000 U.S. Teen Surveys," *The Herald-Sun,* February 3, 2007; Jeanne Halgren Kilde, "Rapture Culture: Left Behind in Evangelical America," *Church History* 74 (June, 2005): 410; David Klinghofer, "Social Issues a Natural for Religion Books," *Publishers Weekly,* May 22, 2006, p. 9.

[13]William Henderson, "Fighting the Christian Fundies," *Advocate,* November 7, 2006, p. 4; Mel White, *Stranger at the Gate: To Be Gay and Christian in America* (New York: Simon & Schuster, 1994).

[14]See Rina Palta, review of *Body Piercing Saved My Life,* by Andrew Beaujon, *Mother Jones,* July/August 2006 <www.motherjones.com/arts/books/2006/07/body_piercing_saved_my_life.html>.

[15]Joseph W. Trigg, "Christianity and the Transformation of the Book: Origen, Eusebius, and the Library of Caesarea," *Church History* 76 (June, 2007): 397.

[16]"The Early History of Harvard University," The Harvard Guide: History, Lore, and More <www.hno.harvard.edu/guide/intro/index.html>.

[17]Frederick Rudolph, *The American College and University: A History* (Athens: University of Georgia Press, 1990), p. 16.

[18]Nathan O. Hatch, *The Democratization of American Christianity* (New Haven, Conn.: Yale University Press, 1989), p. 126.

[19]Earlier American religious fiction is discussed in Matthew T. Herbst, "The Moral Hurt of Novel Reading: Methodism and American Fiction, 1865-1914," *Methodist History* 44 (2006): 239.

[20]Allan Fisher, "D. L. Moody's Contribution to Christian Publishing: He Was the Catalyst for Two of America's Largest Religious Book Publishers," *Christian History* 25 (January 1, 1990): 32-33.

[21]Martin E. Marty, *Pilgrims in Their Own Land: 500 Years of Religion in America* (New York: Penguin, 1984), pp. 378-79.

[22]Allan Fisher, "Five Surprising Years for Evangelical-Christian Publishing: 1998-2002," *Publishing Research Quarterly* 19 (Summer 2003): 20.

[23]Ian S. Rennie, "Fundamentalism and the Varieties of North Atlantic Evangelicalism," in *Evangelicalism: Comparative Studies of Popular Protestantism in North America, the British Isles, and Beyond, 1700-1990,* ed. Mark A. Noll, David W. Bebbington and George A. Rawlyk (New York: Oxford University Press, 1994), pp. 335-37.

[24]Michele Steele, "Christian Fiction Finds a Booming Audience," Columbia News Service <http://jscms.jrn.columbia.edu/cns/2006-01-10/steele-christianfiction/>. Romance novels aimed at evangelicals sold impressively in mainstream bookstores after 2005.

[25]Edward Nawotka, "Singing Nashville's Praises," *Publisher's Weekly,* June 19, 2006, p. 19. Successful sales by evangelicals in mainstream marketplaces are not flukes. In 2004 Thomas Nelson hired Tamara Heim, former president of Borders Bookstores, as chief publishing officer to rethink Nelson's approach to mainstream marketing. That marketplace, Michael Hyatt said in 2005, was one of the fastest growth areas for sales of evangelical books anywhere in the United States (p. 22).

[26]Mark I. Pinsky, "Among the Evangelicals: How One Reporter Got Religion," *Columbia Journalism Review* 43, no. 5 (2005): 8-10.

[27]"Pastor Rick Warren and Jon Meacham of *Newsweek* Discuss Faith in America," *Meet the Press,* NBC News Transcripts, National Broadcasting Company, December 24, 2006.

Chapter 7: Practicing Worship Media Beyond PowerPoint

[1]I use the terms *multimedia, worship media, liturgical media, worship media art* and *liturgical art* interchangeably. Worship media include PowerPoint slides, painting, sculpture, dance, incense and poetry.

[2]Consult Eileen D. Crowley, *Liturgical Art for a Media Culture* (Collegeville, Minn.: Liturgical Press, 2007); Tex Sample, *The Spectacle of Worship in a Wired World: Electronic Culture and Gathered People of God* (Nashville: Abingdon, 1998).

[3]Quentin J. Schultze's *High-Tech Worship? Using Presentational Technologies Wisely* (Grand Rapids: Baker, 2004) offers a thoughtful and comprehensive consideration of slideware in worship.

[4]Software programs like Shout, EasyWorship, Service Builder, Presentation Manager, Adoration Worshipware, SongPro and ZionWorx claim a greater affinity with church mission than the Microsoft juggernaut. Their libraries of stock photos and religious artwork often supplement databases of hymn lyrics and multiple Bible translations. Some even allow simple, moving backgrounds beneath static lines of text.

[5]Some nonprofit image pools and vendors (like Christian Media Association or Worship House

Media) are explicitly Christian, while others (like Digital Hotcakes) package nature footage culled from stock archives.

[6]"*Rocky Balboa* Born Again in Christian Theme," *Day to Day*, NPR, December 20, 2006.

[7]*The Worshipper Magazine*, Spring 2007, p. 5.

[8]Juniper Schneider, interview by author, videotape recording, St. Joseph's Catholic Church, Roseburg, Oregon, October 20, 2003. Many of the interviews cited in this chapter were conducted during the production of *FutureWorship 1.0*, a documentary I directed for the Calvin Institute of Christian Worship. The film chronicles the use of presentational technologies in churches throughout the nation. The featured congregations, selected by Robb Redman and members of *Worship Leader Magazine*'s editorial staff, were seldom over three hundred members.

[9]Mary Hersley, interview by author, videotape recording, Saint Joseph Catholic Church, Roseburg, Oregon, October 18, 2003.

[10]Karen Ward, interview by author, videotape recording, Apostle's Church, Seattle, Washington, September 20, 2003.

[11]Megan Kooistra, interview by author, videotape recording, CentrePointe Christian Reformed Church, Grand Rapids, Michigan, November 9, 2003.

[12]A paraphrased conversation of the worship committee of the Scottsdale Congregational United Church of Christ, facilitated by author, videotape recording, Scottsdale, Arizona, October 4, 2003.

[13]Deborah Bruce, "Key Findings: Who Worships in the U.S.?" U.S. Congregational Life Survey <www.uscongregations.org/key.htm>.

[14]This stereotype is breaking down. May Wong, "Consumer Electronics Companies Woo Women: Women Spent More on Technology Than Men in 2003," *MSNBC*, January 16, 2004 <www.msnbc.msn.com/id/3966261>; Michael Grebb, "Women Want Electronics Too: Closing the Gender Gap," Ecoustics.com (July 28, 2005) <http://forum.ecoustics.com/bbs/messages/34579/151254.html>.

[15]Quentin J. Schultze, interview by author, videotape recording, Grand Rapids, Michigan, November 12, 2003.

[16]Dad once told me, "Keep a tie long enough, it'll come back in style," perhaps paraphrasing Ecclesiastes 1:9.

[17]Carol Palmer, interview by author, videotape recording, Trinity Presbyterian Church, Scotia, New York, October 25, 2003.

[18]Mark Meyer, interview by author, videotape recording, CentrePointe Christian Reformed Church, Grand Rapids, Michigan, November 9, 2003.

[19]Schultze, *High-Tech Worship?* p. 47. Among the eight reasons given for closing the door on presentational technologies, theological concerns and biblical notions of beauty are, sadly, absent.

[20]Ward interview; Kent Wilson, interviews by author, videotape recording, Trinity Lutheran Church, Willard, Ohio, October 20 and 29, 2003.

[21]Andrew Holmes, interview by author, Grand Rapid, Michigan, March 20, 2007.

[22]Ibid. Holmes's observation targets a personal frustration. As I wrote this chapter, most of what I found written on the subject was published by equipment and software manufacturers.

[23]A whopping 84 percent of churches say they use slideware "to gain contemporary relevance." Schultze, *High-Tech Worship?* p. 105.

[24]John Margolies and Emily Gwathmey, *Ticket to Paradise: American Movie Theaters and How We Had Fun* (Boston: Little, Brown, 1991), pp. 49-63. See also Simcha Jacobovici, director, *Hollywoodism: Jews, Movies and the American Dream* (Canadian Broadcasting Corporation, 1998).

[25]Edward Tufte, "PowerPoint Is Evil," *Wired*, September 2003 <www.wired.com/wired/archive/11.09/ppt2.html>.

[26]Article 10 of the Berne Convention—which should be read concurrently with Mark 12:16-18—enumerating allowable free uses of intellectual property, is widely available on the Internet including at <www.law.cornell.edu/treaties/berne/10.html>.

[27]Linda Garmon, director, "Sister Aimee," *American Experience* (Public Broadcasting System, 2007).

[28]Anthony Breznican, "Image and Cruise Control," *USA Today,* June 26, 2005 <www.usatoday.com/life/people/2005-06-26-cruise_x.htm>.

[29]My grandmother, Dora Burgin, is here playing fast and loose with a paraphrase of Saint Jerome attributed to Chaucer in the *Tale of Melibee,* ca. 1386: "Dooth somme good dedes that the devel, which is oure enemy, ne fynde yow nat unoccupied." Richard Hazelton, "Chaucer and Cato," *Speculum* 35 (July 1960): 356.

[30]The pre-credit sequence of the Beatles' *Hard Day's Night,* with the Fab Four on the run from rampaging fans, always put me in mind of the Gospel of Mark.

[31]Philippians 4:8 could be recast for church artists: "Finally, brothers and sisters, whatever is inoffensive, whatever matches your carpet, whatever is inexpensive, whatever is cute, whatever we can agree on at the last moment, whatever is imitative—if anything is safe or derivative—think about such things."

[32]William David Spencer and Aida Besancon Spencer, *God Through the Looking Glass: Glimpses from the Arts* (Grand Rapids: Baker Books, 1998), pp. 152-54.

[33]Martin Luther (1483–1546) wrote that "next to the Word of God, the noble art of music is the greatest treasure in the world. . . . A person who gives this some thought and yet does not regard music as a marvelous creation of God, must be a clodhopper indeed and does not deserve to be called a human being; he should be permitted to hear nothing but the braying of asses and the grunting of hogs." Martin Luther, "Foreword to 'Georg Rhau's Collection, *Symphoniae iucundae*'" <www.eldrbarry.net/mous/saint/luthmusc.htm>.

[34]Roughly a third of the book of Exodus is devoted to the design and execution of worship multimedia.

[35]I have circumspectly chosen the word *army.* Worship is a corporate undertaking, and so was art until sometime during the nineteenth century. "The concept of the artist/author as some kind of asocial being, blessed with genius, waiting for divine inspiration and exempt from all normal rules of social intercourse is therefore very much an ahistorical and limited one. Its kernel of truth lies in the fact that the development of our society *has* marginalized artists. The artist is more likely to be alienated and isolated from society and production today than in any earlier period." Janet Wolff, *The Social Production of Art* (New York: St. Martin's, 1981), p. 12.

[36]With the possible exception of Nehemiah 8, the Bible does not mention preaching as a normative act of worship. Yet today's church has embraced the spoken text as worship's tent pole. Perhaps it is no surprise to see it also embrace PowerPoint, marketed first as a technology of teaching with text, especially bulleted texts.

[37]Gene Veith, *The Gift of Art: The Place of the Arts in Scripture* (Downers Grove, Ill.: InterVarsity Press, 1983), pp. 17-28, 43-61. See also Gene Veith, *State of the Arts: From Bezalel to Mapplethorpe* (Westchester, Ill.: Crossway, 1991), pp. 105-31.

Chapter 8: Going Digital with Contemporary Christian Music

[1]The phrase "contemporary Christian music" was apparently coined by the founder of *CCM Magazine,* a holy version of *Billboard* just for evangelicals. See Don Cusic, *The Sound of Light: A History of Gospel and Christian Music* (New York: Hal Leonard, 2002), p. 294.

[2]Robert M. McManus, "Southern Gospel Music versus Contemporary Christian Music: Compet-

ing for the Soul of Evangelicalism," in *More than Precious Memories,* ed. Michael P. Graves and David Fillingim (Macon, Ga.: Mercer University Press, 2004), pp. 43-56.

[3]Cusic, *Sound of Light,* p. 248. Larry Norman's 1969 album *Upon This Rock* was the first commercially released Jesus rock project, and one cut often served as the unofficial CCM Anthem, "I Wish We'd All Been Ready."

[4]Rich Mullins, a prolific songwriter and composer of such early CCM songs as "Our God Is an Awesome God" (recorded by Michael W. Smith and many other CCM artists) and "Sing Your Praise to the Lord" (recorded by Amy Grant), went on to record and perform his songs in concerts throughout the nation. Like Green, he died young, in a highway accident on the way to a performance.

[5]Megan Livengood and Connie Ledoux Book, "Watering Down Christianity? An Examination of the Use of the Theological Words in Christian Music," *Journal of Media and Religion* 3, no. 2 (2004): 119-29.

[6]William D. Romanowski, "Rock Apostles and Pop Apostasy," *Perspectives,* January 2002, p. 11.

[7]Mark Allan Powell, "The Business of Contemporary Christian Music: Jesus Climbs the Charts," *The Christian Century,* December 2002, pp. 20-26.

[8]The Gospel Music Association (GMA) Dove Awards have imitated the Grammy awards for forty years, giving awards in categories from rap/hip hop and urban to pop, rock, bluegrass and traditional gospel.

[9]Chad Butler in an interview with Dena Ross, "Honest Music for Thinking People," Beliefnet <www.beliefnet.com/story/182/story_18224_1.html>.

[10]For more detail about early CCM, see Paul Baker, *Contemporary Christian Music: Where It Came from, What It Is, Where It's Going* (Westchester, Ill.: Crossway, 1985); Steve Miller, *The Contemporary Christian Music Debate* (Wheaton, Ill.: Tyndale, 1993); Jay R. Howard and John M. Streck, *Apostles of Rock: The Splintered World of Contemporary Christian Music* (Lexington: University Press of Kentucky, 1999); Steve Lawhead, *Rock Reconsidered: A Christian Looks at Contemporary Music* (Downers Grove, Ill.: InterVarsity Press, 1981); Mark Allan Powell, *Encyclopedia of Contemporary Christian Music* (Peabody, Mass.: Hendrickson, 2002).

[11]See Scott Ross, *Scott Free* (Old Tappan, N.J.: Chosen, Revell, 1976), pp. 131-43; Pat Robertson with Jamie Buckingham, *The Autobiography of Pat Robertson: Shout It from the Housetops* (Plainfield, N.J.: Logos, 1972), pp. 202-5.

[12]I spent most of my free time and disposable income in these shops in the 1970s.

[13]McManus, "Southern Gospel Music versus Contemporary Christian Music," pp. 57-58.

[14]I watched this firsthand as I attended many early performances before they could even be considered concerts. Concurrently observing these dynamics as a performer in small coffeehouses such as the Catacombs in Allentown, Pennsylvania, and in local churches, I later saw the same as a music journalist during the years of 1986-2000 while interviewing national and local performers for a variety of music magazines and other publications. For two years I worked part time promoting concerts at the Jersey Shore and was privy to "the way it worked" in small clubs, medium-sized venues and large festivals.

[15]Sally Blake, *The Disciples,* PBS documentary, November 19, 2002 (Discovery Times Channel, 2002).

[16]Many of the anecdotes, perceptions and facts shared in this chapter have been gleaned from primary sources made available to me through the undocumented interviews I conducted with artists such as Amy Grant, Russ Taff, Abe Laboriel and Bill Maxwell of Koinonia, Mylon Le Fevre, GLAD, The Imperials, Kim Boyce, Carman, David and the Giants, Stryper, Ginny Owens, and many others.

[17]There are scores of large CCM festivals and many niche events such as Music Expo East in New York state, Spirit West Coast in California and Godapalooza in Colorado Springs. The Creation

Festival began in Mount Union, Pennsylvania, with a New Jersey pastor, Harry Thomas, and Tim Landis, and expanded to other locations in the US.

[18]John Fisher, "Consider This Column," *CCM Magazine*, August 1988, p. 82.

[19]Livengood and Book, "Watering Down Christianity?" p. 119.

[20]Steven John Camp, "A Call for Reformation in the Contemporary Christian Music Industry," personal website (October 31, 1998) <www.worship.com/steve_camp_107_theses.htm>.

[21]Eric Gormly, "Evangelizing Through Appropriation: Toward a Cultural Theory on the Growth of Contemporary Christian Music," *Journal of Media and Religion* 2, no. 4 (2003): 251.

[22]Howard and Streck, *Apostles of Rock*, p. 217.

[23]Matt Slocum and Leigh Nash, "The Discontent Between Business and Artistry," *Christianity Today*, August 1, 2003 <www.christianitytoday.com/ct/2003/134/43.0.html>.

[24]William D. Romanowski, *Eyes Wide Open: Looking for God in Popular Culture*, rev. and exp. ed. (Grand Rapids: Brazos, 2007), p. 102.

[25]Gormly, "Evangelizing Through Appropriation," pp. 251-65.

[26]Livengood and Book, "Watering Down Christianity?" p. 128.

[27]Mark Joseph, *The Rock & Roll Rebellion: Why People of Faith Abandoned Rock Music—and Why They're Coming Back* (Nashville: Broadman & Holman, 1999).

[28]Charlie Peacock, *At the Crossroads: Inside the Past, Present and Future of Contemporary Christian Music* (Colorado Springs: Shaw, 2004), p. 106.

[29]Rick Warren, "Worship: Planned for God's Pleasure," SelfGrowth.com: The Online Self Improvement Encyclopedia <www.selfgrowth.com/articles/Warren1.html>.

[30]Michael Card, *Scribbling in the Sand* (Lexington: University of Kentucky Press, 2002).

[31]"Behind the Resources," *Relevant Leader*, Summer 2007, pp. 36-41.

[32]Kenneth Burke, "The Range of Rhetoric," in *Landmark Essays on Rhetoric and Literature*, ed. Craig Kallendorf (New York: Lawrence Erlbaum, 1999), pp. 225-42.

[33]Gormly, "Evangelizing Through Appropriation," p. 251.

[34]Peacock, *At the Crossroads*, p. 13.

[35]Susanne Langer, *Philosophy in a New Key: A Study in the Symbolism of Reason, Rite and Art*, 3rd ed. (Cambridge, Mass.: Harvard University Press, 1942), pp. 246-54.

[36]Cusic, *Sound of Light*, p. 35.

[37]GLAD, "Variations on a Hymn," video clip <www.youtube.com/watch?v=3SqQOKr6IAk>.

[38]Daniel Stout, review of *Traces of the Spirit: The Religious Dimensions of Popular Music*, by Robin Sylvan, *Journal of Media and Religion* 2, no. 3 (2003): 66.

[39]McManus, "Southern Gospel Music versus Contemporary Christian Music," p. 58.

[40]Also see Ephesians 1:7-12, Ephesians 4:13-15 and Colossians 1:21-29.

[41]Langer, *Philosophy in a New Key*.

[42]For example, consider the way Saul's jangled emotions were soothed by David's anointed playing as described in 1 Samuel 16:23: "Whenever the spirit from God came on Saul, David would take up his lyre and play. Then relief would come to Saul; he would feel better, and the evil spirit would leave him."

[43]Editorial Staff, ProSound News (New York: Newsbay Media Audio Group, 2007), p. 66.

[44]The proliferation of social networking sites on the Web, such as Facebook, FM, TotalVolume and MySpace, tapping into the potential for participatory media.

[45]Rebecca St. James in an interview with Dena Ross, "Tuning In to the Voice of God," Beliefnet <www.beliefnet.com/story/205/story_20555_1.html>.

[46]As of November 26, 2007, there were 55,300 Christian songs available on YouTube <www.youtube.com/results?search_query=Christian+music>.

[47]Peacock, *At the Crossroads*, p. 7.

Chapter 9: Praising God with Popular Worship Music

[1]Terry York, *America's Worship Wars* (Peabody, Mass.: Hendrickson, 2003).

[2]Christian DJs are becoming the new worship leaders for teens and twentysomethings who want to worship God outside the traditional church. Club Worship in Reading, Pennsylvania, lets teens express themselves in dance to techno-pop music under the direction of the emcee/worship leader. Fusion, in Jacksonville, Florida, is a four-hour, nonstop rave where teens come to dance to house, trance and jungle music under pulsating lights. Participants say they can "hear God in the pulsating techno music." Organizers of these clubs see the opportunity for friendship evangelism. See Sandra K. Chamber, "Our Love Is Loud," *Charisma & Christian Life*, February 2003, pp. 50-55.

[3]Hip-hop is used at Crossover Church in Tampa, Florida. Worship typically begins with worship team singers in chocolate-brown T-shirts leading twenty minutes of praise and prayer. During worship, a dancer spins by, singing "When the Spirit of the Lord moves in my heart, I will dance like David danced." A bank of turntables is on the stage, where a contemporary church might have a keyboard or drum set. See Cathy L. Grossman, "Shouting Hip-Hop's Praises: Churches Put Spin on the Word," *USA Today*, November 28, 2005 <www.crossoverchurch.org/usatoday/usatoday.html>.

[4]Dan A. Kimball, *The Emerging Church: Vintage Christianity for New Generations* (Grand Rapids: Zondervan, 2003); Robert E. Webber, *The Younger Evangelicals: Facing the Challenges of the New World* (Grand Rapids: Baker Books, 2002).

[5]Brian A. Wren, "'Sing It, Preacher!' Thoughts About Contemporary Worship Music," *Journal for Preachers* 24, no. 1 (2000): 45-53.

[6]Jack Hayford, *Worship His Majesty: How Praising the King of Kings Will Change Your Life* (Ventura, Calif.: Gospel Light, 2000), p. 21.

[7]Robert R. Redman, "How I Caught the Worship Bug: And Never Got Over It," *Reformed Worship* 16, no. 59 (2004) <www.reformedworship.org/magazine/article.cfm?article_id=1038>. See also Robb Redman, *The Great Worship Awakening: Singing a New Song in the Postmodern Church* (San Francisco: Jossey-Bass, 2002), p. 8.

[8]Jay R. Howard and John M. Streck, *Apostles of Rock: The Splintered World of Contemporary Christian Music* (Lexington: University Press of Kentucky, 1999); Mark Allan Powell, *Encyclopedia of Contemporary Christian Music* (Peabody, Mass.: Hendrickson, 2002).

[9]John M. Frame, *Contemporary Worship Music: A Biblical Defense* (Philipsburg, N.J.: P & R, 1997), p. 9. Michael Hawn traces CWM back to the "Azusa Street revival in 1906, at the Apostolic Faith Mission, where Pentecostalism broke loose in the U.S. with praise and worship making the heart of the church service." Cited in Joe Orso, "Contemporary Music Slowly Gaining Ground in Churches," *Knight Ridder Tribune Business News*, June 23, 2006, p. 1.

[10]Some popular songs from these Masses became known outside Catholic circles. See William J. Reynolds, Milburn Price and David Music, *A Survey of Christian Hymnody*, 4th ed. (Carol Stream, Ill.: Hope, 1999), chap. 11.

[11]The Barna Group, "Focus on 'Worship Wars' Hides the Real Issues Regarding Connection to God," The Barna Update (November 19, 2002) <www.barna.org/FlexPage.aspx?Page=BarnaUpdate&BarnaUpdateID=126>.

[12]Christian Copyright Licensing International, "CCLI Company Profile" <www.ccli.com/CCLI/CompanyProfile.cfm>. See also, Christian Copyright Licensing International, "Number of License Holders Worldwide" <www.ccli.com/CCLI/LicenseHolders.cfm>.

[13]Simon Gonzalez, "Who Would Have Imagined?" *Decision*, September 2003, p. 14.

[14]Praise and Worship Music Channel, ChristianTuner <www.christiantuner.com/praise/>, Worship Radio Network <www.worshipradio.com/>.

[15]WorshipMusic.com <www.worshipmusic.com>.

[16]WorshipTogether.com <www.worshiptogether.com>.

[17]Worship Together's New Song Café is a popular new addition. See also WorshipMatters: Resources for Leading Worship from Bob Kauflin <www.worshipmatters.com/>; Passion Conferences <www.268generation.com/2.0/splash1.htm>.

[18]Deborah Evans Price, "Praise and Worship Genre Blessed with Global Growth," *Billboard* 115, no. 7 (2003): 1 <www.allbusiness.com/retail-trade/miscellaneous-retail-retail-stores-not/4642267-1.html>.

[19]"U.S. Congregations," The U.S. Congregational Life Survey from April 2001 at <www.USCongregations.org/>.

[20]Barry Liesch, *The New Worship* (Grand Rapids: Baker Books, 2001), pp. 19, 30.

[21]John D. Witvliet, "At Play in the House of the Lord: Why Worship Matters," *Books & Culture,* November/December, 1998; see reprint at <www.calvin.edu/worship/about/staff/jwitvliet/atplay.php>.

[22]Scripture supports repetition. In Isaiah 6 the seraphs use *holy* three times. Revelation 4:8 says that the saints will never stop saying, "'Holy, holy, holy is the Lord God Almighty,' who was, and is, and is to come."

[23]Orso, "Contemporary Music Slowly Gaining Ground in Churches," p. 1.

[24]Edward Miller encouraged the Church of England to sing hymns like the breakaway Methodists. "It is well known that more people are drawn to the temples of Methodists by their attractive harmony, than by the doctrine of their preachers. . . . Where the Methodists have drawn one person from our communion by their preaching, they have drawn ten by their music." "The Golden Age of Hymns," *Christian History* 10 (1991): 3.

[25]Lynne and Bill Hybels, *Rediscovering Church: The Story and Vision of Willow Creek Community Church* (Grand Rapids: Zondervan, 1995), p. 69.

[26]G. A. Pritchard, *Willow Creek Seekers Services: Evaluating a New Way of Doing Church* (Grand Rapids: Baker Books, 1996). See also Harry Boonstra, "The Best of Times? The Worst of Times? Snapshots of Worship Styles," *Reformed Worship* 47 (March 1998): 16-17; Cornelius Plantinga Jr. and Sue Rozeboom, *Discerning the Spirits: A Guide to Thinking About Christian Worship Today* (Grand Rapids: Eerdmans, 2003).

[27]Dan Lucarini and John Blanchard, *Why I Left the Contemporary Christian Music Movement* (Auburn, Mass.: Evangelical, 2002).

[28] Bert Polman's study covered the core repertoire of CWM over a fifteen-year period. His findings are reported in chap. 8 of Robert H. Woods Jr. and Brian Walrath, eds., *The Message in the Music: Studying Contemporary Praise and Worship* (Nashville: Abingdon, 2007), pp. 127-37.

[29]Many songs use male language for God that does not reflect "mainline sensibilities about gender inclusiveness." Also, there may be a "patriarchal and royal image of God inappropriate for use in democratic and egalitarian North America." Robin Knowles Wallace, "Praise and Worship Music: Look at Language," *Hymn* 55 (2004): 27-28.

[30]Wren, *Praying Twice,* p. 221.

[31]Robert Webber, "Is Our Worship Killing Christianity in America?" *Worship Leader,* November/December 2005, p. 10.

[32]Robert Webber, "Where Will All the Songs Go?" *Worship Leader,* March/April 2004, p. 12, and chap. 2, pp. 43-53.

[33]Woods and Walrath, *Message in the Music,* pp. 54-64. See also pp. 43-53.

[34]Webber, "Where Will All the Songs Go?" p. 12.

[35]E.g., explicit trinitarian aspects are largely absent, and themes of God's demands for justice and righteousness in social relationships are lacking. See Woods and Walrath, *Message in the Music,* pp. 29-42; 65-75.

[36]Liesch, *New Worship,* p. 21. For a discussion of the missing role of lament in worship today, see Michael Card, *A Sacred Sorrow: Reaching Out to God in the Lost Language of Lament* (Colorado Springs: NavPress, 2005).

[37]Raymond T. Gawronski, "Why Orthodox Catholics Look to Zen," *New Oxford Review* 60 (July/August 1993): 14.

[38]Marva Dawn, *Reaching Out Without Dumbing Down: A Theology of Worship for the Turn-of-the-Century Culture* (Grand Rapids: Eerdmans, 1995). See also Sally Morgenthaler, *Worship Evangelism: Inviting Unbelievers into the Presence of God* (Grand Rapids: Zondervan, 1995).

[39]Marva Dawn, "Worship Is Not a Matter of Taste," *Creator* 21 (November 1999): 5-9.

[40]Gerhard von Rad, *Old Testament Theology* (New York: Harper, 1962), p. 24.

[41]Donald P. Hustad, *Jubilate II: Church Music in Worship and Renewal* (Carol Stream, Ill.: Hope, 1993), p. 136.

[42]They praised God with resonating tambourines, jubilant dancing, and clashing cymbals (Psalm 150), and clapped their hands and shouted for joy (Psalm 47:1). See Erik Routley, *Church Music and the Christian Faith* (Carol Stream, Ill.: Hope, 1978), p. 6. The Hebrews read Scriptures for three hours and praised God for another three hours (Nehemiah 9:1-6)—so much for short choruses and brief singing!

[43]The persecuted New Testament Church hid for the first three hundred years or so, meeting quietly in homes and catacombs. Consequently, it adopted the synagogue a cappella style of singing versus the professionally performed temple style, which included orchestral accompaniment. See James F. White, *A Brief History of Christian Worship* (Nashville: Abingdon, 1993); Ralph P. Martin, *Worship in the Early Church* (Grand Rapids: Eerdmans, 1974).

[44]Quoted in Eric Werner, "The Conflict Between Hellenism and Judaism in the Music of the Early Church," *Hebrew Union College Annual* 20 (1947): 420.

[45]Lutheran composer J. S. Bach later recounted that his congregation sang up to forty stanzas of a single hymn. See Roland H. Bainton, *A Life of Martin Luther: Here I Stand* (Toronto: New American Library of Canada, 1963), p. 267.

[46]Hustad, *Jubilate II,* pp. 193-94.

[47]"Early Protestant Episcopal bishops were concerned that artistic skill, and performance trumped proper solemnity so characteristic of the ancient church." In a formal letter to ministers, bishops wrote, "The house of prayer is desecrated by a choice of music and a style of performance which are rather suited to the Opera than to the Church—when the organist and the choir seem to be intent only on exciting the admiration of the audience by the display of their artistic skill; and the entertainment of the concert-room is taken as a substitute for the solemn praises of that Almighty Being who searchest the heart." See Jane Rasmussen, *Musical Taste as a Religious Question in Nineteenth-Century America* (Lewiston, N.Y.: Mellen, 1986), p. xvii.

[48]Shannon Dietor-Hartley, "New Music Controversy: Hymns vs. Contemporary Worship (or, Hymns Used to Be Scandalous)," *Church Musician Today* 3 (June 2000): 21.

[49]One source of inspiration for Luther's hymns was traditional folk music. All types of folk songs were composed of four to eight lines of poetry and based on a simple musical structure known as the "Bar form," not on today's "bar" music. He always sought a delightful, singable melody. See Rebecca Wagner Oettinger, *Music as Propaganda in the German Reformation* (London: Ashgate, 2001), p. 21. See also Edward J. Foley, "Martin Luther: A Model Pastoral Musician," *Currents in Theology and Mission* 14 (December 1987): 407.

[50]Dietor-Hartley, "New Music Controversy," p. 21.

[51]Simon Gonzalez, "Who Would Have Imagined?" *Decision,* September 2003, p. 14.

[52]CWM has proliferated in the United Kingdom and Australia as well, mainly through use in

churches and worship events. Many leading worship artists come from these countries, for example, Australian Darlene Zschech, who wrote "Shout to the Lord." Australia's Hillsong Church (Hillsong Music) has been a leader in the worship industry since the 1980s. Most of the major worship labels realize the international potential. Integrity has offices in Singapore, London and Australia; Vineyard in Brazil, New Zealand, South Africa, Holland, Germany, the United Kingdom, Scandinavia and India. These countries are doing native-speaking recordings of what is coming out in their areas. See Price, "Praise and Worship Genre Blessed with Global Growth."

[53]Robert J. Keeley, "What's New in . . . Contemporary Worship Music," *Banner,* December 2001, p. 15.

[54]Powell, *Encyclopedia of Contemporary Christian Music,* pp. 250-52.

[55]The "Absolute Worship" CD collection is one of many examples of CCM labels collecting worship songs from various artists and repackaging them to the public for private worship. "Absolute Worship," Authentic Music (2004). See also "America's Newest Praise and Worship Favorites, Vol. 1," Brentwood (1999).

[56]See the Official Website of Passion Conferences at <http://268generation.com/2.0/splash3.htm>.

[57]Terry York, "Add One Hymn: Recipe for CCM and 'Modern Worship' Congregational Song," *Hymn* 55 (July 2004): 29-33.

[58]Price, "Praise and Worship Genre Blessed with Global Growth."

[59]Steve Rabey, "The Profits of Praise: The Praise and Worship Music Industry Has Changed the Way the Church Sings," *Christianity Today,* July 1999, pp. 32-33.

[60]Price, "Praise and Worship Genre Blessed with Global Growth."

[61]Ibid.

[62]David Crumm, "New Chevrolet Marketing Campaign Takes on Evangelical Note," *Knight Ridder Tribune Business News,* October 23, 2002, p. 1.

[63]Pete Ward, *Selling Worship: How What We Sing Has Changed the Church* (Carlisle, U.K.: Paternoster, 2005).

[64]Pritchard, *Willow Creek Seeker Services.*

[65]Robert E. Webber, *Planning Blended Worship: The Creative Mixture of Old and New* (Nashville: Abingdon, 1998); Robert Webber, *Ancient-Future Faith: Rethinking Evangelicalism for a Postmodern World* (Grand Rapids: Baker Books, 1999); Robert Webber, *Ancient-Future Evangelism: Making Your Church a Faith-Forming Community* (Grand Rapids: Baker Books, 2003).

[66]York, "Add One Hymn," p. 32.

[67]Nicholas Wolterstorff, *Art in Action: Toward a Christian Aesthetic* (Grand Rapids: Eerdmans, 1980), pp. 184-91.

[68]Because the body of Christ is or should be "blended" (see 1 Corinthians 12), blended worship makes sense, according to proponents. For corporate worship to accurately reflect the nature and unity of the body of Christ, it must include the people of God in all of their diversity who are unified by their common focus on worship. Four separate services on any given Sunday may very well work against this kind of unity. See Paul F. M. Zahl and Paul Basden, eds., *Exploring the Worship Spectrum: 6 Views* (Grand Rapids: Zondervan, 2004).

[69]David B. Pass, *Music and the Church: A Theology of Church Music* (Nashville: Broadman, 1989); also David B. Pass, *Music and the Church,* 2nd ed. (Johannesburg: PassWord, 2005).

[70]John D. Witvliet, *Worship Seeking Understanding* (Grand Rapids: Baker Academic, 2003), chap. 9.

[71]Explore the Taizé movement online at <www.taize.fr/>. The site includes a community area that cyberpilgrims can use for daily reflections, prayers and songs.

[72]See Vintage Faith Church at <www.vintagechurch.org/>.

[73]Keith Drury, “Five Recent Worship Trends,” *Thinking Drafts,* November 2001 <www.drury writing.com/keith/1wortren.htm>. See also Webber, *The Younger Evangelicals.*

[74]The Barna Group, “Focus On ‘Worship Wars’ Hides the Real Issues Regarding Connection to God,” The Barna Update (November 19, 2002) <www.barna.org/FlexPage.aspx?Page=BarnaUpd ate&BarnaUpdateID=126>. George Barna reported at a symposium at Baylor University that the coverage afforded the worship wars has exaggerated the scope of the problem while ignoring the real issues regarding worship. “The major challenge,” according to Barna, “is not about how to use music to facilitate worship as much as it is to help people understand worship and have an intense passion to connect with God.” Barna concluded “that relatively few churches have intense musical battles but most churches have too few people who truly engage God in worship.”

[75]Redman, “How I Caught the Worship Bug,” para. 3; see also Robert R. Redman, “Welcome to the Worship Awakening,” *Theology Today* 58, no. 3 (2001): 369-83.

[76]Michael S. Hamilton, “Triumph of the Praise Songs: How Guitars Beat out the Organ in the Worship Wars,” *Christianity Today* 43, no. 8 (1999): 28-35.

Chapter 10: Following Pilgrims into Cyberspace

[1]See Amber L. Anderson, “‘Surf Here Often?’” *Christianity Today,* June 11, 2001, pp. 38-40; Cheryl Green, *World Wide Search: The Savvy Christian's Guide to Online Dating* (Colorado Springs: Waterbrook, 2004).

[2]Books about evangelicals and cyberspace include Douglas Groothuis, *The Soul in Cyberspace* (Grand Rapids: Baker Books, 1997); Quentin J. Schultze, *Habits of the High-Tech Heart: Living Virtuously in the Information Age* (Grand Rapids: Baker Books, 2002); Gene Edward Veith Jr. and Christopher L. Stamper, *Christians in a .com World: Getting Connected Without Being Consumed* (Westchester, Ill.: Crossway, 2000); and Andrew Careaga, *eMinistry: Connecting with the Net Generation,* 2nd ed. (Grand Rapids: Kregel, 2001).

[3]Stewart Hoover, Lynn Schofield Clark and Lee Rainie, “Faith Online: 64% of Wired American Have Used the Internet for Spiritual or Religious Purposes,” Reports: Family, Friends & Community, Pew Internet & American Life Project (April 7, 2004) <www.pewinternet.org/PPF/r/126/ report_display.asp>, p. 10.

[4]Douglas E. Cowan and Jeffrey K. Hadden, “Virtually Religious,” in *The Oxford Handbook of New Religious Movements,* ed. James R. Lewis (New York: Oxford University Press, 2004), p. 120.

[5]Stewart Hoover et al., “Faith Online.”

[6]See, e.g., the search function at BibleGateway.com, a service of Gospel Communications International <www.biblegateway.com>.

[7]See, e.g., the searchable library provided by Christian Classics Ethereal Library <www.ccel.org>.

[8]See, e.g., the film and music reviews at HollywoodJesus <www.hollywoodjesus.com>.

[9]See, e.g., the resources made available by *Christianity Today* online <www.christianitytoday.com>.

[10]See, e.g., the cartoons at ReverendFun <www.reverendfun.org>.

[11]See, e.g., the satire at WittenburgDoor <www.wittenburgdoor.com/>.

[12]See, e.g., the discussions at ThinkChristian <www.thinkchristian.net> and video clips at Quentin J. Schultze's site, An Essential Guide to Public Speaking <www.calvin.edu/go/speaking/>.

[13]Michael J. Laney, “Mediated Religion: Motivations for Religious Web Site Usage; An Exploratory Study of Christian Web Site Users” (Ph.D. diss., University of Tennessee, 1998).

[14]This is why it is important to listen to contemporary critics as well as fans of new media. Evangelicals need to consider how the medium might affect the message. Alan Jacobs, “The Virtues of Resistance,” *Books & Culture,* September/October 2002, pp. 22-23, 40-42.

[15]For more on cyberspace as a mirror, see Jeff Zaleski, *The Soul of Cyberspace* (San Francisco: Harp-

erSanFrancisco, 1997); and Lorne L. Dawson and Douglas E. Cowan, "Introduction," in *Religion Online: Finding Faith on the Internet,* ed. Lorne L. Dawson and Douglas E. Cowan (New York: Routledge, 2004), p. 6.

[16]One Christian group says that the Internet is "the first medium in history that does not care about content, about good or bad, right or wrong, decent or indecent." See World Association for Christian Communication, *Churches and Faith Organisations on the Internet: A General Overview* (London: WACC, 1997), p. 7.

[17]Helen Lee, "The Internet: A Missionary Hotline," *Christianity Today,* April 3, 1995, p. 80.

[18]Lucas Hendrickson, "Surfing the 'Net: Christian Music Jumps into Cyberspace," *CCM,* March 1995, p. 10.

[19]The Barna Group, "More Americans Are Seeking Net-Based Faith Experiences," The Barna Update (May 21, 2001) <www.barna.org/FlexPage.aspx?Page=BarnaUpdate&BarnaUpdateID=90>.

[20]One of the highest-profile attempts to address the issue of evangelicals' addiction to online pornography is <www.xxxchurch.com>.

[21]See, e.g., Tal Brooke, ed., *Virtual Gods* (Eugene, Ore.: Harvest House, 1997).

[22]Jon Katz, review of *Virtual Faith,* by Tom Beaudoin, Slashdot: News for Nerds, Stuff That Matters (February 26, 1999) <slashdot.org/articles/99/02/26/107210.shtml>.

[23]Heidi Campbell, "'This Is My Church': Seeing the Internet and Club Culture as Spiritual Space," in *Religion Online: Finding Faith on the Internet,* ed. Lorne L. Dawson and Douglas E. Cowan (New York: Routledge, 2004), p. 107. Also see Heidi Campbell, *Exploring Religious Community Online: We Are One in the Network* (New York: Peter Lang, 2005).

[24]Mia Lövheim, "Young People and the Use of the Internet in Transitional Space," *Heidelberg Journal of Religions on the Internet* 1, no. 1 (2005): 7 <www.ub.uni-heidelberg.de/archiv/5826/>.

[25]George D. Randels Jr., "Cyberspace and Christian Ethics: The Virtuous and/in/of the Virtual," *Annual of the Society of Christian Ethics* 20 (2000): 167.

[26]Christopher Helland, "Popular Religion and the World Wide Web: A Match Made in (Cyber) Heaven," in *Religion Online: Finding Faith on the Internet,* ed. Lorne L. Dawson and Douglas E. Cowan (New York: Routledge, 2004), p. 23.

[27]"Finding God on the Web," *Time,* December 16, 1996, p. 63. This article is part of an issue dedicated to "Jesus Online."

[28]Douglas E. Cowan, "Contested Spaces: Movement, Countermovement, and E-Space Propaganda," in *Religion Online: Finding Faith on the Internet,* ed. Lorne L. Dawson and Douglas E. Cowan (New York: Routledge, 2004), p. 266.

[29]Elizabeth Bromstein, "How to Start Your Own Religion," personal blog <www.otoons.com/eso/Start_Your_Own_Religion.htm>.

[30]Sterling Huston, quoted in A. Scott Moreau and Mike O'Rear, "Doing Evangelism on the Internet," *Evangelical Missions Quarterly* 36 (April 2002): 218.

[31]Steven Waldman, quoted in Mindy Sink, "Spiritual Issues Lead Many to the Net," *New York Times,* September 6, 2003.

[32]Scholars and reporters dedicated an entire conference to blogging and religion, focusing partly on the question of whether the apostle Paul would have been a blogger in today's world. See "Convergence and Society: Ethics, Religion, and New Media," College of Mass Communications and Information Studies, University of South Carolina, October 19-21, 2006 <newsplex.sc.edu/newsplex_con06.html>.

[33]See Marv Knox, "Internet 'Gossip' Undermines Christians' Credibility," EthicsDaily.com (June 5, 2002) <www.ethicsdaily.com/article_detail.cfm?AID=929>.

[34]See, e.g., "How Your Church Can Use MySpace," Church Marketing Sucks, Center for Church Communication (April 6, 2006) <www.churchmarketingsucks.com/archives/2006/04/how_your_church_1.html>.

[35]Tom Beaudoin, "Spiritual Quests Move Online, out of the Church and into the Chat Room," *Business 2.0,* September 26, 2000, p. 186. Beaudoin's book on the topic is *Virtual Faith: The Irreverent Spiritual Quest of Generation X* (San Francisco: Jossey-Bass, 1998).

[36]Geoff Boucher, quoted in "Illegal Downloads Hit Christian Music Industry," *Manatee Herald-Tribune,* October 11, 2006. The original study is summarized in The Barna Group, "Fewer Than 1 in 10 Teenagers Believe That Music Piracy Is Morally Wrong," The Barna Update (April 26, 2004) <www.barna.org/FlexPage.aspx?Page=BarnaUpdate&BarnaUpdateID=162>.

[37]Andy Crouch, "Promises, Promises," *Christianity Today,* February 19, 2001, p. 72.

[38]Wendell Berry, *What Are People For?* (New York: North Point, 1990), p. 172.

[39]A few websites track Christian myths and urban legends, including: <www.new-life.net/myths.htm>, <www.truthminers.com/>, and <www.snopes.com/religion/religion.asp>.

[40]Earlier mass media have not been particularly effective for evangelism. See Quentin J. Schultze, *Televangelism and American Culture: The Business of Popular Religion* (Grand Rapids: Baker Books, 1989), pp. 187-90.

[41]Helen A. Berger and Douglas Ezzy, "Internet as Virtual Spiritual Community: Teen Witches in United States and Australia," in *Religion Online: Finding Faith on the Internet,* ed. Lorne L. Dawson and Douglas E. Cowan (New York: Routledge, 2004), p. 175.

[42]Lorne L. Dawson and Jenna Hennebry, "New Religions and the Internet: Recruiting in a New Public Space," in *Religion Online: Finding Faith on the Internet,* ed. Lorne L. Dawson and Douglas E. Cowan (New York: Routledge, 2004), p. 151.

[43]A well-argued Roman Catholic perspective can be found in Pierre Babin and Angela Zukowski, *The Gospel in Cyberspace: Nurturing Faith in the Internet Age* (Chicago: Loyola Press, 2002).

[44]I attempted to summarize some of these various perspectives in terms of the common agreement that the Internet will never be better than the people who use it, and that each of the virtues emphasized by various Christian and Jewish traditions can be meaningfully used to evaluate cyberculture. See Quentin J. Schultze, *Habits of the High-Tech Heart: Living Virtuously in the Information Age* (Grand Rapids: Baker Academic, 2004).

[45]Paul A. Soukup, "On-Line Religion," *America,* May 8, 1999, pp. 8-10.

[46]Graham Ward, "Between Virtue and Virtuality," *Theology Today,* 59 (April 2002): 55-70.

[47]Keith Howard, "The Impact of New Communication Technologies on the Church," *Touchstone* 19 (January 2001): 36.

Chapter 11: Evangelicals in Theater

[1]Her name has been changed to protect her privacy, but she does still have letters from Kirk Douglas begging her to reconsider entering the acting conservatory.

[2]The significance of both Orlin Corey's and Jeannette Clift George's pioneering work as directors, playwrights and producers cannot be overestimated. Corey is the first recipient of the Lifetime Achievement Award from Christians in Theatre Arts (CITA), and Clift George is the second.

[3]See Peter Senkbeil, "Why Christian Theater Is Exploding," *Christianity and the Arts* 4, no. 1 (1997): 4-7.

[4]Ibid. Senkbeil's article is of seminal importance in understanding the growth of theater involvement in the evangelical tribe.

[5]Learn about Covenant Players at <www.covenantplayers.org/>.

[6]Information about the play can be found at "*Toymaker & Son* Training & Licensing Info" on Colin

Harbinson's website <www.colinharbinson.com/toymakerandson/training.html>.

[7]Learn about Christians in Theatre Arts at <www.cita.org/>.

[8]See Lillenas publications at <www.nph.com/nphweb/html/lmol/index.jsp>.

[9]A very helpful book of introductory insights regarding drama ministry and training principles is Steve Pederson, *Drama Ministry* (Grand Rapids: Zondervan, 1999).

[10]Learn about Saltworks Theatre Company at <www.saltworks.org>. Theater-in-education is a performance medium employed by several regional, professional theaters run by Christians. It has become a standard arm of community outreach and a very steady source of income for these theaters.

[11]Perhaps evangelicals did not formerly attend live theater performances because they did not see themselves in the protagonist on stage; few plays were written *about* the evangelical tribe and *for* the tribe. The newer evangelical habit of theater attendance was spurred by the regional theaters' incremental willingness to stage plays pertinent to the evangelical experience.

[12]Dan Wilson, "How to Stage a Drama Ministry," *Christianity and the Arts* 7 (Fall 1994): 28.

[13]David Riemenschneider, "'Life Illustrated' Stories Offer Added Focus to Sermons," *Preaching Resources,* July-August 1997, p. 30.

[14]See Kimberly R. Messer's "Playwright's Guidelines and Program Builder Contributor's Guidelines" at <http://www.nph.com/nphweb/html/ldol/articleDisplay.jsp?mediaId=2351652&catSecCd=PLAYG&nid=ban&articleReview=false>. Messer, Lillenas Publishing's drama publishing editor, also provides a valuable website for church dramatists, listing downloadable dramatic sketches, articles with a variety of acting/directing tips, and even a Christian drama networking forum at <www.nph.com/nphweb/html/ldol/index.jsp?nid=navlm>.

[15]For a substantive context for understanding the pastoral care model in theater ministry, see Dietrich Bonhoeffer, *Life Together,* trans. John W. Doberstein (New York: Harper & Row, 1954).

[16]I was introduced to the theater and its possibilities while serving as a pastor at Trinity Church in Livonia, Michigan. I was intrigued by theater as an arena for pastoral care more than theater as art, founding Trinity House Theater in 1981. My questions regarding art as evangelism and biblically informed aesthetics came later.

[17]Laura Collins-Hughes, "Articles of Faith: Can Conservative Christianity Find Expression on the Stage? And Is There Even Such a Thing as Christian Theatre?" *American Theater,* September 2006, p. 61.

[18]Quoted in Bernard F. Dukore, *Dramatic Theory and Criticism: Greeks to Grotowski* (Fort Worth: Harcourt Brace Jovanovich College, 1974), pp. 85-86.

[19]Ibid., p. 89.

[20]Ibid., pp. 90-91.

[21]Ibid., p. 94

[22]Augustine, *The Confessions of Saint Augustine,* trans. D. B. Pusey, 3rd ed. (New York: Pocket Books, 1959), pp. 31-32.

[23]See Edmund S. Morgan, "Puritan Hostility to the Theater," in *Proceedings of the American Philosophical Society* 110, no. 3 (1966): 340-47. The Quakers also possessed an "anti-theatrical prejudice." See Michael P. Graves, "The Anti-Theatrical Prejudice and the Quakers in *Truth's Bright Embrace: Essays and Poems in Honor of Arthur O. Roberts,* ed. Paul N. Anderson and Howard R. Macy (Newberg, Ore.: George Fox University Press, 1996).

[24]Morgan, "Puritan Hostility to the Theater," p. 340. Morgan points out that hostility to the theater was not exclusively Puritan, and suggests other explanations for the riot—such as the art form's distracting the pre-Revolutionary audience from the focus of the rebellion against England.

[25]One compelling challenge from a fundamentalist-separatist perspective comes from Kevin T.

Bauder, "Fundamentalism and Theater: Act One, Whatever Happened?" SharperIron <www.sharperiron.org/2007/01/02/fundamentalist-and-theater-acts-three-say-what/>.

[26]Joseph H. Hellerman, *The Ancient Church as Family* (Minneapolis: Augsburg Fortress, 2001), pp. 184-86.

[27]Oscar G. Brockett and Franklin J. Hildy, "European Theatre in the Middle Ages," in *History of the Theater,* 9th ed. (Boston: Allyn & Bacon, 2003), p. 72.

[28]For an excellent overview of the Christian history of narrative drama and the aesthetics of the image, see Terry Lindvall, *Sanctuary Cinema: Origins of the Christian Film Industry* (New York: New York University Press, 2007), pp. 28-36.

[29]See a list of past productions by Theater 315 at <www.theatermania.com/content/theater.cfm?intTheaterID=3632>.

[30]Learn about The Lamb's Theatre Company at <www.lambstheatre.org/>.

[31]Learn about Lamb's Players Theatre at <www.lambsplayers.org/>.

[32]Learn about Taproot Theatre Company at <www.taproottheatre.org>.

[33]Learn about A. D. Players at <www.adplayers.org/>.

[34]Learn about the Acacia Theatre Company at <www.acaciatheatre.com>.

[35]"Our Name & Mission," Sight and Sound Theatres <www.sight-sound.com>.

[36]Malcomb Goldstein, *The Political Stage: American Drama and Theater of the Great Depression* (New York: Oxford University Press, 1974), pp. 82-85.

[37]See Paul D. Patton, "The Sacred Use of the Profane?" *Christianity and Theater* 25 (Spring 2004), pp. 47-53. Thanks to John Peck for this point.

[38]The phrases "poetic aesthetic" and "rhetorical aesthetic" are attributed to Stuart Scadron-Wattles and quoted in Senkbeil, "Why Christian Theatre Is Exploding," p. 7.

[39]Learn about Art Within at <http://artwithin.org/index_popup.html>.

[40]See New Works Series, Threads Productions, Center for Faith & Work, Redeemer Presbyterian Church <www.faithandwork.org/new_works_series_page732.php>.

Chapter 12: Faith-Based Theme Parks and Museums

[1]Paul Lomartire, "What Would Jesus View?" *Palm Beach Post,* June 17, 2004.

[2]Marvin J. Rosenthal, a Jewish convert to Christianity who became a Baptist minister, founded the organization Zion's Hope in 1989 to reach Jews with the gospel. In February of 2001 he opened the gates of Holy Land Experience to controversy from charismatics (who could not work there because the doctrinal statement excluded them) and condemnation by Jews (who believed the park sought to trick them into hearing the gospel presentations). Vic Eliason's interview of Rosenthal, "Zion's Hope," on Crosstalk America (April 12, 2007) <www.crosstalkamerica.com/shows/2007/04/zions_hope.php>. See also Valerie G. Lowe, "Sparks Fly After Opening of Holy Land Theme Park," *Charisma,* May 2001, pp. 26-28.

[3]Olivia Barker, "'Holy Land' as Theme Park," *Chicago Sun-Times,* February 11, 2001.

[4]Timothy K. Beal, *Roadside Religion: In Search of the Sacred, the Strange, and the Substance of Faith* (Boston: Beacon, 2005).

[5]Christopher Boyd, "Biblical Theme Park Seeks to Get the Word Out," *Orlando Sentinel,* October 16, 2006.

[6]Margaret J. King, "Theme and Amusement Parks," in *Encyclopedia of Recreation and Leisure in America,* ed. Gary S. Cross (Woodbridge, Conn.: Charles Scribner's Sons, 2004), 2:363-68.

[7]Mark I. Pinsky, "Six Flags over Israel," *Christianity Today,* March 5, 2001, pp. 101-3.

[8]Ibid., p. 103.

[9]For example, in 2004 revenue was $8.7 million while expenses were $9.2 million. As of July 2006

they still had not made a profit. See Jeff Brumley, *Florida Times-Union* (Jacksonville), July 3, 2006.

[10]Mark I. Pinsky, "Holy Land's Debts Erased in Christian Network Deal," *Orlando Sentinel,* June 6, 2007. Note the irony of TBN, a Pentecostal group, taking over the Holy Land Experience, an organization that initially would not employ charismatics.

[11]Not quite as elaborate a destination, Ave Maria Grotto in Cullman, Alabama, bills itself "Jerusalem in Miniature." It has replicas of significant historical buildings as well as a Jerusalem hillside. See <www.avemariagrotto.com/> for more information. Christus Gardens, in operation since 1960 in Gatlinburg, Tennessee, boasts of its "inspirational and educational" experience with over one hundred life-sized figures and tells stories of the life of Christ. See <www.christusgardens.com/about_christus_gardens.html>.

[12]John Greco, Roman Catholic, willed the park to an order of nuns who still own the property. For information about Holy Land U.S.A., see <http://roadsideamerica.com/holy/index.html>. See also Mary E. Ladd and Julie Wiskirchen, "Onward Christian Tourists," *Hermenaut* 15 (December 2000) <www.hermenaut.com/a6.shtml>.

[13]Beal, *Roadside Religion,* pp. 25-48.

[14]Alexander Provan, "Watching Jesus Rise, Twice an Hour," *Seattle Times,* August 4, 2006. See also Juan Mabromata, "Life of Jesus Is Main Attraction at Buenos Aires Theme Park," *Sawf News,* April 9, 2006.

[15]Chris Branam, "Christ of Ozarks Marks 40 Years Atop Mountain," *Arkansas Democrat-Gazette,* June 4, 2006; see also "About Our Ministry," The Great Passion Play <www.greatpassionplay.com/about/htm>.

[16]Campbell Gray, "Museums," in *Encyclopedia of Religion, Communication, and Media,* ed. Daniel A. Stout (New York: Routledge, 2006), pp. 271, 273.

[17]Chris Kenning, "Science and Religion: Creation Museum Opens," *Courier-Journal, USA,* Religion News Blog (May 29, 2007) <www.religionnewsblog.com/18374/creation-museum-2>.

[18]Mark Looy, interview by author, Petersburg, Kentucky, June 12, 2007.

[19]Stephen Asma, "Dinosaurs on the Ark: The Creation Museum," *The Chronicle Review,* May 18, 2007, p. B13.

[20]Dmitry Kiper, "Creationism: A Museum for Middle America," *Newsweek/MSNBC,* April 11, 2007 <www.msnbc.msn.com/id/18061154/site/newsweek/print/1/displaymode/1098/>.

[21]The criticism and wide press coverage served the museum well. Less than two months after it opened it had already had over 100,000 visitors. "Business Booming at Controversial Creationism Museum," *USA Today,* August 2, 2007 <www.usatoday.com/travel/destinations/2007-08-02-Kentucky-creation-museum_N.htm>.

[22]See Stephanie Simon, "Billy Graham, Tourist Attraction," *Los Angeles Times,* May 28, 2007.

[23]Other creation museums exist, including one at Eureka Springs, Arkansas. For a significant listing, see Creation Museums at <http://nwcreation.net/museums.html>. The Explorations in Antiquity Center in Georgia is run by a biblical archaeologist and billed as "a museum of daily life in biblical times." With full-scale archeological replicas, the center seeks to educate visitors about everything from houses of worship to a Bedouin tent, and from the life of a shepherd to a crucifixion tree. Opened in June 2006, it also includes the requisite food stop and museum shop. See information at <www.explorationsinantiquity.com>. Word Spring Discovery Center at Wycliffe headquarters in Orlando is a small hands-on museum designed to educate about the need for and complexity of Bible translation. I was impressed by its ability to inspire the audience to support its work. See <www.wycliffe.org/Wordspring/>.

[24]Other roadside religion attractions and museums include the Golgotha Fun Park in Cave City, Kentucky; biblical mini-golf in Lexington, Kentucky; a reconstruction of Noah's Ark in Frost-

burg, Maryland; the World's Largest Ten Commandments in Murphy, North Carolina; a cross garden in Prattville, Alabama; and the Precious Moments Inspiration Park in Carthage, Missouri, with a painted chapel loosely inspired by the Sistine Chapel.

[25]Oscar G. Brockett with Franklin J. Hildy, *History of the Theatre,* 8th ed. (Boston: Allyn & Bacon, 1999), pp. 8-9.

[26]Ibid., pp. 13-48.

[27]Carol Harrison, *Augustine: Christian Truth and Fractured Humanity* (Oxford: Oxford University Press, 2000), pp. 136-38.

[28]Brockett and Hildy, *History of the Theatre,* pp. 49-79.

[29]Ibid., pp. 81-120. See also A. M. Nagler, *A Source Book in Theatrical History* (New York: Dover, 1952), pp. 38-53.

[30]Ellen Hirzy, "History of Museums," *Microsoft Encarta Online Encyclopedia* <http://encarta.msn .com>.

[31]Harrison, *Augustine,* pp. 141-42. For an interesting description of key worldwide pilgrimage sites today, see Jennifer Westwood's *Sacred Journeys: An Illustrated Guide to Pilgrimages Around the World* (New York: Henry Holt, 1997).

[32]Luigi Tomasi, "*Homo viator:* From Pilgrimage to Religious Tourism via the Journey," in *From Medieval Pilgrimage to Religious Tourism: The Social and Cultural Economics of Piety,* ed. William H. Swatos Jr. and Luigi Tomasi (Westport, Conn.: Praeger, 2002), pp. 1-24.

[33]Boris Vukonić, *Tourism and Religion,* trans. Sanja Matešić (Trowbridge, U.K.: Redwood Book, 1996), p. 190.

[34]"Holy Land," Modiya: Jews/Media/Religion, New York University, accessed May 30, 2007, at <http://modiya.nyu.edu/handle/1964/54>.

[35]Barbara Kirshenblatt-Gimblett, "A Place in the World: Jews and the Holy Land at World's Fairs," in *Encounters with the 'Holy Land': Place, Past, and Future in American Jewish Culture,* ed. Jeffrey Shandler and Beth S. Wenger (Hanover, N.H.: University Press of New England, 1998), p. 60.

[36]Burke O. Long, *Imagining the Holy Land: Maps, Models, and Fantasy Travels* (Bloomington: Indiana University Press, 2003), pp. 43-87.

[37]See Marilyn Mathews Bendiksen, "The Endless Summers of Chautauqua," *New York Archives Magazine,* Chautauqua Institution; download the reprint at <www.ciweb.org/history.html>; "Palestine Park," Chautauqua Institution <http://exhibit.chautauqua-inst.org/palestine.html>. For an in-depth analysis see Burke O. Long, *Imagining the Holy Land: Maps, Models, and Fantasy Travels* (Bloomington: Indiana University Press, 2003), pp. 7-41.

[38]Long, *Imagining the Holy Land,* pp. 33, 39.

[39]James A. Albert, *Jim Bakker: Miscarriage of Justice?* (Chicago, Ill.: Carus, 1998), pp. 2, 17, 19-30. Heritage USA had a residential area with homes, apartments and condominiums, a petting zoo, store, motel, lakes, swimming pools, restaurants, tennis courts, miniature golf, recreational fields and trails, campgrounds, an enormous television studio, a five-thousand-seat church, a lakeside theater, a prayer room, a huge water park, a main street of shops attached to the five-hundred-room Heritage Grand Hotel, an indoor mall, live entertainment, Bible studies, and worship services. This was a safe, self-contained and isolated Christian getaway intricately dependent on the TV ministry. Today, MorningStar Ministries is restoring the hotel and main street, hoping to revive some of the earlier glamour. See information about the H.I.M. Conference Center at MorningStar's website <www.morningstarministries.org/>.

[40]"About Us," Herschend Family Entertainment <www.hfecorp.com/aboutus/>; Joel Kilpatrick, "Branson Theme Park Owners Say Christ Is at the Core of Their Business," *Charisma,* August 1999, pp. 20-21.

[41]Another example of a mainstream park is Visionland, renamed Alabama Adventure, which began as a safe family environment and whose name was inspired by Proverbs 29:18: "Where there is no vision, the people perish" (KJV). Today, it still monitors attendees' dress and language. See "Bible Inspires New Alabama Theme Park, Visionland," *Star-Ledger* (Newark, N.J.), June 21, 1998, p. 3.

[42]Aaron K. Ketchell, "'I Would Much Rather See a Sermon Than Hear One': Experiencing Faith at Silver Dollar City," in *The Business of Tourism: Place, Faith, and History,* ed. Philip Scranton and Janet F. Davidson (Philadelphia: University of Pennsylvania Press, 2007), p. 134.

[43]Dahleen Glanton, "Showbiz Has a Star in Jesus: Religion Sells—and Sells—as Christians Fuel a $4 Billion Entertainment Industry," *Chicago Tribune,* November 12, 2006.

[44]Walt Kallestad, *Entertainment Evangelism: Taking the Church Public* (Nashville: Abingdon, 1996); Tex Sample, *The Spectacle of Worship in a Wired World: Electronic Culture and the Gathered People of God* (Nashville: Abingdon, 1998).

[45]William E. Schmidt, "TV Minister Calls His Resort 'Bait' for Christianity," *New York Times,* December 24, 1985.

[46]Bill Jones, interview by author, Orlando, Florida, January 18, 2007.

[47]Paul Lomartire, "What Would Jesus View?" *Palm Beach Post,* June 17, 2004.

[48]See Eric Michael Mazur and Tara K. Koda, "The Happiest Place on Earth: Disney's America and the Commodification of Religion," in *God in the Details: American Religion in Popular Culture,* ed. Eric Michael Mazur and Kate McCarthy (New York: Routledge, 2001), p. 313.

[49]Ken Myers, "Letter to Listeners," Mars Hill Audio (December 2003) <www.marshillaudio.org/contribute/Fall_03_FR_Letter.pdf>.

[50]Michael Linton, "Bible Park U.S.A.," *First Things: The Journal of Religion, Culture, and Public Life,* May 31, 2007 <www.firstthings.com/onthesquare/?p=757>; Lisa Marchesoni, "Bible Park U.S.A.," *Murfreesboro* (Tennessee) *Post,* April 15, 2007.

[51]Reggie White dreamed of building a $100-million Bible theme park, attracted investors, and was exploring sites when he died. See Marcia Ford, "Investors Plan Bible Theme Park," *Charisma,* September 1994, p. 94. Proposals have come and gone for a Catholic theme park in the Philippines (see Luz Rimban, "Planned Philippines Catholic Theme Park," *Albion* (Maryland) *Monitor,* February 2, 1998) and a religious theme park near Las Vegas (Susan Greene, "Religious Theme Park Proposed near Mesquite," *Las Vegas Review-Journal,* July 19, 1997). The English park is discussed in Andrew Norfolk, "Slay Goliath, Sail the Ark—It Will Be a Hell of a Ride at Holyland," (London) *Times Online,* March 28, 2005 <www.timesonline.co.uk/tol/news/uk/article438726.ece>.

[52]Conal Urquhart, "Plans for Holy Land Theme Park on Galilee Shore Where Jesus Fed the 5,000," (London) *Guardian Unlimited,* January 4, 2006 <www.guardian.co.uk/israel/Story/0,2763,1677557,00.html>. Reportedly that location was chosen to minimize commercialization and to focus on a teaching center, multimedia presentations, hiking trails and gardens, all for tourists. The Reverend M. G. "Pat" Robertson's untimely comments about the prime minister, however, caused the Israeli government to refuse to work with him, although other investors are involved. See Steven G. Vegh, "Israel Cuts Robertson from Galilee Tourist Park," *Virginian-Pilot,* January 12, 2006 <http://content.hamptonroads.com/story.cfm?story=98012&ran=31875>.

[53]Mark I. Pinsky, *A Jew Among Evangelicals: A Guide for the Perplexed* (Louisville: Westminster John Knox, 2006), pp. 133-42.

[54]Barker, "'Holy Land' as Theme Park."

[55]Nancy L. Stockdale, "'Citizens of Heaven' versus 'The Islamic Peril': The Anti-Islamic Rhetoric of Orlando's Holy Land Experience Since 9/11/01," *American Journal of Islamic Social Sciences* 21, no. 3 (2004): 89-90.

[56]Long, *Imagining the Holy Land,* p. 5.

[57]Frank Burch Brown, *Good Taste, Bad Taste, and Christian Taste: Aesthetics in Religious Life* (New York: Oxford University Press, 2000), p. 147.
[58]The new Billy Graham Library does not charge a fee.
[59]For example, when a white Anglo-Saxon is presented as the epitome of what Jesus, a middle-eastern Jew, looks like, critics rightly question if the Bible teaches racism.
[60]Long, *Imagining the Holy Land,* pp. 5, 45.

Chapter 13: Merchandising Jesus Products

[1]Books about Christian merchandising include Lynn Schofield Clark, ed., *Religion, Media, and the Marketplace* (New Brunswick, N.J: Rutgers University Press, 2007); Heather Hendershot, *Shaking the World for Jesus: Media and Conservative Evangelical Culture* (Chicago: University of Chicago Press, 2004); Mark A. Knoll, *God and Mammon: Protestants, Money, and the Marketplace, 1790-1860* (New York: Oxford University Press, 2001); Colleen McDannell, *Material Christianity: Religion and Popular Culture in America* (New Haven, Conn.: Yale University Press, 1995); and Betty Spackman, *A Profound Weakness: Christians & Kitsch* (Carlisle, U.K.: Piquant, 2005).
[2]Spackman, *Profound Weakness,* p. 5.
[3]Ibid., p. 167.
[4]Debbie Howell, "Christian Retailing Ascending to New Heights," *DSN Retailing Today,* April 19, 2004, p. 4; Laura Smith-Spark, "Faith-Based Toys to Hit US Stores," *BBC News,* July 30, 2007 <http://news.bbc.co.uk/1/hi/world/americas/6916287.stm>.
[5]Heather Grimshaw, "An Almighty Market: God Is Big Business in the Publishing World, as long as Writers Steer Clear of Any Forbidden Territory," *The Denver Post,* July 10, 2005.
[6]Rob Moll, "Hurt by Success: Christian Bookstores Hit Hard by Competition from Wal-Mart," *Christianity Today,* November 2004, p. 21.
[7]Smith-Spark, "Faith-Based Toys."
[8]Tim Ferguson and Josephine Lee, "Spiritual Reality," *Forbes,* January 1997, p. 70.
[9]"Demand for Religious Games, Toys Grows: Entrepreneurs Mix Fun with Serious Themes and Find a Niche, Even Though Few Mass Retailers Carry Their Products," *Christian Post,* December 24, 2006 <www.christianpost.com/article/20061224/24487_Demand_for_Religious_Games,_Toys_Grows.htm>.
[10]Other merchandise accounted for sales as follows: 19 percent gifts, 16 percent music, 11 percent Bibles, 8 percent stationery and cards, 3 percent church supplies, 3 percent videos, and 15 percent other. Fred Hiers, "Christian Retailers Combine Faith and Business," *Ocala* (Florida) *Star-Banner,* January 21, 2007.
[11]Rachel Elinsky, "Religious Publishing for the Red State Consumers and Beyond," *Publishing Research Quarterly* 21, no. 4 (2005): 11-29. Joan Harrison, "Religious Products Market Lures Buyers," *Mergers & Acquisitions* 41, no. 11 (2006): 46.
[12]Smith-Spark, "Faith-Based Toys."
[13]See promotions at the website for the Christian toy company One2Believe at <www.one2believe.com>.
[14]"Demand for Religious Games."
[15]Julie Salamon, "Market Strategy Splits the Sacred and Secular," *New York Times,* December 27, 2003.
[16]Cathy Lynn Grossman, "Faith's Purchasing Power," *USA Today,* December 12, 2006 <www.usatoday.com/news/religion/2006-12-12-faiths-purchasing-power_x.htm>.
[17]Ibid.
[18]See promotions on the website for One2Believe <www.one2believe.com>.

[19]William Fisher, "Death to Infidels via Video Games," *Scoop*, December 15, 2006 <www.scoop.co.nz/stories/HL0612/S00225.htm>.

[20]For a discussion of the relationship between community and consumption, see Laura Miller, "Shopping for Community: The Transformation of the Bookstore into a Vital Community Institution," *Media, Culture & Society* 21, no. 3 (1999): 385-407.

[21]McDannell, *Material Christianity*, p. 45.

[22]Ibid.

[23]Religious artifacts can express and validate one's own faith. See Charles E. Swann, *The Communicating Church* (Atlanta: Office of Media Communication of the Presbyterian Church in the U.S., 1981).

[24]Anne E. Borden, "Making Money, Saving Souls: Christian Bookstores and the Commodification of Christianity," in *Religion, Media, and the Marketplace*, ed. Lynn Schofield Clark (New Brunswick, N.J.: Rutgers University Press, 2007), p. 69.

[25]Anna Kaplan, "Bold, Stylish Look Gives Fashion Sense to Religious Apparel," *The Record*, March 17, 2007 <www.recordnet.com/apps/pbcs.dll/article?AID=/20070317/A_LIFE/703170306/-1/A_NEWS13>.

[26]These product promotions have been seen on the website for C28: Not of This World <www.c28.com>.

[27]John Ma, "Christian Concerts and Memorabilia Finds Its Way in Youth Culture," *SpiritHit News*, July 6, 2004 <http://news.spirithit.com/index/culture_art/print/christian_concerts_and_memorabilia>.

[28]Lauren F. Winner, "Nurturing Today's Teen Spirit," *Publishers Weekly*, March 12, 2004, p. 30.

[29]See the promotions at Lord Mart: Jesus Junk and Holy Hardware . . . for LESS <www.dougbeaumont.org/Lord%20Mart/index.html>.

[30]See the advocacy at the website for One2Believe <www.one2believe.com/battleforthetoybox.asp>.

[31]Sandy Shore, "Christian Retailers Ecumenical About Competition," *Naples Daily News*, July 31, 2006.

[32]Charles M. Brown, "The Culture of Culture Industries: Art, Commerce, and Faith in the Christian Retailing Industry" (Ph.D. diss., Southern Illinois University, 2002), p. 105.

[33]Ibid., p. 168.

[34]Vivian S. Park, "Jesus in Today's Fashion Trend Raises Debates," *Christian Post*, May 10, 2004 <www.christianpost.com/article/20040510/20193_Jesus_in_Today%27s_Fashion_Trend_Raises_Debates.htm>.

[35]Adam Graham, "What A Trend We Have in Jesus," *Detroit News*, March 8, 2004 <www.religionnewsblog.com/6387/what-a-trend-we-have-in-jesus>.

[36]Jeremy D. Lawson, Michael J. Sleasman and Charles A. Anderson, "The Gospel According to Safeway: The Checkout Line and the Good Life," in *Everyday Theology: How to Read Cultural Texts and Interpret Trends*, ed. Kevin J. Vanhoozer, Charles A. Anderson and Michael J. Sleasman (Grand Rapids: Baker Books, 2007), pp. 63-80.

[37]Phil Cooke, "Jesus Junk," Crosswalk.com (2006) <www.crosswalk.com/1409402>.

[38]Hendershot, *Shaking the World for Jesus*, p. 18.

[39]See their website at <www.c28.com>.

[40]Ashley Boyer, "T-Shirts with a Purpose: Did You Know You Can Look Stylish and Give to Those in Need?" *Brio*, July 2007, p. 12.

[41]Rose French, "In the Grip of Goliaths: Though Religious Books Leading Sales in the Publishing Industry, Christian Booksellers Struggle," *The Houston Chronicle*, February 11, 2006, p. 2.

[42]Peg Tyre, "The Almighty Dollar: Christian Bookstores Go Bust After Chains Find Religion," *Newsweek,* January 24, 2005, p. 68.

[43]French, "In the Grip of Goliaths," p. 2.

[44]Ibid.

[45]Stephen Bates, "The Jesus Market: Christianity May Be Struggling in the Public Square, but It's Prospering in the Public Bazaar," *The Weekly Standard,* December 16, 2002, p. 27.

[46]Hendershot, *Shaking the World for Jesus,* pp. 20-22.

[47]Ibid.

[48]Borden, "Making Money, Saving Souls."

[49]Ibid.

[50]Ibid.

[51]Hendershot, *Shaking the World for Jesus,* p. 22.

[52]Bo Cassell, "What Would Jesus Think of . . . WWJD?" *Group,* March/April 1999 <http://findarticles.com/p/articles/mi_qa3835/is_199903/ai_n8852263>.

[53]"Hell in a Handbasket," *Chico News & Review,* May 13, 2004 <www.newsreview.com/chico/Content?oid=30421>.

[54]Ferguson and Lee, "Spiritual Reality."

[55]Grossman, "Faith's Purchasing Power."

[56]Spackman, *Profound Weakness,* p. 167.

[57]Brown, "Culture of Culture Industries."

[58]Sharon Tubbs, "Religious Tees Start Fashion Trend," < http://www.signonsandiego.com/uniontrib/20040621/news_1c21jesus.html >.

[59]Spackman, *A Profound Weakness,* p. 167.

[60]Jason Janz, "Jesus Junk," SharperIron (August 24, 2006) <www.sharperiron.org/2006/08/24/jesus-junk>.

Chapter 14: Converting Comic Books into Graphic Novels and Digital Cartoons

[1]Scott McCloud, *Understanding Comics: The Invisible Art* (New York: HarperCollins, 1993), p. 3.

[2]Greg Garrett, *Holy Superheroes! Exploring Faith & Spirituality in Comic Books* (Colorado Springs: Piñon, 2005), p. 25.

[3]One website specifically designed to aid Christians with evangelism through comics is "Using Cartoons in Outreach," Guide <http://guide.gospelcom.net/resources/cartoon-outreach.php>.

[4]McCloud, *Understanding Comics,* p. 9. See also Will Eisner, *Comics and Sequential Art* (Princeton, Wis.: Kitchen Sink Press, 1992).

[5]Edirin Ibru, "Beyond Boy Wonders: The Evolution of Comics," *The Banner,* May 2007 <www.thebanner.org/magazine/article.cfm?article_id=1023>.

[6]C. L. Cowan, "Comic Books for the Kingdom," *Mission Frontiers: The Bulletin of the U.S. Center of World Mission,* July-August 1998 <www.missionfrontiers.org/1998/0708/ja9812.htm>.

[7]Ibid.

[8]Ibid. To understand how the same technique was used in the United States in the nineteenth century by the American Tract Society and the American Sunday School Union, see David Morgan, *Protestants and Pictures: Religion, Visual Culture, and the Age of American Mass Production* (New York: Oxford University Press, 1999), p. 28.

[9]The most famous or infamous examples were developed by Jack Chick in the late 1960s and became most popular in the 1970s. In subsequent years the topics of these tracts changed from a simple evangelistic message to conspiratorial polemics against certain Christian denominations or various translations of the Bible. See Chick Publications at <www.chick.com>.

[10]Cowan, "Comic Books for the Kingdom"; United Bible Societies, "Record Distribution Predicted for Bible Comics," September 2001. To see the latter article, use the search function at <www.biblesociety.org/index2.htm>.

[11]Nanami Minami, *America! Why Is It That Way?* (Tokyo: Word of Life Press, 2003) and *Down the Road of the Narrow Gate* (Tokyo: Word of Life Press, 1997). Both works are in Japanese. See information at WLPM Book Catalog <www.wlpm.or.jp/english/index_bo.htm>.

[12]United Bible Societies, "Record Distribution Predicted for Bible Comics."

[13]For further information and links to the various Bible Societies currently using comics evangelistically, see "United Bible Societies" <www.biblesociety.org/index2.htm>.

[14]There is a special collection of John Lawing's work at Regent University in Virginia Beach, Virginia. See a description of the Christian Cartooning Collection of the Regent University Library at <www.regent.edu/general/library/services/collections/specialcollresourcedevpol2003.htm>. There is also a film based on his life. See *Drawn Together* at Reelgood.TV <www.reelgood.tv/filminfo.php?film=392DRAWNT>.

[15]Dave Walker, *The Dave Walker Guide to the Church* (London: Canterbury Press Norwich, 2006), introduction.

[16]Beverly Rykerd, "Graphic Novel Puts a Face on the Future of Left Behind Series," Left Behind Series News (July 5, 2001) <www.leftbehind.com/channelnews.asp?channelID=17&pageid=462>.

[17]This description has been used in promoting the graphic novels by Robert James Luedke. See ordering information at Head Press Publishing <www.headpress.info/>.

[18]Ibid.

[19]To see more examples of Christian graphic novels, see Christianbook.com at <www.christianbook.com>.

[20]Rana Foroohar, "Literature: Graphic Novels as Serious Art," *Newsweek,* August 22, 2005.

[21]*Manga* is the Japanese word for "comic book" or "graphic novel."

[22]See description of products at "Zondervan's Manga Debut: *Z Graphic Novels*" <www.zondervan.com/Cultures/en-US/Product/Kidz/Kidz+ZGraphic+Novels.htm?QueryStringSite=Zondervan>.

[23]Terry Mattingly, "Graphic Novels, Big Questions," On Religion (January 31, 2007) <http://tmatt.gospelcom.net/column/2007/01/31/>.

[24]Ibid.

[25]Ibid.

[26]See Scott McCloud, *Reinventing Comics: How Imagination and Technology Are Revolutionizing an Art Form* (New York: HarperCollins, 2000).

[27]*The New Yorker,* long famous for its cartoons, now has an animated cartoon on its website. See the Humor page of the *The New Yorker* website at <www.newyorker.com/humor>.

[28]For a collection of digital tracts produced in partnership with the American Tract Society, see Digitracts: Online Evangelism Presentations and Resources at <www.digitracts.com>.

[29]A website launched in 1996 and dedicated to evangelistic Christian comics claims that it is "the Internet's Original, Longest-Running, and Most Complete Online Guide of Its Kind," Christian Comics International <www.christiancomicsinternational.org/>. The website Comix35 also claims that it is "using the world's most popular literature to tell the world's most vital message" and provides training for individuals and ministries around the world in the production and effective use of comics-style literature. See <www.comix35.org>.

[30]See "Using Cartoons in Outreach," Guide <http://guide.gospelcom.net/resources/cartoon-outreach.php>. Another how-to book to assist aspiring comic book creators is Scott McCloud, *Making Comics: Storytelling Secrets of Comics, Manga and Graphic Novels* (New York: HarperCollins, 2006).

[31]Robert L. Short, *The Gospel According to Peanuts* (Louisville: Westminster John Knox Press,

1965); Joe Maxwell, "Johnny Hart: Not Caving In," *Today's Christian*, March/April 1997 <www.christianitytoday.com/tc/7r2/7r2018.html>; Terry Mattingly, "Pastor Will B. Dunn—RIP," On Religion (July 18, 2007) <http://tmatt.gospelcom.net/column/2007/07/18/>; Rick Newcombe, "Johnny Hart in Memoriam (1931-2007)," Creators Syndicate (April 7, 2007) <www.creators.com/news/10.html>.

[32]Rik Offenberger, "Royden Lepp: Shepherding Comics," SBC Interviews, <www.silverbulletcomicbooks.com/features/111950300964378,print.htm>.

[33]McCloud, *Understanding Comics*, p. 10-20.

[34]David Bratcher, "The Cross as a Journey: The Stations of the Cross for Protestant Worship," CRI/The Voice: Biblical and Theological Resources for Growing Christians <www.crivoice.org/stations.html>. See also Mark D. Roberts, "The Stations of the Cross: A Devotional Guide for Lent and Holy Week" (2007) <www.markdroberts.com/htmfiles/resources/stationsofthecross.htm>.

[35]See biographies of Andrea Pisano and Ghiberti Lorenzo at the Web Gallery of Art <www.wga.hu/index1.html>.

[36]Sonia Halliday and Laura Lushington, *The Bible in Stained Glass*, ed. Tim Dowley (Ridgefield, Conn.: Morehouse, 1990), p. 8.

[37]Ibid.

[38]David Morgan, *Protestants and Pictures: Religion, Visual Culture, and the Age of American Mass Production* (New York: Oxford University Press, 1999).

[39]B. J. Oropeza, ed., *The Gospel According to Superheroes: Religion and Popular Culture* (New York: Peter Lang, 2005), p. 4.

[40]Stan Lee, "Foreword," *The Gospel According to Superheroes: Religion and Popular Culture*, ed. B. J. Oropeza (New York: Peter Lang, 2005), p. xii.

[41]Stephen Skelton, *The Gospel According to the World's Greatest Superhero* (Eugene, Ore.: Harvest House, 2006), p. 22.

[42]One scholar argues that Batman is portrayed in the 1989 film as a schizophrenic rather than as a biblical savior. See Robert E. Terrill, "Put on a Happy Face: *Batman* as Schizophrenic Savior," *The Quarterly Journal of Speech* 79, no. 3 (1993): 319-35.

[43]Skelton, *Gospel According to the World's Greatest Superhero*, p. 30.

[44]Garrett, *Holy Superheroes!* p. 11.

[45]For a very interesting website that discusses the religious affiliations of many comic book characters: see "The Religious Affiliations of Comic Book Characters," Comic Book Religion, created July 27, 2005 <www.adherents.com/lit/comics/comic_book_religion.html>.

[46]Some Christians formed a comic arts society to share their love of comics: see The Christian Comic Arts Society at <www.christiancomicarts.com/>.

Chapter 15: Evangelicals' Quest to Find God's Place in Games

[1]Brad King and John Borland, *Dungeons and Dreamers: The Rise of Computer Game Culture from Geek to Chic* (New York: McGraw-Hill/Osborne, 2003).

[2]Paul Cardwell Jr. "The Attacks on Role-Playing Games," *Skeptical Inquirer* 18, no. 2 (1994): 157-65; Kurt Lancaster, "Do Role-Playing Games Promote Crime, Satanism and Suicide Among Players as Critics Claim?" *Journal of Popular Culture* 28, no. 2 (1994): 67-79.

[3]See a well-known 1984 cartoon from Chick Ministries that makes a similar claim: Jack T. Chick, *Dark Dungeons* (Ontario, Calif.: Chick Publications, 1984) <www.chick.com/reading/tracts/0046/0046_01.asp>.

[4]Cardwell, "Attacks on Role-Playing Games"; Steve Weese, "Christians Playing Dungeons and

Dragons," Fans for Christ <www.fansforchrist.org/phpBB2/articles/article03.htm>; M. Joseph Young, "Confessions of a Dungeons & Dragons Addict," personal website <www.mjyoung.net/dungeon/confess.html>.

[5]Nancy Justice, "The Pokémon Invasion," *Charisma,* February 2000, pp. 58-65.

[6]The Electronic Software Association says that 2006 sales of computer and video games reached $7.4 billion in the United States alone: see "Top 10 Industry Facts" at the ESA website <www.theesa.com/facts/top_10_facts.php>.

[7]Both the academic field of game studies and intellectual game designers have struggled to define the term *game.* The best summary overview of a wide range of definitions is in Eric Zimmerman and Katie Salen, *Rules of Play: Game Design Fundamentals* (Cambridge, Mass.: MIT Press, 2003), pp. 71-83.

[8]"Welcome to Cactus Game Design," Cactus Game Design Inc. website <www.cactusgamedesign.com/>.

[9]One example among many: "Nintendo Surgeons More Precise?" Wired News, December 19, 2004 <www.wired.com/medtech/health/news/2004/12/66086>.

[10]See James Paul Gee, *What Video Games Have to Teach Us About Learning and Literacy* (New York: Palgrave Macmillan, 2003).

[11]Brian Belknap, "Reaching the Gamer Gens," *Group,* May/June 2005, pp. 66-70.

[12]"Company History, Mission Statement and Vision," Brethren Entertainment <www.brethren-et.com/BEWebsite/aboutus/company.html>.

[13]See, for example: the Tribe of Judah <www.toj.cc/>; The Forgiven: Terenas Alliance Guild <www.theforgiven.net/>; gamers4God <gamers4god.com/>; D.o.G., Disciples of God <http://d-o-g-clan.com/>. Guilds and clans are not exclusively Christian phenomena. Most MMOG players join guilds, and most of these groups are mainstream.

[14]Men of God International <www.menofgod.us/>.

[15]Fans for Christ <www.fansforchrist.org/>; Christian Gamers Alliance <www.cgalliance.org/>.

[16]Lynette R. F. Cowper, Mark Joseph Young, Paul Cardwell et al., "Frequently Asked Questions by Christians About Role-playing Games," Christian Gamers' Guild <www.christian-gamers-guild.org/chaplain/cfaq.html>.

[17]J. R. R. Tolkien, "On Fairy-Stories," in *The Monsters and the Critics and Other Essays,* ed. Christopher Tolkien (London: Allen & Unwin, 1983), pp. 109-61.

[18]C. S. Lewis, "On Stories" and "Tolkien's *The Lord of the Rings,*" in *C. S. Lewis: Essay Collection and Other Short Pieces,* ed. Lesley Walmsley (London: HarperCollins Publisher, 2000), pp. 491-504, 519-25.

[19]Weese, "Christians Playing Dungeons and Dragons."

[20]"About Us," Spirit of Elijah, Tribe of Judah <www.toj.cc/gw/index.php?option=com_content&task=view&id=34&Itemid=35>. Note that some believe outright proselytizing to be bad form and possibly to be against game conduct rules. See a discussion at Andy Rau, "A Light to the Virtual Worlds," Think Christian (December 7, 2005) <www.thinkchristian.net/?p=459>.

[21]Young, "Confessions of a Dungeons & Dragons Addict."

[22]Editorial, "Deadening of the Heart," *Christianity Today,* October 2005, p. 31.

[23]Adam Holz, "Life or Something Like It," *Plugged In,* November 2004, p. 12.

[24]John Northbrooke, *A Treatise Against Dicing, Dancing, Plays, and Interludes: With Other Idle Pastimes* (1577; repr. London: F. Shoberl, 1843). The original title was *A Treatise wherein Dicing, Dauncing, Vaine playes, or Enterluds, with other idle pastimes, &c., commonly ysed on the Sabboth day, are reproued by the Authoritie of the word of God and auntient writers.*

[25]Belknap, "Reaching the Gamer Gens."

[26]Adam Holz, "Grand Theft Auto is Back in the News," *Plugged In,* September 2005, p. 12.

[27]Justice, "Pokémon Invasion."

[28]See, e.g., Mary and Elizabeth Van Nattan, "Did You Know? Number 1: Playing Cards," Balaam's Ass Speaks, personal website <www.balaams-ass.com/journal/homemake/playcard.htm>; J. D. Carlson, "Should Christian People Play Cards?" European-American Evangelistic Crusades <www.eaec.org/bibleanswers/playing_cards.htm>.

[29]Elizabeth Wirth, "For Mine Is the Kingdom: Playing God with Computer Games," *Re:Generation Quarterly* 7, no. 3 (2001): 21.

[30]Michael Jindra, "Video Game Worlds," *Society* 44, no. 4 (2007): 67-73; Michael Jindra, "The Passions of Alternate Media Universes," in *Passions in Economy, Politics, and the Media,* ed. Wolfgang Palaver and Petra Steinmair-Pösel (Münster: LIT Verlag, 2005), pp. 434-35.

[31]*A Letter from a Minister to His Friend Concerning the Games of Chesse* (1680), cited in *Francis Willughby's Book of Games: A Seventeenth-Century Treatise on Sports, Games and Pastimes,* ed. David Cram, Jeffrey L. Forgeng and Dorothy Johnston (Aldershot, England: Ashgate, 2003), p. 67.

[32]Belknap, "Reaching the Gamer Gens."

[33]See, e.g., Elliot M. Avedon and Brian Sutton-Smith, *The Study of Games* (New York: Wiley & Sons, 1971).

[34]*Francis Willughby's Book of Games.*

[35]Northbrooke, *Treatise Against Dicing.*

[36]Alfonso X, *Book of Games,* trans. Sonja Musser Golladay, available online at <www.u.arizona.edu/~smusser/ljtranslation.html>.

[37]Several game historians cite Death Race in 1976 as the first game to wade into media-violence controversies. See, for example, Rusel DeMaria and Johnny L. Wilson, *High Score! The Illustrated History of Electronic Games* (Berkeley: McGraw-Hill, 2002), pp. 27-28.

[38]Steven L. Kent, *The Ultimate History of Video Games: From Pong to Pokemon and Beyond—The Story Behind the Craze That Touched Our Lives and Changed the World* (Roseville, Calif.: Prima, 2001), pp. 461-80; J. C. Herz, *Joystick Nation: How Videogames Ate Our Quarters, Won Our Hearts, and Rewired Our Minds* (Boston: Little, Brown, 1997), pp. 183-95.

[39]Two standard news articles on this story: Dirk Johnson and James Brooke, "Portrait of Outcasts Seeking to Stand Out from Other Groups," *New York Times,* April 22, 1999; Paul Duggan, Michael D. Shear and Marc Fisher, "Shooter Pair Mixed Fantasy, Reality," *Washington Post,* April 22, 1999. Here are some interesting related items: Janelle Brown, "Doom, Quake and Mass Murder," *Salon,* April 23, 1999 <www.salon.com/tech/feature/1999/04/23/gamers/index.html>; Barbara Mikkelson, "The Harris Levels," Snopes.com (January 1, 2005) <www.snopes.com/horrors/madmen/doom.asp>.

[40]"Video game 'sparked hammer murder,' " CNN, July 29, 2004 <http://www.cnn.com/2004/WORLD/europe/07/29/uk.manhunt/index.html>. Tor Thorsen, "San Andreas Rated AO, Take-Two Suspends Production," GameSpot News (July 20, 2005) <www.gamespot.com/news/6129500.html>.

[41]Some Christians have testified at U.S. congressional hearings, such as the Reverend Steve Strickland and Daphne White of the now-defunct Lion & Lamb Project website. See the hearing notice for U.S. Senate Committee on the Judiciary, "What's in a Game? State Regulation of Violent Video Games and the First Amendment," 109th Congress, 2nd session, March 29, 2006 <judiciary.senate.gov/hearing.cfm?id=1824>; Barbara F. Meltz, "Legislation Would Target Violence in Video Games," *Boston Globe,* May 22, 2003. Jack Thompson is a conservative Christian who is very prominent in most video-game controversies (and widely reviled in the gaming community). He does not have his own website, but he is mentioned in dozens, if not hundreds, of news stories, blog postings, etc. A supposedly neutral site called JackThompson.org archives many of

his statements: see "It's About Video Games," JackThompson.org, an open source project <www.jackthompson.org>.

[42]Young, "Confessions of a Dungeons & Dragons Addict."

[43]James D. Hargrove, "Review of Dragonraid Adventure Learning System," RPGnet (November 7, 2005) <www.rpg.net/reviews/archive/11/11723.phtml>.

[44]Randy Frame, "Is Bible Knowledge Becoming Just Another Trivial Pursuit?" *Christianity Today,* October 5, 1984, p. 62.

[45]Game history database MobyGames lists Wisdom Tree releases from 1991 through 1994 at <www.mobygames.com/game-group/wisdom-trees-bible-themed-games>.

[46]Rob Anderson, "The History Behind Redemption and Cactus Game Design, Inc.," Cactus Game Design Inc. <www.cactusgamedesign.com/red_game_history.php>.

[47]*Wired* pegged Christian video-game revenue at $200 million in 2002; by comparison, in the same year, the Entertainment Software Association pegged overall U.S. sales of computer and video games at $7.0 billion. The late 2006 release of *Left Behind: Eternal Forces* may have altered this ratio slightly, but probably not significantly. See "What Would Jesus Play?" *Wired,* December, 2003 <www.wired.com/wired/archive/11.12/play.html?pg=8>; "Sales and Genre Data," Entertainment Software Association <www.theesa.com/facts/sales_genre_data.php>; John Gartner, "Christians Code Heavenly Games," *Wired,* August 4, 2005 <www.wired.com/gaming/gamingreviews/news/2005/08/68401>; John Gartner, "God Games Seek Souls, Not Profit," *Wired,* August 4, 2005 <www.wired.com/gaming/gamingreviews/news/2005/08/68402>.

[48]Evangelical and mainstream companies publish a wide array of explicitly Christian board and card games, many of which are Christian or at least Bible-themed versions of other games, such as the Bible version of Apples to Apples or Settlers of Canaan, which is a knockoff of the extremely popular Settlers of Catan. Some, however, are original, like the long-running trading card game Redemption. While the games are interesting and worth examining, their market and cultural impact are small and impossible to gauge. Also, most media and public attention focuses on the higher-profile mainstream digital-game industry.

[49]The category of children's games is not a strictly unique genre, only a market segment. Children's games can be puzzles, action-oriented RPGs or more. In practice, however, games specifically targeted at children receive different marketing and critical attention from other types of games, and thus function much like a genre.

[50]"Convert-Em-Up," *Wired,* April 18, 2001 <www.wired.com/culture/lifestyle/news/2001/04/43116>; Randy Dotinga, "Video Games Where Prayer Triumphs over Sword," *USA Today,* August 25, 2005 <www.usatoday.com/tech/products/games/2005-08-25-christian-video-games_x.htm>.

[51]See one rather typical article: Ilene Lelchuk, "'Convert or Die' Game Divides Christians," *San Francisco Chronicle,* December 12, 2006. For a less-balanced report on conservative Jack Thompson's negative reaction to the game, see Jonathan Hutson, "Apocalypse, Now a Lawsuit (Part 5)," Talk to Action (June 12, 2006) <www.talk2action.org/story/2006/6/12/31011/1474>.

[52] For example, one of the erroneous but widespread accusations was that the Tribulation Force hunted down and slaughtered gays, Jews and other minority groups. The main source of the accusation might be from Jonathan Hutson, "The Purpose Driven Life Takers (Part 1)," Talk to Action (May 29, 2006) <www.talk2action.org/story/2006/5/29/195855/959>.

[53]It's possible to find Christians in the mainstream industry. For example, a local Canadian paper ran a story in 2006 about a devout Catholic working at giant game publisher and developer EA: Jeff Graham, "Finding God in the Exploding Video Game Industry," *BC Christian News,* December 2006, p. 14. Former Methodist minister James Wyatt is a game-maker who writes about his experiences and ideas on his website; see, e.g., James Wyatt, "Art and Faith (and D&D?)," Aquela.

com, personal blog (December 13, 2005) <http://aquela.com/blog/C590336757/index.html>. Jay Moore of GarageGames, a prominent developer of software for small-game companies, is a member of the ACE and a poster at the Christian Coders Network Web forums. The Christian Gamers' Guild has a remarkable list of accomplished game-makers (mostly in nondigital games) who profess to be Christian, although not always evangelical. See Lynette R. F. Cowper, M. Joseph Young and Paul Cardwell, "Christian Game Designers, Writers, and Publishers," Christian Gamers' Guild <www.christian-gamers-guild.org/chaplain/xians.html>.

[54]Josh Giesbrecht, interview by author, Abbotsford, Canada, June 2007.

[55]Eric Tiansay, "Not Just Fun and Games," *Charisma,* November 2003, pp. 86-90.

[56]Games and their popularity ebb and flow, and they do so even faster in the digital realm. Likewise, enthusiast groups form, shift and disband at remarkable speeds—busy communities can die off in a year from struggles, neglect or the release of new games. For a fascinating account of one group's struggles with longevity, see "History of Redeemed," Redeemed <christiangaming.org/redeemed/history.php>.

[57]See "Welcome to PureFun!" PureFun <pure-fun.com/>; "Christ-centered Game Review—Christian Gaming Perspective," Christ-centered Game Reviews <www.ccgr.org/>.

[58]Victorino Matus, "'Civilization' and Its Contents: A Video Game for the Ages," *The Weekly Standard,* February 26, 2007 <www.weeklystandard.com/content/public/articles/000/000/013/305yuvkp.asp>.

[59]TenNapel posts often on his forum, and a search there will reveal quite a few discussions about his faith and his art. A good example (even though the subject is graphic novels, the principles are applicable to games): "Question for Doug: Where did you start . . . ," Doug TenNapel Works, music contact forum (November 17, 2004) <tennapel.nomoretangerines.com/viewtopic.php?t=861&>.

[60]Jon Carroll, "D(Riven)," *Wired,* September 1997 <www.wired.com/wired/archive/5.09/riven.html?topic=&topic_set>; DeMaria and Wilson, *High Score!* pp. 258-61.

[61]There is no single, authoritative, simple, publicly accessible list of PC bestsellers of all time. (There *is* a well-documented and researched list at Wikipedia, but of course this changes with user contributions. See "List of Best-selling Video Games," Wikipedia <http://en.wikipedia.org/wiki/List_of_best-selling_video_games>.) Myst shows up in the top five or ten of every list I have ever seen. An article from 2001 pegged the sales at six million units (Michael Guilfoil, "Beyond the Myst," *Spokane Spokesman Review,* May 22, 2001 <www.spokesmanreview.com/pf.asp?date=052201&id=s966647>).

[62]Carroll, "D(Riven)."

[63]Any number of games can do this, but the genre of "god games" provides some of the best examples. In Black & White, the player takes on the role of a deity who gains the worship of villagers via acts of love or terror. The Civilization series of games allows the player to shepherd a culture from rudimentary beginnings to global domination. The list could go on.

[64]See part II of Steve Weese's article "Christians Playing Dungeons and Dragons" <www.fansforchrist.org/phpBB2/articles/article03a.htm>, which is a careful, step-by-step dismantling of some articles by self-proclaimed former witch William Schnoebelen: William Schnoebelen, "Straight Talk on Dungeons and Dragons," Chick Publications <www.chick.com/articles/dnd.asp>; William Schnoebelen, "New Updated Research: Should a Christian Play Dungeons & Dragons?" (2001) <www.chick.com/articles/frpg.asp>.

[65]See William D. Romanowski, *Eyes Wide Open: Looking for God in Popular Culture,* rev. and exp. ed. (Grand Rapids: Brazos, 2007); Craig Detweiler and Barry Taylor, *A Matrix of Meanings: Finding God in Pop Culture* (Grand Rapids: Baker Academic, 2003). For a much briefer and less academic take on Christians and pop culture, see the introduction to this youth ministry site: "All About Ministry and Media," Ministry and Media <www.ministryandmedia.com/about.asp>.

[66]TenNapel, "Question for Doug."

[67]Thanks to Michael Jindra for significant help in crafting this point.

[68]Of course, the same can be said about other pastimes, such as knitting, outdoor activities and cooking. The real modification in the past several decades has been that games have invaded our electronic media and added a degree of sociability and interactivity that is harder to achieve with other electronic media.

Chapter 16: Advertising

[1]"Advertising Campaign Seeks to Ignite Church's Ministry," United Methodist Church, 2001 News Archives <http://archives.umc.org/umns/news_archive2001.asp?ptid=2&story=%7B1A4E8E9C7A5F-49CB-931C-FCA139E0029E%7D&mid=3365>.

[2]Similarly, the United Church of Christ launched a $30-million promotional campaign: "God is still speaking," according to Alan Cooperman. "Churches Go Commercial to Spread Their Message: TV Campaigns Bring Denominations to Homes," *Washington Post*, July 11, 2004, p. A01.

[3]Stephanie Simon, "God's Call Comes by Cell Phone: Bible Verses on a Blackberry, Sermons on an MP3; An Explosion in Digitalized Spirituality Is Making True Believers of Online E-vangelists," *Los Angeles Times*, May 16, 2006.

[4]The lead singer for U2, Bono, was born Paul Hewson and grew up in Dublin with a Protestant mother and Catholic father. He attends the Church of Ireland, an Episcopal church, which bridges the gap between the faiths of his parents. See James Traub, "The Statesman," *New York Times Magazine*, September 18, 2005. In 1997 Bono joined with a church-sponsored campaign to urge governments to cancel debts of impoverished nations. After educating himself about the issue, he began to lobby the U.S. government and created the ONE campaign to encourage governments to give 1 percent of their budgets to poverty relief in Africa. The Red Campaign, which uses the tools of contemporary marketing and advertising, followed in 2006.

[5]Red itself spends nothing on marketing. "We count on our brave partners to market their own products. Our goal is to create a model where private companies can do good and make money at the same time." See Bobby Shriver, "CEO: Red's Raised Lots of Green," *Advertising Age*, March 12, 2007, p. 8.

[6]Mya Frazier, "Costly Red Campaign Reaps Meager $18 Million," *Advertising Age*, March 5, 2007, pp. 1, 43.

[7]Associated Press, "Lutheran Condemns Prosperity Gospel," *The Lynchburg News & Advance*, March 31, 2007, p. D3.

[8]Rich Silverstein, a founder of Goodby Silverstein & Partners, the San Francisco-based agency famed for the "Got milk?" campaign, says that his agency does not pay for posting viral ads on the video-sharing site YouTube. He stresses that ads should be so engaging that they are uploaded and passed around by consumers themselves. "If it's worthy, if it's pass-around worthy, it's going to do good for your brand," Silverstein says. Devin Leonard, "Viral Ads: It's an Epidemic," *Fortune*, October 2, 2006 <http://money.cnn.com/magazines/fortune/fortune_archive/2006/10/02/8387416/index.htm>.

[9]Donald E. Parente, *Advertising Campaign Strategy: A Guide to Marketing Communication Plans*, 4th ed. (Mason, Ohio: Thomson Higher Education, 2006), pp. 5-9.

[10]Rick Warren, *The Purpose-Driven Church: Growth Without Compromising Your Message & Mission* (Grand Rapids: Zondervan, 1995).

[11]Rob Anderson and Chris Gautreau, *The Greater Baton Rouge Business Report* 17, no. 12 (1999): 30.

[12]While checking my email during the editing of this chapter, AOL placed a timely World Vision

side banner ad on my email page which encouraged me to "end a child's hunger" and receive two free CDs.

[13]While on a mission trip in 2007 to a large homeless shelter in Washington, D.C., youth from my church and I were told by the director of the shelter that our red T-shirts were one of the best ways to advertise the love of Christ as we walked the streets of the city.

[14]Kenneth E. Clow and Donald Baack, *Integrated Advertising, Promotion, and Marketing Communications,* 3rd ed. (Upper Saddle River, N.J.: Prentice Hall, 2007), p. 55.

[15]For discussion of evangelical branding practices and politics, see Kenneth M. Cosgrove, *Branded Conservatives: How the Brand Brought the Right from the Fringes to the Center of American Politics* (New York: Peter Lang, 2007).

[16]Ted Hart, James M. Greenfield and Michael Johnston, *Nonprofit Internet Strategies: Best Practices for Marketing, Communications, and Fundraising* (Hoboken, N.Y.: Wiley & Sons, 2005), p. 72.

[17]One of the earliest examples of Christian symbols was the fish logo, a secret sign used by the early Christians. The Greek word for fish (ΙΧΘΥΣ) forms an acronym, which means Jesus Christ (ΙΧ), Son of God (ΘΥ) and Savior (Σ). This acronym functioned like today's corporate logos by forming a group identity. Companies with high brand equity need only have their logos appear in media in order to benefit from logos: Nike's swoosh or McDonald's arches. Christian universities may also have their own logos. In 2007, Liberty University placed its brand or logo, a giant LU, on the mountain near campus, causing a spirited dialogue between fans and critics of such marketing practices.

[18]Douglas B. Holt, *How Brands Become Icons* (Boston: Harvard Business School Press, 2004).

[19]Hart et al., *Nonprofit Internet Strategies,* p. 183.

[20]Holt, *How Brands Become Icons,* stresses that iconic brands "become tremendously desirable as the result of a few masterful performances rather than a bevy of consistent communiqués. When Coke took a hillside of beautiful young people and taught the world to sing in 1971, Americans understood that they must come together to overcome the divisive war effort" (p. 10). In "The Evangelist as Star: The Billy Graham Crusade in Australia, 1959," *Journal of Popular Culture* 33, no. 1 (1999): 165-75, Judith Smart refers to Christine Gledhill's definition of a "star" as ". . . a social sign, carrying cultural meanings."

[21]Martyn Percy, "The Church in the Market Place: Advertising and Religion in a Secular Age," *Journal of Contemporary Religion* 15, no. 1 (2000): 97.

[22]Dan Gilgoff, *The Jesus Machine* (New York: St. Martin's Press, 2007), pp. 67-68.

[23]Warren, *Purpose-Driven Church,* p. 171.

[24]Joel Kirkpatrick, winner of the Gospel Music Association's 2005 top humor award for his website, devotes a special section to humorous tribal bumper stickers in his book *A Field Guide to Evangelicals and Their Habits* (San Francisco: Harper Collins, 2006), pp. 28-30.

[25]Susan D. Brandenburg, "The 'Imperfect' CrossRoad Church Celebrates 10 Years; Ministry Uses Music and Telemarketing to Reach Out to Those Without God," *The Florida Times Union,* April 22, 2006, p. S-5.

[26]Product placement in films and TV programs is common in mainstream marketing.

[27]Kevin Jackson, "Rise of Christian Games Creates Buzz Ahead of Developers Conference," *Christian Post,* July 19, 2007 <www.christianpost.com/pages/print.htm?aid=28521>.

[28]G. Jeffrey MacDonald, "Mainstream Churches Take a Leap of Faith into TV Advertising," *Christian Science Monitor,* March 16, 2004 <www.csmonitor.com/2004/O316/p0S03-USSC.html>.

[29]Malcolm Gladwell's groundbreaking book, *The Tipping Point* (New York: Little, Brown, 2002), p. 7, describes how this process works: "the best way to understand the emergence of fashion trends, the ebb and flow of crime waves, or, for that matter, the transformation of unknown books

into bestsellers, or the rise of teenage smoking, or the phenomena of word of mouth, or any number of the other mysterious changes that mark everyday life is to think of them as epidemics. Ideas and products and messages and behaviors spread just like viruses do."

[30]A 2001 survey found that only 6 percent visited a church for the first time because of advertising. While advertising can raise awareness of the congregation and make current members "feel proud of their congregation," personal contact is the most effective means of encouraging new worshipers. See more about the U.S. Congregational Life Survey at <www.pcusa.org/uscongregations/aboutus.htm>.

[31]For example, according to the Congressional Budget Office's 2004 figures, households in the lowest quintile of the country were making only 2 percent more (adjusted for inflation) than they were in 1979; those in the second quintile, 11 percent; the third, 15 percent; the fourth (upper-middle-class with average yearly income of $82,000), 23 percent; and the top, 63 percent, according to Roger Lowenstein, "The Inequality Conundrum," *New York Times Magazine,* June 10, 2007.

[32]Simon, "God's Call Comes by Cell Phone."

[33]Clarence Walton, referenced in Richard Johannesen, *Ethics in Human Communication,* 3rd ed. (Prospect Heights, Ill.: Waveland, 1990), pp. 43-44.

[34]The search was for "webby awards." The Christian organization World Vision received a Webby Award in 2007.

[35]Matthew Schulz and Jordana Borensztzjn, "Fury at Church Signs," *Herald Sun* (Australia), February 2, 2007 <www.news.com.au/heraldsun/story/0,21985,21156374-661,00.html>.

[36]For a discussion of techniques which facilitate persuasion and which can be applied to Christian witness and nurture, see Em Griffin, *The Mind Changers: The Art of Christian Persuasion* (Wheaton, Ill.: Tyndale, 1976).

[37]Henry Chadwick, preface to *Saint Augustine's Confessions* (New York: Oxford University Press, 1998), p. x.

[38]Augustine, *On Christian Doctrine, in Four Books,* e-text, book 4, chaps. 2 and 5 <www.ccel.org/ccel/augustine/doctrine.txt>.

[39]Rodney Clapp, "The Theology of Consumption & the Consumption of Theology," in *The Consuming Passion: Christianity & the Consumer Culture,* ed. Rodney Clapp (Downers Grove, Ill.: InterVarsity Press, 1998), pp. 180-81.

[40]Jackson Lears, quoted in Clapp, "Theology of Consumption," p. 181.

[41]Ibid., p. 182. Coca-Cola, one of the first massively advertised products, in 1912 was declared the best-advertised product by the Advertising Club of America.

[42]Daniel Boorstin, *Democracy and Its Discontents* (New York: Random House, 1974), pp. 26-42.

[43]Clapp, "Theology of Consumption," p. 169.

[44]Bono, "A Time for Miracles," *Time,* April 2, 2007, p. 70.

[45]"The Vatican's View," *Marketing Magazine* 102, no. 37 (1997): 16-18. Likewise, the Presbyterian Church (U.S.A.) wrestled with guidelines for responsible advertising. A statement from the PCUSA Social Justice and Peacemaking Unit notes that national media have "high visibility" and that the church has not taken advantage of such high-visibility media. The statement goes on to recommend that "the Presbyterian Church (U.S.A.) resolves to begin high-visibility advertising in the national media that will present the gospel in an appealing way to secular people." "Advertising the Gospel," *Church and Society* 84 (July-August 1994): 98.

[46]Quoted in "Vatican's View," p. 16.

[47]Pontifical Council for Social Communications, "Ethics in Advertising," February 22, 1997 <www.vatican.va/roman_curia/pontifical_councils/pccs/documents/rc_pc_pccs_doc_22021997_ethics-in-ad_en.html>.

[48]Ibid., sec. V (a) 5, quoting Pope Paul IV's 1977 World Communications Day Message.

[49]Thomas Garrett, referenced in Johannesen, *Ethics in Human Communication*, p. 41.

[50]The Vatican in its 2007 "Ten Commandments for Drivers" includes the statement, "Cars shall not be for you an expression of power and domination, and an occasion of sin." Based on this commandment, using the "power and domination" appeal would be unethical. Associated Press, "Vatican Issues '10 Commandments' for Drivers," MSNBC, June 20, 2007 <www.msnbc.msn.com/id/19308664/>.

[51]In 1962 a committee of the Illinois Synod of the Presbyterian Church published a statement on "Ethics in Advertising" that included these ethical guidelines:

- Advertising methods should not dull perception and judgment through harassing or wearing down the mind.
- Appeals should be to "higher" emotions rather than "lower" ones, such as vanity, status, lust for power, etc.
- Products advertised should meet genuine needs in consumers' lives; extravagant consumption should not be stimulated.
- Merits and features of products should be presented honestly without distorting the facts.
- Appeals should be in good taste (no blatant sounds that irritate to capture attention, no words or pictures that debase, exploit or mock things we commonly accept as private or sacred).
- Advertising methods should be fair and honorable rather than unfair and dishonorable (no unfounded comparison or exaggerated claims).

Referenced in Johannesen, *Ethics in Human Communication*, pp. 92-93.

[52]World Vision's 2007 website won an international Webby Award; see Reuters, "Webby Award Honors World Vision's Interactive AIDS Experience," AlertNet, June 6, 2007, <www.alertnet.org/thenews/fromthefield/477686/117856718929.htm>.

[53]See the application of the apostle Paul's criteria in Gary Scott Smith, "Evangelicals Confront Corporate Capitalism: Advertising, Consumerism, Stewardship, and Spirituality, 1880-1930," in *More Money, More Ministry: Money and Evangelicals in Recent North American History*, ed. Larry Eskridge and Mark A. Noll (Grand Rapids: Eerdmans, 2000), pp. 39-80.

[54]Ibid., p. 80.

Chapter 17: Promoting Public Relations in a New-Media Environment

[1]Ben Witherington III, "Churches Closed on Christmas?" personal blog (December 4, 2005) <http://benwitherington.blogspot.com/2005/12/churches-closed-on-christmas.html>.

[2]Laurie Goodstein, "When Christmas Falls on Sunday, Megachurches Take the Day Off," *New York Times*, December 9, 2005 <www.nytimes.com/2005/12/09church.html>.

[3]"Closed for Christmas 2: The Megachurch Response," Out of Ur: Following God's Call in a New World (December 15, 2007) <http://blog.christianitytoday.com/outofur/archives/2005/12/closed_for_chri_1.html>.

[4]C. E. Swann, *The Communicating Church* (Atlanta: Office of Media Communications of the Presbyterian Church in the U.S., 1981). Swann proposes a functional method of analyzing religious communication. He notes that church use of communication falls under one of three headings, according to the purpose of the communication: evangelism, nurture of believers and public relations.

[5]This is especially true in light of James 4:11: "Brothers and sisters, do not slander one another. Anyone who speaks against a brother or sister or judges them speaks against the law and judges it. When you judge the law, you are not keeping it, but sitting in judgment on it." That the reputation of Christianity is declining is evidenced by the fact that fewer people claim the faith, dropping from 86.2 percent of Americans in 1990 to 76.5 percent in 2001. To see more on how reli-

gion changes in a market system, see Barry Kosmin and Ariela Keysar, *Religion in a Free Market* (Ithaca, N.Y.: Paramount, 2006).

[6]David Guth and Charles Marsh, *Public Relations: A Values-Driven Approach,* 3rd ed. (Boston: Allyn & Bacon, 2006), p. 5.

[7]Many churches have turned to newer media such as blogs, email and Internet sites to disseminate information to their own congregations, giving believers everything from justification for church or program closures to current events and child-rearing tips. However, this internal discussion leaves the rest of society out of the communication loop and therefore uninformed about the rationale behind controversial decisions.

[8]Biblical metaphors, imagery and partial quotations abounded. Lutz in his *The Origins of American Constitutionalism* (Baton Rouge: Louisiana State University Press, 1988) performed a ten-year study of fifteen thousand colonial documents and found the Bible was the most-quoted text (34 percent), followed by the works of Charles-Louis de Secondat Montesquieu (8.3 percent), Sir William Blackstone (7.9 percent) and John Locke (2.9 percent).

[9]Alexis de Tocqueville, *Democracy in America* (London: Fontana Press, 1994).

[10]David Barton, "The Founding Fathers," audiotape of lecture (Aledo, Tex.: Wallbuilders, 1992), cassette number 0-925279-2-6. Also see Phyllis Grenet, "American Life: A Comparison of Colonial Life to Today's Life," Yale-New Haven Teachers Institute <www.yale.edu/ynhti/curriculum/units/1990/5/90.05.04.x.html>.

[11]George Barna, *Revolution: Worn Out on Church?* (Carol Stream, Ill.: Tyndale, 2005), p. 118.

[12]George Gerbner, *Media and Democracy in the 21st Century* (Northampton, Mass.: Media Education Foundation, 1997).

[13]Bob Briner, *Roaring Lambs: A Gentle Plan to Radically Change Your World* (Grand Rapids: Zondervan, 2000), p. 34.

[14]James Engel, "The Great Commission Advertising Campaign: Misuse of the Mass Media in World Evangelism," *Transformation* 9, no. 4 (1992): 21-23.

[15]Cal Thomas and Ed Dobson, *Blinded by Might: Can the Religious Right Save America?* (Grand Rapids: Zondervan, 1999).

[16]Peter Kerr and Patricia Moy, "Newspaper Coverage of Fundamentalist Christians 1980-2000," *Journalism & Mass Communication Quarterly* 79, no. 1 (2002): 54-73. This longitudinal study of more than three hundred newspapers across the country found politics was the main topic for nearly a quarter of all stories mentioning fundamentalist Christians.

[17]Philip Yancy, "Honest Church Marketing," *Christianity Today,* October 22, 2001, p. 112.

[18]Bob Briner, *Final Roar* (Nashville: Broadman & Holman, 2000), pp. 116-17.

[19]Yancy, "Honest Church Marketing," p. 112.

[20]Doron Mendels, *The Media Revolution of Early Christianity: An Essay on Eusebius's Ecclesiastical History* (Grand Rapids: Eerdmans, 1999), p. 241.

[21]Including "Disputation of Doctor Martin Luther on the Power and Efficacy of Indulgences" (1517), "An Open Letter to the Christian Nobility" (1520), and "On Translating" (1530).

[22]Charles Finney, *The Memoirs of Charles G. Finney: The Complete Restored Text* (Grand Rapids: Academie Books, 1989).

[23]For more on social movements spear-headed by evangelicals, see Donald Dayton, *Discovering an Evangelical Heritage* (Peabody, Mass.: Hendrickson, 2000).

[24]Christian organizations backing social change had to invent ways to get out their messages to mass publics, and the PR profession sprang from this need to reach mass audiences and to spread democratic ideals, using the new technologies that made such communication possible. See Guth and Marsh, *Public Relations.*

[25]Guth and Marsh, *Public Relations*, p. 63.

[26]Ibid.

[27]Morely Safer, interview by author, New York, New York, May 22, 2006. Safer of *60 Minutes* said that news has turned into "infotainment," which means the media wish to have more news stories that read like narratives. Gary Putka, Boston bureau chief of the *Wall Street Journal,* explained that "a good 50 percent" of stories in his newspaper come from news releases. Quoted in Dennis Wilcox and Glen Cameron, *Public Relations Strategies and Tactics,* 8th ed. (Boston: Allyn & Bacon 2006), p. 357.

[28]Joe Fuiten, senior pastor of Cedar Park Church, interview by author, Bothell, Washington, April 20, 2007.

[29]Ibid.

[30]Debra Childers, interview by author, Louisville, Kentucky, March 23, 2007.

[31]Wal-Mart restricted bell ringers to fourteen days a year, and Target banned them from soliciting in front of their stores in 2004. See Dan Benson and Peter Maller, "Target Bans Salvation Army Kettles," *Milwaukee Journal-Sentinel,* October 18, 2004 <www.jsonline.com/story/index.aspx?id=2675457>.

[32]American Political Science Association, "Symposium: The Politics of Same-Sex Marriage," April 2005 <www.apsanet.org/content_15728.cfm>.

[33]For more discussion see Mark I. Pinsky, *The Gospel According to Disney: Faith, Trust, and Pixie Dust* (Louisville: Westminster John Knox, 2004).

[34]For a discussion of this event see Barbara Mikkelson, "Wal-Mart and the NGLLC" (November 21, 2006) <www.snopes.com/politics/sexuality/walmart.asp>.

[35]The church has many diocesan Communications Offices, a Catholic News Agency and a Vatican Press Office. To see the Vatican Web presence, go to <www.vatican.va/phome_en.htm>.

[36]Many denominations have developed news services, though these suffer from lack of funds and offer no coherent evangelical voice. For links to many of these organizations, see <www.toad.net/~andrews/jreldenom.html>.

[37]See Doug Underwood, *From Yahweh to Yahoo! The Religious Roots of the Mass Media and the Rise of the Skeptical Press* (Urbana, Ill.: University of Illinois Press, 2002). Underwood suggests that the media give only a quarter as much coverage to liberal Christians as they give to conservative ones, partly because most journalists share sentiments with liberal Christians and so do not see liberal issues as controversial/newsworthy.

[38]Briner, *Final Roar,* p. 121.

[39]Eilene Wollslager, Karen Legg and John Keeler, "A Typology of Crisis Communication in the Local Church," paper presented at Campbell University Faith and Communication Conference, May 19, 2007, Campbell University, Buies Creek, North Carolina.

[40]The Ted Haggard scandal may have been a blow to evangelicals, but it was well handled from a media perspective. Within days of the accusations, elders released statements and invoked real punishment. Bad media coverage should be seen like dirty laundry: it smells worse if you hide it, but it can quickly get better if it is aired out.

[41]Galatians 5:22-23: "But the fruit of the Spirit is love, joy, peace, patience, kindness, goodness, faithfulness, gentleness and self-control."

[42]Churches and organizations may also need to seek legal advice, and ministries should be familiar with the disclosure prohibitions delineated in the Privacy Act.

[43]Barna, *Revolution,* p. 109.

[44]Carl Henry, *Carl Henry at His Best* (Portland, Ore.: Multnomah, 1990), p. 149.

Chapter 18: Internationalizing Evangelical Media

[1]"Pastor Nabbed with Married Woman," *Red Pepper* <http://redpepper.ug/news.php?item=963>.

[2]Henry Lubega, "Uganda: Churches Declare Billions," *New Vision,* August 18, 2007 <allafrica .com/stories/200708200241.html>.

[3]Obed Minchakpu, "Muslims Aim to End Televangelism," *Christianity Today,* March 2, 1998 <www.christianitytoday.com/ct/1998/march2/8t378c.html>.

[4]See Walter Ihejirika, "Media and Fundamentalism in Nigeria," World Association for Christian Communication <www.wacc.org.uk/wacc/regional_associations/africa/african_articles/media_ and_fundamentalism_in_nigeria>.

[5]See "Islamic Televangelism," Arab Bloggers, Televangelists, Music Videos, Reality TV and More series, *Day to Day* (July 22, 2005) <www.npr.org/about/press/050718.arab.html>.

[6]See Donald Wagner, "Beyond Armageddon," Middle East Window (2005) <http://middleeast window.com/node/300>.

[7]See Manuel M. Marzal, "Transplanted Spanish Catholicism," in *South and Meso-American Native Spirituality: From the Cult of the Feathered Serpent to the Theology of Liberation,* ed. Gary H. Gossen and Miguel Leon-Portilla (New York: Crossroad, 1993), pp. 140-69; Thomas M. Cohen, *The Fire of Tongues: Antonio Vieira and the Missionary Church in Brazil and Portugal* (Stanford: Stanford University Press, 1998); Glen Caudill Dealy, *The Latin Americans: Spirit and Ethos* (Boulder, Colo.: Westview Press, 1992); Anthony Gill, "The Struggle to Be Soul Provider: Catholic Responses to Protestant Growth in Latin America," in *Latin American Religion in Motion,* ed. Joshua Prokopy and Christian Smith (New York: Routledge, 1999), pp. 17-42; Liesl Haas, "The Catholic Church in Chile: New Political Alliances," in *Latin American Religion in Motion,* ed. Joshua Prokopy and Christian Smith (New York: Routledge, 1999), pp. 43-66.

[8]Amy L. Sherman, *The Soul of Development: Biblical Christianity and Economic Transformation in Guatemala* (New York: Oxford University Press, 1997), pp. 6-8.

[9]See Alvin M. Goffin, *The Rise of Protestant Evangelism in Ecuador, 1895-1990* (Gainesville: University Press of Florida, 1994); Harvey Cox, *Fire from Heaven: The Rise of Pentecostal Spirituality and the Reshaping of Religion in the Twenty-First Century* (Cambridge, Mass.: Perseus, 1995), especially chap. 9; Everett A. Wilson, "Sanguine Saints: Pentecostalism in El Salvador," *Church History* 52 (1983): 197.

[10]Robert S. Fortner, *International Communication: History, Conflict and Control of the Global Metropolis* (Belmont, Calif.: Wadsworth, 1993), p. 105.

[11]For a history of Radio Vatican, see Marilyn J. Matelski, *Vatican Radio: Propagation by the Airwaves* (Westport, Conn.: Praeger, 1995).

[12]Marie Friedman Marquardt and Manuel A. Vasquez, *Globalizing the Sacred: Religion Across the Americas* (New Brunswick, N.J.: Rutgers University Press, 2003), pp. 42-44, 55.

[13]Simon Coleman, *The Globalisation of Charismatic Christianity: Spreading the Gospel of Prosperity* (Cambridge: Cambridge University Press, 2000), pp. 184-85.

[14]For instance, there are an estimated 570 tribes in Sudan, representing 56 ethnic groups and 113 vernacular languages in addition to the dominant Arabic language. See James Mabor Gatkuoth, "Ethnicity and Nationalism in the Sudan—Ethnicity and Nationalism: A Challenge to the Churches," *The Ecumenical Review* 47 (April 1995): n.p.

[15]"Missionaries often worked hand in hand with colonial administrators to effect this domination, convinced as they were that Western control would ultimately benefit 'backward' peoples. Christianization has most often assumed Westernization, and such was the overt attitude of most missionaries." Brian Wilson, *Christianity* (New York: Routledge, 1999), p. 84.

[16]T. O. Beidelman, *East African Mission at the Grassroots* (Bloomington: Indiana University Press,

1982), p. 87: "The C. M. S., like all English Evangelicals, entertained a consuming hatred of the Roman Catholic Church. They contrasted 'people of the Pope and people of the Book,' and they referred to the Pope as a devil, to the beliefs of Catholics as 'tyrannical' and 'superstitious,' and to Catholic missionizing as 'Jesuit aggression.'"

[17]Adrian Hastings, "Politics and Religion in Southern Africa," in *Politics and Religion in the Modern World,* ed. George Moyser (New York: Routledge, 1991), pp. 162-88.

[18]For information on corruption and the impacts of tribalism, poverty and lack of education, see Martin Meredith, *The Fate of Africa: From the Hopes of Freedom to the Heart of Despair* (New York: Public Affairs, 2005).

[19]Philip Jenkins, "The Next Christianity," *Atlantic Monthly,* October 2002 <www.theatlantic.com/doc/200210/jenkins>.

[20]Ibid.

[21]Much of the growth of Christianity in China through the nineteenth century was the result of proselytization among the Chinese diaspora, who then carried their new religion back to the mainland through kinship networks, bypassing the control of the government that had banned Christianity from 1724 to 1860. See Joseph Tse-Hei Lee, "The Overseas Chinese Networks and Early Baptist Missionary Movement Across the South China Sea," *The Historian* 63, no. 4 (2001): 752-68.

[22]See Wayne Fife, "Creating the Moral Body: Missionaries and the Technology of Power in Early Papua New Guinea," *Ethnology* 40 (2001): 251-69; Eng Kuah Khun, "Maintaining Ethno-Religious Harmony in Singapore," *Journal of Contemporary Asia* 28, no. 1 (1998): 103-21.

[23]See the church's TV website at <http://english.fgtv.com/>.

[24]Jane Lampman, "How Korea Embraced Christianity," *The Christian Science Monitor,* March 7, 2007 <www.csmonitor.com/2007/0307/p14s01-lire.html>.

[25]Norimitsu Onishi, "Korean Missionaries Carrying Word to Hard-to-Sway Places," *New York Times,* November 1, 2004 <www.nytimes.com/2004/11/01/international/asia/01missionaries.html>.

[26]There are millions of Christians in China, Korea, Vietnam, Indonesia and the Philippines. Leslie E. Sponsel, *Endangered Peoples of Southeast and East Asia: Struggles to Survive and Thrive* (Westport, Conn.: Greenwood Press, 2000), p. 15.

[27]David Aiken, *Jesus in Beijing: How Christianity Is Transforming China and Changing the Global Balance of Power* (Washington, D.C.: Regnery, 2003), p. 8.

[28]Ibid., p. 266.

[29]Ibid., p. 12.

[30]Spengler [pseudonym], "Christianity Finds a Fulcrum in Asia," *Asia Times Online,* August 7, 2007 <www.atimes.com/atimes/China/IH07Ad03.html>.

[31]Roland Platz, "Buddhism and Christianity in Competition? Religious and Ethnic Identity in Karen Communities in Northern Thailand," *Journal of Southeast Asian Studies* 34 (2003): 473-90.

[32]Ibid.

[33]Joel Robbins, *Becoming Sinners: Christianity and Moral Torment in a Papua New Guinea Society* (Berkeley: University of California Press, 2004), pp. 26-27.

[34]As in Africa and Latin America, much of the growth of Christianity in Asia is the result of an alignment of a charismatic or Pentecostal health-and-wealth gospel with people's needs for healing and reduced poverty. I witnessed an Australian guest preacher in a Pentecostal church in Ulaan Bataar, Mongolia, who ran overtime in her sermon, so she stretched her hands over a congregation numbering in the hundreds to heal them of all diseases, from blindness to cancer. She told them they would not have to see a doctor or a hospital again.

[35]Such messianic motives are informed by a desire for the culmination of human history at Armageddon, the provocation of Christ's second coming or the expectation of the rapture.

[36]See Robert S. Fortner, *Communication, Media, and Identity: A Christian Theory of Communication* (New York: Rowman & Littlefield, 2007), pp. 197-99.

[37]Witnesses demonstrate the reality of Christ through their behavior and attitudes, witnessing to his central role in their lives. Tent-makers, like Paul, support their witness through nonevangelistic occupations.

[38]For a Muslim evaluation of Christian missionary work in the Middle East, see Sheikh Salman al-Oadah, "Christian Missionaries Sweeping the Islamic World," Lesson 66, on Monday 12th of Safar, 1413 Hijra, transcript of tape <www.islamworld.net/tanseer.htm>.

[39]See Colin Shindler, "Likud and the Christian Dispensationalists: A Symbiotic Relationship," *Israel Studies* 5 (2000): 155-84.

[40]See "Media Pioneer: Pat Builds a Broadcast Ministry that Stretches around the World," M. G. "Pat" Robertson official website <www.patrobertson.com/mediapioneer/>.

[41]One major difficulty with evangelization in the Middle East may be the result of the "secular retraining of the ear" that occurred during the Enlightenment and consequently informs Christian expectations of media. See Charles Hirshkind, *The Ethical Soundscape: Cassette Sermons and Islamic Counterpublics* (New York: Columbia University Press, 2006), p. 24.

[42]"When traveling in Europe, I am always astonished to see churches abandoned by their congregations, especially those that are transformed into pubs, clubs, shops or places of secular activity. There is something deeply deplorable in this sorry spectacle." Hilarion Alfeyev, "Christian Witnessing to Uniting Europe: A View from a Representative of the Russian Orthodox Church," *The Ecumenical Review* 55 (2003): 76.

[43]Kevin Sullivan, "Foreign Missionaries Find Fertile Ground in Europe," *The Washington Post,* June 11, 2007, A01.

[44]Mary Jordan, "Albanians Rediscover God, If Not Old-Time Religion," *The Washington Post,* April 4, 2007, A01.

[45]Jonathan Luxmoore and Jolanta Babiuch-Luxmoore, "New Myths for Old: Proselytism and Transition in Post-Communist Europe," *Journal of Ecumenical Studies* 36 (1999): 43.

[46]Paul Mojzes, "Proselytism in the Successor States of the Former Yugoslavia," *Journal of Ecumenical Studies* 36 (1999): 221-42.

[47]For an explanation of how and why Europeans see the world, including faith, so differently from Americans, see George Weigel, *The Cube and the Cathedral: Europe, America and Politics Without God* (New York: Basic Books, 2005).

[48]To learn more about these broadcasting companies, see the following websites: <www.twr.org>, <www.feba.org> and <www.febc.org>.

[49]See the CBN WorldReach goal, in the introduction under "About Us" on their website <www.cbnworld.com>.

[50]"Jesus," Wikipedia <http://en.wikipedia.org/wiki/Jesus>.

[51]EV Free churches (as they are popularly known) sponsor missionaries from many locations. See, e.g., <www.firstfreechurch.org/missions/conrad/>.

[52]M. G. "Pat" Robertson's reported call for the assassination of Venezuelian president Hugo Chavez was just one controversial remark. See Kenneth D. MacHarg, "What Was Robertson Thinking?" *Christian Science Monitor,* August 25, 2005 <www.csmonitor.com/2005/0825/p09s01-coop.html>.

[53]See "About Us" on the TBN website <www.tbn.org> for Trinity's claims. See <www.inplainsite.org/html/tbn.html> for the claims of heresy within TBN.

[54]CBN websites highlighting its international connections include <www.cbnasia.org>, <www.cbneurope.com>, <www.cbnafrica.org> and <www.club700hoy.com>.

[55]See "Internet Evangelism: Taking the Gospel of Jesus Christ to the World" at <http://internetevangelism.org/>.

[56]"The Jesus Film Project: Reaching Every Nation, Tribe, People and Tongue" at <www.jesusfilm.org/> includes streaming audio and video in multiple languages. See also The Internet Evangelism Coalition's website <www.webevangelism.com>, including papers or PowerPoint presentations on Internet evangelism.

[57]See, e.g., "Text Messaging Listeners Seeking Christ," Mission Network News (March 7, 2007) <www.mnnonline.org/article/9667>.

[58]See "mTracts—Using Mobile Phones to Spread the Gospel!" American Tract Society <www.atstracts.org/mtracts.php>.

[59]Joint Working Group Between the World Council of Churches and the Catholic Church, "The Challenge of Proselytism and the Calling to Common Witness," *The Ecumenical Review* 48, no. 2 (1996): 212-21.

Chapter 19: Energizing Media Ethics

[1]Jean Porter, "Virtue Ethics," in *The Cambridge Companion to Christian Ethics*, ed. Robin Gill (New York: Cambridge University Press, 2001), p. 99.

[2]Walter Brueggemann, *First and Second Samuel* (Louisville: John Knox, 1990), pp. 1-2.

[3]Stephen C. Barton, "The Epistles and Christian Ethics," in *The Cambridge Companion to Christian Ethics*, ed. Robin Gill (New York: Cambridge University Press, 2001), p. 63.

[4]Referenced in Porter, "Virtue Ethics," p. 100.

[5]David Fergusson, *Community, Liberalism and Christian Ethics* (New York: Cambridge University Press, 1998), p. 24.

[6]Pope John Paul II, *Veritatis Splendor*, August 6, 1993 <www.vatican.va/holy_father/john_paul_ii/encyclicals/documents/hf_jp-ii_enc_06081993_veritatis-splendor_en.html>. The encyclical is discussed in David Hollenbach, *The Common Good and Christian Ethics* (New York: Cambridge University Press, 2002), p. 48.

[7]Several contemporary neurological studies associate brain development with cultural constructions of the good. See Michael S. Gazzaniga, *The Ethical Brain* (New York: Dana, 2005).

[8]Thomas Aquinas, *Summa Theologiae* 2.1, ques. 91 and 94.

[9]Porter, "Virtue Ethics," pp. 103-4.

[10]George Lindbeck is discussed in Fergusson, *Community, Liberalism and Christian Ethics*, p. 12; and Bernard T. Adeney, *Strange Virtue: Ethics in a Multicultural World* (Downers Grove, Ill.: InterVarsity Press, 1995), pp. 58, 85-87.

[11]Clifford G. Christians, John P. Ferré and P. Mark Fackler, *Good News: Social Ethics and the Press* (New York: Oxford University Press, 1993).

[12]Two of the most strident voices challenging the message today are Sam Harris, *Letters to a Christian Nation* (New York: Knopf, 2006), and Richard Dawkins, *The God Delusion* (New York: Mariner, 2007).

[13]See, e.g., Ian A. McFarland, *The Divine Image: Envisioning the Invisible God* (Minneapolis: Fortress, 2005).

[14]Sissela Bok, *Lying: Moral Choice in Public and Private Life* (New York: Vintage, 1999).

[15]The malaise is poignantly expressed in Federico Mayor and Jerome Binde, *The World Ahead: Our Future in the Making* (New York: Zed Books, 2001), p. 5.

[16]David Craig and John P. Ferré, "Agape in the Service of Journalism," in *Ethics and Evil in the Public Sphere*, ed. Robert S. Fortner and Mark Fackler (New York: Hampton, forthcoming).

[17]Richard Harries, *Reinhold Niebuhr and the Issues of Our Time* (Grand Rapids: Eerdmans, 1986).

[18]See, e.g., Geffrey B. Kelly and F. Burton Nelson, ed., *A Testament of Freedom: The Essential Writings of Dietrich Bonhoeffer* (New York: HarperCollins, 1990).

[19]Walter Lippmann, *Public Opinion* (New York: Macmillan, 1961), pp. 398ff.

Chapter 20: Considering a Catholic View of Evangelical Media

[1]Teresa Malcolm, "Fearful Faith in End Times Novels," *National Catholic Reporter*, June 15, 2001 <http://natcath.org/NCR_Online/archives2/2001b/061501/061501a.htm>; Joyce Donohoe, "Left Behind: Crossing the Threshold of Fear," *The Living Light* 40, no. 2 (2003): 15-26; Paul Thigpen, "'Rapture Fever' May Be Injurious to One's Spiritual Health," *The Living Light* 40, no. 2 (2003): 33-43.

[2]Richard B. Gregg, "The Ego-Function of the Rhetoric of Protest," *Philosophy & Rhetoric* 4 (1971): 71-91.

[3]See the Catholic Library Association's Catholic Periodical and Literature Index at <www.cathla .org/cpli.php>.

[4]See the Southern Baptist Periodical Index at <www.sbuniv.edu/library/SBPI.htm>.

[5]Elizabeth L. Eisenstein, *The Printing Revolution in Early-Modern Europe* (Cambridge: Cambridge University Press, 1983); Mark U. Edwards Jr., *Printing, Propaganda, and Martin Luther* (Berkeley: University of California Press, 1994).

[6]Walter J. Ong, *Orality and Literacy: The Technologizing of the Word* (New York: Methuen, 1982), pp. 78-116.

[7]David Payne, "Characterology, Media, and Rhetoric," in *Media, Consciousness, and Culture: Explorations of Walter Ong's Thought*, ed. Bruce E. Gronbeck, Thomas J. Farrell and Paul A. Soukup (Newbury Park, Calif.: Sage, 1991), pp. 223-36.

[8]Walter J. Ong, "Literacy and Orality in Our Times," *ADE Bulletin* 58 (1978): 1-7.

[9]At least from a media ecology perspective. See Lance Strate, "A Media Ecology Review," *Communication Research Trends* 23, no. 2 (2004): 1-48.

[10]One major movement within evangelicalism that takes into account the nonliteral sense of Scripture and new, more oral modes of communication and worship is the "emerging church" movement. Adherent Brian D. McLaren has written a book whose title captures this: *A Generous Orthodoxy: Why I Am a Missional, Evangelical, Post/Protestant, Liberal/Conservative, Mystical/Poetic, Biblical, Charismatic/Contemplative, Fundamentalist/Calvinist, Anabaptist/Anglican, Methodist, Catholic, Green, Incarnational, Depressed-Yet-Hopeful, Emergent, Unfinished Christian* (Grand Rapids: Zondervan, 2004).

[11]Robert A. White, "The Media, Culture, and Religion Perspective," *Communication Research Trends* 26, no. 1 (2007): 1-24.

[12]Elisabeth Arweck and William Keenan, eds., *Materializing Religion: Expression, Performance, and Ritual* (Aldershot, Hampshire, UK: Ashgate, 2006).

[13]William Keenan and Elisabeth Arweck, "Introduction: Material Varieties of Religious Expression," in *Materializing Religion: Expression, Performance, and Ritual*, ed. Elisabeth Arweck and William Keenan (Aldershot, U.K.: Ashgate, 2006), p. 2.

[14]Gregor T. Goethals, *The Electronic Golden Calf: Images, Religion, and the Making of Meaning* (Cambridge, Mass.: Cowley, 1990); Bernice Martin, "The Aesthetics of Latin American Pentecostalism: The Sociology of Religion and the Problem of Taste," in *Materializing Religion: Expression, Performance, and Ritual*, ed. Elisabeth Arweck and William Keenan (Aldershot, U.K.: Ashgate, 2006), pp. 138-60; "Religious Rejections of the World and Their Direction," in *From Max Weber*, ed. Hans Gerth and C. Wright Mills (London: Routledge, 1948), pp. 323-59.

[15]Richard A. Blake, *Afterimage: The Indelible Catholic Imagination of Six American Filmmakers* (Chicago: Loyola Press, 2000).

[16]Ibid., p. 9. One could argue that a confluence of theological conviction and communication technology led to both the fact of usage and the pattern of use of the various communication media: Protestants, seeking private interpretation of the Scripture, more readily adopted the printing press, something Eisenstein, *Printing Revolution,* demonstrates. On the other hand, the spread of literacy and biblical translations because of the printing press further encouraged the Protestant tradition of individual Bible reading and interpretation.

[17]Blake's argument follows Richard P. McBrien, *Catholicism* (New York: Harper & Row, 1981); and Andrew M. Greeley, *The Catholic Imagination* (Berkeley: University of California Press, 2000).

[18]Gerard Manley Hopkins, "God's Grandeur," in *The Poems of Gerard Manley Hopkins,* 4th ed., ed. W. H. Gardner and N. H. McKenzie (Oxford: Oxford University Press, 1970), p. 66.

[19]Blake, *Afterimage,* p. 14.

[20]Ibid., pp. 15-20.

[21]Max Weber, *The Protestant Ethic and the Spirit of Capitalism* (London: Allen & Unwin, 1930).

Chapter 21: Looking with a Jew at Evangelical Popular Culture

[1]Mark I. Pinsky, "*Passion* Has Made Christianity the Talk of the Town," *Orlando Sentinel,* March 14, 2004, F.1.

[2]Ibid.

[3]Daniel Wolpe, interview by author, email, July 8, 2007.

[4]Douglas Hartmann, Xuefeng Zhang and William Wischstadt, "One (Multicultural) Nation Under God? Changing Uses and Means of the Term 'Judeo-Christian' in the American Media," *Journal of Media and Religion* 4 (Winter 2005): 208-9.

[5]Martin E. Marty, interview by author, email, March 14, 2007.

[6]Simcha Weinstein, interview by author, email, May 2 May, 2007. Weinstein is the author of *Up, Up, and Oy Vey! How Jewish History, Culture, and Values Shaped the Comic Book Superhero* (Baltimore: Leviathan, 2006).

[7]Phil Vischer, interview by author, email, February 22, 2007.

[8]Weinstein interview.

[9]You can see the box office records at "*Jonah: A VeggieTales Movie,*" Internet Movie Database <http://imdb.com/title/tt0298388/business>.

[10]Mike Nawrocki, interview by author, email, February 21, 2007.

[11]Phil Vischer, *Jonah* DVD commentary (Big Idea Productions, 2002).

[12]Weinstein interview.

[13]Wolpe interview.

[14]Weinstein interview.

[15] Reg Grant, interview by author, email, February 25, 2007. Grant is on the faculty of Dallas Theological Seminary and specializes in popular culture.

[16]Mark I. Pinsky, *A Jew Among the Evangelicals: A Guide for the Perplexed* (Louisville: Westminster John Knox, 2006), pp. 129-44. I have provided an extensive account from the Jewish perspective in my book, including visits I made with Orthodox rabbi Sholem Dubov and others.

[17]Quoted in Naomi Pfefferman, "The Rabbi and the Reverend," Jewishjournal.com (February 22, 2002) <www.jewishjournal.com/home/preview.php?id=8142>.

[18]Ellen Gray, "Stroke Survivor Kirk Douglas Makes Rare Appearance on 'Touched by an Angel,'" *Philadelphia Daily News,* March 11, 2000.

[19]Mark I. Pinsky, *The Gospel According to the Simpsons: BIGGER (and Possibly Even) BETTER! EDI-*

TION (Louisville: Westminster John Knox, 2007), pp. 46-69. Jews are also portrayed favorably, if marginally in *The Simpsons.* Two full episodes and part of a third are devoted to Judaism, but a Jewish sensibility pervades the series.

Index